Brill's Arab and Islamic Laws Series

Edited by

Dr. Khaled Abou El Fadl
University of California, Los Angeles, School of Law

VOLUME 8

The titles published in this series are listed at *brill.com/bail*

War and Law in the Islamic World

War and Law in the Islamic World

By

Matthias Vanhullebusch

BRILL
NIJHOFF

LEIDEN | BOSTON

Library of Congress Cataloging-in-Publication Data

Vanhullebusch, Matthias, author.
War and Law in the Islamic World / By Matthias Vanhullebusch.
pages cm — (Brill's Arab and Islamic laws Series)
Based on author's thesis (doctoral) – School of Oriental and African Studies, University of London, 2011
Includes bibliographical references and index.
ISBN 978-90-04-29825-5 (hardback : alk. paper) — ISBN 978-90-04-29824-8 (e-book) 1. War (Islamic law)
I. Title.

KBP2416.V36 2015
341.60917'67—dc23

2015015430

ISSN 1871-2894
ISBN 978-90-04-29825-5 (hardback)
ISBN 978-90-04-29824-8 (e-book)

This book is printed on acid-free paper.

MIX
Paper from responsible sources
FSC www.fsc.org
FSC® C109576

Printed by Printforce, the Netherlands

To my grandfather Lucien D'hondt

To arms he rushes at all times and in all places;
no bounds to his fury, no end to his destructive vengeance.
Together they engage, nation with nation, city with city, king with king;
and to gratify the folly or greedy ambition of two poor puny mortals,
who shortly shall die by nature, like insects of a summer's day—
all human affairs are disarranged, and whirled in confusion.
I will pass over the sad tragedy of war,
acted on the bloody stage of the world in times long past.

DESIDERIUS ERASMUS, *Querela Pacis* (1521)

Contents

Foreword

Dr Matthias Vanhullebusch has produced an impressive study examining a subject that retains considerable contemporary value and interest. This book—initially produced as a doctoral thesis for the School of Oriental and African Studies, University of London—engages with the issues of identity, power and change with reference to the interpretation and application of international humanitarian law and the Islamic humanitarian laws. The study examines the genesis and the development of the two distinct systems in their efforts to regulate conflicts and violence and in so doing explores critical areas of contradictions and complexities.

This book is divided into three substantive parts with each part presenting a comparative survey of the various strands of jurisprudence within Western and Islamic traditions on the laws of war. Chapter I examines the principles of protection as provided within *siyar* and Islamic laws of war. A similar exercise is conducted as regards the principles emerging from international humanitarian law in Chapter II. Part II of the book (consisting of Chapters III and IV) provides a highly engaging survey of the divergent yet interrelated progression of the "Western" and "Islamic" civilizations respectively. Part III, which represents chapters V and VI, tests the tenacity of the two systems from the prism of jurisdictional issues as well as through approaches towards contentious aspects of the laws of war including proportionality and military necessity. The study concludes with a number of thought-provoking though highly significant reflections on the subject.

There are many virtues of this research: authoritative in its approach and substantiated through a detailed reading and understanding of the subject, the arguments in this book are carefully constructed. The writing style is crisp and fluent which undoubtedly facilitates the exposition of complexities inherent in the debate surrounding the interpretation and application of Islamic laws of war as well as international humanitarian law. Probably the most admirable quality of the work is that amidst tensions of identity, power and change prevalent in the competing systems of both the Islamic laws of war and international humanitarian law, it takes forward a message of reconciliation, rapprochement and mutual coexistence. It is this approach of advocacy for humanitarianism and humanity, which presents the reader with the most profound and positive message. As Vanhullebusch notes the "[s]tudy asserts that there is also another reality beyond the text as well, namely the world as such in which human beings live. This world necessarily can never be fully captured or represented by the text though it can control the knowledge of how one looks at this world, namely in conflictual terms. In this way, it is possible to transcend the divisions which the texts have produced and which have started to live their own violent realities within this human world." (Conclusions)

With such maturity of analysis and originality of arguments, Dr Matthias Vanhullebusch has produced an excellent study. The work will be of enormous value not only to students of Islamic laws of war and international humanitarian law, but would greatly assist all those seeking to comprehend and unravel the apparent contradictions between Islamic conception of peace-building and the secularised or Westernised model of conflict resolution. I wholeheartedly commend this monograph, which in my view will prove to be a reference point for the future.

Professor Javaid Rehman
Brunel University
London, United Kingdom
February 2015

Preface

This book explores the genesis and development of International Humanitarian Law (IHL) and Islamic Law of War (ILW), from their origins to today's conflicts in the Islamic and Middle Eastern world. From a positivist perspective, it compares the different principles pertaining to protection, i.e. distinction and proportionality, as opposed to military necessity. A historical analysis will expose the ideological foundations and contexts that have influenced IHL and ILW throughout the ages. In doing so, it highlights that strategies of divide and rule and of the dehumanisation of the enemy Other are reflected accordingly in the interpretation and application of the principles of protection. The conflictual reading of protection v. necessity and of the Self v. the enemy Other is inherent in the respective systems and establishes that both are designed to consolidate power. Beyond the positivist and historical approaches to the laws of war and the principles of protection, a naturalist legal reading will foster the spirit of the laws, which is, obviously, the saving of human life. In order for humanity as a whole to survive, both the Western and Islamic legal traditions on warfare have always had the potential to serve that end. However, throughout history, polarisations have prevented to challenge traditional positivist and historical readings of the laws which themselves are denouncing each other for respectively the absence and/or lack of agency and of contextualisation in the interpretation and application of those principles of protection. This undermines the humanitarian spirit of the laws of armed conflict which the naturalist legal approach seeks to promote. In order to transcend the vicious circles of violence across the Islamic world, it offers a unique perspective to interpret and apply the laws of war when grounding humanity in the biological and creationary realm of existence and belonging in favour of humanitarian protection.

Acknowledgements

This book project—whose roots can be traced back to my master studies in International Politics (CERIS-Paris Sud-XI/2006), International Law (Leiden/2007) and my PhD thesis (SOAS/2011)—wouldn't come to fruition without the continued support of my wife, Dorothy Zhang, and my family. My deepest thank goes to my former PhD supervisors Prof. Mashood A. Baderin and Prof. Matthew Craven (SOAS) for their guidance and supervision, Prof. Peter Muchlinski—my research tutor—and Prof. Martin Lau and the late Prof. Eugene Cotran—my former colleagues on the Yearbook of Islamic and Middle Eastern Law (Brill), and Prof. Javaid Rehman (Brunel)—my colleague on the Journal of Islamic State Practices in International Law. I owe a special debt of gratitude to Prof. Werner Menski (SOAS) who has led various discussion groups with our peers and to my friends at SOAS when discussing this project: Abdulbari Altami (Albaha), Nesrine Badawi (AUC), Mwanakitina Bakari (SOAS), Mohammad Nazmuzzaman Bhuian (Dhaka), Muin Boase (SOAS), Vincent Depaigne (European Commission), Sarah Elibiary (SOAS), Jonathan Ercanbrack (SOAS), Taymour Harding (Oxford), John Haskell (Mississippi), Vivian Ibrahim (Mississippi), Amie Kamanda (Portsmouth), Ayla Karmali (Afridi & Angell), Zakiah Hanum Kassim (Celcom), Emir Kaya (YBU), Victor Kattan (NUS), Carool Kersten (KCL), Kai Kreutzberger (Herbert Smith), Mara Malagodi (LSE), Faris Nasrallah (Baker Botts), Rose Parfitt (Melbourne), Abdur Rauf (Bahria), Mohammad Shahabuddin (Keele) and Gus Waschefort (UNISA).

I am indebted to my other friends and colleagues who have been supportive of this project in numerable ways, including Ademola Abass (ISS Africa), Ceren Abi (UCLA), Awn Shawkat Al-Khasawneh (ICJ/ILA), Freya Baetens (Leiden), Khaled Bashir (Aberdeen), Niels Blokker (Leiden), Pascal Bongard (Geneva Call), Olivier Corten (ULB), James Crawford (ICJ), Eric David (ULB), Jean d'Aspremont (Manchester), Koen De Feyter (Antwerp), Bruno Demeyere (ICRC), Katherine Derderian (Amnesty International), Eric Drybooms (RMA Belgium), John Dugard (Leiden), Horst Fischer (EIUC/GTZ), Pierre Hazan (CHD), Joost Herman (NOHA/RUG), Stanislas Horvart (RMA Belgium), Weidong Ji (SJTU), David Kennedy (Harvard), Ben Klappe (MOD Netherlands), Jann Kleffner (SNDC), Sari Kouvo (EEAS), Angharad Laing (PHAP), Rick Lawson (Leiden), Fork Yow Leong (ICRC), Edouard Mancini (IPB/Italia) Alexander Mattelaer (VUB/IES), Naz Modirzadeh (Harvard), André Miroir (CERIS), Muhammad Munir (IIUI/Islamabad), Frederik Naert (Council of the EU), Yoshinobu Nagamine (ICRC), Salem Hikmat Nasser (FGV Direito SP), Inger Österdahl (Uppsala), Bruce Oswald (Melbourne), Noëlle

Quénivet (West England), Cedric Ryngaert (KUL), Marco Sassòli (Geneva), Iain Scobbie (Manchester), Hesti Setyowati (Chevron), Niaz Shah (Hull), Prakash Shah (QMU), Mohamed Shahabuddeen (ICTY/ICTR), Thomas Skouteris (AUC), Stefaan Smis (VUB), Carsten Stahn (Leiden), Lisa Tabassi (OSCE), Ruti Teitel (NY Law), David Tolbert (ICTJ), Kim Van der Borght (VUB), Anicée Van Engeland (SOAS), Alfons Vanheusden (MOJ Belgium), Frans Viljoen (Pretoria), and William Worster (The Hague University).

I am particularly grateful to the Series Editor of Brill's Arab and Islamic Laws Series—Khaled Abou El Fadl (UCLA)—for the constructive feedback and to my colleagues-editors at Brill Academic Publishers, Marie Sheldon, Jill Zumbach, Paige Sammartino and Ingeborg van der Laan for their professionalism and for overseeing the production of this volume. Special thanks also to my student Muhemmed Amin (SJTU) for his editorial assistance.

Matthias Vanhullebusch
Shanghai Jiao Tong University
Shanghai, China
Spring 2015

Table of Legal Materials and Cases

International Humanitarian Law

Legal Materials

1863 Instructions for the Government of Armies of the United States in the Field, General Orders No. 100 (Lieber Code).

1868 Declaration of St. Petersburg.

1874 Examen de la Déclaration de Bruxelles, Institut de Droit International, Session de la Haye 1875.

1885 General Act of the Berlin Conference.

1899 Final Act of the International Peace Conference.

1899 Convention with Respect to the Laws and Customs of War on Land and its Annex: Regulations concerning the Laws and Customs of War on Land (1899 Hague II).

1899 Convention for the Adaptation to Maritime Warfare of the Principles of the Geneva Convention of 22 August 1864 (1899 Hague III).

1899 Declaration to Prohibit, for the Term of Five Years, the Launching of Projectiles and Explosives from Balloons, and Other Methods of Similar Nature (1899 Hague IV, 1).

1899 Declaration concerning Asphyxiating Gases (1899 Hague IV, 2).

1899 Declaration concerning Expanding Bullets (1899 Hague IV, 3).

1907 Final Act of the Second Peace Conference.

1907 Convention respecting the Laws and Customs of War on Land and its Annex: Regulations concerning the Laws and Customs of War on Land (1907 Hague IV).

1907 Convention relative to the Laying of Automatic Submarine Contact Mines (1907 Hague VIII).

1907 Convention concerning Bombardment by Naval Forces in Time of War (1907 Hague IX).

1907 Convention for the Adaptation to Maritime Warfare of the Principles of the Geneva Convention (1907 Hague X).

1907 Declaration Prohibiting the Discharge of Projectiles and Explosives from Balloons (1907 Hague XIV).

1919 Covenant of the League of Nations.

1922–1923 Rules concerning the Control of Wireless Telegraphy in Time of War and Air Warfare, Commission of Jurists at the Hague, December 1922–February 1923.

1925 Protocol for the Prohibition of the Use of Asphyxiating, Poisonous or Other Gases, and of Bacteriological Methods of Warfare.

1945 UN Charter.

1949 Convention for the Amelioration of the Condition of the Wounded and Sick in Armed Forces in the Field (GC I).

1949 Convention for the Amelioration of the Condition of Wounded, Sick and Shipwrecked Members of Armed Forces at Sea (GC II).

1949 Convention relative to the Treatment of Prisoners of War (GC III).

1949 Convention relative to the Protection of Civilian Persons in Time of War (GC IV).

1972 Convention on the Prohibition of the Development, Production and Stockpiling of Bacteriological (Biological) and Toxin Weapons and on their Destruction.

1976 Convention on the Prohibition of Military or any Hostile Use of Environmental Modification Techniques.

1977 Protocol Additional to the Geneva Conventions of 12 August 1949, and relating to the Protection of Victims of International Armed Conflicts (AP I).

1977 Protocol Additional to the Geneva Conventions of 12 August 1949, and relating to the Protection of Victims of Non-International Armed Conflicts (AP II).

1980 Convention on Prohibitions or Restrictions on the Use of Certain Conventional Weapons Which May be Deemed to be Excessively Injurious or to Have Indiscriminate Effects.

1980 Protocol on Non-Detectable Fragments (Protocol I).

1980 Protocol on Prohibitions or Restrictions on the Use of Mines, Booby-Traps and Other Devices (Protocol II).

1980 Protocol on Prohibitions or Restrictions on the Use of Incendiary Weapons (Protocol III).

1993 Convention on the Prohibition of the Development, Production, Stockpiling and Use of Chemical Weapons and on their Destruction.

1995 Protocol on Blinding Laser Weapons (Protocol IV).

1996 Amended Protocol on Prohibitions or Restrictions on the Use of Mines, Booby-Traps and Other Devices.

1997 Convention on the Prohibition of the Use, Stockpiling, Production and Transfer of Anti-Personnel Mines and on their Destruction.

2001 Draft Articles on Responsibility of States for Internationally Wrongful Acts, International Law Commission.

2001 Draft Articles on Responsibility of States for Internationally Wrongful Acts, with Commentaries, 2001 Yearbook of the International Law Commission, Vol. II, Part II.

2003 Protocol on Explosive Remnants of War (Protocol V).

2006 Counterinsurgency Manual, United States Government Interagency Counterinsurgency Initiative, at http://www.usgcoin.org/library/doctrine/COIN-FM3-24.pdf (Last accessed on 15 February 2015)

2008 Convention on Cluster Munitions.

Cases

The Case of the S.S. "Lotus", PCIJ, Judgment, 7 September 1927, PCIJ Series A, Case No. 10, 1927, at http://www.icj-cij.org/pcij/serie_A/A_10/30_Lotus_Arret.pdf (Last accessed on 15 February 2015)

Ex parte Quirin et al., US Supreme Court, Judgment, 31 July 1942, 317 US [Supreme Court Reports] 1 (1942).

Nuremberg Trial Proceedings, Vol. 1, Indictment: Count Three: War Crimes: VIII. Statement of the Offence.

Judgment of the International Military Tribunal for the Trial of German Major War Criminals, International Military Tribunal of Nuremberg, War Crimes and Crimes against Humanity, General, 30 September–1 October 1946, at http://avalon.law.yale.edu/imt/judwarcr.asp#general (Last accessed on 15 February 2015)

USA v. Krupp et al., International Military Tribunal of Nuremberg, Tribunal III, Judgment, 31 July 1948, Case No. 10, at http://www.loc.gov/rr/frd/Military_Law/pdf/NT_war-criminals_Vol-IX.pdf (Last accessed on 15 February 2015)

Prosecutor v. Tadić, ICTY, Appeals Chamber, Judgment, 15 July 1999, Case No. IT-94-1-A, at www.icty.org (Last accessed on 15 February 2015)

Prosecutor v. Tadić, ICTY, Trial Chamber, Judgment, 7 May 1997, Case No. IT-94-1-T, at www.icty.org (Last accessed on 15 February 2015)

Prosecutor v. Tadić, ICTY, Appeals Chamber, Decision on the Defence Motion for Interlocutory Appeal on Jurisdiction, 2 October 1995, Case No. IT-94-1-AR72, at www.icty.org (Last accessed on 15 February 2015)

Legality of the Threat or Use of Nuclear Weapons in Armed Conflict, ICJ, Advisory Opinion, 8 July 1996, I.C.J. Reports 1996, at http://www.icj-cij.org/docket/files/95/7495.pdf (Last accessed on 15 February 2015)

Prosecutor v. Delalić and Delić, ICTY, Trial Chamber, Judgment, 16 November 1998, Case No. IT-96-21-T, at www.icty.org (Last accessed on 15 February 2015)

Prosecutor v. Galić, ICTY, Trial Chamber, Judgment, 5 December 2003, Case No. IT-98-29-T, at www.icty.org (Last accessed on 15 February 2015)

Prosecutor v. Kordić and Čerkez, ICTY, Appeals Chamber, Judgment, 17 December 2004, Case No. IT-95-14/2-A, at www.icty.org (Last accessed on 15 February 2015)

Prosecutor v. Strugar, ICTY, Trial Chamber, Judgment, 31 January 2005, Case No. IT-01-42-T, at www.icty.org (Last accessed on 15 February 2015)

Prosecutor v. Halilović, ICTY, Trial Chamber, Judgment, 16 November 2005, Case No. IT-01-48-T, at www.icty.org (Last accessed on 15 February 2015)

Banković and Others v. Belgium and 16 Others Contracting States, ECHR, Grand Chamber, Decision as to the Admissibility of Application No. 52207/99, 12 December 2001, Application No. 52207/99, at www.echr.coe.int (Last accessed on 15 February 2015)

Islamic Law of War

Legal Materials

1968 Palestine National Covenant

1972 Organisation of the Islamic Conference Charter

1990 Cairo Declaration on Human Rights in Islam

Cases

The State Bank of India Ltd. v. The Custodian of Evacuee Property, West Pakistan, High Court of Lahore, P.L.D. 1969, 1050.

Introduction

More than ever humanity is lost in today's conflicts where different actors on the international plane are fighting each other. In the Muslim world in general and the Middle East in particular, states, non-state actors and military alliances are involved in armed hostilities. Uninterruptedly, conflicts are fought on the basis of different political claims for human dignity. Their different expressions—as translated by the responsibility to protect on behalf of the international community of states, the right of self-defence of the state and the right of self-determination of peoples—have too often a common denominator in terms of their realisation, namely human suffering. In past and on-going conflicts in Islamic countries—such as Afghanistan, Chad, Indonesia, Iraq, Mali, Libya, Pakistan, Somalia, Sudan, Syria and Yemen—or in countries with Muslim populations—such as China, India, Nigeria and the Philippines—innocent civilians are still and have been subjected to oppression and violence. Increasingly, international and regional organisations—such as the United Nations (UN), the North Atlantic Treaty Organisation (NATO), the Arab League, the African Union (AU) or the Economic Community of West African States (ECOWAS)—are no longer immune to what is happening in the internal affairs of sovereign states. The protection of human rights and human dignity and the fight against terrorism obfuscate the respective positions of all involved and potential parties to the conflict when calling for humanitarian intervention and the respect of sovereign equality. While prospects for positive change on the international plane come to fruition, the ever-returning stalemate between international and regional organisations, states as well as non-state actors demonstrates that—traditionally—the strongest party to the conflict continues to dictate the law. To find a peaceful way out of armed conflicts and to pave the way to a transitional justice, the substantial and real costs of losing humanity towards these goals must be accounted for. If the price for peace can only be measured through violence then humanity can call upon the other half of its human nature, namely to balance the long-term benefits of such actions.

The dehumanisation of the enemy Other however has even further increased the polarisation between the warring parties and has influenced the actual application of the principles of protection during warfare. Distinction and proportionality are the key principles of protection under the laws of war that are present in the Western and Islamic legal traditions. These same principles have often been curtailed by military necessity. This apparent tension as witnessed in practice between humanitarian principles and military necessity has repeatedly been preceded by dichotomous discourses that increase

 | DOI 10.1163/9789004298248_002

the gap between both sides to the conflict. This book challenges the polarisation between humanity and necessity, between the Self and the enemy Other as well as the analyses that reinforce and perpetuate such polarisation that puts humanity as a whole at risk. A comparative study between International Humanitarian Law (IHL) and Islamic Law of War (ILW) is suggested to be an appropriate methodology to facilitate a dialogue between these different legal regimes. Finding a common basis such as a common humanity can reinforce humanitarian protection in its interpretation and on the battlefield. Advancing such dialogue on humanity is one possible avenue to engage all humanitarian actors, international and regional organisations, states, rebel forces, non-governmental organisations (NGOs) and civil society in such endeavour. Here, a naturalist legal reading of IHL and ILW shall find that common ground that serves as the basis for a positivist legal reading of the principles of protection and military necessity. A shared humanity found within nature or the creation will be a new starting point to interpret and apply the principles of protection towards the enemy Others and constitutes the most powerful expression of its own humanity.

In those regions of the world, unfortunately, too often conflicting arguments can not be settled peacefully and despair leads to violence. A vicious circle of violence instead inexplicably finds its way each time again in the resolution of conflicts. Law legitimises and regulates these different claims but power infiltrates and assimilates the enemy Other with a dehumanised counterpart unworthy of the law's protection. While the regulation on the use of force, i.e. jus ad bellum, is not part of this study, the narratives present at the time of those decisions to settle conflicting claims through violence and force necessarily permeates the debates on the actual conduct of hostilities, i.e. jus in bello, and even on the applicable law in the aftermath of the conflict, i.e. jus post bellum. Jus ad bellum, jus in bello and jus post bellum are intimately linked and their respective values of peace, humanity and accountability are each time at stake when violence is given the authority and function to defend these values in the first place. These contradictions—present in the law and reflected on the battlefield—have led to such despair in the Muslim world in general and the Middle East in particular. Jus in bello prompts important questions that affect the course of events after the conflict in particular in terms of accountability and transitional justice. Faith and commitment to peaceful transition after conflicts cannot be compelled in those societies if agreement on accountability for past abuses is not reached. Therefore, this book calls upon such humanitarian conscience to comply with the underlying moral values of the global legal and political order and the scope of its research needs to be situated as part of such endeavour. In addition, this comparative study of IHL and ILW highlights the contemporary relevance and practice of Islamic law in the regulation and resolution of armed conflicts beyond its past historical dimensions.[1]

Identity on the battlefield triggers important questions regarding the legitimacy of belligerency and the applicable law to the different types of armed conflict. In terms of the positivist principle of distinction, civilians and combatants ought to distinguish from each other and each of them have their respective protection under IHL and ILW. Depending on the nature of the participants to the armed hostilities, different legal regimes apply. From the IHL perspective, one distinguishes between international armed conflicts where the belligerent parties are states and non-international armed conflicts where states and non-state actors are fighting each other or between the latter. From the ILW perspective, two legal regimes exist and regulate accordingly conflicts amongst Muslims in internal warfare and between Muslims and non-Muslims in a context of external warfare. In spite of this categorisation of the applicable laws to different contexts of warfare depending on the nature of the belligerent parties, in theory, the principle of distinction between civilians and those participating in armed hostilities applies without reservation in the Western and Islamic legal tradition. In reality however, one witnesses that—partly due to the lack of precautionary measures—belligerent parties too often violate this fundamental principle of warfare as well as the principle of proportionality that restrains military necessity in the conduct of military operations. In this humanitarian context, law and politics are interchangeably used, as argues Stephens in the following words:

> The application of policy to heighten humanitarian objectives in terms entirely consistent with apparently settled propositions of the law is not usually controversial. The point being advanced is that policy adherence to a particular position per se does not oblige legal compliance. Whereas invoking or denying a legal claim invites a particular justificatory discourse within a framework of pre-existing institutional norms, an argument of policy remains within the largely unstructured political realm where pointed assertions of national interest and preference are more

1 See Special Issue on Afghanistan in Vincent Bernard (ed), 'Humanitarian debate: law, policy, action. Conflict in Afghanistan II—Part 2: Law and humanitarian action', (2011) 93 International Review of the Red Cross, 1. See also Mohamed Elewa Badar, 'Jus in bello under Islamic international law', (2013) International Criminal Law Review, 593.

> validly contended. Most critically, policy positions and directions can be withdrawn and re-deployed without any formal restraint.[2]

Clearly, applying and understanding the law are two different things. On the one hand, the lack of uniformity and consistency between the laws of war and their practice only confirms the difficulties which the frontline presents to the humanitarian principles. On the other hand, the law of war itself isn't enforceable enough to guarantee its further relevance and existence, especially in today's asymmetrical conflicts.[3] Within such atmosphere of indeterminacy and uncertainty in law and on the battlefield, realism and idealism, necessity and humanity are in open conflict. The apparent unitary character of the principles of protection, i.e. distinction and proportionality, are not applied regardless of the nature of the adversary party.[4] In this regard, the respect for these fundamental principles has been criticised by deconstructivist approaches to the laws of war. In their view, the application of the law is subject to an inherent contradiction between the principles of protection and military necessity. While the principles of protection in warfare seem to aspire universal ambitions—either from a Western and Islamic legal perspective—their content is characterised by two opposing values, i.e. descending (community-based) and ascending (sovereignty-based). The indeterminedness of those principles' language allows both sets of respectively liberal and realist arguments to seek justification for their objectives. This openness and contradiction are structural features of any legal system and its interpretation and application as points out Koskenniemi in the following words:

> It should not be difficult to recognize the normative/concrete oppositions in these two argumentative patterns. The descending pattern privileges normativity over concreteness while the ascending pattern does the reverse. Under the descending pattern, law becomes effectively constraining. Justification is not received from mere factual power but from

2 Dale Stephens, 'Blurring the lines: the interpretation, discourse and application of the law of armed conflict', (2009) 12 Yearbook of International Humanitarian Law, 85, at 89–90.

3 M. Cherif Bassiouni, 'The new wars and the crisis of compliance with the law of armed conflict by non-state actors', (2008) 98 Journal of Criminal Law and Criminology, 711; Nicolas Lamp, 'Conceptions of war and paradigms of compliance: the "new war" challenge to international humanitarian law', (2011) 16 Journal of Conflict and Security Law, 225.

4 James Turner Johnson, 'Maintaining the protection of non-combatants (part 1)', in David Kinsella & Craig L. Carr (eds), The morality of war: a reader (Lynne Rienner Publishers 2007), at 267.

> normative 'ideals' called rules. Under the ascending pattern, the justifiability of rules is derived from the facts of State behaviour, will or interest. The patterns oppose each other as they regard each other too subjective. From the ascending perspective, the descending model falls into subjectivism as it cannot demonstrate the content of its aprioristic norms in a reliable manner (i.e. it is reliable to the objection of utopianism). [...] From the descending perspective, the ascending model seems subjective as it privileges State will or interest over objectively binding norms (i.e. it is vulnerable to the charge of apologism). [...] Consequently, international legal discourse cannot fully accept either of the justificatory patterns. It works so as to make them seem compatible. The result, however, is an incoherent argument which constantly shifts between the opposing positions while remaining open to challenge from the opposite argument. This provides the dynamics for international legal argument.[5]

Other critical legal scholars such as Anghie, Berman, Kennedy, and Orford (IHL)[6] and El Fadl, Hassan, Khan and Mahmassani (ILW)[7] denounce the underlying motivations of the creation of IHL and ILW and its conflicting positivist legal arguments. Here, the juxtaposition of the positivist and deconstructivist approaches on the laws of war will expose the alleged conflict going on between both methodologies which analyse the world in conflictual terms, namely along sovereignty-based and community-based interests. The positivist and deconstructivist approaches encourage this conflict to take place respectively in the positive law of war and in the context of the law of war,

---

5 Martti Koskenniemi, From apology to utopia: the structure of international legal argument (Cambridge University Press 2005), at 60.

6 Antony Anghie, Imperialism, sovereignty, and the making of international law (Cambridge University Press 2005); Nathaniel Berman, 'Privileging combat? Contemporary conflict and the legal construction of war', (2004–2005) 43 Columbia Journal of Transnational Law, 1; David Kennedy, Of war and law (Princeton University Press 2006); Anne Orford, Reading humanitarian intervention: human rights and the use of force in international law (Cambridge University Press 2003).

7 Khaled Abou El Fadl, Rebellion and violence in Islamic law (Cambridge University Press 2001); Syed Riazul Hassan, The reconstruction of legal thought in Islam: a comparative study of the Islamic and the Western systems of law in the latter's terminology with particular reference to the Islamic laws suspended by the British rule in the sub-continent (Law Publishing Company 1974); Ali K. Khan, A theory of international terrorism: understanding Islamic militancy (Martinus Nijhoff Publishers 2006); S. Mahmassani, Les principes du droit international à la lumière de la doctrine islamique (Recueil des Cours. Académie de Droit International 1966).

or respectively between necessity v. protection and the Self v. the Other. In this debate on the application of the laws of war in an armed conflict, military necessity from the realist perspective has been invoked to counter liberal protection and vice versa. In addition, regarding the structural contradiction within the laws of war, critical legal scholarship seeks to explain the context and the discourses that inform their application. In this respect, legal histories on the identities and the narratives on the Self and the enemy Other provide valuable insights on how the dehumanisation of the enemy Other influences the actual creation, interpretation and application of those principles and structures in law. In the Western and Islamic traditions, dichotomies have conquered the public mind-set through fear and have artificially divided humanity in the world of the Self and its Other. Universally, throughout human history, humanity has tried to orient itself to be oneself and to be part of a collectivity.[8] Such historicity refers to individual and collective selfhood.[9]

A deconstructivist reading of the laws of war demonstrates that discourses prevent the mutuality between human beings to become partly a Self in their encounter with the Other[10] and to recognise their interrelationship—even on the battlefield. The categorisation of the applicable law to different contexts of warfare shows proof of such distinction based on the nature of the belligerent parties as defined along the lines of presence or absence of respectively state-hood in IHL or Muslim-hood in ILW. Within each jurisdictional regime, the interpretation and application of the principles of distinction and proportionality are equally subjected to narratives that divide and rule over the dehumanised Other. From this historical perspective, the state of behaviour of one community against its enemy Other—upon whose negation the Self is built—presents these utilitarian and instrumentalising narratives as being unsustainable and self-destructive. Consequently, the division between the Self and the Other as engrained in the jurisdictional regimes of the Western and Islamic legal traditions reveals the dividing consequences of the overall conflictual structure of the legal arguments that restrain interconnectedness in the human face of the enemy Other.

Incidentally, violence has been given a function and meaning within this conflictual paradigm where protection and necessity, the Self and the enemy Other are diametrically opposed respectively in the law and the context.

---

8 Paul Tillich, The courage to be (Collins Clear-Type Press 1962).

9 Vytautas Kavolis, 'Histories of selfhood, maps and sociability', in Vytautas Kavolis (ed), Designs of selfhood (Associated University Press 1984), at 20.

10 Martin Buber & Maurice Stanley Friedman, The knowledge of man (George Allen & Unwin 1965), at 71.

Accordingly, it is considered as the only possible means to fully settle these differences that cannot possibly be transcended through peaceful means.[11] The law of the strongest imposes its will upon the weaker parties. Power is a crucial parameter in the decision-making process to engage in armed hostilities. The stalemate between international, regional, national and subnational actors in the Middle East further played into such paradigm where compromise is impossible and violence is the answer to solving conflicts. Such explanation—having the ambition to provide an all-inclusive explanation of reality—actually tames violence to a meaning or a theory and normalises discriminatory practices as inevitable.[12] Behind an apparent natural order, human nature is rationalised along the lines of those divisive discourses on the Self and the enemy Other that create and facilitate the conditions that justify violence. From a deconstructivist approach, the indeterminacy of the law—as expressed through its structural contradictions—is informed by those underlying narratives that create such division in the first place.

While from a positivist perspective, the legitimation of violence through the law has its constraints, its deconstructivist reading further limits the prospects of protection within the laws of war. Except for violence, no proper space is available within the laws of war to mark its application in favour of humanity as its interpretation has been fraud by dehumanising narratives on the enemy Other. Such conflictual interpretative framework prevents humanity from asking the right questions as it preconceives violence to be the answer; while balancing the duality of human nature involves the responsibility to compromise between opposing interests, behaviours, desires and conditions of human beings. Instead, describing human nature in paradoxical terms denies the acceptance of its duality and reinforces its conflictual and vicious reasoning. Criticisms on such indeterminacy highlight the inability and incapacity to push the legal and political boundaries to challenge the inevitability of human suffering. For the victims of violence and oppression, such explanation erodes the value of their lives and thus reduces the infringements to their human dignity to meaningless proportions. Moreover, violence and its legitimation

11 See for example Article 42, United Nations (UN) Charter, which provides that: "Should the Security Council consider that measures provided for in Article 41 would be inadequate or have proved to be inadequate, it may take such action by air, sea, or land forces as may be necessary to maintain or restore international peace and security. Such action may include demonstrations, blockade, and other operations by air, sea, or land forces of Members of the United Nations."

12 See also Tim Jacoby, Understanding conflict and violence: theoretical and interdisciplinary approaches (Routledge 2008), at 72.

through the text is senseless as it will always infringe upon the life of human beings and consequently upon the survival of the human species: *dulce bellum inexpertis*.

Therefore, dialoguing in terms of inclusion and exclusion is irrelevant for the purpose of protecting everybody who is entitled to protection during armed conflicts. Arguing outside the interpretative framework of this apologetic exclusion and its inclusive idealistic counterpart might truly contribute to the universal—liberal—ambitions of protection accessible for all. Allowing the rationalisation of inclusion as the solution to these objectives would ignore the entire construction of the conflictual paradigm which is built upon the dividing terms of inclusion and exclusion in the first place. Such attempt towards inclusion would inherently reproduce such discrimination. Not all means justify these ends. Debates on universalist and cultural relativist stances on human dignity are also construed along those dividing lines, though as this comparative study intends to establish, they offer important insights on the presence of such notion in each legal system. In order to avoid reproducing such conflictual paradigm, this comparative study does not envisage engaging on universalist and cultural relativist accounts on the protection of humanity and its dignity.[13] It rather takes a common humanity as the starting point from which rules on the principles of protection in IHL and ILW can be deduced as opposed to the historical narratives on the Self and the enemy Other that have and have been curtailing the genuine scope of their application. In this regard, humanity belongs to all human beings and all human beings are members of humanity.

Humanity, therefore, needs to be reminded of this in order to live up its potential of *homo sapiens sapiens*. A naturalist legal reading gives humanity back its agency to engage in a dialogue between different legal traditions that will propel and reconcile positivist and deconstructivist approaches towards them in order to enhance humanitarian protection in theory but most importantly on the battlefield. Interpreting and applying the laws of war ought to take on a more complementary approach when it comes to furthering the dialogue on humanitarian protection in favour of all human beings affected and

13 Ebrahim Afsah, 'Contested universalities of international law: Islam's struggle with modernity', (2008) 10 Journal of the History of International Law, 259; Ann Elizabeth Mayer, 'The Islam and human rights nexus: shifting dimensions', (2007) 4 Muslim World Journal of Human Rights, 1; Heidi Morrison, 'Beyond universalism', (2004) 1 Muslim World Journal of Human Rights, 1; Rohimi B. Shapiee, 'Revitalising the siyar (Islamic international law): a challenge for the Muslims', (2008) 4 Journal of Islamic State Practices in International Law, 1.

involved by armed conflict. Challenges are not specific to one or another legal tradition but rather common to humanity as a whole that doesn't expect to be treated differently on the battlefield. Such pragmatism however is not only aiming at a dialogue between and a reconciliation of positivist principles of protection as found in different legal systems, it is also driven by a humanitarian conscience that aims to create such space where all subjects of law are protected accordingly. As opposed to the vacuum of that space which the deconstructivist approach denounces to be inherently indeterminate enough to be oriented by the dictates of the most powerful and their self-destructive violence. The latter's descriptive order presupposes that the absence of human agency and belonging prevents human beings to challenge its interpretative tools and to find back its common humanity and conscience that protects human life instead.

Therefore, in this comparative study on IHL and ILW, humanity will be defined respectively from the biological/evolutionary and creationary perspective. In this regard, a determinate definition and identity will be given to such human belonging in both legal traditions that serves the purpose of humanitarian protection of all human beings on the battlefield. On the one hand, from the Western and secular perspective, humanity is defined as the common belonging to the human race that has evolved through evolution and that is grounded in the natural realm. By their biological belonging, all human beings are members of the human race. On the other hand, from the Islamic and religious perspective, all human beings belong to the creation as made by God. Grounding the definition and the knowledge of humanity and its livelihood within the natural realm presents a new starting point which accommodates differences as found in nature or the creation. Such unity in diversity finds the socially undetermined realm to be grounded in a naturally deterministic order of common biological or creationary belonging. A naturalist legal reading of the principles of protection will necessarily have a transcendental angle. It strikes the interpretation and the application of the principles of protection outside the positivist and deconstructivist approaches to them as it introduces a common humanity beyond their conflictual readings.

From this "life" paradigm that puts human life central to its definition and methodology, tensions, however, between realism, i.e. necessity, and idealism, i.e. protection, within this complementary approach do not necessarily have to be tolerated as the relativist position sees it, but rather have to be settled carefully with respect for the natural order in which these arguments are being raised. Such moral approach would transcend the divisions introduced by humanity upon humanity which should respect the world described and experienced in complementary and interdependent terms instead. Thus, humanity should no longer be an agent and a victim at the same time of its own violence. This study, therefore, aims at demonstrating that human beings across Western and Islamic civilisations can awaken their consciousness with regard to their biological membership and/or membership of God's creation, respectively, and consequently to the survival of humanity; and stems in part from an ambition to facilitate dialogue between cultures, legal and religious alike. Within the "life paradigm"—advanced in this book—humanity can find again the meaning of life which is at the roots of its existence and survival. In that regard, particularly to the experiences and encounters of the Western and Islamic civilisations, according to Mignolo and Schwiwy, "a change of directionality in the work of translation and transculturation [...] could help in thinking and moving beyond dichotomies, politically and ethically".[14]

Besides the unity of humanity as found in nature or in the creation, lies perhaps a stronger bound among human beings which would denounce the rationalisation of violence and its correlative and inevitable suffering.[15] The exercise of a humanitarian conscience in particular would be the natural outcome of such responsibility whose descriptive order prescribes sustainability for the sake of the survival of the human species. It is the human(itarian) conscience, which is the other part of humanity's attributes and which can give a voice within the man-made conflictual paradigm to survive the human species. The necessarily transcendental nature of this conscience connects human beings with each other and necessarily accepts its interconnectedness and intersubjectivity. From a naturalist legal perspective,[16] as will be submitted, such conscience gives guidance to apply the laws of armed conflict beyond the positivist and deconstructivist approaches within the conflictual paradigm. This deontological approach seeks to read a morality or "natural law ethics",[17] as grounded in (human) nature without which no life can be conceived, inside the present

14 Walter D. Mignolo & Freya Schiwy, 'Beyond dichotomies: translation/transculturation and the colonial difference', in Elisabeth Mudimbe-Boyi (ed), Beyond dichotomies: histories, identities, cultures, and the challenge of globalization (State University of New York Press 2002), at 252.

15 Michael Nicholson, Rationality and the analysis of international conflict (Cambridge University Press 1992), at 105; Soli Özel, 'The inevitability of violence?', (2004) 9 Journal of Islamic Law and Culture, 27.

16 See Amanda Russell Beattie, 'Absolute ends and dynamic rules: being political as human beings', in Anthony F. Lang & Amanda Russell Beattie (eds), War, torture, and terrorism: rethinking the rules of international security (Routledge 2009); Frank Griffel, 'The harmony of natural law and Shari'a in Islamist theology', in Abbas Amanat & Frank Griffel (eds), Shari'a: Islamic law in the contemporary context (Stanford University Press 2007).

17 Robert P. George, In defense of natural law (Oxford University Press), at 84.

legal positivist framework. From this perspective, the "life paradigm" can embrace the Self and enemy Other as complementary to its existence in order to limit the human suffering even within the framework of the laws of war. It is not the contradictory nature of the present legal paradigm between considerations of humanity and military necessity, as established by deconstructivists, but the failure to foster such a morality that, according to Cohen, "constitutes the main impediment to civilized conduct in this area".[18] The balance of these allegedly conflicting interests within the "life paradigm" will be guided by such humanitarian conscience. Such empowerment recognises the biological or creationary and ontological common grounds of the human species and its agency to respect its unity at least for the sake of its own survival.

Nonetheless, the discursive and social discriminations introduced by humanity are necessarily part of human nature. Their deconstruction however leads to another debate about nothingness which is left after the deconstruction of these discriminatory discourses. Therefore, deconstruction in particular would be able to expose, as Cornell puts it, "the nakedness of power struggles and, indeed, of violence masqueraded as the rule of law"[19] as well as the indeterminacy of inherent conflicting arguments as rationalised within the structure of law and its doctrines.[20] Obviously, this methodology starts from the premise that law is deconstructible and recognises that there also exists a reality beyond the text, namely the one of life.[21] Therefore, the actual exercise of deconstruction is itself an act of justice as it necessarily strikes the law from the outside.[22] If violence has been informing the law from outside, then a human(itarian) conscience can counter that violence in that same outside realm of the law in order to transcend the meaning of violence given within the law. From this literary perspective, this book aims at understanding the strategies of representation within the conflictual paradigm in the Western and Islamic traditions. Only then can deconstruction transcend the perverse effects of rationalising violence—which gives meaning to violence within that paradigm—by trying to give meaning to life instead beyond the text and

---

18 Marshall Cohen, 'Morality and the laws of war', in Virginia Held, Sidney Morgenbesser & Thomas Nagel (eds), Philosophy, morality, and international affairs (Oxford University Press 1974), at 88.

19 Drucilla Cornell, 'The violence of masquerade: law dressed up as justice', (1990) 11 Cardozo Law Review, 1047, at 1047.

20 Michel Rosenfeld, 'Deconstruction and legal interpretation: conflict, indeterminacy and the temptations of the new legal formalism', (1990) 11 Cardozo Law Review, 1211, at 1212.

21 Frank R. Ankersmit, Historical representation (Stanford University Press 2001), at 282–84.

22 Jacques Derrida, 'Force de la loi: le "fondement mystique de l'autorité" ', (1990) 11 Cardozo Law Review, 920, at 943–45.

especially on the battlefield. Humanity cannot be divided as far as human suffering is concerned. Both the realist self-interested behaviour of human beings and the idealist potential to make them respect the unity of humanity are part of the intrinsic duality of human nature. Its true value in the end can only be known subjectively and be manipulated along both characteristics however outside the existing structure/paradigm of the legal argument. No real justice can exist without life, i.e. the nature of things.

Therefore, this book has a broad focus because it aims at bringing together different lines of enquiry about the representation and construction of different identities, about the shaping of aspirations of protection in the laws of war and about the relationship between law and politics; it offers a blueprint that complements positivist and deconstructivist approaches to IHL and ILW by advancing a naturalist legal reading that seeks to promote their humanitarian spirit. Apart from this introductory chapter, this book substantively consists of three main Parts, each of them comparing the relevant subject matter to be discussed. Within each Part, a separate Chapter will be dedicated to the Western and Islamic tradition on the laws of war respectively. Finally, the concluding chapter will summarise the findings of this research.

Firstly, Part I, consisting of Chapters I and II, will address the laws of war as such by focusing on the jurisdictional regimes having legalised the historical divisions of the Self and the Other as well as the principles of protection (distinction, i.e. between combatants and non-combatants, and proportionality, i.e. not inflicting more human suffering than necessary). From a positivist perspective, Chapter I will explore how the jurisdictional regimes under ILW have reflected the division of political spheres of influences. The latter division has no textual support whatsoever under the primary sources of Islamic law, i.e. the Qur'an and the Sunnah. But these divisions were legalised into an abode of Islam, i.e. the *dar al-Islam*, and of war, i.e. the *dar al-harb*. Depending on which enemies of Islam were fought, the territorial and temporal jurisdiction of external and internal *jihad* will be examined. In addition, the application of the principles of distinction and proportionality will be assessed for both types of *jihad*. Being influenced by ILW, IHL as described under Chapter II will prove a similar distinction of jurisdiction and use of the principles of protection. Hence, a closer look upon the territorial and temporal jurisdiction of international and non-international armed conflicts will be made. Also an analysis on how the principles of distinction and proportionality in the respective jurisdictional regimes operate will be given.

Secondly, Part II, consisting of Chapters III and IV, will give a critical legal historical—and thus deconstructivst—analysis of the Self and the Other by looking at each context having determined the division and consecutive categorisation of the Self and the Other. In Chapter III, the narrative on the Western Self and its Other will be traced back to the role of the Christian religion as the basis for determining the Self. Consecutively, the Enlightenment period had set aside the Christian conscience for Science and Reason categorising the Self and the Other along a standard of civilisation. Western powers found their justification for nationalistic and imperialist ambitions within the progress narrative to conquer the world and to put their humanitarianism at its disposal. History, however, proved that the West rather suppressed the Other's particularism and tradition in spite of its universal message of liberalism. Even after decolonisation, the West continued to manifest itself as the moralising saviour of the unprivileged peoples in particular when they were subjected to authoritarian and terrorist leaderships. Obviously, Chapter IV on the Islamic legal history on the Self and its Other will start from the period of Revelation onwards. The early Islamic emperors and their jurists had divided the world into different spheres of influence determined by the religious affiliation of its inhabitants and which had to be included under their authority; until the Western powers were challenging the Islamic rule and introduced the modern state system dividing the Islamic territories along racial and ethnic lines. Disagreement remained as to how emancipate and become sovereign from the Western colonial powers through nationalism, modernism or revivalism. Ultimately, these discussions proved to be vain as rebellious, local and terrorist groups revolted against the despotic regimes within the Muslim world.

Finally, Part III, consisting of Chapters V and VI, will look at the structure of the legal argument with reference to the jurisdictional regimes and the principles of proportionality and military necessity in order to demonstrate the inherent contradiction of this structure. It will also emphasise the need to argue outside this structure, from the "life paradigm", for the sake of the survival of the human species. Chapter V will examine the question of legitimate belligerency of warring parties in external and internal *jihad* as informed by the division between Islamic leaderships and their opponents. Also the principle of proportionality is subject to the discretion of the military commander to invoke military necessity during armed hostilities. It would seem contradictory to raise a communitarian legal argument advocating overall protection against its self-interested counterpart of necessity. Within this paradigm it is impossible to respect God's creation of humanity, but it remains possible to fight the so-called inner *jihad* to overcome this (rationalisation and legitimation of) violence in theory and practice by raising one's human(itarian) conscience. Similarly, Chapter VI will address how the determination of the jurisdictional regime under IHL throughout the structure of the legal arguments has been affected by the underlying historical division between the Self and the Other.

The Other's recognition of legitimate belligerency remains at the discretion of the Western Self to allow it to participate on the international plane and to benefit from its legal order. However, regardless of the lawful participation in armed hostilities, the conduct of belligerent parties continues to jeopardise the protection of those affected by the conflict—combatants and civilians alike. In spite of the legal developments expanding the scope of protection and limiting the atrocities of warfare, military necessity at one side of the equation in the structure of the legal arguments curtails the efforts of the principles of protection. Clearly, no protection is available, both in theory and in practice, in such endless circle of violence which has put humanity as a whole at risk. Therefore, a call for facing these hierarchies of humanity could bring further awareness in the secular West in order for humanity to survive.

The concluding chapter will submit that the conflictual reasoning in the Western and Islamic traditions on the laws of war is not sustainable to embrace the diversity which is present in the evolution and creation of humanity. Moreover, the positivist and deconstructivist approaches towards those traditions reinforce the same conflictual nature of humanity's behaviour towards its Others. Instead, a complementary perspective on such human nature as guided by a humanitarian conscience would actually transcend those divisions in the structure of the legal argument in order for humanity to safeguard its humanity and survival.

PART I

Positivist Analysis of the Principles of Protection in Warfare

CHAPTER I

Principles of Protection in Warfare under Islamic Law of War

1.1 Introduction

The aim of this chapter is to analyse—from a positivist perspective—the principles of protection, i.e. distinction and proportionality, under ILW. Although some extensive work has been undertaken by different scholars in the field with respect to the general evolution of ILW,[1] the principles of protection have not been really examined in detail. The principles of distinction and proportionality (which are also found in the traditions of IHL, i.e. jus in bello) will be examined herein from the outlook of the primary sources of Islamic law, i.e. the Qur'an and the Sunnah. These primary sources provide the basis for understanding state conduct during peace and war times, i.e. the so-called *siyar*.[2] Without entering into the debate on the origins of IHL and ILW,[3] this structure will facilitate an understanding of past and ongoing conflicts with perpetrators and victims from Islamic and Western origins. The chapter will firstly categorise the territorial and temporal jurisdiction of ILW, secondly its

1 For example: Muhammad Hamidullah, Muslim conduct of state (Sh. Muhammed Ashraf 1961); James Turner Johnson, The holy war idea in Western and Islamic traditions (Pennsylvania State University Press 1997); James Turner Johnson & John Kelsay, Cross, crescent, and sword: the justification and limitation of war in Western and Islamic tradition (Greenwood Press 1990); Majid Khadduri, War and peace in the law of Islam (Johns Hopkins Press 1955); Rudolph Peters, Jihad in classical and modern Islam (Markus Wiener 1996); Niaz A. Shah, Islamic law and the law of armed conflict: the armed conflict in Pakistan (Routledge 2011).

2 Richard C. Martin, 'The religious foundations of war, peace, and statecraft in Islam', in James Turner Johnson & John Kelsay (eds), Just war and jihad: historical and theoretical perspectives on war and peace in Western and Islamic traditions (Greenwood Press 1991), at 91. *Siyar*, however, is not strictly limited to these primary sources but include others like arbitral awards, orders of commanders, treaties, etc. The latter are also often based on the Qur'an and the Sunnah.

3 See Karima Bennoune, '"As-Salamu Alaykum" humanitarian law in Islamic jurisprudence', (1993–1994) 15 Michigan Journal of International Law, 605; Carolyn Evans, 'The double-edged sword: religious influences on international humanitarian law', (2005) 6 Melbourne Journal of International Law, 1.

 | DOI 10.1163/9789004298248_003

subjects, and finally the conduct of hostilities in order to give a clearer picture of certain principles present within the Qur'anic experience but whose juristic interpretations have blurred the straightforwardness by which the Prophet Muhammad had spread the message of Islam. This latter historical context will be dealt with in Part II (Chapter IV), where a closer look at the narratives of the Islamic Self and its Other will try to expose how—over time—such divisions seem to have influenced the law to reflect such discourse.

Before dealing with the substantive issues in this chapter, a closer look upon the sources of Islamic law is mandatory. Traditionally, the sources of Islamic law are categorised into the Qur'an, the Sunnah, *ijma* (consensus among the jurists) and *qiyas* (analogy). However, not all *madhahib* agree upon the latter two sources and rather treat them as methodologies to interpret the primary divine sources of Islamic law, i.e. the Qur'an and the Sunnah which override all the other sources of Islamic law. The Qur'an constitutes of the Revelation to the Prophet Muhammad. Very few verses in the Qur'an refer to fighting. Therefore, the need to analyse the Sunnah which constitutes of the Traditions of the Prophet Muhammad, namely the things He has done, said and acquiesced to during His lifetime. These Traditions have been transmitted through the *hadiths* which are collections of those Traditions. Their credibility and authenticity depend on the chain of narration and the people involved in collecting these Traditions.[4] For those reasons, we will use the collection of *hadiths* from Al-Bukhari (d. 870), called the *Sahih*[5] which, generally, has been accepted by jurists as being of high authenticity.[6]

1.2 Territorial and Temporal Jurisdiction

1.2.1 *On War and Peace*

Before analysing ILW and its jurisdictional regimes, its historical development will be briefly dealt with. ILW has been formulated by the jurists in terms of historical progress made by the Islamic community, i.e. the *ummah*, from the

4 Wael B. Hallaq, An introduction to Islamic law (Cambridge University Press 2009), at 16–9; Arif Ali Khan & M.H. Syed, Concept of Islamic law (Pentagon Press 2007), at 60–1.

5 See M. Muhsin Khan, Translation of Sahih Bukhari, at http://www.iiu.edu.my/deed/hadith/bukhari/index.html. (Last accessed 15 February 2015)

6 Jonathan A.C. Brown, Hadith: Muhammad's legacy in the medieval and modern world (Oneworld Publications 2009), at 7 and 39.

period of Revelation onwards[7] through the early battles of Islam.[8] The establishment of the first Islamic community was accompanied and guided by the Revelation to the Prophet and the teachings of the Prophet. The Qur'an and the Traditions would adapt to the challenges which the first Muslims were facing both from within and outside their community.[9] In the first instance, the Islamic faith had to be propagated peacefully. Until the Meccans continued to persecute the Muslims in Medina after their migration there, the *ummah* needed to be defended accordingly against their aggressive enemies. The moment the new Muslim state gained more power, it could afford to pursue an offensive policy in the Arabian Peninsula rather than a defensive one.[10] After the victories of the Islamic armies within this territory, an expansionist desire would spread the message around the rest of the world[11] with the aim of inviting the non-Muslims to embrace this new religion or otherwise subject them to the Islamic rule while permitting them to continue their own religious practices.[12] In that regard, the so-called "peace verses"[13] though they precede those of the "sword", were set aside.[14] Hence, the theory of abrogation, i.e. *naskh*,[15] was particularly useful for setting aside the initial engagement of

---

7 Ann Elizabeth Mayer, 'War and peace in the Islamic tradition and international law', in James Turner Johnson & John Kelsay (eds), Just war and jihad: historical and theoretical perspectives on war and peace in Western and Islamic traditions (Greenwood Press 1991), at 197.

8 Towqueer Alam Falahi, The Quranic concept of war and peace (Kanishka Publishers 2004), at 90–101.

9 Mayer, in, at 197.

10 Abdullahi Ahmed An-Na'im, Toward an Islamic reformation: civil liberties, human rights, and international law (Syracuse University Press 1996), at 158.

11 Bernard K. Freamon, 'Martyrdom, suicide, and the Islamic law of war: a short legal history', (2003–2004) 27 Fordham International Law Journal, 299, at 314–15.

12 Wael B. Hallaq, Shari'a: theory, practice, transformations (Cambridge University Press 2009), at 327.

13 While the "peace verses" are indicative of the message of peace which the Revelation stands for, the "sword verses" on the other hand, which were revealed after the peace ones, are rather interpreted to justify a continuous warfare with the unbelievers. See Sohail H. Hashmi, 'Interpreting the Islamic ethics of war and peace', in Sohail H. Hashmi (ed), Islamic political ethics: civil society, pluralism, and conflict (Princeton University Press 2002), at 206.

14 See David Bukay, 'Peace or jihad? Abrogation in Islam', (2007) 14 Middle East Quarterly, 3.

15 As an interpretive technique, the theory of abrogation justifies to repeal particular Quran'ic verses by others based upon the assertion that some verses are contradicting each other and that clarity needs to be achieved when reading the Qur'an by giving preference to only one side of the conflicting verses. Here, the "sword verses" have benefited

peaceful understanding with the non-Muslim communities and affirming the waging of war with them instead.[16] For example, the "peace verse" in Q8:61 "But if the enemy incline towards peace, do thou (also) incline towards peace, and trust in Allah. For He is One that heareth and knoweth (all things)" was considered by early Islamic jurists to have been abrogated. Thus, by virtue of the theory of abrogation the "peace verse" was replaced by the later "sword verse" in Q9:29 "Fight those who believe not in Allah nor the Last Day, nor hold that forbidden which hath been forbidden by Allah and His Messenger, nor acknowledge the religion of Truth, (even if they are) of the People of the Book, until they pay the Jizya with willing submission, and feel themselves subdued".[17] Kamali has argued that the use of the theory of abrogation by early Islamic jurists to sweepingly supersede the "peace verses" with the "sword verses" was influenced "by the prevailing pattern of hostile relations with non-Muslims" at the time.[18] Clearly, such interpretations set aside the defensive wars which would preserve the *ummah* for the sake of an aggressive *jihad* which became legally justified by the jurists as being the normal and universal condition of the Islamic state's relations with its rivals[19] at that particular time in history.[20]

The earliest codified sources on *siyar*—i.e. the law on the conduct and behaviour of the Islamic state in peace and war times[21]—already dated from

---

from such abrogation at the expense of the "peace verses". See John Burton, The sources of Islamic law: Islamic theories of abrogation (Edinburgh University Press 1990).

16 Hashmi, in, at 206.

17 This research is using the translation of the Holy Qur'an by Yusuf Ali. See Yusuf Ali, The Holy Quran, at http://www.harunyahya.com/Quran_translation/Quran_translation_index.php. (Last accessed 8 March 2012) Any citation to the Qur'anic verses are made to the above mentioned translation and will be implied from now onwards as a reference work.

18 Muhammad H. Kamali, Principles of Islamic jurisprudence (The Islamic Texts Society 2003), at 223.

19 Mohammad Tal'at al-Ghunaimi, The Muslim conception of international law and the Western approach (Martinus Nijhoff Publishers 1968), at 137; Hashmi, in, at 205; Hilmar Krüger, Fetwa und Siyar: zur internationalrechtlichen Gutachtenpraxis der osmanischen Seyh ül-Islâm vom 17. bis 19. Jahrhundert unter besonderer Berücksichtigung des "Behcet ül-Fetâvâ" (Harrassowitz 1978), at 119; Abdul Hamid Ahmad Abu Sulayman, Towards an Islamic theory of international relations: new directions for methodology and thought (1993) (Revision of a thesis (PhD), International Institute of Islamic Thought, University of Pennsylvania, 1973), at 43.

20 Mashood A. Baderin, 'The evolution of Islamic law of nations and the modern international order: universal peace through mutuality and co-operation', (2000) 17 American Journal of Islamic Social Sciences, 57, at 67.

21 Hamidullah, at 10.

1240.[22] They dealt *inter alia* with non-Muslim subjects within—i.e. in the *dar al-Islam* (the abode of Islam, outside Muslim territory, i.e. in the *dar al-harb* (the abode of war)), and with treaty partners, i.e. in the *dar al-sulh* (the abode of the covenant).[23] These territorial divisions, from the offensive *jihad* perspective, were functionally only temporary as they would seize to exist when all peoples belonged to the same Muslim state through imperial jihadist and annexation policies.[24] These aggressive policies were presented as being part of a religious obligation.[25] According to Khadduri, it was a permanent struggle until the *dar al-harb* was overcome by the *dar al-Islam* not only militarily and politically but also psychologically.[26] Nonetheless, a number of political practices in Islamic history could be given that would prove the contrary[27] as they conflict with the values of peace and justice which Islam stands for.[28] Regardless of the hostile environment of tribal warfare in the Arabian Peninsula[29] and where threatening empires and their ideologies in their turn could have overrun their newly emerging Islamic competitor,[30] the categorisations of non-Muslim peoples in opposition to the *ummah*[31] would approve the use of force[32] against the non-Muslims in order to dominate and rule against them in future hostile situations. If one advocates peaceful coexistence among peoples where sovereignty is to be respected, war can only be of a defensive nature.[33]

---

22 Khaled Abou El Fadl, Rebellion and violence in Islamic law (Cambridge University Press 2001), at 144.

23 Abu Sulayman, at 7.

24 Khadduri, at 44; Isam Kamel Salem, Islam und Völkerrecht: das Völkerrecht in der islamischen Weltanschauung (Express Edition 1984), at 98.

25 Mayer, in, at 202.

26 Majid Khadduri, The Islamic law of nations: Shaybani's Siyar (John Hopkins Press 1966), at 16–7; Maulana Muhammad Ali, A manual of hadith (Curzon Press 1988), at 252.

27 Baderin, at 59.

28 See also Niaz A. Shah, Self-defense in Islamic and international law: assessing Al-Qaeda and the invasion in Iraq (Palgrave Macmillan 2008), at 31.

29 An-Na'im, at 142.

30 Baderin, at 67.

31 Syed Riazul Hassan, The reconstruction of legal thought in Islam: a comparative study of the Islamic and the Western systems of law in the latter's terminology with particular reference to the Islamic laws suspended by the British rule in the sub-continent (Law Publishing Company 1974), at 136.

32 An-Na'im, at 142.

33 Id., at 153; al-Ghunaimi, at 180; Majid Khadduri, 'The Islamic theory of international relations and its contemporary relevance', in J. Harris Proctor (ed), Islam and international relations (Pall Mall 1965), at 31.

Evidently, this "territorial demarcation" should also be seen in the light of "the war-prone tendencies of those times",[34] as Baderin argues. Consequently, *siyar* kept its importance to regulate this state of affairs and appeared to have become part of the eternal problem.[35] Such man-made corpus of Islamic law of nations resulting from the juristic efforts of different schools of law[36] has been misappropriated in reality and started to live its own life. Theoretically, states which are not in factual war with the Muslim state would be at war anyhow.[37] The bifurcation of the world order into different spheres was a legal fiction[38] having no textual support whatsoever in the primary sources.[39] These divisions were developed by the jurists as the "*ex post facto* legitimation of the early conquests"[40] from the eighth century onwards.[41] In this regard, peace could no longer be considered to be an interval of recess[42] and war would be a transitory condition.[43] The Qur'an however demands the Muslims not to be aggressors in any case; they shall only fight for the cause of God against the injustices inflicted upon Muslims,[44] namely to repel aggression, to protect the historic mission of Islam and to defend religious freedom. Fights for such cause as opposed to those fights for worldly political reasons are the only fights which are sanctioned religiously.[45] Or in the words of the Prophet: "He who

---

34 Baderin, at 67–8.

35 Majid Khadduri & Herbert J. Liebesny, Law in the Middle East / Vol. 1, Origin and development of Islamic law (Middle East Institute 1955), at 350.

36 Gamal M. Badr, 'A survey of Islamic international law', (1982) 76 American Society of International Law Proceedings, 56, at 56.

37 al-Ghunaimi, at 183–84.

38 Hashmi, in, at 207.

39 Niaz A. Shah, 'Self-defence in Islamic law', (2005–2006) 12 Yearbook of Islamic and Middle Eastern Law, 181, at 193.

40 Abdulaziz A. Sachedina, 'The development of jihad in Islamic revelation and history', in James Turner Johnson & John Kelsay (eds), Cross, crescent, and sword: the justification and limitation of war in Western and Islamic tradition (Greenwood Press 1990), at 37.

41 Fred M. Donner, 'The sources of Islamic conceptions of war', in James Turner Johnson & John Kelsay (eds), Just war and jihad: historical and theoretical perspectives on war and peace in Western and Islamic traditions (Greenwood Press 1991), at 50.

42 Khadduri & Liebesny, Law in the Middle East / Vol. 1, Origin and development of Islamic law, at 354.

43 Abu Sulayman, at 121–22.

44 Bassam Tibi, 'War and peace in Islam', in Sohail H. Hashmi (ed), Islamic political ethics: civil society, pluralism, and conflict (Princeton University Press 2002), at 178.

45 Abou El Fadl, at 63; Rudolph Peters, Jihad in medieval and modern Islam: the chapter on jihad from Averroes' legal handbook "Bidayat al-mudjtahid" and the treatise "Koran and fighting" by the late Shaykh al-Azhar Mahmud Shaltut (E.J. Brill 1977), at 55 and 85.

fights that Allah's Word (i.e. Islam) should be superior, fights in God's cause."[46] Therefore, only an aggression, i.e. a first attack,[47] against the Islamic community necessitates the collective response or obligation (as seen by the Sunni schools of law, i.e. Hanafi, Hanbali, Maliki and Shafi)[48] of the Muslims defending[49] their so-called "Islamic world order"[50] and its "doctrine of monotheism".[51] First aggressive armed attacks by Muslims are prohibited and constitute a provocation and thus a transgression as illustrated in different verses of the Qur'an:[52]

> Fight in the cause of Allah those who fight you, but do not transgress limits; for Allah loveth not transgressors. (Q2:190)
>
> And fight the Pagans all together as they fight you all together. But know that Allah is with those who restrain themselves. (Q9:36)
>
> And fight them on until there is no more Tumult or oppression, and there prevail justice and faith in Allah. But if they cease, let there be no hostility except to those who practise oppression. (Q2:193)
>
> Allah forbids you not, with regard to those who fight you not for (your) Faith nor drive you out of your homes, from dealing kindly and justly with them: for Allah loveth those who are just. (Q60:8)
>
> Allah only forbids you, with regard to those who fight you for (your) Faith, and drive you out of your homes, and support (others) in driving you out, from turning to them (for friendship and protection). It is such as turn to them (in these circumstances), that do wrong. (Q60:9)

---

46 Al-Bukhari, Vol. 4, Book 52, Number 65. (Narrated by Abu Musa)

47 Ali, A manual of hadith, at 265.

48 al-Ghunaimi, at 141; S. Mahmassani, Les principes du droit international à la lumière de la doctrine islamique (Recueil des Cours. Académie de Droit International 1966), at 281.

49 M. Raquibuz Zaman, 'Islamic perspectives on territorial boundaries and autonomy', in Sohail H. Hashmi (ed), Islamic political ethics: civil society, pluralism, and conflict (Princeton University Press 2002), at 95.

50 Sachedina, in, at 36.

51 Peters, Jihad in medieval and modern Islam: the chapter on jihad from Averroes' legal handbook "Bidayat al-mudjtahid" and the treatise "Koran and fighting" by the late Shaykh al-Azhar Mahmud Shaltut, at 43.

52 al-Ghunaimi, at 167; Ali ibn Muhammad Mawardi & Asadullah Yate, al-Ahkam as-Sultaniyyah: the laws of Islamic governance (Ta-Ha Publishers 1996), at 63; Peters, Jihad in classical and modern Islam, at 74.

> It may be that Allah will grant love (and friendship) between you and those whom ye (now) hold as enemies. For Allah has power (over all things). And Allah is Oft-Forgiving, Most Merciful. (Q60:7)

The classical Islamic jurists institutionalised the dichotomy between the good and the evil in their respective abodes of peace and war. *Jihad*, initially the fight against aggression, has later become the instrument not "in the fulfilment of the divine promise",[53] as understood by Sachedina, but rather the strategy to gain political control over its Muslim and non-Muslim adversaries. A universal Islam[54] with peaceful coexistence among peoples and religions[55] on equal footing[56] would be set aside by political ambitions for power. The consolidation of universal Islam whose extinction by its enemies has been feared by the Islamic establishment could possibly explain the violations of ILW towards Islam's Others.[57] As a result, such division has appropriated and reproduced itself within the realities in which Muslims had to interact with their internal and external enemies. This early juristic polity and its legally instituted fiction of division of the world and its subjects will be object of the rest of this study. It will constitute the benchmark against which the Qur'anic experience and the Sunnah needs to be reflected. These man-made elucidations contrast with the Qur'an which explains the diversity of humanity in religious terms not in military-political territorialities. Against this brief historical background on the relationship between war and peace in Islam, we will now examine how this relationship is also translated into legal terms and in particular what the territorial and temporal jurisdictional scopes of ILW are.

1.2.2 *During External Warfare*

1.2.2.1 Territorial Jurisdiction

A territory becomes part of the abode of war and *jihad* has to be waged, as al-Ghunaimi states, whenever "Muslim rule and directions are not applied

53 Sachedina, in, at 36–7.

54 al-Ghunaimi, at 156.

55 Khadduri, 'The Islamic theory of international relations and its contemporary relevance', in, at 31.

56 Javaid Rehman, Islamic state practices, international law and the threat from terrorism: a critique of the "clash of civilizations" in the new world order (Hart 2005), at 49.

57 Ahmed Zaki Yamani, 'Humanitarian international law in Islam: a general outlook', in Hisham M. Ramadan (ed), Understanding Islamic law: from classical to contemporary (Rowman & Littlefield Publishers 2006), at 66.

therein, or if the Muslims and their *dhimmis*[58] can find no protection and their residence is not safe".[59] This would happen when, for example Friday prayers and the Festivals, i.e. the *'Ids*, are prevented to take place and consequently their religious freedom is being undermined.[60] Of course, the full exercise of the five individual obligations of every Muslim have to be ensured as well, namely the recognition of one God, the prayers, the Ramadan, the payment of *zakat*, i.e. tax benefiting the needy, and the pilgrimage to the holy places. In anticipation of violations by non-Muslims towards Muslims living in their territory, the non-Muslim political instances which reject an invitation to embrace Islam or in second instance are reluctant to sign *dhimmah* agreements recognising their personal laws under Islamic sovereign rule, become a threat. Their people would be considered to be belligerents.[61] *Siyar* accommodated these two nations, i.e. those of the Muslims and non-Muslims, at war and prescribes the laws of war to be respected in their encounters.[62]

Siyar would also provide an appropriate definition of *dar al-Islam*, as opposed to *dar al-harb*, in order for Islamic territories to be delimitated. There, Islamic rule would prevail or Muslim subjects and their *dhimmis* could have safe residence under non-Islamic sovereigns. Hanafis did not accept the latter situation and required full incorporation of Muslims subjects and their *dhimmis* in Islamic territory through conquest. Successful secession of a territory which used to belong to the *dar-Islam*, according to the jurist al-Shafi (d. 820), becomes *dar al-harb*.[63] However, the jurist Abu Hanifa (d. 767) argues that such rebellion would remain part of the *dar al-Islam* "except when it is not separated from *dar al-harb* by a Muslim territory".[64] For the purpose of protecting the territorial integrity of the abode of Islam, so-called "military

58 Those with whom Islamic authorities have concluded a treaty allowing them to continue to exercise their own religious practice in exchange for a taxation (poll tax), *i.e.* the *jizya*, guaranteeing their protection in case of war. See Abu Sulayman, at 28–9.

59 al-Ghunaimi, at 156; see also Adel Théodor Khoury, Toleranz im Islam (Kaiser; Grünewald 1980), at 105.

60 Saghir Ahmad Khan & Abdur Rahim, Islamic jurisprudence (Mansoor 1986), at 120; Abdur Rahim, The principles of Islamic jurisprudence, according to the Hanafi, Maliki, Shafi'i and Hanbali schools (Kitab Bhavan 1994), at 376; Khoury, at 104.

61 An-Na'im, at 148; Sheikh Wahbeh al-Zuhili, 'Islam and international law', (2005) 87 International Review of the Red Cross, 269, at 278; Abu Sulayman, at 19–20; Hashmi, in, at 207; Ameur Zemmali, Combattants et prisonniers de guerre en droit islamique et en droit international humanitaire (E. Pedone 1997), at 31.

62 Hassan, at 136.

63 al-Ghunaimi, at 155–58; see also An-Na'im, at 150.

64 al-Ghunaimi, at 158.

jihad" mandates the collective obligation, i.e. *levée en masse*, or the individual struggle of every capable believer against non-Islamic threats.[65] Evidently, anyone who prevents and opposes Muslims to flourish within their territory and outside as Muslim aliens, could be considered to be in a state of war, i.e. *harb*, and *jihad* could rectify this unjust situation. It could be done through *al-fath*, i.e. conquest, in order for righteousness to prevail and God's message to be conveyed to everybody. However, such occupation and its transfer of sovereignty to the *dar al-Islam* differ from a military invasion wanting to realise specific strategic objectives with no intention whatsoever to annex the *dar al-harb*.[66] The Qur'an refers to this wrong-doing to be addressed in the latter case:

> To those against whom war is made, permission is given (to fight), because they are wronged—and verily, Allah is most powerful for their aid. (Q22:39)

> (They are) those who have been expelled from their homes in defiance of right,—(for no cause) except that they say, "our Lord is Allah". Did not Allah check one set of people by means of another, there would surely have been pulled down monasteries, churches, synagogues, and mosques, in which the name of Allah is commemorated in abundant measure. Allah will certainly aid those who aid his (cause); for verily Allah is full of Strength, Exalted in Might, (able to enforce His Will). (Q22:40)

In order for these adversaries of Islam[67] to be fought in an external *jihad* they would need to be based in the *dar al-harb* and have become non-Muslims through their behaviour if they were it before;[68] whether they are Muslims, i.e. the rebels/disserters, or not, i.e. the polytheists, non-Muslims, and in particular the Peoples of the Book/Scriptuaries (Christians, Jews, Magians (Zorostrians), and Sabians), or not anymore, i.e. the apostates. However, in practice, rebels and apostates despite the apostates' denunciation of Islam and of (one of) its five individual obligations are technically still Muslims. A war waged against

---

65 Freamon, at 307; at 454; Hilmi M. Zawati, Is jihad a just war? War, peace, and human rights under Islamic and public international law (Edwin Mellen Press 2001), at 16.

66 Zawati, at 18–9.

67 Nikolai Egorovich Tornau, Das moslemische Recht: aus den Quellen dargestellt (Rodopi 1970), at 51.

68 al-Ghunaimi, at 138–39; Hashmi, in, at 205–6.

rebels and apostates will be examined under internal warfare against enemies of Islam from within, although their treatment will not be that different from the external rivals of Islam.[69]

1.2.2.2 Temporal Jurisdiction

1.2.2.2.1 *The Opening of the War*

Declarations of war are necessary and in particular against the signatory party to a treaty which has threatened to violate its terms; except in the case of self-defence against an attack regardless of the existing treaty relations with the aggressor or in the case of retaliation against an effective breach of treaty.[70] The following verses in the Qur'an imply a reference to such a (possible) violation of a treaty by the enemy which would have to be denounced or even fought against:

> If thou fearest treachery from any group, throw back (their covenant) to them, (so as to be) on equal terms: for Allah loveth not the treacherous. (Q8:58)

> But if they violate their oaths after their covenant, and taunt you for your Faith,—fight ye the chiefs of Unfaith: for their oaths are nothing to them: that thus they may be restrained. (Q9:12)

> Will ye not fight people who violated their oaths, plotted to expel the Messenger, and took the aggressive by being the first (to assault) you? Do ye fear them? Nay, it is Allah Whom ye should more justly fear, if ye believe! (Q9:13)

Obviously, sympathetic and humanitarian assistance to those who seek help against injustice regardless whether they are Muslim or not and wars for idealistic reasons to spread Islam necessitate a declaration.[71] In the case of humanitarian intervention the Qur'an provides that:

---

69 An-Na'im, at 150.

70 Hamidullah, at 191.

71 Hassan, at 171; Mahmassani, at 290; see also Matthias Vanhullebusch, 'Islamic law and the responsibility to protect', (2010) 4 Human Rights and International Legal Discourse, 191.

> And why should ye not fight in the cause of Allah and of those who, being weak, are ill-treated (and oppressed)?—Men, women, and children, whose cry is: "Our Lord! Rescue us from this town, whose people are oppressors; and raise for us from thee one who will protect; and raise for us from thee one who will help!" (Q4:75)

> If any one slew a person—unless it be for murder or for spreading mischief in the land—it would be as if he slew the whole people: and if any one saved a life, it would be as if he saved the life of the whole people. (Q5:32)

However, wars cannot be fought during the sacred months, nor can they be started in this period, unless the very existence of the Islamic community is at stake. This ruling has been a reminiscent of pre-Islamic Arabian tribal society in order to, on the one hand, facilitate peace and let trade flourish, and on the other hand, grant time and resources to (re)organise for the battle afterwards. The Qur'an provides in that regard:

> The prohibited month for the prohibited month,—and so for all things prohibited,—there is the law of equality. If then any one transgresses the prohibition against you, Transgress ye likewise against him. But fear Allah, and know that Allah is with those who restrain themselves. (Q2:194)

> The number of months in the sight of Allah is twelve (in a year)—so ordained by Him the day He created the heavens and the earth; of them four are sacred: that is the straight usage. So wrong not yourselves therein, and fight the Pagans all together as they fight you all together. But know that Allah is with those who restrain themselves. (Q9:36)

> They ask thee concerning fighting in the Prohibited Month. Say: "Fighting therein is a grave (offence); but graver is it in the sight of Allah to prevent access to the path of Allah, to deny Him, to prevent access to the Sacred Mosque, and drive out its members." Tumult and oppression are worse than slaughter. (Q2:217)

> But when the forbidden months are past, then fight and slay the Pagans wherever ye find them, an seize them, beleaguer them, and lie in wait for them in every stratagem (of war); but if they repent, and establish regular prayers and practise regular charity, then open the way for them: for Allah is Oft-forgiving, Most Merciful. (Q9:5)

1.2.2.2.2 *The End of the War*

The belligerent parties can simply cease the armed hostilities without agreeing upon the terms of a truce or an armistice. Of course, war can also be settled through treaties of peace respecting the respective sovereignties and independence of both parties. Thus, the former enemies enter into the abode of the covenant, envisaging some long-term peace.[72] There is disagreement among jurists whether the treaty is only valid for ten years as was the case of the Hudaibiyah treaty (d. 628) signed by the Prophet or whether it can be renewed as any other contract.[73] The Qur'an warns Muslims to remain vigilant whenever eternal friendship with non-Muslims has to be concluded:

> Should they intend to deceive thee,—verily Allah sufficeth thee: He it is that hath strengthened thee with His aid and with (the company of) the Believers. (Q8:62)

> O ye who believe! Take not the Jews and the Christians for your friends and protectors: They are but friends and protectors to each other. And he amongst you that turns to them (for friendship) is of them. Verily Allah guideth not a people unjust. (Q5:51)

> And those who believe will say: "Are these the men who swore their strongest oaths by Allah, that they were with you?" All that they do will be in vain, and they will fall into (nothing but) ruin. (Q5:53)

Whenever the non-Muslim enemy was defeated and its territory was annexed after all into the *dar al-Islam*, preference would be given to the ruler and its people who embraced Islam or accepted the suzerainty of the Islamic victor. In return they could continue to practice their own religion and personal laws.[74] Once the persecution had ceased and freedom of religion could be fully professed, according to Ali, the "sword had to be sheathed".[75] In this regard, the Qur'an reminds of God's omnipotence to unite peoples of different beliefs:

> And (moreover) He hath put affection between their hearts: not if thou hadst spent all that is in the earth, couldst thou have produced that affection, but Allah hath done it: for He is Exalted in might, Wise. (Q8:63)

---

72 Hamidullah, at 266; al-Zuhili, at 278.

73 Hamidullah, at 267.

74 Id., at 265–66; An-Na'im, at 148.

75 Ali, A manual of hadith, at 253.

> It may be that Allah will grant love (and friendship) between you and those whom ye (now) hold as enemies. For Allah has power (over all things). And Allah is Oft-Forgiving, Most Merciful. (Q60:7)

1.2.3 *During Internal Warfare*

1.2.3.1 Territorial Jurisdiction

In principle, no wars could be fought within the *dar al-Islam* and obedience to the Islamic leadership had to be ensured.[76] In reality, wars from within have been waged by the *murtaddun*, i.e. the apostates, by the *muharibun*, i.e. the bandits, brigands, highway robbery men, and by the *bughah*, i.e. the rebels.[77] Generally, each of their behaviours is variably detrimental and subversive to the interests and values of the Islamic community.[78] On the one hand, rebels challenge the righteous authority of the Islamic established authorities within the *dar al-Islam*.[79] On the other hand, apostates have renounced their Islamic faith or have refrained from observing one of their individual religious obligations and are therefore a threat which needs to be cured. Thus, apostasy wars were justified.[80] Some verses in the Qur'an speak about those tensions within the *ummah*. For example:

> Those who turn back as apostates after Guidance was clearly shown to them,—the Evil One has instigated them and busied them up with false hopes. (Q47:25)

With respect to the bandits, they also operate within the abode of Islam but for the sake of personal and pecuniary benefits they terrorise the helpless population, and in particular travellers on highways across that territory.[81] The Shi'i jurist Abu Ja'far al-Tusi (d. 1067) however, believes that also other motives can drive the actions of bandits which can terrorise on land, for example in cities and deserts, or on sea.[82] *Muharaba*, i.e. brigandage, has been regulated by the *ahkam al-hiraba*, i.e. the laws relating to the crime of bandits and brigands.

---

76 Zemmali, at 165.

77 Abou El Fadl, at 32.

78 An-Na'im, at 150.

79 John Kelsay, 'Al-Shaybani and the Islamic law of war', (2003) 2 Journal of Military Ethics, 63, at 67.

80 Yamani, in, at 71.

81 Abou El Fadl, at 205–6.

82 Id., at 220.

Thus, Islamic criminal law is the applicable law and not ILW. However, divergence exists on the nature of this activity whether it truly corrupts the (territorial) integrity and sovereignty of the *ummah* or the Islamic faith. The *hiraba* verse does not necessarily provide more answers.

> The punishment of those who wage war against Allah and His Messenger, and strive with might and main for mischief through the land is: execution, or crucifixion, or the cutting off of hands and feet from opposite sides, or exile from the land: that is their disgrace in this world, and a heavy punishment is theirs in the Hereafter. (Q5:33)

In the tenth and eleventh century, most of the Hanafi jurists considered rebellion as a sin.[83] In this respect, rebellion differed from the crime of banditry as these alleged rebels were waging a "war against Allah and His Messenger"[84] within the *dar al-Islam*. The Islamic establishment easily accused those who opposed their rule of causing *fitnah* i.e. disbelief[85] which needed to be brought to an end as part of the maxim of "enjoining the good and forbidding the evil".[86] The treatment of these Muslims fighting against the Islamic leadership for theological reasons instead of worldly ones, which are impermissible,[87] falls under the *ahkam al-bughat*, i.e. the laws relating to rebels under an Islamic public order.[88] Other jurists classified it under many branches of Islamic law, including under *siyar* and *jihad*.[89] The Hanbali jurist Ibn Taymiyya (d. 1327–1328), however, dismisses the different regulations as to the permissiveness of rebellion and describes any fighting among Muslims as *fitnah*. According to him, rebellion should be forbidden irrespective of the reasons why they are fought; whether, on the one hand, to defend against unjust rulers and their illegal commands, i.e. the theological war, or, on the other hand, to overthrow those rulers in order to crown oneself to merely gain power, i.e. the political war.[90] The Qur'an also refers to strives among Muslims:

---

83 Id., at 189–90.

84 Q5:33.

85 Abou El Fadl, at 196.

86 Id., at 196; see also Q7:199.

87 Id., at 272.

88 Khaled Abou El Fadl, 'Ahkam al-bughat: irregular warfare and the law of rebellion in Islam', in James Turner Johnson & John Kelsay (eds), Cross, crescent, and sword: the justification and limitation of war in Western and Islamic tradition (Greenwood Press 1990), at 150.

89 Id., in, at 154–55.

90 Abou El Fadl, Rebellion and violence in Islamic law, at 271–72.

> If two parties among the Believers fall into a quarrel, make ye peace between them: but if one of them transgresses beyond bounds against the other then fight ye (all) against the one that transgresses until it complies with the command of Allah; but if it complies then make peace between them with justice and be fair: for Allah loves those who are fair (and just). (Q49:9)

> The Believers are but a single Brotherhood: so make peace and reconciliation between your two (contending) brothers; and fear Allah, that ye may receive Mercy. (Q49:10)

Generally, the jurists also supported reconciliatory means of dealing with the righteousness of conflicting and relative claims of the two groups. Despite the type of actions pursued by the rebels, punishments were discouraged.[91] Still, the Maliki judge Ibn 'Abd al-Barr (d. 1070) argues that terrorising for the propagation of their cause could disqualify rebels from their protective status and could be treated as common criminals instead.[92] No matter in which territory the rebels are conducting their struggle against the Islamic leadership, they remain subjected to Islamic law having personal and thus universal jurisdiction over Muslims; whether they are in the *dar al-Islam*, the *dar al-harb*, the *dar al-baghy*, i.e. the abode of rebels enjoying partial recognition, or in the *dar ahl al-'adl*, i.e. the abode of the loyalists claiming full legitimacy.[93] However, non-Muslims who have effective control over territory within and who fight against the Islamic state, are treated as rebels under Islamic law; whereas Muslim rebels who border the *dar al-harb* and fight against the Islamic authorities, are supposed to be non-Muslims given the presumption of aid provided by their neighbours from the *dar al-harb*.[94]

1.2.3.2 Temporal Jurisdiction

As for the beginning of war, similar rules of external *jihad* apply for internal *jihad*. In this regard, in terms of alleged disbelief, the apostates and rebels are also *mushrikun*.[95] On the one hand, as for apostasy wars, converted Muslims

91 John Kelsay, 'Civil society and government in Islam', in Sohail H. Hashmi (ed), Islamic political ethics: civil society, pluralism, and conflict (Princeton University Press 2002), at 27; Abou El Fadl, Rebellion and violence in Islamic law, at 292 and 336.

92 Abou El Fadl, Rebellion and violence in Islamic law, at 222, 257 and 262.

93 Id., at 176–77.

94 Hamidullah, at 185.

95 See Q9:36.

who have signed any type of covenant which has ended a previous war between them (as non-Muslims) and the Islamic army and which has sanctioned their conversion to Islam, are liable from the moment they break this treaty and its obligations and risk retaliation. On the other hand, regarding rebellion, the Hanafi jurist Abu Bakr al-Sarakhsi (d. 1090–1091) adds that pre-emptive strikes are permissible by the loyalist Islamic army even before the rebels attacked the established Islamic authorities. Still, the commission of some overt acts on behalf of the rebels indicating their intent to rebel such as regrouping in particular locations can justify such pre-emptive action.[96] Bandits, however, fall under the specific jurisdiction of the laws relating to brigandage.

1.3 The Principle of Distinction

1.3.1 *On Discrimination*

The Qur'an, the Sunnah and the practice of the successors of the Prophet Muhammad demand a strict adherence to the principle of distinction during armed hostilities.[97] As a general rule Q2:190 "Fight in the cause of Allah those who fight you" makes this distinction clear.[98] Such restriction on Islamic warfare in respect of permitted targets[99] and the associated regimes of non-combatant immunities reveal functional caution[100] to be exercised when dealing with non-combatants, i.e. those who are not (longer) participating in armed hostilities. This distinction and classification behind the enemies' lines can limit the number of atrocities of war as these persons cannot be attacked, killed or molested.[101] The pre-Islamic rule of *shahama*, i.e. "man's boldness",[102] clearly has influenced and prohibited violent demonstrations of men's power against the weaker parties in societies under Islamic leadership.[103] However, military necessity can override this protection for civilians and their property as allowed under the precept *al-darura tubih al-mahzurat* ("necessity makes

96 Abou El Fadl, Rebellion and violence in Islamic law, at 197.

97 Hashmi, in, at 211; see also Ella Landau-Tasseron, "Non-combatants" in Muslim legal thought, at http://www.futureofmuslimworld.com/research/pubID.60/pub_detail.asp. (Last accessed 15 February 2015)

98 Shah, Islamic law and the law of armed conflict: the armed conflict in Pakistan, at 35.

99 Tibi, in, at 180; Salem, at 121.

100 Johnson, The holy war idea in Western and Islamic traditions, at 119–20.

101 Zawati, at 43; Ali, A manual of hadith, at 253.

102 Tibi, in, at 181.

103 Id., in, at 181.

the prohibited acts permissible"),[104] whenever non-combatants are participating in the fighting, planning or supplying.[105] Anyone who helps the enemy looses this protection[106] and can be killed in self-defence or for reasons of belligerent reprisal.[107] In case of wrong-doing against the Muslims, the Qur'an refers to reciprocity:

> And so for all things prohibited,—there is the law of equality. If then any one transgresses the prohibition against you, transgress ye likewise against him. But fear Allah, and know that Allah is with those who restrain themselves. (Q2:194)

The category of non-combatants[108] include children younger than 15 years, women, slaves, old men, disabled and sick persons, both physically and mentally, because they would be incapable of bearing arms.[109] Children until puberty could not yet have been infected by disbelief, i.e. as understood in terms of non-Muslim, apostasy or sinful rebellion, and consequently cannot be attacked. A *hadith* on the teachings of the Prophet and a command of Abu Bakr, the first caliph after the death of the Prophet, prescribe this very issue:[110] "During some of the Ghazawat of the Prophet a woman was found killed. Allah's Apostle disapproved the killing of women and children."[111] However, Abbasid jurists argue that women, children and old men may not be killed except when they die for a just cause leading to the victory of the Islamic state; for example in case they are commanders of, advisors to the army, or are rulers.[112]

Other civilians benefiting from immunities to be attacked are diplomats, merchants, and peasants given their important role as so-called "builders of prosperity"[113] within the Muslim society and with its neighbours.[114] Monks

---

104 Id., in, at 180.

105 Khadduri & Liebesny, Law in the Middle East / Vol. 1, Origin and development of Islamic law, at 355; Hamidullah, at 223.

106 Krüger, at 18. In particular the High Court of Lahore's decision: *The State Bank of India Ltd. v. The Custodian of Evacuee Property, West Pakistan* P.L.D. 1969, 1050.

107 al-Zuhili, at 282.

108 Hassan, at 173; al-Zuhili, at 277 and 280–81; An-Na'im, at 149.

109 Zawati, at 43; Johnson, The holy war idea in Western and Islamic traditions, at 119–20.

110 al-Zuhili, at 282.

111 Al-Bukhari, Vol. 4, Book 52, Number 257. (Narrated by 'Abdullah)

112 Hamidullah, at 223.

113 Yamani, in, at 82.

114 Zawati, at 44; Numan ibn Muhammad Ibn Hayyun, Ismail Kurbanhusien Poonawala & Asaf Ali Asghar Fyzee, The pillars of Islam: Da'a'Im al-Islam of al-Qadi al-Nu'man (Oxford University Press 2002), at 453.

and hermits living in religious or spiritual isolation cannot be attacked either upon the condition that they do not take part in combat and remain in their churches, monasteries or cells.[115] In this respect, places of worship are immune from attack. So are combatants who are no longer fighting because they are wounded or sick and thus are no longer participating in combat. None of these persons can be used as human shields when captured or taken hostage.[116]

This general principle of distinction is accused by Abdul Hamid Ahmad Abu Sulayman of lacking appreciation for the changing circumstances and modernisation of warfare,[117] such as air strikes which are nowadays regulated by international conventions and have become part of Islamic law in the respective signatory states.[118] Irrespective of the indiscriminate nature of modern weaponry, distinction shall guide the choice of targets as a first test during military operations. Unless military necessity mandates otherwise, the latter action requires the respect of the principle of proportionality, as a second test, in order to avoid unnecessary suffering to be inflicted upon any of the victims of armed attacks regardless whether they are combatants or not. Perfidious and treacherous actions blurring the distinction between lawful participants in combat are forbidden as well[119] and are to be distinguished from ruses of war, such as surprise attacks, infiltration among enemy lines, spreading rumours among the latter, etc.[120]

1.3.2 *In External Warfare*

The principle of distinction is applicable in any armed conflict regardless whether the war is waged among believers or against unbelievers. Non-combatants on the one hand, cannot be the objects of attack; they deserve protection.[121] When these non-combatants have suffered damages, the Muslim combatants can only be held responsible and liable under their laws of war when having intentionally ignored discriminate action on the battlefield. Hence, Muslim fighters are accountable for acts surpassing their belligerency.[122] Others try to avoid any liability on behalf of the Islamic soldiers and accuse the leaders of the *dar al-harb* for having implicated their innocent population in

115 Zawati, at 43; Hamidullah, at 204; Yamani, in, at 82.

116 Hamidullah, at 206; David Aaron Schwartz, 'International terrorism and Islamic law', (1991) 29 Columbia Journal of Transnational Law, 629, at 649.

117 Abu Sulayman, at 77.

118 Hamidullah, at 229.

119 Id., at 204.

120 Yamani, in, at 76.

121 Freamon, at 323–24.

122 Hamidullah, at 202–3.

this struggle.[123] The jurist al-Shafi in particular, continues that all of them can be killed because of their state of disbelief regardless of the Prophet's injunction to save their lives.[124] In addition, both on land or at sea, Islamic warriors can attack respectively the castles or ships of their enemies even when they are shielded with Muslim subjects; thus, military necessity prevails.[125]

Muslim combatants on the other hand, should distinguish themselves from non-combatants. Even at the Prophet's time and in particular at one of the early battles, namely the Battle of Badr (d. 624), conducted for the defence of the *ummah* against the unbelievers, Muslim warriors were urged to wear distinctive signs or uniforms, such as woollen cloaks. Not only for the sake of telling them apart from their adversaries but also to receive the help of angels standing on their side. Cries of specific watchwords would facilitate the discrimination between friends from foes during campaigns at night.[126]

1.3.3 *In Internal Warfare*

With regard to the apostasy wars, only those who truly renounce the Islamic faith, whether they are men or women, can be the objects of targeting as only they are a threat to the stability and order of the Islamic community. Given the lack of supporting evidence, disagreement exists as to whether apostates should be executed or not unless they are remorseful for their actions of disbelief.[127] Enslavement of apostates and confiscation of their property are not possible.[128] The following verses in the Qur'an refer to open disbelief and hypocrisy:

> The Hypocrites, men and women, (have an understanding) with each other: they enjoin evil, and forbid what is just, and are close with their hands. They have forgotten Allah. So He hath forgotten them. Verily the Hypocrites are rebellious and perverse. (Q9:67)

123 John Kelsay, 'Islam and the distinction between combatants and noncombatants', in James Turner Johnson & John Kelsay (eds), Cross, crescent, and sword: the justification and limitation of war in Western and Islamic tradition (Greenwood Press 1990), at 205.

124 Abu Sulayman, at 12.

125 Khadduri, War and peace in the law of Islam, at 114.

126 Hamidullah, at 235; Lodewijk William Christiaan Van den Berg, Principes du droit musulman (A. Jourdan 1896), at 227.

127 Abou El Fadl, Rebellion and violence in Islamic law, at 32.

128 Yamani, in, at 71.

> Those who break Allah's Covenant after it is ratified, and who sunder what Allah has ordered to be joined, and do mischief on earth: these cause loss (only) to themselves. (Q2:27)

> Fight them, and Allah will punish them by your hands, cover them with shame, help you (to victory) over them, heal the breasts of Believers. (Q9:14)

The terrorisation of the population by bandits is not necessarily that different from the actions of a group of rebels which have a *ta'wil*, i.e. a cause, a justification for rebellion based on religious grounds, and who are, according to Tabassum, "striving to replace the existing illegitimate and unjust system with a legitimate and just order".[129] The rebels located in a distinct territory over which they have effective control,[130] can violate the rules of the Islamic regime through their acts of rebellion.[131] The bandits, however, are prosecuted under criminal law. The rebels were rather treated at the discretion of the Islamic authorities assessing the legitimacy of their ideological claims[132] for the purpose of justifying the use of force on their behalf.[133] Depending on the qualification of the rebellion as being sinful or not, i.e. advocating disbelief or not, killing would be respectively permitted or prohibited.[134] Rebels could also be killed whenever they sought refuge in their stronghold and were preparing for consecutive combats against the central Islamic authority.[135]

Generally, rebels could only be fought and killed as long as they disturb the peace and violate the loyalists' laws of order; restoring this does not imply their extermination.[136] Whenever they were not able to fight through illness, injury, capitulation or capture, according to the jurist al-Shafi and the Shafi judge al-Mawardi (d. 1058), they would enjoy non-combatant immunity and were no longer objects of military targeting.[137] Nonetheless, those supporting

129 Sadia Tabassum, 'Combatants, not bandits: the status of rebels in Islamic law', (2011) 93 International Review of the Red Cross 121, at 126.

130 Abou El Fadl, Rebellion and violence in Islamic law, at 168.

131 Kelsay, 'Civil society and government in Islam', in, at 26; Abou El Fadl, Rebellion and violence in Islamic law, at 150.

132 Abou El Fadl, Rebellion and violence in Islamic law, at 202.

133 Abou El Fadl, 'Ahkam al-bughat: irregular warfare and the law of rebellion in Islam', in, at 163.

134 Abou El Fadl, Rebellion and violence in Islamic law, at 32.

135 Hamidullah, at 178; Abou El Fadl, Rebellion and violence in Islamic law, at 243.

136 Hamidullah, at 178; Abou El Fadl, Rebellion and violence in Islamic law, at 243.

137 Abou El Fadl, Rebellion and violence in Islamic law, at 150, 152 and 171.

the rebels or standing idly by can be considered as being as guilty and become legitimate objects of attack. Respect for the principle of distinction might just become subject to ideological concerns.[138] As a response, insurgency or asymmetrical warfare tends to employ irregular tactics denying protection to non-combatants for the sake of winning the minds of the peoples to turn against the Islamic government.[139]

1.4 The Principle of Proportionality

1.4.1 *On Means and Methods of War*

The use of particular weaponry or military tactics which cause unnecessary suffering or bloodshed have to be limited in order to reduce the cruelties of warfare.[140] The battles fought to preserve and to universalise the Islamic faith cannot ignore the humanity which Islam truly stands for and invoke (military) necessity to circumvent its basic principles of protection.[141] Thus, the principle of necessity earlier referred to is curtailed by the precept *al-darurat tuqdaru bi qadariha* ("necessity would be limited by proportionality"). Instead of expanding on those rules on the use of force during armed hostilities (jus in bello), the jurists have rather prioritised the development of the doctrine on the right to go to war (jus ad bellum).[142] However, the regulation and restriction of human behaviour in order to fully develop in harmony within society and beyond, is the essence of the Qur'anic teachings. In this respect, any turbulence needs to be denounced regardless whether it takes place in peace or in war times.[143] The Qur'an teaches on the limits to be respected in armed struggles:

---

138 Kelsay, 'Islam and the distinction between combatants and noncombatants', in, at 208.

139 Khaled Abou El Fadl, 'Ahkam al-bughat: irregular warfare and the law of rebellion in Islam', in see id., at 163.

140 Hamidullah, at 225; Yamani, in, at 72.

141 Khadduri, War and peace in the law of Islam, at 102; Krüger, at 18 and in particular the High Court of Lahore's decision: *The State Bank of India Ltd. v. The Custodian of Evacuee Property*, *West Pakistan*, High Court of Lahore, P.L.D. 1969, 1050.

142 Christopher Gregory Weeramantry, Islamic jurisprudence: an international perspective (Macmillan 1988), at 138; Charles E. Butterworth, 'Al-Fârâbî's statecraft: war and the well-ordered regime', in James Turner Johnson & John Kelsay (eds), Cross, crescent, and sword: the justification and limitation of war in Western and Islamic tradition (Greenwood Press 1990), at 80.

143 Falahi, at 88; al-Zuhili, at 282.

> And if ye do catch them out, catch them out no worse than they catch you out: but if ye show patience, that is indeed the best (course) for those who are patient. (Q16:126)

> Fight in the cause of Allah those who fight you, but do not transgress limits; for Allah loveth not transgressors. (Q2:190)

Mutilation and torture of the enemy and its animals with eventually death as a result are forbidden.[144] As a *hadith* prescribes: "The Prophet [...] forbade mutilation (or maiming) of bodies."[145] In addition, "unnecessary devastation, destruction of harvest",[146] as Hamidullah lists, as well as the cutting of trees during the hostilities or the commission of massacres among the defeated are not contributing to the objectives set to win the war and thus they are prohibited acts.[147] The Prophet Muhammad and the consecutive caliphs also commanded these injunctions to their Islamic armies. It was excluded that the destruction or extermination of the enemy could ever be a goal to be pursued in particular when there is enough good reason that this would not contribute to the victory of the Islamic armies.[148] These policies do not only reflect humanitarian and moral considerations but are also driven by functional motivations;[149] the potential values of captured enemies and their properties would serve the Islamic community unless the *ummah* would benefit from their annihilation; and this in spite of the verses on belligerent reprisals in the Qur'an.[150] Therefore, the use of certain weaponry, such as so-called "poisonous arrows"[151] and fire, which belong to the prerogatives of God only,[152] were outlawed whereas others, such as smoke or gases, were permitted by some; however, "poisonous arrows" were permitted by others too, depending on

144 Hamidullah, at 204; Hassan, at 173; Peters, Jihad in classical and modern Islam, at 37.

145 Al-Bukhari, Vol. 3, Book 43, Number 654. (Narrated by 'Abdullah bin Yazid Al-Ansari)

146 Hamidullah, at 205.

147 Hassan, at 173.

148 Hallaq, Shari'a: theory, practice, transformations, at 329.

149 See Khaled Abou El Fadl, 'Between functionalism and morality: the juristic debates on the conduct of war', in Jonathan E. Brockopp (ed), Islamic ethics of life: abortion, war, and euthanasia (University of South Carolina Press 2003).

150 Johnson, The holy war idea in Western and Islamic traditions, at 122–24; Khadduri, War and peace in the law of Islam, at 107; for example Q2:194 and Q16:126.

151 Hamidullah, at 207; Hassan, at 173.

152 Salem, at 123.

the circumstances.[153] Surprise attacks were encouraged as well because they would facilitate victory and reduce bloodshed.[154]

With regard to the captives made during the armed hostilities, the same prohibitions apply to these individuals. Thus, they cannot be killed, decapitated, nor burned and should be treated with human dignity and without unnecessary suffering.[155] Rape of women in detention is considered as an act of adultery or fornication and Muslim combatants would be liable for such action under Islamic criminal law.[156] In addition, public curiosity upon the dead bodies of the enemy is disliked.[157] These instructions reveal significant progress made compared to the pre-Islamic custom of *lex talionis*, i.e. retaliation.[158] Violators of these rules will be severely prosecuted under Islamic law. The Qur'an mentions how to treat captives:

> Therefore, when ye meet the Unbelievers (in fight), smite at their necks; at length, when ye have thoroughly subdued them, bind a bond firmly (on them): thereafter (is the time for) either generosity or ransom: until the war lays down its burdens. (Q47:4)

> And they feed, for the love of Allah, the indigent, the orphan, and the captive. (Q76:8)

Suicide attacks in particular raise greater concerns in terms of their legitimacy[159] in situations of asymmetrical armed conflict where this method of war, i.e. martyrdom, has mobilised many jihadists.[160] According to some, fighting for the cause of God would justify any method of warfare against an impenetrable military adversary. Others would disagree and uphold the prohibition of acts of suicide in any event.[161] The Islamic combatant has the intention to take away

153 Hamidullah, at 226.

154 Id., at 225.

155 Zemmali, at 450; Mohamed M. El Zeidy & Ray Murphy, 'Islamic law on prisoners of war and its relationships with international humanitarian law', (2004) 14 Italian Yearbook of International Law, 53, at 62.

156 Hamidullah, at 204–6; Hassan, at 173.

157 Mawardi & Yate, at 80.

158 Hamidullah, at 315.

159 Abou El Fadl, 'Ahkam al-bughat: irregular warfare and the law of rebellion in Islam', in, at 163.

160 Freamon, at 302.

161 Ali K. Khan, A theory of international terrorism: understanding Islamic militancy (Martinus Nijhoff Publishers 2006), at 200–1; Muhammed Munir, 'Suicide attacks and Islamic law', (2008) 90 International Review of the Red Cross, 71, at 79.

his or her own life[162] and generally commits perfidy by not distinguishing him- or herself from non-combatants. These actions usually ignore any principles of distinction or proportionality and deviate from the values supported by the *ummah*.[163] Only God has the sole authority to create life and destroy it; He shall only award those who die in His cause and punish these sinful martyrs who fought for it.[164] Generally, treacherous acts of warfare and mutilation are forbidden but can be permitted during reprisal actions.[165] The Qur'an further elaborates on those being killed in action:

> Fighting is prescribed for you, and ye dislike it. But it is possible that ye dislike a thing which is good for you, and that ye love a thing which is bad for you. But Allah knoweth, and ye know not. (Q2:216)
>
> And if ye are slain, or die, in the way of Allah, forgiveness and mercy from Allah are far better than all they could amass. (Q3:157)
>
> Let those fight in the cause of Allah Who sell the life of this world for the hereafter. To him who fighteth in the cause of Allah,—whether he is slain or gets victory—Soon shall We give him a reward of great (value). (Q4:74)
>
> And We should have shown them the Straight Way. (Q4:68)
>
> Nor kill (or destroy) yourselves: for verily Allah hath been to you Most Merciful! (Q4:29)
>
> If any do that in rancour and injustice,—soon shall We cast them into the Fire: and easy it is for Allah. (Q4:30)

1.4.2 *During External Warfare*

When the unbelievers did not want to embrace Islam or pay *jizya*, i.e. the tax for *dhimmis* who live within the Islamic territory, in the first place, war was the last resort to subjugate them to Islam upon the condition of course that the Islamic armies were victorious. In this regard, the destruction of the

---

162 Freamon, at 308.

163 Tamara Sonn, 'Irregular warfare and terrorism in Islam: asking the right questions', in James Turner Johnson & John Kelsay (eds), Cross, crescent, and sword: the justification and limitation of war in Western and Islamic tradition (Greenwood Press 1990), at 138.

164 Freamon, at 308; Franz Rosenthal, 'On suicide in Islam', (1946) 66 Journal of the American Oriental Society, 239, at 244.

165 Mahmassani, at 303.

unbelievers would be useless and would violate ILW.[166] The general principle of proportionality for reasons of humanity and functionality are applicable as well. Nonetheless, sea jihadists can throw their captives and property into the sea, except if they are Muslims.[167] However, the enemy combatants who are made prisoners of war and who deserve a kind treatment,[168] can be (ab)used for political ends in order to undermine the morale of the adversary party.[169] They could be executed when safe conduct could not be guaranteed.[170] So, in accordance with the teachings of the Prophet, two prisoners of war at the Battle of Badr were decapitated because their trial proved that they committed crimes beyond their belligerency.[171]

1.4.3 *During Internal Warfare*

The use of certain weaponry, like flame-throwers, mangonels or other weapons of mass destruction, is not allowed in inter-Muslim strives unless military necessity requires so.[172] This would be the case of first attacks on behalf of the rebels or when the loyalist armed forces are in the impossibility to defeat the rebels' stronghold upon the condition that innocent women and children not sharing the views of any of the parties to the conflict are not exposed to any risks.[173] According to the Zahiri jurist Ibn Hazm (d. 1064), in case of the use of fire or flooding against the rebels, they must be evacuated safely in order to "escape death and surrender".[174] Judge al-Mawardi continues that their homes cannot be burned nor flooded.[175] Both Shafi and Hanafi jurists advocate a preferential treatment of captured rebels; they may not be killed even when rebels executed loyalists[176] because the rebels would not be considered to be sinners.[177] The rebels' moral claims are as relative to those of the Islamic authorities whose righteousness can only be appraised subjectively.[178] In spite of being

166 Tibi, in, at 181.

167 Khadduri, War and peace in the law of Islam, at 115.

168 al-Ghunaimi, at 148; al-Zuhili, at 283.

169 Abu Sulayman, at 102.

170 Averroes, Imran Ahsan Khan Nyazee & Muhammad Abdul-Rauf, The distinguished jurist's primer: a translation of Bidayat al-mujtahid (Garnet Publishing 1994), at 457.

171 Hamidullah, at 214; Weeramantry, at 135.

172 Abou El Fadl, Rebellion and violence in Islamic law, at 152 and 160.

173 Id., at 152, 216 and 259.

174 Id., at 216.

175 Id., at 172.

176 Id., at 173 and 194.

177 Id., at 175.

178 Id., at 126.

considered to be believers, Maliki jurists accept that the wounded rebels and fugitives may be killed unless the rebellion ends or its reinforcement stops.[179] Needless to say, the power of rhetoric as retained by the jurists can as easily be manipulated to put any internal adversary to the Islamic regime outside the protection of ILW. As a consequence, rebels could have recourse to irregular means and methods of war instead.

1.5 Conclusion

Although the development of ILW and its application was intended to respect the universal message of Islam, on several occasions this message of peace has been interpreted differently given the specific circumstances of warfare at a particular time in the history of Islam. The introduction of the bipolar world as translated into the different jurisdictional regimes, i.e. the *dar al-Islam* and the *dar al-harb*, by the juristic community created an interpretation beyond the Revelation. Evidently, this theorisation further influenced the appreciation of the principles of distinction (between combatants and non-combatants) and of proportionality during armed hostilities to be applied therein. ILW has proven to be very sophisticated in its evolution and application during armed conflicts both against external or internal enemies of Islam. General principles of distinction and proportionality have become the object of juristic interpretation and are subject to communitarian and sovereignty propositions. The communitarian one advocates a more inclusive protection of the belligerent parties and non-combatants. The sovereignty position rather advances military necessity at the expense of the protection of the most vulnerable groups.

The structure of this Islamic legal argument is common to the secular national or international ones. This becomes clearer in Chapter II on IHL. Such positivistic dialogue between ILW and IHL may draw interesting conclusions in terms of recognition of their similarities. Although the degree of differences attributed by jurists across their borders accuses their antagonists, its outcome might mirror the non-observance of their own traditions against its own subjects and also toward its Others. Sufficient reasons can be given to understand this essentialist stance; in particular Part II will deal with this. Humanity, however, as will be pointed out in Part III, cannot afford to wait for these answers as each individual deserves to be protected from the cruelties and necessities of warfare. Therefore, even Chapter I's positivist account might advance the basic principles serving these ends to be applied accordingly, regardless of

179 Id., at 258.

the artificial divisions of humanity which were constructed in order to rule over it. Such inventions have contributed to the establishment and defence of Islamic empires and communities. However, the different abodes across which the universal message of Islam can be carried out have no textual support in the primary sources. Instead, the Qur'an is clear about the unity of humanity and about its diversity:

> Mankind was one single nation, and Allah sent Messengers with glad tidings and warnings; and with them He sent the Book in truth, to judge between people in matters wherein they differed. (Q2:213)

> O mankind! We created you from a single (pair) of a male and a female, and made you into nations and tribes, that ye may know each other (not that ye may despise (each other)). (Q49:13)

CHAPTER II

Principles of Protection in Warfare under International Humanitarian Law

2.1 Introduction

The aim of this chapter is to analyse from a positivist perspective the principles of protection under the IHL regime. In this regard, this chapter will adopt a similar structure as the one presented in Chapter I where the principles of protection under ILW were examined. In this chapter, the principles of distinction and proportionality as applied in the different jurisdictional regimes of international and non-international armed conflict will be looked upon. Both primary sources, i.e. treaties, customs and other general principles, as well as secondary, i.e. (inter)national jurisprudence and legal doctrines, will be used to determine those protective standards' evolution and application. This analysis is particularly important for Part III, in Chapter VI, where this positivist account will be juxtaposed with the historical analysis as examined in Part II, in Chapter III. It will be submitted that the narrative on the "Western" Self and its Other have influenced the interpretation and application of the rules of armed conflict. Moreover, determining these universal principles of protection will assist a future reading on the structure of the legal arguments in IHL considerably. The chapter will firstly deal with the territorial and temporal jurisdiction, secondly with the principle of distinction and thirdly with the principle of proportionality.

Before beginning with the above-mentioned, some explanation on the sources of IHL is necessary. The codified branch of IHL consists of the so-called 1899–1907 Hague Regulations[1] and 1949 Geneva Conventions.[2] The former limit

1 1899 Final Act of the International Peace Conference, 1899 Convention with Respect to the Laws and Customs of War on Land and its Annex: Regulations concerning the Laws and Customs of War on Land (1899 Hague II), 1899 Convention for the Adaptation to Maritime Warfare of the Principles of the Geneva Convention of 22 August 1864 (1899 Hague III), 1899 Declaration to Prohibit, for the Term of Five Years, the Launching of Projectiles and Explosives from Balloons, and Other Methods of Similar Nature (1899 Hague IV, 1), 1899 Declaration concerning Asphyxiating Gases (1899 Hague IV, 2), 1899 Declaration concerning Expanding Bullets (1899 Hague IV, 3), 1907 Final Act of the Second Peace Conference, 1907 Convention respecting the Laws and Customs of War on Land and its Annex: Regulations concerning the Laws and Customs of War on Land 1907 (1907 Hague IV), 1907 Convention relative to the

 | DOI 10.1163/9789004298248_004

or prohibit the means and methods of warfare whereas the latter protect the victims of war, i.e. non-combatants and persons no longer taking direct part in the armed hostilities. The 1977 Additional Protocols[3] to the 1949 Geneva Conventions provide a more detailed account on the principles of protection as applicable both during international and non-international armed conflicts. A great number of those limitations on warfare and on the protection of victims have become customary international law or even peremptory norms and conversely many customary rules have been codified as well. These customary rules have been listed in the customary law study on IHL as commissioned by the International Committee of the Red Cross (ICRC).[4] Also weapons conventions[5] contribute to these ends and will be referred to where necessary.

Laying of Automatic Submarine Contact Mines (1907 Hague VIII), 1907 Convention concerning Bombardment by Naval Forces in Time of War (1907 Hague IX), 1907 Convention for the Adaptation to Maritime Warfare of the Principles of the Geneva Convention (1907 Hague X), 1907 Declaration Prohibiting the Discharge of Projectiles and Explosives from Balloons (1907 Hague XIV).

2 1949 Convention for the Amelioration of the Condition of the Wounded and Sick in Armed Forces in the Field (GC I), 1949 Convention for the Amelioration of the Condition of Wounded, Sick and Shipwrecked Members of Armed Forces at Sea (GC II), 1949 Convention relative to the Treatment of Prisoners of War (GC III), 1949 Convention relative to the Protection of Civilian Persons in Time of War (GC IV).

3 1977 Protocol Additional to the Geneva Conventions of 12 August 1949, and relating to the Protection of Victims of International Armed Conflicts (AP I), 1977 Protocol Additional to the Geneva Conventions of 12 August 1949, and relating to the Protection of Victims of Non-International Armed Conflicts (AP II).

4 See Jean-Marie Henckaerts & Louise Doswald-Beck, Customary international humanitarian law (Cambridge University Press 2005).

5 1925 Protocol for the Prohibition of the Use of Asphyxiating, Poisonous or Other Gases, and of Bacteriological Methods of Warfare, 1972 Convention on the Prohibition of the Development, Production and Stockpiling of Bacteriological (Biological) and Toxin Weapons and on their Destruction, 1980 Convention on Prohibitions or Restrictions on the Use of Certain Conventional Weapons Which May be Deemed to be Excessively Injurious or to Have Indiscriminate Effects, 1980 Protocol on Non-Detectable Fragments (Protocol I), 1980 Protocol on Prohibitions or Restrictions on the Use of Mines, Booby-Traps and Other Devices (Protocol II), 1980 Protocol on Prohibitions or Restrictions on the Use of Incendiary Weapons (Protocol III), 1993 Convention on the Prohibition of the Development, Production, Stockpiling and Use of Chemical Weapons and on their Destruction, 1995 Protocol on Blinding Laser Weapons (Protocol IV), 1996 Amended Protocol on Prohibitions or Restrictions on the Use of Mines, Booby-Traps and Other Devices, 1997 Convention on the Prohibition of the Use, Stockpiling, Production and Transfer of Anti-Personnel Mines and on their Destruction, 2003 Protocol on Explosive Remnants of War (Protocol V), 2008 Convention on Cluster Munitions.

In addition, as this chapter will demonstrate, (inter)national jurisprudence[6] on the principles of protection and on the different jurisdictional regimes has further elucidated on their interpretation and application in several cases and has denounced their difficulties as well as their potentials to reconcile jus ad bellum, i.e. the law on the use of force, and human rights law with the jus in bello, i.e. IHL.

2.2 Territorial and Temporal Jurisdiction

2.2.1 *On the Fragmentation of International (Humanitarian) Law*

The aims of international law to restrict the use of force on the international arena, i.e. jus ad bellum, and those of IHL to regulate the conduct of warfare among the warring parties, i.e. jus in bello, have to be seen in close relationship.[7] The idealist enterprise to enhance peace among nations and the so-called "human necessity"[8] to provide protection in case of violation of peace are not necessarily paradoxical but are intertwined. In this respect, as stipulated in the Preamble of 1899 Hague II, "while seeking means to preserve peace and prevent armed conflicts among nations, it is likewise necessary to have regard to cases where an appeal to arms may be caused by events which their solicitude could not avert".[9] From this realist perspective, if the ends to go to war would justify the means used during war, then certain means could make those ends beyond reach.[10] A state might assert its sovereignty by attacking or defending itself but it has to give a normative justification in accordance with the existing international law on the use of force. With regard to this law on the use of force, different regimes existed before and after the 1928 Kellogg-Briand Pact and the 1945 UN Charter.[11] Both the idealist and realist categories

6 In particular of the International Criminal Tribunal for the Former Yugoslavia (ICTY).

7 See Ryan Goodman, 'Controlling the recourse to war by modifying jus in bello', (2009) 12 Yearbook of International Humanitarian Law, 53; Robert D. Sloane, 'The costs of conflation: preserving the dualism of jus ad bellum and jus in bello in the contemporary law of war', (2009) 34 Yale Journal of International Law, 47.

8 Hilaire McCoubrey, International humanitarian law: modern developments in the limitation of warfare (Ashgate 1998), at 5.

9 Preamble, 1899 Hague II; see also Preamble, 1907 Hague IV having substituted the 1899 Hague II and its Annex (i.e. Regulations respecting the Laws and Customs of War on Land).

10 Geoffrey Francis Andrew Best, War and law since 1945 (Oxford University Press 1994), at 244.

11 David Rodin, War and self-defense (Oxford University Press 2002), at 119–20.

of asserting power are, however, often manipulated along both ends to justify states' behaviour.[12] In spite of the relativity of the moral claims on the use of force on the international plane, all parties to the conflict must, nevertheless, respect the same IHL.[13] Hence, all combatants, whether lawful or unlawful, are morally equal before the laws of armed conflict.[14]

The use of force within non-international armed conflicts, however, is not regulated by international mechanisms as such. As the organs of the state have the sole prerogative to use force,[15] they would rather treat the use of force by non-state actors against the state as so-called "situations of internal disturbances and tensions", as put by Article 1(2) of AP II. In this respect, states would avoid these situations to be defined as non-international armed conflicts and would keep them outside the realm of IHL. Consequently, the application of IHL would depend on the recognition of the belligerent parties in internal armed conflicts.[16] Although the rebels' cause is subject to domestic jurisdiction, Cassese finds that their "legal standing"[17] also has an international aspect, in particular toward the international community and other states. In spite of this attempt to broaden the international protection of IHL within internal armed conflicts, the ICTY in its *Tadić* case stated that "(i) only a number of rules and principles governing international armed conflicts have gradually been extended to apply to internal conflicts; and (ii) this extension has not taken place in the form of a full and mechanical transplant of those rules to internal conflicts; rather, the general essence of those rules, and not the detailed regulation they may contain, has become applicable to internal

12 Id., at 195.

13 Marco Sassòli, 'Jus ad bellum and jus in bello: the separation between the legality of the use of force and humanitarian rules to be respected in warfare: crucial or outdated?' in Michael N. Schmitt & Jelena Pejic (eds), International law and armed conflict: exploring the faultlines: essays in honour of Yoram Dinstein (Martinus Nijhoff Publishers 2007), at 246; Hortensia D.T. Gutierrez Posse, 'The relationship between international humanitarian law and the international criminal tribunals', (2006) 88 International Review of the Red Cross, 65, at 79.

14 Jeff McMahan, Killing in war (Oxford University Press 2009), at 4.

15 Sassòli, in, at 255.

16 Hans Kelsen, 'Recognition in international law: theoretical observations', (1941) 35 American Journal of International Law, 605, at 617; see also Sylvain Vité, 'Typology of armed conflicts in international humanitarian law: legal concepts and actual situations', (2009) 91 International Review of the Red Cross, 69.

17 Antonio Cassese, 'Status of rebels under the 1977 Geneva Protocol on non-international armed conflict', (1981) 30 International and Comparative Law Quarterly, 416, at 429.

conflicts".[18] However, so-called wars of national liberation for the right of self-determination by the colonial peoples against the colonial powers are also considered to be justified by the international law on the use of force.[19] These wars of national liberation would become subjected to the laws of armed conflict under AP I and would no longer be considered to be non-international armed conflicts.[20] Here again, given its interconnection, grounds under the jus ad bellum would allow such conflict to become internationalised under the jus in bello.

Despite the legal characterisation of different armed conflicts, state practices would seem to demonstrate certain uniformity in applying IHL. Such state practice would seem to make different regulations for both international and non-international armed conflicts undesirable.[21] Nonetheless, during the Global War on Terror, the indeterminacy of the conflict would appear to undermine the application of IHL to take place. Hence, as noted by Quénivet, international jurisprudence would help "in appraising whether an armed conflict is, in fact, taking place".[22] For example, in the *Tadić* case, the ICTY's Appeals Chamber specified that "an armed conflict exists whenever there is a resort to armed force between States or protracted armed violence between governmental authorities and organised armed groups or between such groups within a State".[23] In stating so, the Tribunal blurred the legal distinction between both types of conflict for so-called "compelling humanitarian reasons".[24] Nonetheless, this compartmentalisation between the two distinct

18 *Prosecutor v. Tadić*, ICTY, Appeals Chamber, Decision on the Defence Motion for Interlocutory Appeal on Jurisdiction, 2 October 1995, Case No. IT-94-1-AR72, at www.icty.org, para. 126. (Last accessed on 15 February 2015)

19 Elisabeth Chadwick, Self-determination, terrorism and the international humanitarian law of armed conflict (Martinus Nijhoff Publishers 1996), at 9.

20 Article 1(4), AP I.

21 Emily Crawford, 'Unequal before the law: the case for the elimination of the distinction between international and non-international armed conflicts', (2007) 20 Leiden Journal of International Law, 441, at 457.

22 Noëlle Quénivet, 'The applicability of international humanitarian law to situations of a (counter-)terrorist nature', in Roberta Arnold (ed), International humanitarian law and the 21st century's conflicts: changes and challenges (Editions universitaires suisses 2005), at 33.

23 *Prosecutor v. Tadić*, ICTY, Appeals Chamber, Decision on the Defence Motion for Interlocutory Appeal on Jurisdiction, 2 October 1995, Case No. IT-94-1-AR72, at www.icty.org, para. 70. (Last accessed on 15 February 2015)

24 Crawford, at 443.

laws of armed conflict prevents "the principle of natural justice",[25] as understood by Cryer, and thus equality as described by Hart to "secure that the law is applied to all those and only those who are alike in the relevant respect marked out by the law itself".[26] How could different jurisdictional regimes ever do justice to the victims of war?

Also, peremptory norms of IHL and human rights law would further advance the basic humanitarian considerations during peacetime and wartime. In spite of their protective measures respectively during wartime and peacetime, the discrepancy between those legal regimes of international armed conflict and non-international armed conflict[27] has also tried to divide IHL, i.e. *lex specialis*, and human rights law, i.e. *lex generalis*.[28] This unnecessary dichotomy has been criticised by Best in the following words:

> The idea of humankind upon which it is founded is, after all, an even bolder one than that of human rights law, its twin in this matter. IHL and human rights law, proclaiming the same truth, sing from different scores. The human rights score, on the sunnier side, proclaims that humankind, for all its admitted subspecies diversity and notwithstanding the red herrings of cultural relativism, is one moral community and that its individual members, from whatever part of it they come, can respond to that community's demands and normally wish to do so. The IHL score in more sombre tones, perceiving that the groups composing that community continue to get into deadly quarrels with one another, prudently prescribes rules for their conduct and punishments for breaking them.[29]

Clearly, the fragmentation of the laws on the use of force and the laws of armed conflict would seem to be artificial in the sense that their interconnection is manifestly present when it comes to determining legitimate belligerency and the applicable law during armed conflict. Though the separation of IHL from human rights law appears to be more justifiable, the protection that victims

25 Robert Cryer, Prosecuting international crimes: selectivity and the international criminal law regime (Cambridge University Press 2005), at 195.

26 Herbert L.A. Hart, The concept of law (Clarendon 1994), at 160.

27 Heather A. Wilson, International law and the use of force by national liberation movements (Clarendon Press 1988), at 34.

28 Ingrid Detter De Lupis, The law of war (Cambridge University Press 1987), at 131; see also Jorge Cardona Llorens, 'Libération ou occupation? Les droits et devoirs de l'état vainqueur', in Karine Bannelier (ed), L'intervention en Irak et le droit international (Pedone 2004), at 234.

29 Best, at 293.

of war deserve might go beyond the actual wartime and peacetime.[30] Still, the current legal paradigm makes these divisions and, therefore, the next sections will, firstly, determine the rules on the different jurisdictional regimes of international and non-international armed conflict both territorially and temporally (in a chronological order in terms of the date of the creation of the different sources of IHL); secondly, analyse how the principles of distinction and proportionality operate within those different jurisdictional regimes.

2.2.2 *International Armed Conflicts*

2.2.2.1 Territorial Jurisdiction

From the territorial perspective, the laws of international armed conflict and occupation start to apply, according to the 1899–1907 Hague Regulations, whenever the territory "is actually placed under the authority of the hostile army".[31] Common Article 2 of the 1949 Geneva Conventions stipulates that the "partial or total occupation of the territory of a High Contracting Party" brings about their application. Article 1(3) of AP I confirms its application with reference to common Article 2 of the 1949 Geneva Conventions. In practice, a lot of ambiguity remains as to when the belligerent occupation commences. Most

30 For more on the discussion on the relationship between IHL and human rights law, see Robert Cryer, 'The interplay of human rights and humanitarian law: the approach of the ICTY', (2009) 14 Journal of Conflict and Security Law, 511; Christopher Greenwood, 'Human rights and humanitarian law: conflict or convergence', (2010) 43 Case Western Reserve Journal of International Law, 491; Hans-Joachim Heintze, 'On the relationship between human rights law protection and international humanitarian law', (2004) 86 International Review of the Red Cross, 789; Jean-Marie Henckaerts, 'Concurrent application of international human rights law and international humanitarian law: victims in search of a forum', (2007) 1 Human Rights and International Legal Discourse, 95; Robert McLaughlin, 'The law of armed conflict and international human rights law: some paradigmatic differences and operational implications', (2010) 13 Yearbook of International Humanitarian Law, 213; Alexander Orakhelashvili, 'The interaction between human rights and humanitarian law: fragmentation, conflict, parallelism or convergence?', (2008) 19 European Journal of International Law, 161; Marco Sassòli & Laura M. Olson, 'The relationship between international humanitarian and human rights law where it matters: admissible killing and internment of fighters in non-international armed conflicts', (2008) 90 International Review of the Red Cross, 599; Iain Scobbie, 'Principle or pragmatics? The relationship between human rights law and the law of armed conflict', (2009) 14 Journal of Conflict and Security Law, 449; Kenneth Watkin, 'Controlling the use of force: a role for human rights norms in contemporary armed conflict', (2004) 98 American Journal of International Law, 1.

31 Article 42, 1899 Hague II; Article 42, 1907 Hague IV.

would agree that the control and thus the authority over a particular territory entail the respect for the laws of occupation.[32]

AP I introduced another ground for the use of force in the international arena[33] whose conduct of hostilities is subjected to its own provisions and to those of the 1949 Geneva Conventions. In this regard, Article 1(4) of AP I includes "armed conflicts in which peoples are fighting against colonial domination and alien occupation and against racist regimes in the exercise of their right of self-determination, as enshrined in the Charter of the United Nations and the Declaration on Principles of International Law concerning Friendly Relations and Co-operation among States". These peoples fighting for their right of self-determination would be treated as other High Contracting Parties. They would have to assume the same treaty obligations as the High Contracting Parties upon the condition that the authorities representing their peoples, according to Article 96(3) of AP I, unilaterally declare to "apply the [1949 Geneva] Conventions and this Protocol in relation to that conflict". The armed forces of this party shall respect Article 43(1) of AP I and thus comply "with the rules of international law applicable in armed conflict". The interaction between jus ad bellum and jus in bello is obvious; respectively, the authority to declare compliance with IHL leads to the "recognition of belligerency"[34] whereas the latter's capacity is a requirement for "legitimate combatancy".[35] McCoubrey and White have argued that "although it may be strongly contended that, where an 'internationalized' international humanitarian regime is made applicable, the generality of 'Hague' norms should also be applied".[36] Clearly, the internationalisation of armed conflicts has an impact upon the applicability of a jurisdictional regime with a greater territorial scope.

In spite of these attempts to internationalise so-called wars of national liberation, to provide protections to victims of war and to impose limitations on the conduct of hostilities of all parties to such conflicts, their real scope would seem to be very limited.[37] The decolonisation era as focused upon by Article 1(4) of AP I was almost completely finished at the moment AP I was adopted;

---

32 Hilaire McCoubrey & Nigel D. White, International law and armed conflict (Dartmouth 1992), at 282–3.

33 Christopher Greenwood, Essays on war in international law (Cameron May 2007), at 215.

34 Wilson, at 48.

35 Id., at 48.

36 McCoubrey & White, International law and armed conflict, at 199.

37 See also Detlev F. Vagts & Theodor Meron, 'The Geneva Conventions of 1949 and wars of national liberation', in Detlev F. Vagts, Theodor Meron, Stephen M. Schwebel & Charles Keever (eds), Humanizing the laws of war: selected writings of Richard Baxter (Oxford University Press 2013), at 279.

besides, the ratification of AP I by the member states of the international community took place predominantly after the Cold War—more than one decade later than its adoption.[38] In addition, when considering the cumulative conditions of resistance "against colonial domination and alien occupation and against racist regimes", practically speaking and in a restrictive sense, only the past fight against the Apartheid regime in South Africa and Namibia could be aimed at. Moreover, when acknowledging the application of this Protocol to those limited armed conflicts, Article 96(3) stating that "the authority representing a people engaged against a High Contracting Party [...] may undertake to apply the Conventions and this Protocol" presumes that the compliance with the Geneva Conventions and AP I are two different obligations; whereas, AP I "supplements the Geneva Conventions";[39] it cannot be dissociated from the latter; and thus supplements "in all circumstances".[40]

2.2.2.2 Temporal Jurisdiction

From the temporal point of view, armed conflicts between High Contracting Parties start traditionally by a declaration of war[41] or by "an ultimatum with conditional declaration of war".[42] AP I, as intended, supplements the situations as referred to in common Article 2 of the 1949 Geneva Conventions.[43] Nowadays, declarations of war are in desuetude.[44] In this regard, the *Tadić* definition of armed conflict as mentioned above is useful in determining when an international armed conflict actually commences and from which moment IHL is applicable, namely "whenever there is a resort to armed force between States".[45] For wars of national liberation, according to Article 96(3) of AP I, from the moment of receipt of the declaration of the authority representing those peoples warring against their oppressors by the depositary, "the conventions

---

38 See website of the ICRC: ICRC, at http://www.icrc.org/IHL.nsf/%28SPF%29/party_main_treaties/$File/IHL_and_other_related_Treaties.pdf. (Last accessed 15 February 2015).

39 Article 1(3), AP I.

40 Article 1(1), AP I.

41 Article 1, 1907 Hague III; Common Article 2, GC I-IV.

42 Article 1, 1907 Hague III.

43 Article 3, AP I.

44 Christopher Greenwood, 'Scope of application of humanitarian law', in Dieter Fleck (ed), The handbook of international humanitarian law (Oxford University Press 2010), at 49.

45 *Prosecutor v. Tadić*, ICTY, Appeals Chamber, Decision on the Defence Motion for Interlocutory Appeal on Jurisdiction, 2 October 1995, Case No. IT-94-1-AR72, at www.icty.org, para. 70. (Last accessed on 15 February 2015)

and this Protocol are equally binding upon all"[46] High Contracting Parties to the internationalised armed conflict.

With respect to the conclusion of war and the application of relevant rules of IHL, such as belligerent occupation, international law has provided many mechanisms leading to the termination of war, such as cease-fire, truce and armistice, peace agreements, etc.[47] It remains, however, difficult to assess the legal status of a territory whether it is "de jure occupied [or] de facto self-governing", as put by Alonzo-Maizlish.[48] Neither is it clear when control over those territories has to be handed over to the sovereign.[49] Though, the scope of protection to civilians in the territories of the High Contracting Parties as guaranteed in Article 6 of GC IV continues beyond the actual "general close of military operations" or "in the case of occupied territory" beyond "one year after the general close of military operations". Thus, "protected persons whose release, repatriation or re-establishment may take place after such dates shall meanwhile continue to benefit by the present Convention".[50] Article 5 of GC III provides a similar extended protection to prisoners of war. Article 3 of AP I somehow combines and confirms such protection for two protected categories of individuals, i.e. civilians and prisoners of war; it seemingly extends the protection not only after "the general close of military operations" but also beyond "the termination of the occupation".

2.2.3 *Non-International Armed Conflicts*

2.2.3.1 Territorial Jurisdiction

The fulfilment of the requirements of legal combatancy, paralleling those of the internationalised armed conflicts,[51] imposed upon the rebel armed forces would be a sign of quasi-governmental authority, "albeit unrecognized",[52] to implement the provisions of AP II. Article 1(1) of AP II expects "dissident armed forces or other organized armed groups which, under responsible command, exercise such control over a part of its territory as to enable them to

46 Article 96(3)(c), AP I.

47 Michael I. Handel, 'War termination: a critical survey', in Nissan Oren (ed), Termination of wars: processes, procedures and aftermaths (The Magnes Press 1982), at 23.

48 David Alonzo-Maizlish, 'When does it end? Problems in the law of occupation', in Roberta Arnold (ed), International humanitarian law and the 21st century's conflicts: changes and challenges (Editions universitaires suisses 2005), at 99.

49 Eyal Benvenisti, The international law of occupation (Princeton University Press 1993), at 145.

50 Article 6, GC IV.

51 See Article 43, AP I.

52 McCoubrey & White, International law and armed conflict, at 200.

carry out sustained and concerted military operations and to implement this Protocol". Consequently, the provisions of AP II are applicable within the territory controlled by the rebel armed forces. As for the armed forces of the High Contracting Party, AP II shall apply within the whole of the territory. Also common Article 3 to the 1949 Geneva Conventions is applicable in such internal armed conflicts and is "equally binding on all parties to the conflict, irrespective of their share of responsibility for the breakdown of social harmony and for starting the struggle", as seen by Bugnion.[53] With regard to the 1899–1907 Hague Regulations, their application is, according to McCoubrey and White, "more questionable since it is not claimed that a full jus in bello regime would apply to such internal conflicts. Nonetheless many violations of 'Hague' law in such a context might well be argued to contravene general human rights and in some cases might even attract international attention."[54]

Of course, these non-international armed conflicts can have international dimensions as well. AP II clearly forbids that anything in its provisions can be invoked as a pretext for "intervening, directly or indirectly, for any reason whatever, in the armed conflict or in the internal or external affairs of the High Contracting Party in the territory of which that conflict occurs".[55] In this respect, territorial sovereignty and integrity as well as the national unity of the respective state cannot be challenged. The involvement of external powers in non-international armed conflicts was greatly feared by the decolonised territories after the Second World War. They once used the right of self-determination as advocated by the UN Charter as a new ground of jus ad bellum to get protection as legitimate belligerents, but it would seem that they now invoke limitations on the use of force which the same Charter provides in its Article 2(4). Regardless of the altruistic or egoistic intentions of humanitarian intervention in such territories, IHL in such situations has become the object of conflicting interests. Falk's description of this tension between sovereignty and communitarian arguments is still relevant in today's world where spheres of influence are likely to be divided by the most powerful on the international plane but whose cost is shifted towards the international community as a whole:

> Internal wars present expanding nations and blocs with opportunities for strategic expansion that do not involve the high risks of reaching those

53 François Bugnion, 'Jus ad bellum, jus in bello and non-international armed conflicts', (2003) 6 Yearbook of International Humanitarian Law, 167, at 186.

54 McCoubrey & White, International law and armed conflict, at 200.

55 Article 3(2), AP II.

> self-destructive levels of conflict that are likely to attend major armed attacks across international boundaries. This political characteristic places heavy pressure upon nonintervention norms that are designed to restrain partisan foreign participation in domestic strife. This pressure is accentuated by the moral commitments that are held currently by many important international actors. Can there be any relevance of international law to internal war in such a situation?[56]

Indeed, in its *Tadić's* appeals judgment, the Tribunal argued that a non-international armed conflict becomes internationalised when one of the non-state armed groups is acting on behalf of a third State.[57] The latter however should exercise overall control over the former.[58] The judgment continued that the intervention of a third State through its troops in an existing non-international armed conflict also internationalised that armed conflict—yet dependent on the circumstances such international armed conflict may coexist alongside the existing non-international armed conflict.[59]

2.2.3.2 Temporal Jurisdiction

As opposed to international(ised) armed conflicts—at least traditionally, the issuance of declarations of war during non-international armed conflicts is irrelevant. The asymmetrical so-called "structural power"[60] disadvantage of rebel armed forces against armed forces of the state pushes the rebels to have recourse to surprise and unnotified attacks. In the case of non-international armed conflicts, IHL, according to the ICTY in the *Tadić* case, "applies from the initiation of such armed conflicts [...] until [...] a peaceful settlement is achieved".[61] However, as Article 1(2) of AP II stipulates, "this Protocol shall not apply to situations of internal disturbances and tensions, such as riots, isolated and sporadic acts of violence and other acts of a similar nature, as not being armed conflicts". Also the ICTY in its *Tadić* trial judgment refined the thresh-

---

56 Richard Falk, 'Janus tormented: the international law of internal war', in James N. Rosenau (ed), International aspects of civil strife (Princeton University Press 1964), at 188–89.

57 *Prosecutor v. Tadić*, ICTY, Appeals Chamber, Judgment, 15 July 1999, Case No. IT-94-1-A, at www.icty.org, para. 84. (Last accessed on 15 February 2015)

58 Id., para. 120. See also Tom Gal, 'Unexplored outcomes of Tadić: applicability of the law of occupation to war by proxy', (2014) 12 Journal of International Criminal Justice, 1.

59 Id., para. 84.

60 Detter De Lupis, at 15.

61 *Prosecutor v. Tadić*, ICTY, Appeals Chamber, Decision on the Defence Motion for Interlocutory Appeal on Jurisdiction, 2 October 1995, Case No. IT-94-1-AR72, at www.icty.org, para. 70. (Last accessed on 15 February 2015)

old to establish the existence of non-international armed conflict, namely "the intensity of the conflict and the organization of the (non-state) parties to the conflict" for the purpose to distinguish such non-international armed conflict "from banditry, unorganized and short-lived insurrections, or terrorist activities".[62]

Still, the limited encouragement of the applicability of rules of international armed conflict towards the rebels,[63] as stated by the ICTY in the same *Tadić* case, does not "imply a partial or complete acknowledgement of their government"[64] and thus upholds the essentially unequal relationship between the warring parties. At the end of non-international armed conflicts, according to Article 2(2) of AP II, "all the persons who have been deprived of their liberty or whose liberty has been restricted for reasons related to such conflict, as well as those deprived of their liberty or whose liberty is restricted after the conflict for the same reasons, shall enjoy the protection of Article 5 and 6 until the end of such deprivation or restriction of liberty". Article 25 of AP II, however, does not specify the end of the hostilities, and in particular with regard to detained individuals. It says that:

> In case a High Contracting Party should denounce this Protocol, the denunciation shall only take effect six months after the receipt of the instrument of denunciation. If, however, on the expiry of six months, the denouncing Party is engaged in the situation referred to in Article 1, the denunciation shall not take effect before the end of the armed conflict. Persons who have been deprived of liberty, or whose liberty has been restricted, for reasons related to the conflict shall nevertheless continue to benefit from the provisions of this Protocol until their final release.

2.3 The Principle of Distinction

2.3.1 *On Status and Privileges*

The early industrial war campaigns in Europe and the industrial rate at which they were killing peoples soon became, according to Prins, "morally intolerable

62 *Prosecutor v. Tadić*, ICTY, Trial Chamber, Judgment, 7 May 1997, Case No. IT-94-1-T, at www.icty.org, para. 562. (Last accessed on 15 February 2015)

63 Theodor Meron, War crimes law comes of age: essays (Oxford University Press 1998), at 138.

64 Article 152, 1863 Instructions for the Government of Armies of the United States in the Field, General Orders No. 100 (Lieber Code).

and politically useless".[65] During the First World War, IHL did not conceptualise a civilian population which could be distinguished from combatants as such and for those reasons it did not receive the protection it deserved if this had been the case.[66] The technological developments of aerial warfare in particular enabled not only to destroy but also to inflict terror upon the civilians who were considered to be part of the enemy forces. Civilians were considered to be giving their support to the industrial warfare machine of the enemy.[67] Such perception of civilian involvement dominated the discourse of warfare for a long time. This alleged behaviour of the civilian population would, in the eyes of the soldiers, become the benchmark against which they had to assess their actions. Later, however, this approach on such alleged behaviour turned its focus on the status of the individual instead. Although, in this shift, "civilians clearly have not done anything to warrant attacks or to warrant immunity from attacks",[68] as understood by May, the principle of distinction would seem to be constructed upon those moral and conceptual grounds. Hence, the inherent vulnerability and the status of the civilian population would transcend the accusations of their alleged behaviour and actions.[69]

In this respect, IHL's ambitions to advance the standard of civilisation by granting non-combatant immunity, i.e. immunity from attack, to civilians and those no longer participating in armed hostilities, i.e. *hors de combat*, do not necessarily reflect the moral, military and political necessities in armed conflict. This latter argument based on necessity might justify any means to be used to win the war and to defend one's survival. For example, as Best continues, "war's new weapons of mass destruction and means of delivering them made it horribly easy to maximize non-combatant *non*-protection".[70] Nonetheless, in its *Nuclear Weapons* advisory opinion, the International Court of Justice (ICJ) endorsed the principle of distinction and its corresponding prohibition to attack civilians and to inflict unnecessary suffering upon combatants.[71] The

65 Gwyn Prins, 'Civil and uncivil wars', in Gwyn Prins & Hylke Tromp (eds), The future of war (Kluwer Law International 2000), at 215.

66 Amanda Alexander, 'The genesis of the civilian', (2007) 20 Leiden Journal of International Law, 359, at 365.

67 Id., at 369.

68 Larry May, War crimes and just war (Cambridge University Press 2007), at 175.

69 Id., at 187.

70 Best, at 260. (Emphasis added by Best)

71 Jan Wouters & Frederik Naert, 'Shockwaves through international law after 11 September: finding the right responses to the challenges of international terrorism', in Cyrille Fijnaut, Jan Wouters & Frederik Naert (eds), Legal instruments in the fight against international terrorism: a transatlantic dialogue (Martinus Nijhoff Publishers 2004), at 478.

Court stated that these "cardinal principles [...] constitute intransgressible principles of international customary law".[72] However, the idealist endeavour to protect civilians during warfare would still need to be balanced against the realist nature of war which makes full protection impossible.[73]

The disproportionate number of civilian casualties during the Second World War as compared to military ones in previous wars[74] would call for a restriction on the use of so-called "inherently indiscriminate"[75] weapons. Prior to the application of the protections granted by the principle of discrimination,[76] the determination of the civilian or military purpose of the object of target would need to be addressed first.[77] The customary IHL study of the ICRC states that "military objectives are limited to those objects which by their nature, location, purpose or use make an effective contribution to military action and whose partial or total destruction, capture or neutralisation, in the circumstances ruling at the time, offers a definite military advantage".[78] This definition clearly upholds that the only "legitimate object"[79] of warfare is the weakening of the opponent's armed forces. Consequently, no positive definition of civilian objects would be necessary as they would be the negation of the only legitimate objects of attack, i.e. the military objectives.[80] This theoretical distinction is particularly important on the battlefield. According to Kalshoven, "the abstract concept of general protection of the civilian population against the dangers of hostilities can be clarified somewhat by distinguishing two situations. One is that of the attack on the civilian population, or on members of the civilian population, as such. The other situation is that of the attack on

72 *Legality of the Threat or Use of Nuclear Weapons in Armed Conflict*, ICJ, Advisory Opinion, 8 July 1996, I.C.J. Reports 1996, at http://www.icj-cij.org/docket/files/95/7495.pdf, paras. 78–9. (Last accessed on 15 February 2015)

73 Best, at 325.

74 Robert J. Mathews & Timothy L.H. McCormack, 'The relationship between international humanitarian law and arms control', in Helen Durham & Timothy L.H. McCormack (eds), The changing face of conflict and the efficacy of international humanitarian law (Martinus Nijhoff Publishers 1999), at 72.

75 Id., in, at 73.

76 Kenneth Watkin, '21st century conflict and international humanitarian law: status quo or change?' in Michael N. Schmitt & Jelena Pejic (eds), International law and armed conflict: exploring the faultlines: essays in honour of Yoram Dinstein (Martinus Nijhoff Publishers 2007), at 284.

77 Detter De Lupis, at 233 and 239.

78 Henckaerts & Doswald-Beck, at 29. See also Article 52(2), AP I.

79 1868 Declaration of St. Petersburg.

80 Henckaerts & Doswald-Beck, at 32.

a military objective which affects the civilian population."[81] Therefore, civilian categorisations are ambiguous for the belligerent parties whose enmity towards each other trumps the harmlessness of civilian identities.[82]

Similar difficulties have risen when characterising the status of non-combatants and combatants. The non-combatants include all "persons who are not members of the armed forces"[83] and those combatants *hors de combat*, i.e. no longer taking part in armed hostilities.[84] Although the vulnerable position of civilians was unquestionable in doctrine, in practice the definition of combatancy turned the civilian's status back to its alleged behaviour. According to customary IHL, civilians are immune from attack "unless and for such time as they take a direct part in hostilities".[85] The ICRC "Interpretive Guidance on the Notion of Direct Participation in Hostilities under International Humanitarian Law" corroborates this customary rule: "For the purposes of the principle of distinction in international armed conflict, all persons who are neither members of the armed forces of a party to the conflict nor participants in a *levée en masse* are civilians and, therefore, entitled to protection against direct attack unless and for such time as they take a direct part in hostilities."[86] In any given circumstance, it is impossible to dissociate the protective status from the actual conduct. Or as Dinstein puts it, "a person is not allowed to wear simultaneously two caps: the hat of a civilian and the helmet of a soldier".[87] IHL does not accommodate part-time or unlawful combatancy[88] which in practice

---

81 Frits Kalshoven, The law of warfare: a summary of its recent history and trends in development (Henry Dunant Institute 1973), at 60.

82 Hugo Slim, Killing civilians: method, madness and morality in war (Hurst & Co. 2007), at 184.

83 Henckaerts & Doswald-Beck, at 17.

84 Detter De Lupis, at 243; For further discussion on direct participation in armed hostilities, see Michael N. Schmitt, 'The interpretive guidance on the notion of direct participation in hostilities: a critical analysis', (2010) 1 Harvard National Security Journal, 5; Michael N. Schmitt, 'Deconstructing direct participation in hostilities: the constitutive elements', (2009–2010) 42 New York University Journal of International Law and Politics, 697; Kenneth Watkin, 'Opportunity lost: organized armed groups and the ICRC "Direct Participation in Hostilities" interpretive guidance', (2009–2010) 42 New York University Journal of International Law and Politics, 641.

85 Henckaerts & Doswald-Beck, at 19.

86 ICRC, Interpretive Guidance on the Notion of Direct Participation in Hostilities under International Humanitarian Law (ICRC 2009), at 16.

87 Yoram Dinstein, The conduct of hostilities under the law of international armed conflict (Cambridge University Press 2004), at 29.

88 Jelena Pejic, '"Unlawful/Enemy combatants": interpretations and consequences', in Michael N. Schmitt & Jelena Pejic (eds), International law and armed conflict: exploring

has often taken place. Such so-called "strategic instrumentalization"[89] of those legal categories in practice undermines the clearly defined nature of such stable legal categories. Therefore, IHL as it stands, treats protected civilians who commit "belligerent acts"[90] as unprivileged and they loose their non-combatant immunity; while the privileged combatants can be prosecuted for certain acts beyond their belligerency when violating IHL.

Upon capture and imprisonment of those unlawful combatants, the United States Supreme Court before its 1942 *Quirin* case argued that these "are subject to trial and punishment by military tribunals for acts which render their belligerency unlawful".[91] Hence, such treatment denies the favourable prisoner of war's entitlements[92] and, as Baxter argues, "neglects to protect unprivileged belligerents because of the danger their acts present to their opponents".[93] Against this background, Maxwell and Watts conclude that "only by removing the fighter entirely from the classification system of the existing positive law of war can one reasonably posit that he is not entitled to the fundamental due process guarantees of the law of war and simultaneously is criminally liable merely on the basis of his extra-conventional status".[94] The latter situation has been rejected by the United States Supreme Court in its *Hamdan v. Rumsfeld* ruling as such narrow interpretation would breach the 1949 Geneva Conventions.[95] Though, such military practices have until today further destabilised IHL at the so-called "level of participant identity";[96] these same military practices have again confirmed the close interaction between the legal

---

the faultlines: essays in honour of Yoram Dinstein (Martinus Nijhoff Publishers 2007), at 338.

89 Nathaniel Berman, 'Privileging combat? Contemporary conflict and the legal construction of war', (2004–2005) 43 Columbia Journal of Transnational Law, 1, at 54.

90 Charles H.B. Garraway, '"Combatants": substance or semantics?' in Michael N. Schmitt & Jelena Pejic (eds), International law and armed conflict: exploring the faultlines: essays in honour of Yoram Dinstein (Martinus Nijhoff Publishers 2007), at 331.

91 *Ex parte Quirin et al.*, US Supreme Court, Judgment, 31 July 1942, 317 US [Supreme Court Reports] 1 (1942), at 30–1.

92 Knut Dörmann, 'The legal situation of "unlawful/unprivileged combatants"', (2003) 85 International Review of the Red Cross, 45, at 46.

93 Richard R. Baxter, 'So-called "unprivileged belligerency": spies, guerrillas, and saboteurs', (1951) 28 British Yearbook of International Law, 321, at 328.

94 Mark David Maxwell & Sean M. Watts, '"Unlawful enemy combatant": status, theory of culpability, or neither?', (2007) 5 Journal of International Criminal Justice, 19, at 23–4.

95 Michael C. Dorf, 'The Orwellian Military Commissions Act of 2006', (2007) 5 Journal of International Criminal Justice, 10, at 18.

96 Berman, at 51.

standing of their adversaries to use force, i.e. jus ad bellum, and their legitimate belligerency, i.e. jus in bello.[97]

2.3.2 *International Armed Conflicts*

Despite the customary nature of the principle of distinction,[98] it was for the first time in history that this principle and its related immunity for non-combatants have been explicitly codified by a legal instrument, namely by AP I, in its Article 48:[99] "In order to ensure respect for and protection of the civilian population and civilian objects, the Parties to the conflict shall at all times distinguish between the civilian population and combatants and between civilian objects and military objectives and accordingly shall direct their operations only against military objectives."[100] In addition, Article 3(2) of the 1980 Protocol on Prohibitions or Restrictions on the Use of Mines, Booby-Traps and Other Devices (Protocol II), Article 3(7) of its 1996 amended version and Article 2(1) of the 1980 Protocol on Prohibitions or Restrictions on the Use of Incendiary Weapons (Protocol III) have also legalised this distinction. Nevertheless, as Article 52(3) of AP I establishes, "in case of doubt whether an object is normally dedicated to civilian purposes [...] is being used to make an effective contribution to military action, it shall be presumed not to be so used". Apparently, this Article 52(3) of AP I relativises the definition of military objectives.[101] Even a later precision of military objectives in Article 52(2) of AP I remains as abstract and non-specific.[102] Still, Articles 51(4)–(5) of AP I further elaborate on indiscriminate attacks. According to Article 54(2) of AP I,

> it is prohibited to attack, destroy, remove or render useless objects indispensable to the survival of the civilian population, such as foodstuffs, agricultural areas for the production of foodstuffs, crops, livestock, drinking water installations and supplies and irrigation works, for the specific purpose of denying them for their sustenance value to the civilian population or to the adverse Party, whatever the motive, whether in order to starve out civilians, to cause them to move away, or for any other motive.

---

97 Id., at 56–7.

98 Peter Rowe, Defence: the legal implications: military law and the laws of war (Brassey's Defence Publishers 1987), at 148.

99 Judith Gail Gardam, Non-combatant immunity as a norm of international humanitarian law (Martinus Nijhoff Publishers 1993), at 109.

100 Article 48, AP I.

101 Best, at 272.

102 Dinstein, at 83.

Also attacks on "works or installations containing dangerous forces"[103] are prohibited given the risk of release of dangerous forces would indiscriminately affect the civilian population. Linked with this, according to Article 55 of AP I, is the protection of the natural environment from those attacks which cause "widespread, long-term and severe damage" and thereby "prejudice the health or survival or the population". This so-called "interrelationship of man and nature"[104] and the protection of nature[105] was already validated by the 1976 Convention on the Prohibition of Military or any Hostile Use of Environmental Modification Techniques; whereas Article 35(3) of AP I exclusively deals with the environment.[106] The 1923 Hague Rules of Air Warfare which give a more illustrative exposition of allowed and prohibited targets as well as the 1954 Convention for the Protection of Cultural Property in the Event of Armed Conflict (as referred to by Article 53 of AP I) can also be seen in this light. In addition, no military objectives, according to Article 51(7) of AP I can be shielded with civilians and thus similarly reaffirms Article 28 of GC IV which prohibits their presence "to render certain points or areas immune from military operations". The same prohibition also applies for prisoners of war.[107]

With regard to individuals licensed to kill and their privilege to commit legitimate belligerent acts, Article 51(3) of AP I corroborates the customary rule on the exception to non-combatant immunity in case of direct participation in armed hostilities.[108] Non-combatants simply cannot legally take part in combat.[109] In case of ambiguity, there exists, according to Article 50(3) of AP I, a presumption that everybody "who does not come with the definition of civilians" remains under the protective status of the civilian (population) upon the condition of course that no belligerent acts have been committed. In international armed conflicts, the protection of captured civilians would be complementary to the one of prisoners of war as this protection would rely on that

---

103 Article 56, AP I.

104 Preamble, 1976 Convention on the Prohibition of Military or any Hostile Use of Environmental Modification Techniques.

105 Karen Hulme, War torn environment: interpreting the legal threshold (Martinus Nijhoff Publishers 2004), at 21.

106 McCoubrey, International humanitarian law: modern developments in the limitation of warfare, at 229.

107 Article 23, GC III.

108 Pejic, in, at 337.

109 Margaret D. Stock, 'Detainees in the hands of America: new rules for a new kind of war', in Michael N. Schmitt & Gian Luca Beruto (eds), Terrorism and international law: challenges and responses (International Institute of Humanitarian Law 2003), at 120.

negative definition.[110] Again, the status of protection has become dependent upon the perspective of the combatant, as enshrined in Article 4 of GC III; the civilian would be its negation. However, GC III does not refer to combatants when defining prisoners of war.[111] Moreover, according to Naqvi, "it is submitted that the underlying principle establishing a general presumption of prisoner-of-war status for those participating in hostilities is developing into a customary rule".[112] Until such time, human treatment has to be guaranteed.[113]

In its *Delalić* and *Delić* judgment,[114] the ICTY stated that any individual apprehended by the adversary armed forces shall benefit from the protective status of the civilian under GC IV or of the prisoner of war under GC III.[115] Nonetheless, unlawful combatancy enters again into the picture whenever such protection needs to be guaranteed by the High Contracting Parties. Although, according to Article 5 of GC III, combatants who have acted beyond their belligerency and whose belonging to any of the categories entitled to prisoner of war as outlined in Article 4 of GC III is doubtful, they shall continue to enjoy the protection of prisoner of war "until such time as their status has been determined by a competent tribunal". Or in more general terms, any "person who takes part in hostilities and falls into the power an adverse Party shall be presumed to be a prisoner of war".[116] On the contrary, all perfidious actions would be indicative of the lack of central command on those members of such armed forces. These violators, in case of capture, do not deserve the full privileges which AP I and GC III provide.[117] In addition, mercenaries, according to Article 47 of AP I, "shall not have the right to be a combatant or a

110 José Luis Rodríguez-Villasante y Prieto, 'Terrorist acts, armed conflicts and international humanitarian law', in P.A. Fernández-Sánchez (ed), The new challenges of humanitarian law in armed conflicts: in honour of professor Juan Antonio Carrillo-Salcedo (Martinus Nijhoff Publishers 2005), at 33.

111 Detter De Lupis, at 117.

112 Yasmin Naqvi, 'Doubtful prisoner-of-war status', (2002) 84 International Review of the Red Cross, 571, at 592.

113 Horst Fischer, 'Protection of prisoners of war', in Dieter Fleck (ed), The handbook of international humanitarian law (Oxford University Press 2008), at 378.

114 *Prosecutor v. Delalić and Delić*, ICTY, Trial Chamber, Judgment, 16 November 1998, Case No. IT-96-21-T, at www.icty.org, para. 271. (Last accessed on 15 February 2015)

115 Luigi Condorelli & Yasmin Naqvi, 'The war against terrorism and jus in bello: are the Geneva Conventions out of date?' in Andrea Bianchi & Yasmin Naqvi (eds), Enforcing international law norms against terrorism (Hart Publishing 2004), at 35.

116 Article 45(1), AP I.

117 Henckaerts & Doswald-Beck, at 384; in particular Article 44(4), AP I.

prisoner of war"; the 1989 International Convention against the Recruitment, Use, Financing and Training of Mercenaries further deals with this matter.

Clearly, the legitimacy of combatancy has particularly been favourable for professional armies and the *levée en masse,*[118] i.e. the "inhabitants of a non-occupied territory, who on the approach of the enemy spontaneously take up arms to resist the invading forces, without having had time to form themselves into regular armed units, provided they carry arms openly and respect the laws and customs of war".[119] While there is no obligation under IHL to wear uniforms,[120] wearing civilian clothing is only illegal when killing and wounding treacherously those individuals who belong "to the hostile nation or army".[121] However, outside the actions of the *levée en masse,* Article 44(3) of AP I, considers the lack of other visible criteria to be perfidious, except for the carrying of arms openly. Particularly, in the context of occupation and decolonisation without real military fronts,[122] the immunity of such conduct of those combatants or their legitimate belligerency under the jus in bello would recognise the legitimacy of their insurgency or cause under the jus ad bellum against the occupying or colonial armies.[123] The lack of true distinction by a potentially growing army of irregular armed forces might produce even more civilian casualties.

2.2.3 *Non-International Armed Conflicts*

Although common Article 3 to the 1949 Geneva Conventions provides a minimum standard of protection to civilians and combatants *hors de combat,* it does not explicitly reveal the principle of distinction. This principle could be inferred from the prohibited acts mentioned in the same Article 3(1)(a), i.e. "violence to life and person". Similarly, the same fundamental standards of humane treatment have been reproduced within Article 4(2) of AP II, i.e. "violence to the life [...] of persons". Consequently, AP II did not truly remedy this gap of protection; its Article 13 would only be a restatement of Article 51 of AP I's first paragraphs. Moreover, the non-combatant immunity as codified

---

118 Karma Nabulsi, Traditions of war: occupation, resistance, and the law (Oxford University Press 2005), at 16–7; see also Articles 49 and 51, Lieber Code and Article 2, Annex 1907 Hague IV.

119 Article 4(A)(6), GC III.

120 Toni Pfanner, 'Military uniforms and the law of war', (2004) 86 International Review of the Red Cross, 93, at 104.

121 Article 23(b), Annex to 1907 Hague IV.

122 Michel Veuthey, Guérilla et droit humanitaire (Institut Henry-Dunant 1983), at 21.

123 Berman, at 56.

by Article 48 of AP I does not have its equivalent international recognition in non-international armed conflicts.[124] However, according to Kalshoven,[125] a limited recognition of this privilege can be deduced from Article 7 of AP II: "All the wounded, sick and shipwrecked, whether or not they have taken part in the armed conflict, shall be respected and protected."

Nonetheless, as reaffirms the customary IHL study by the ICRC, "the lawfulness of direct participation in hostilities in non-international armed conflicts is governed by national law".[126] Article 1(1) of AP II, on the international legal dimension, only specifies that "dissident armed forces of other organized armed groups" should be "under responsible command". Hence, civilians are again defined negatively as opposed to the membership to one of these groups. Their protection, however, according to Article 13(3) of AP II finishes "for such a time they take a direct part in hostilities". According to Berman, "common Article 3 and Protocol II are thus consistent with the statist and governmentalist biases that inform the legal construction of war".[127] Such fewer criteria of combatant status' can lead to more indiscriminate attacks[128] and a lesser "sense of duty towards international obligations agreed to by the very government to which [the rebels] are so violently opposed", as Moir continues.[129] In addition, the customary IHL protection of the principle of humanity and the dictates of public conscience as referred to in Article 1(2) of AP I for international armed conflicts have no legally binding equivalent for internal armed conflicts despite its reference in the Preamble of AP II.[130]

124 Gardam, at 128.

125 Frits Kalshoven, 'Reaffirmation and development of international humanitarian law applicable in armed conflicts: the Diplomatic Conference, Geneva, 1974–1977, Part I: combatants and civilians', (1977) 8 Netherlands Yearbook of International Law, 106, at 118–19.

126 Henckaerts & Doswald-Beck, at 13.

127 Berman, at 20.

128 Detter De Lupis, at 117.

129 Lindsay Moir, The law of internal armed conflict (Cambridge University Press 2002), at 53; see also

130 Michael Bothe, Karl Josef Partsch & Waldemar A. Solf, New rules for victims of armed conflicts: commentary on the two 1977 protocols additional to the Geneva Conventions of 1949 (Martinus Nijhoff Publishers 1982), at 620.

2.4 The Principle of Proportionality

2.4.1 *On Humanity and Necessity*

Whenever the principle of distinction and its corollary non-combatant immunity have been considered by the armed forces for their military actions, the principle of proportionality shall continue to direct their conduct. It is a customary rule of IHL that "launching an attack which may be expected to cause incidental loss of civilian life, injury to civilians, damage to civilian objects, or a combination thereof, which would be excessive in relation to the concrete and direct military advantage anticipated, is prohibited".[131] Also strategic motivations to take advantage of the substantial value of the civilian resources guided the conquering armies during and after the war.[132] Consequently, as so-called "ethical baselines",[133] proportionality and the protection of civilians through humane treatment are inseparable.[134] Besides, the positive obligation of humane treatment and the negative one of proportionality and necessity would cancel each other out. Moreover, as Kennedy continues, the "injuries of wartime are also permissible, privileged, structured by law".[135]

Despite the aim to fully comply with protective norms, collateral damage remains difficult to avoid.[136] Though, from an utilitarian perspective,[137] the means of warfare would have to rationally bring about the anticipated military purpose with the least possible injurious harm.[138] However, the principle of necessity seems to destroy, as May argues, "the possibility of there being any absolute, or near absolute, prohibitions during war, because a war may be

131 Henckaerts & Doswald-Beck, at 46. See also Article 51(5)(b), Article 57(2)(a)(iii) & Article 57(2)(b), AP I.

132 Geoffrey Francis Andrew Best, 'Restraints on war by land before 1945', in Michael Howard (ed), Restraints on war (Clarendon Press 1977), at 20–8.

133 David Kennedy, 'Reassessing international humanitarianism', in Anne Orford (ed), International law and its others (Cambridge University Press 2006), at 138.

134 Edward K. Kwakwa, The international law of armed conflict: personal and material fields of application (Kluwer Academic Publishers 1992), at 39.

135 David Kennedy, Of war and law (Princeton University Press 2006), at 114.

136 Jean Pictet, Development and principles of international humanitarian law: course given in July 1982 at the University of Strasbourg as part of the courses organized by the International Institute of Human Rights (Martinus Nijhoff Publishers 1985), at 88.

137 May, at 211.

138 Amichai Cohen & Yuval Shany, 'A development of modest proportions: the application of the principle of proportionality in the Targeted Killings case', (2007) 5 Journal of International Criminal Justice, 310, at 312.

merely a series of military necessities".[139] Again, such entitlement legitimises to violate both jus ad bellum and jus in bello. The principles of proportionality and humanity would only be functional to limit the instrumental necessities of war. In addition, customary IHL states that "all feasible precautions must be taken to avoid, and in any event to minimise, incidental loss of civilian life, injury to civilians and damage to civilian objects".[140] Hence, as restatements of the principle of necessity,[141] the precaution by which necessity operates would, as Duffy puts it, "ensure the lawfulness of a military attack".[142] In this way, possible future reconciliation[143] between the warring parties might be guaranteed and might offer "a better peace", as seen by Howard.[144] The cornerstone of humanity in the jus in bello is inextricably linked with accountability under the jus post bellum.

More concretely, whenever the object of targeting has been determined, proportionality shall prohibit particular weaponry causing "superfluous injury and unnecessary suffering"[145] and shall affect the way weaponry is being used in particular circumstances.[146] Thus, as another customary rule of IHL stipulates, "each party to the conflict must take all feasible precautions in the choice of means and methods of warfare with a view to avoiding, and in any event to minimise, incidental loss of civilian life, injury to civilians and damage to civilian objects".[147] But, so-called technologically "advanced military powers"[148] actually possess such banned and other indiscriminate weapons. Best argues that the "risk of horrors accompanying [their] use"[149] would remain "a matter of regret".[150] In this respect, arms control treaties in general could provide

139 May, at 197.

140 Henckaerts & Doswald-Beck, at 51.

141 Kwakwa, at 37.

142 Helen Duffy, The "war on terror" and the framework of international law (Cambridge University Press 2005), at 235.

143 Michael Howard, 'Temperamenta belli: can war be controlled?' in Michael Howard (ed), Restraints on war: studies in the limitation of armed conflict (Oxford University Press 1979), at 14.

144 Id., in, at 14.

145 Mathews & McCormack, in, at 71.

146 Detter De Lupis, at 136.

147 Henckaerts & Doswald-Beck, at 56.

148 Best, War and law since 1945, at 324.

149 Id., at 306.

150 Id., at 306.

less industrially advanced parties to escape an arms race[151] of such inhumane weaponry. At the same time, such treaties could also "increase mistrust and spiralling expenditures", as seen by Keefer.[152] Moreover, it is most likely that the technological inferior parties would have recourse to less conventional and indiscriminate methods and means of warfare[153] in order to ultimately compete for the support of the civilian population.[154]

Evidently, the issue of precision-guided weaponry is *de facto* linked with the requirements of proportionality it wants to safeguard. Schmitt, however, argues that "the extent of harm and damage is relevant only in relation to the military advantage reasonably expected as the attack was launched".[155] In this respect, indiscriminate attacks with civilian casualties as a result are necessarily condemned of being reckless. Consequently, another spiral of indiscriminate warfare will spur out of this asymmetrical violence. Nonetheless, in spite of the rapid technological evolution in military affairs,[156] the Martens clause is part of customary IHL.[157] But, according to the 1868 Declaration of St. Petersburg, "the Contracting or Acceding Parties reserve to themselves to come hereafter to an understanding whenever a precise proposition shall be drawn up in view of future improvements which science may effect in the armament of troops, in

151 Scott Andrew Keefer, 'Building the palace of peace: The Hague Conference of 1899 and arms control in the progressive era', (2006) 8 Journal of the History of International Law, 1, at 8.

152 Id., at 65.

153 Michael N. Schmitt, 'The impact of high and low-tech warfare on the principle of distinction', in Roberta Arnold (ed), International humanitarian law and the 21st century's conflicts: changes and challenges (Editions universitaires suisses 2005), at 177; See also Gabriella Blum, 'On a differential law of war', (2011) 52 Harvard International Law Journal, 163.

154 Karine Bannelier, 'L'influence de la guerre asymétrique sur les règles du jus in bello', in Karine Bannelier (ed), L'intervention en Irak et le droit international (Pedone 2004), at 148.

155 Michael N. Schmitt, 'Precision attack and international humanitarian law', (2005) 87 International Review of the Red Cross, 445, at 457.

156 *Legality of the Threat or Use of Nuclear Weapons in Armed Conflict*, ICJ, Advisory Opinion, 8 July 1996, I.C.J. Reports 1996, at http://www.icj-cij.org/docket/files/95/7495.pdf, para. 78. (Last accessed on 15 February 2015)

157 Robin M. Coupland, 'The SIrUS Project: towards a determination of which weapons cause "superfluous injury or unnecessary suffering"', in Helen Durham & Timothy L.H. McCormack (eds), The changing face of conflict and the efficacy of international humanitarian law (Martinus Nijhoff Publishers 1999), at 103; see also a discussion by Antonio Cassese, 'The Martens clause: half a loaf or simply pie in the sky?', (2000) 11 European Journal of International Law, 187.

order to maintain the principles which they have established, and to conciliate the necessities of war with the laws of humanity."[158] However, the determination of necessity remains at the discretion of the military commander.[159]

2.4.2 *International Armed Conflicts*

During international armed conflicts, proportionality shall also govern the treatment of the adversaries' combatants and civilian population in order to minimise their suffering. With regard to the situation of non-combatants, "each High Contracting Party shall allow the free passage of all consignments of medical and hospital stores, [...] of essential foodstuffs, clothing and tonics intended for children under fifteen, expectant mothers and maternity cases".[160] As a corollary to the customary prohibition of "starvation of civilians as a method of warfare" confirmed by Article 54(1) of AP I, the protection of such collective relief schemes has to be guaranteed by the High Contracting Parties.[161] Article 23 and 59 of GC IV, however, continue that the free passage of those goods enabling the humane treatment and survival of those vulnerable groups is subjected to the fear that they "may accrue to the military efforts or economy of the enemy".[162] The latter contrasts with the general observations of Article 27 of GC IV which states that all protected persons "shall at all times be humanely treated". Moreover, denying such humanitarian goods in particular would circumvent the minimum humane treatment as spelled out in Article 75 of AP I, inspired by common Article 3 to the 1949 Geneva Conventions and obey the more general prohibition of Article 32 of GC IV where:

> The High Contracting Parties specifically agree that each of them is prohibited from taking any measure of such a character as to cause the physical suffering or extermination of protected persons in their hands. This prohibition applies not only to murder, torture, corporal punishment, mutilation and medical or scientific experiments not necessitated by the medical treatment of a protected person, but also to any other measures of brutality whether applied by civilian or military agents.

158 1868 Declaration of St. Petersburg.

159 Mika Nishimura Hayashi, 'The Martens clause and military necessity', in Howard M. Hensel (ed), The legitimate use of military force: the just war tradition and the customary law of armed conflict (Ashgate 2009), at 139–40.

160 Article 23, GC IV.

161 Article 59, GC IV and Article 70(4) AP I.

162 Article 23(c), GC IV.

Such provisions are closely associated with the principle of distinction which in this particular context refer to the prohibition of collective punishment against civilians[163] and individuals *hors de combat*[164] as a disproportionate measure which sets aside the individual responsibility of the members of the civilian populations for their wrong-doing. With regard to the prisoners of war, humane treatment and protection are mandatory "at all times [...] against acts of violence or [...] physical mutilation or [...] medical or scientific experiments of any kind which are not justified by the medical, dental or hospital treatment of the prisoner concerned and carried out in his interest".[165] Also alimentary, clothing, medical, sanitary and shelter obligations are imposed upon the Detaining Power.[166]

Not only general treaties[167] on the conduct of hostilities during international armed conflicts prohibit the use of such "means and methods of warfare which are of a nature to cause superfluous injury or unnecessary suffering",[168] also certain weapons conventions[169] reflect this customary rule of IHL. However, the protocols on incendiary and blinding laser weapons[170] do not prohibit

---

163 Article 50, Annex 1907 Hague IV; Article 33, para. 1, GC IV; Article 75(2)(d), AP I.

164 Article 87, para. 3, GC III.

165 Article 13, GC III.

166 See Articles 20–32, GC III; Articles 10–11, AP I.

167 1868 Declaration of St. Petersburg; 1899 Hague IV, 2; 1899 Hague IV, 3; Article 23(e), Annex 1899 Hague II, Article 23(e); Annex 1907 Hague IV; Article 35(2), AP I.

168 Henckaerts & Doswald-Beck, at 237. See also Article 35(3), AP I.

169 Preamble, 1980 Convention on Prohibitions or Restrictions on the Use of Certain Conventional Weapons Which May be Deemed to be Excessively Injurious or to Have Indiscriminate Effects; 1980 Protocol on Non-Detectable Fragments (Protocol I); Article 6(2), 1980 Protocol on Prohibitions or Restrictions on the Use of Mines, Booby-Traps and Other Devices (Protocol II); Article 3(3), 1996 Amended Protocol on Prohibitions or Restrictions on the Use of Mines, Booby-Traps and Other Devices; Preamble, 1997 Convention on the Prohibition of the Use, Stockpiling, Production and Transfer of Anti-Personnel Mines and on their Destruction. The 1925 Protocol for the Prohibition of the Use of Asphyxiating, Poisonous or Other Gases, and of Bacteriological Methods of Warfare is inspired by the same prohibition already present within Article 70, Lieber Code and Article 23(e), Annex 1899 Hague II and 1907 Hague IV. It has been reproduced by later conventions such as the 1972 Convention on the Prohibition of the Development, Production and Stockpiling of Bacteriological (Biological) and Toxin Weapons and on their Destruction and the 1993 Convention on the Prohibition of the Development, Production, Stockpiling and Use of Chemical Weapons and on their Destruction.

170 Articles 1(5) and 2(3), 1980 Protocol on Prohibitions or Restrictions on the Use of Incendiary Weapons (Protocol III); Article 2, 1995 Protocol on Blinding Laser Weapons (Protocol IV).

their use but insist instead on the so-called "precautionary measures"[171] to be taken when employing them; and this to avoid a violation of the princicple of proportionality in the conduct of armed hostilities. In this regard, according to Article 51(5)(b) of AP I, indiscriminate attacks "which may be expected to cause incidental loss of civilian life, injury to civilians, damage to civilian objects, or combination thereof, which would be excessive in relation to the concrete and direct military advantage anticipated". Besides the "constant care"[172] to incalculate proportionality in attack and "against the effects of attack"[173] during international armed conflicts, weapons conventions continue to play an important role in the aftermath of warfare. Because, also the remnants of war cause, according to the 2003 Protocol on Explosive Remnants of War, "serious post-conflict humanitarian problems".[174] Moreover, these remnants of war have "severe consequences"[175] to the security of civilian population. Therefore, on the level of the reconciliation process, any disproportionate military action like the ones mentioned above shall affect the accountability for those violations.[176]

2.4.3 *Non-International Armed Conflicts*

Common Article 3 to the 1949 Geneva Conventions and Part II of AP II explicitly deal with the humane treatment at all times of "all persons who do not take a direct part or who have ceased to take part in hostilities".[177] The protection of the civilian population against starvation and the prohibition of all means and methods of war having this direct or indirect influence upon the former are regulated both by customary and treaty law. In spite of this prohibition enacted by Article 14 AP II, no provisions safeguard the actual "access of humanitarian relief even though such access is clearly a *conditio sine qua non* for relief actions".[178] However, the "freedom of movement of authorised humanitarian relief personnel",[179] as a customary rule of IHL, remains "subject

---

171 Article 51(8), AP I.

172 Article 57 (1), AP I.

173 Article 58, AP I; see also Article 3(10), 1996 Amended Protocol on Prohibitions or Restrictions on the Use of Mines, Booby-Traps and Other Devices.

174 Preamble, 2003 Protocol on Explosive Remnants of War (Protocol V).

175 Preamble, 2008 Convention on Cluster Munitions; Preamble, 1997 Convention on the Prohibition of the Use, Stockpiling, Production and Transfer of Anti-Personnel Mines and on their Destruction.

176 Article 50, GC I; Article 51, GC II; Article 130, GC III; Article 147, GC IV; Article 85, AP I.

177 Article 4(1), AP II.

178 Henckaerts & Doswald-Beck, at 194–95.

179 Id., at 200.

to the consent of the High Contracting Party" as stipulated by Article 18(2) of AP II. Consequently, military necessity can still be invoked by the warring parties in order to curtail such obligation under customary IHL. Although state practice gives sufficient support to a customary rule in those situations, the limited legal certainties which IHL gives to those helpless individuals can, as during international armed conflicts, be supplemented by human rights law applicable during peacetime and wartime.

Regarding the conduct of hostilities, no explicit reference has been made in AP II to the principle of proportionality nor to the precautionary measures during and against the effects of attack. Nowadays, given the customary nature of their obligation, they are, however, applicable in non-international armed conflicts. Also the customary prohibition on "the use of means and methods of warfare which are of a nature to cause superfluous injury or unnecessary suffering"[180] applies in non-international armed conflicts. Although these principles and prohibitions were initially deliberately omitted in AP II,[181] the same calculations as during international armed conflicts have to be made when using particular weaponry in armed conflicts of a non-international character. In this regard, the ICTY in its *Tadić* case brought solace: "Indeed, elementary considerations of humanity and common sense make it preposterous that the use by States of weapons prohibited in armed conflicts between themselves be allowed when States try to put down rebellion by their own nationals on their own territory. What is inhumane, and consequently proscribed, in international wars cannot but be inhumane and inadmissible in civil strife."[182]

2.5 Conclusion

From this positivist perspective on the jurisdictional regimes of IHL and the principles of protection, it seems that these categorical imperatives conflict with the exigencies of military necessity and emergency situations. The structure of the legal arguments in IHL consists of these two opposing values, namely the communitarian (humanity) and sovereignty (necessity) ones. It is necessary to understand why these values have been formulated in those conflictual terms. In this regard, Chapter III in Part II will try to analyse a history of

180 Id., at 237.

181 Id., at 48, 52 and 239.

182 *Prosecutor v. Tadić*, ICTY, Appeals Chamber, Decision on the Defence Motion for Interlocutory Appeal on Jurisdiction, 2 October 1995, Case No. IT-94-1-AR72, at www.icty.org, para. 119. (Last accessed on 15 February 2015)

divide and rule against which the rules of armed conflict can be understood. A contextualisation of the narrative on the "Western" Self and its Other which have accompanied and informed the creation, interpretation and application of IHL might be useful to understand how the laws of war legitimise warring parties to have recourse to necessity in the first place. Both violence and the law seem to feed into each other's ambitions to assert their power.

Consequently, if any binding nature is to be expected from IHL in order to protect the victims of warfare, it appears that those hopes might be vain in reality because the structure of the legal arguments in IHL, as it stands, might never be fully conclusive when it comes to achieving those ends. Nonetheless, the laws of humanity which the Martens clause is referring to might be a possible guidance towards compliance of IHL. As Chapter VI in Part III will try to demonstrate, such humanitarian conscience might transcend the divisive nature of the structure of the legal arguments in IHL as possibly set up and influenced by the divisive narrative of the "Western" Self and its Other as will be examined in Chapter III. Such conscience might give an answer to this strategy to divide and rule over the legal protections as promised by humanitarian safeguards and foster that necessary change beyond the divisive structure of the legal arguments in IHL, so IHL could be truly humanitarian again in its spirit.

PART II

Historical Analysis of the Self and the Other

CHAPTER III

The "Western" Self and the Other

3.1 Introduction

The aim of this chapter is to trace back the history of the discourses on the "Western" Self and its Other. As opposed to the positivist analysis of IHL as discussed in Chapter II, this chapter will examine, from a deconstructivist perspective, the historical background of identity formation and exclusion in the Western civilisation. As Part I of this book has analysed the similarities between existing principles of protection, namely those of distinction and proportionality, in the Islamic and Western traditions on laws of war, respectively, Part II of this book is aimed at establishing that the instrumentalisation of the narratives on the Self and the Other within Western and Islamic discourses shows equally proof of a strategy to divide and rule over their internal and external enemies. Although the Western discourse of inclusion and exclusion already dates from the early beginnings of Christianity,[1] this chapter will predominately focus on the continuation of that early conscience from the nineteenth century onwards, when IHL was formally developing.

From its Christian origins, the West's civilising mission spread across the overseas territories of the European colonial powers. In the light of the duality of human nature, the fruits of this enterprise brought different civilisations in contact with each other in multiple dimensions. As will be submitted, a relationship on equal footing was never fully envisaged as the Western "civilized" and modern Self would negate its primitive Other. Throughout the West's history, the Western need for unity amongst its own ranks did face many internal challenges from different interest groups. Despite these different claims of legitimacy within, the Western powers had agreed upon their responsibility to assist the unprivileged peoples and nations around the world. From the colonial missions, through the Mandate System, and the wars of national liberation, the decolonised peoples were granted, progressively, a greater responsibility

1 David Archard, Paul Gifford, Nigel Rapport & Trevor A. Hart (eds), 2000 years and beyond: faith, identity, and the common era (Routledge 2003); Christian Duquoc & Casiano Floristán (eds), Christian identity (T. & T. Clark 1988); Hans Küng, Christianity: its essence and history (SCM Press 1995); Jacob Neusner (ed), Religious foundations of Western civilization: Judaism, Christianity, Islam (Abingdon Press 2006).

 DOI 10.1163/9789004298248_005

to assume their position amongst the international community of sovereign states.

The civilisational and rational standards of Western powers which this Other had to adhere to, went hand in hand with violence. Within these struggles for more self-determination, the "Western" Other remained subjected to similar divisions which it witnessed from the beginning of its colonisation by imperial powers. In addition, the division along racial and ethnic lines created even more disunity and violence amongst themselves and kept them deprived of a better political, economic and social future. Capitalist and communist ideologies competed to provide a right answer to the Other's concerns. The end of the Cold War, however, solidified a liberal narrative which promised to restructure and improve the humanitarian and developmental situation of some of the desperate nations and of their peoples. But such modes of Western intervention became unacceptable for certain groups in society whose dehumanisation would lead them to resist this form of continuous tutelage. As a self-fulfilling prophecy, the resistance on behalf of the Other against the social and economic discrepancies which the West had instituted, appears to justify the West's military response against such resistance.

3.2 From Christianity to Colonialism

3.2.1 *Religious Conscience versus Rationalism*

From the beginning of Christianity, the growing community of followers was seeking unity against the threats of persecution from outside their community. As a matter of survival they had to organise themselves through the institution of the Church. From the fourth century onwards—under the Roman emperor Constantine—Christianity became the official religion in the Roman Empire. At the end of Roman Empire, during the so-called Middle Ages, Western and Byzantine Christians were respectively fighting amongst each other and against the rising Islamic Empire in the Middle Eastern region. At least for the Byzantines, the obsession with unity[2] of humanity would denounce the nomadism of the Arab tribes and invaders of a so-called "degeneration of humankind".[3] Meanwhile, Europe itself was divided, but its cultural revolution from the fifteenth century onwards brought new incentives to redress

2 Jacques Ellul, La subversion du christianisme (Seuil 1984), at 58.

3 Brian Stanley, 'Christian missions and the Enlightenment: a reevaluation', in Brian Stanley (ed), Christian missions and the Enlightenment (Eerdmans 2001), at 187.

its violent past and reunite its territory under one rule of law.[4] In addition, this renaissance of Europe's classical past as well as the decline of the Islamic Empire would stimulate Christian European rulers and particularly the Papacy to spread their universal morality across the globe.[5] Europe's ambition for internal unity could also have been a pretext to advancing such consciousness of social responsibility towards all members of humanity.

In view of unifying humanity under such a Christian morality, the Church faced many challenges to submit humanity's natural inclination to self-preservation.[6] Nevertheless, Christianity's so-called "message of eternal redemption"[7] offered enough potentiality for the Church to redirect, control and anticipate human behaviour even outside Europe. Despite such views of predestination, the doctrines as developed by the righteous Christian authorities, however, did not infringe upon humanity's self-determination and its liberties.[8] According to Khoury, "dans cette perspective, le critère de la foi religieuse devient la foi en l'homme, et le critère de la foi vivante et agissante, de la pratique religieuse, devient la pratique politique".[9] And so it did, the European scientific inventions and discovery of the Americas at the end of the fifteenth century onwards showed proof of humanity's autonomy. Also on the religious scene, this belief in humanity enabled it to propose other religious claims against the central Christian authorities. In this respect, the Protestant Reformation and the Catholic Counter-Reformation led again to religious wars in the heart of Europe's different kingdoms fighting for their own Christian justice and social responsibility.[10]

---

4 Paul Khoury, Islam et christianisme: dialogue religieux et défie de la modernité (Heidelberg Press-Lebanon 1973), at 117.

5 Brett Bowden, 'The colonial origins of international law, European expansion and the classical standard of civilization', (2005) 7 Journal of the History of International Law, 1, at 8.

6 Ellul, at 86.

7 Helder Camara, The Church and colonialism: the betrayal of the Third World (Dimension Books 1969), at 103.

8 Véronique Hervouët, L'enjeu symbolique: islam, christianisme, modernité: interprétation psychanalytique des fondements religieux et idéologiques et de leurs conflits (L'Harmattan 2004), at 141.

9 Khoury, at 12. Free translation: "From this perspective, the criteria of religious faith becomes the faith in man, and the criteria of lively faith and of religious practice, becomes the political practice."

10 Shadia B. Drury, Terror and civilization: Christianity, politics, and the Western psyche (Palgrave Macmillian 2004), at 70 and 85.

Apparently, this evolution which should have set humanity free led to even more competition and division on the European political scene between Anglican, Catholic and Lutheran adherents. Within this struggle for power, according to Drury, the Christian conscience had internalised terror through the fear for each Other.[11] In this regard, the European political and religious establishments instilled fear in the minds of their subjects within and beyond Europe. Returning back to such predestined views of humanity, these establishments would further legitimise their socio-economic domination over their subjects. In addition, they would foster the illusion that this brutality and violence, as noted by Drury, was "the key to the civilizing process".[12] This process would set their subjects ultimately free.

From the end of the sixteenth century, natural lawyers like de Vitoria and Grotius, were developing another international legal order whose binding character had its roots within God's natural world.[13] The difference was that this law of peoples could be rationally elucidated from the natural divine law which embodied the limitations upon humanity's unbounded drive for survival.[14] However, only the European peoples could possibly settle the competing rights of those members of human society to their survival; simply because their civilisational development allowed them to judge rationally and objectively about the competing claims between them and the "uncivilised" savages.[15] Grotius found that the Church would no longer have jurisdiction to settle such disputes in the universal natural legal order. Under this *jus gentium*, the state or the independent sovereign instead would have these jurisdictional prerogatives as well as the authority to contribute to this new corpus of law.[16] If, however, the "uncivilised" peoples would resist or defy this legal order, in which they initially were participants, Europeans would inevitably have recourse to war to redress such violations within certain boundaries; something which de Vitoria highlighted in the following words:

> If after the Spaniards have used all diligence, both in deed and in word, to show that nothing will come from them to interfere with the peace and

11 Id., at 123.

12 Id., at 99.

13 Antony Anghie, Imperialism, sovereignty, and the making of international law (Cambridge University Press 2005), at 17.

14 Richard Tuck, The rights of war and peace: political thought and the international order from Grotius to Kant (Oxford University Press 2001), at 100.

15 Id., at 135.

16 Id., at 96.

> well-being of the aborigines, the latter nevertheless persist in their hostility and do their best to destroy the Spaniards, they can make war on the Indians, no longer as an innocent folk, but as against forsworn enemies and may enforce against them all the rights of war, despoiling them of their goods, reducing them to captivity, deposing their former lords and setting up new ones, yet withal with observance of proportion as regards the nature of the circumstances and of the wrongs done to them.[17]

Clearly, the independent European sovereigns ensured the respect for this universal natural and moral order. This order established at least some kind of stability on the international scene at that time. From the seventeenth century onwards, however, Hobbes in particular rather found that states would not accept any universal justice and would, like human beings, rationally justify their preferences of self-interest and self-preservation to be served before those of others. Nonetheless, according to Hobbes, the duality of human nature necessarily required a balance between humanity's freedom against the interests of others.[18] There seemed to be a tension between humanity's utilitarian behaviour which would inherently produce a struggle between competing interests and humanity's need for respecting the Other. These self-centred interests might be informed by identities on the Self and the Other as well. Consequently, these interests would be served through this division and rule. In spite of these divisions, Pufendorf, another seventeenth century natural lawyer, believed that out of necessity human beings had to be sociable, transcend those divisions and be aware of the responsibilities human beings have in each others' well-being.[19] In the eighteenth century, Kant argued that as a matter of evolution, cosmopolitan peace could rise out of disputes where self-preservation was initially at stake. Still, he remained realistic that war was the "*status naturalis*" between human beings.[20] Rousseau, another eighteenth century liberal thinker, was of the opinion that the state which incorporated the sovereignty of its people had to accommodate the different liberties of its citizens. The social contract would be a manifestation of the general will of the

17 Franciscus de Vitoria, De Indis et de ivre belli (Carnegie Institution of Washington 1917), at 155.

18 Thomas Hobbes, De Cive (Kessinger Publishing 2004), at 37–8.

19 Samuel Pufendorf, Of the law of nature and nations: eight books (The Lawbook Exchange, Ltd. 2005), at 233.

20 Immanuel Kant, Perpetual peace (Filiquarian Publishing, LLC 2007), at 13.

sovereign people.[21] Montesqieu, however, warned about the possible tyranny of the governing authorities through violence and censorship.[22]

These Enlightenment ideas made it possible to rationally construct a human society of solidarity which could manage the conflicting selfish interests of human beings.[23] As previously done by religious authorities, now state institutions regulated human liberties and project their standards of moral behaviour upon their citizens in their social interactions.[24] In this respect, the state was an indispensable tool to further these Enlightenment principles whose morality benefited the whole of humanity.[25] Under the protection of the sovereign against external foreign threats,[26] civil society could flourish within a so-called "civilised space"[27] of inclusion. As opposed to the sixteenth century natural legal order amongst European sovereigns, from the mid-nineteenth century, European states developed positive international law. These rules adopted by consent, at least in theory, protected sovereignty within a territorially determined nation state order and were binding upon states.[28] In practice, however, the rational explanation on individual human behaviour and its violent nature also applied to states.[29] Moreover, the systematic rationalisation of profit laid the foundation for Western capitalism[30] and its unlimited drive to conquer the world and impose its industrious mode of planning.[31] In this imperial economic process, according to Cobban, "tyranny at home and aggression abroad were the logical and historical consequences of the attempt to put the theory

21 Jean-Jacques Rousseau, Du contrat social ou principes du droit politique (MetaLibri 2008), at 38.

22 Charles-Louis de Secondat de Montesqieu, De l'esprit des lois (Librairie de Paris 1777), at 187.

23 Lester Gilbert Crocker, Nature and culture: ethical thought in the French Enlightenment (Johns Hopkins University Press 1963), at 328.

24 Hilary Putnam, Enlightenment and pragmatism (Koninklijke Van Gorcum 2001), at 33.

25 Janis Langins, Conserving the Enlightenment: French military engineering from Vauban to the Revolution (MIT Press 2004), at 211.

26 Wayne Morrison, Criminology, civilisation and the new world order: rethinking criminology in a global context (Routledge Cavendish 2006), at 19.

27 Id., at 18.

28 Robert Howse, 'Europe and the New World Order: lessons from Alexandre Kojève's engagement with Schmitt's "Nomos der Erde" ', (2006) 19 Leiden Journal of International Law, 93, at 94.

29 Penelope Simons, 'The emergence of the idea of the individualized state in the international legal system', (2003) 5 Journal of the History of International Law, 293, at 298.

30 Danièle Hervieu-Léger & Françoise Champion, Vers un nouveau christianisme? Introduction à la sociologie du christianisme occidental (Cerf 1986), at 210.

31 Robert Delavignette, Christianisme et colonialisme (Fayard 1960), at 23.

of popular sovereignty into practice".[32] Hence, the actions of the sovereign to divide and rule domestically and overseas were attributed to its own people in whose name these crimes were committed. Also Hume, an eighteenth century philosopher, illustrated the utilitarian, though brutal, exercise of such sovereignty on behalf its people:

> The rage and violence of public war; what is it but a suspension of justice among the warring parties, who perceive, that this virtue is now no longer of any use or advantage to them? The laws of war, which then succeed to those of equity and justice, are rules calculated for the advantage and utility of that particular state, in which men are now placed. And were a civilized nation engaged with barbarians, who observed no rules even of war; the former must also suspend their observance of them, where they no longer serve to any purpose; and must render every action or encounter as bloody and pernicious as possible to the first aggressors.[33]

3.2.2 *Nationalism and Orientalism*

At the end of the eighteenth century, Western sovereign states started to establish their "imagined political community—and imagined as both inherently limited and sovereign", as put by Anderson.[34] As opposed to the nonmembers of this community,[35] this national belonging was rationalised by the concept of *Volksgeist*, i.e. the spirit of the people. The people's sovereignty unified the power of the people which rested in the state. Despite the protective and inward-looking nature of such national identity, it necessarily remained influenced by a continuously changing world conscience, i.e. *Weltgeist*.[36] The industrial revolutions of the nineteenth century for example might have shaped these identities. In view of the self-preserving nature of humanity, the scientific and industrial inventions done by European nations caused tension among other nations to compete over this progress within Europe and beyond. Each European nation wanted to be, according to Hobson, "the sole carrier

32 Alfred Cobban, In search of humanity: the role of the Enlightenment in modern history (George Braziller 1960), at 194.

33 Tom L. Beauchamp (ed), An enquiry concerning the principles of morals: a critical edition / David Hume (Clarendon Press 2006), at 16.

34 Benedict Anderson, Imagined communities: reflections on the origin and spread of nationalism (Verso 1991), at 5.

35 Eric J. Hobsbawn, Nations and nationalism since 1780: programme, myth, reality (Cambridge University Press 1993), at 91.

36 Simons, at 329.

of civilisation and human progress, in the economic, intellectual and political realms".[37] Though European peoples had already discovered and conquered some parts of the world since the sixteenth century, the unrivalled technological capability[38] accelerated and consolidated these colonial expeditions. With respect to the colonisation of overseas and oriental territories, de Vattel, a nineteenth century Swiss international lawyer, further elaborated on the law of survival of the fittest which allowed the use of force to impose its order: "The earth was designed to feed its inhabitants; and he who is in want of everything is not obliged to starve, because all poverty is vested in others ... Extreme necessity revives the primitive communion, the abolition of which ought to deprive no person of the necessaries of life."[39] It appears that there were no limits to the European man's existence; its drive to survive made him very pragmatic in achieving its goals.

In this regard, Commager observed that the scientific classification of Europe's findings on their colonial territories gave "new dimensions to both Nature and Man".[40] New empirical evidence as interpreted by the modern scientific enterprise produced new truths. However, these truths could impossibly reduce the complexity of the realities found outside the West.[41] According to Prakash, these "changes in knowledge had direct implications for the technologies of rule".[42] Hence, the relationship of power between the colonial Self and the colonised Other was affected;[43] even beyond the mere essentialisation of the Other as the negation of the "Western" Self[44] and the embodiment

37 J.M. Hobson, The Eastern origins of Western civilization (Cambridge University Press 2004), at 222.

38 Stanley, in, at 10.

39 Emmerich de Vattel, The law of nations or the principles of natural law (J. Chitty 1839), at 107–8.

40 Henry Steele Commager, The empire of reason: how Europe imagined and America realized the Enlightenment (Anchor Press/Doubleday 1977), at 49.

41 John Gray, Enlightenment's wake: politics and culture at the close of the modern age (Routledge 1995), at 152; Colin Gunton, Enlightenment and alienation: an essay towards a Trinitarian theology (Marshall Morgan & Scott 1985), at 12.

42 Gyan Prakash, 'Writing post-orientalist histories of the Third World: Indian historiography is good to think', in Nicholas B. Dirks (ed), Colonialism and culture (University of Michigan Press 1992), at 357.

43 Ann Laura Stoler, 'Rethinking colonial categories: European communities and the boundaries of rule', in Nicholas B. Dirks (ed), see id., at 322.

44 Ashis Nandy, The intimate enemy: loss and recovery of self under colonialism (Oxford University Press 1988), at 72.

of difference.[45] Lorimer, one of the leading international lawyers of the nineteenth century, said that "no modern contribution to science seems destined to influence international politics and jurisprudence to so great an extent as that which is known as ethnology, or the science of races".[46] Despite the unity of humanity, early biologists did advance biological distinctions of the human species into different racial groups as promoted by their colleagues in anthropology.[47] These subdivisions called "races" were based upon anatomical traits. They could impossibly cover large segments of the human population given the continuous migration and intermingling of peoples. The differentiation of individual characteristics would be set aside to establish hierarchies based on the imagined idea of race.[48] The status of a (sub-)race was determined in relation towards other races. The white man was the point of reference against which others had to be judged on a scale of civilisational progress yet expressed in biological terms. Social Darwinism in particular explained why certain populations have occupied higher positions within society as opposed to their inferior others.[49] Man, at least the Western one, has taken over the laws of nature and imposed its own rule on it. Russel Wallace, i.e. Darwin's counterpart, noticed that these human interventions could have uncontrollable outcomes:

> This victory which he has gained for himself gives him a directing influence over other existences. Man has not only escaped "natural selection" himself, but he actually is able to take away some of that power from nature which, before his appearance, she universally exercised. We can anticipate the time when the earth will produce only cultivated plants and domestic animals; when man's selection shall have supplanted "natural selection".[50]

---

45 Joshua Paul Dale, 'Cross-cultural encounters through a lateral gaze', in Inge E. Boer (ed), After orientalism: critical entanglements, productive looks (Rodopi 2003), at 64.

46 James Lorimer, The institutes of the law of nations (William Blackwood and Sons 1883), at 93.

47 L.C. Dunn, 'Race and biology', in Leo Kuper (ed), Race, science and society (The Unesco Press 1975), at 31.

48 Benjamin H. Isaac, The invention of racism in classical antiquity (Princeton University Press 2004), at 29–35.

49 E.U. Essien-Udom, 'Tribalism and racism', in Leo Kuper (ed), Race, science and society (The Unesco Press 1975), at 236.

50 Alfred Russel Wallace, 'The origin of human races and the antiquity of man deduced from the theory of "natural selection"', in Michael D. Biddis (ed), Images of race (Leicester University Press 1979), at 52.

Racism would serve the white man's objective to impose its own scientific order and to justify its authority which was based upon the scientific representations of their dehumanised subjects.[51] These acclaimed rationalised and objective perceptions of the world made it almost impossible to challenge this new order from within.[52] Moreover, geographic distances between Western and non-Western cultures were indicative of their divergence in terms of temporal and evolutionary progress.[53] Hence, the universalisms of the Enlightenment are, according to Muthu, "imperializing ideologies that are fundamentally antagonistic toward cultural diversity".[54] The destruction of those cultures might actually free the impoverished inhabitants of the overseas colonial territories from their cultural backwardness.[55] In addition, supplied with missionary confidence,[56] Western progress could now be spread around the world in order to transform the Other in accordance with its own Western image.[57] Within these ancient lands, European nations were not only scrambling for territories but were also defining the extent of their own natural right to civilise the Other.[58] By denying sovereignty to the local peoples and by controlling their territories, the colonisers assumed these peoples' sovereignty and territorial control instead. Lawrence, a nineteenth century international lawyer, underscored that responsibility: "International Law regards states as political units possessed of proprietary rights over definite portions of the earth's surface. So entirely is its conception of a state bound up with the notion of territorial possession that it would be impossible for a nomadic tribe, even if highly organised and civilized, to come under its provisions."[59] Westlake, however, found that there

51 Robert W. Rydell, 'Science in the service empire: empire in the service of science', in Gregory Blue, Martin Bunton & Ralph Croizier (eds), Colonialism and the modern world: selected studies (Sharpe 2002), at 231.

52 Alain Touraine, Critique de la modernité (Fayard 1992), at 179.

53 Jan-Erik Lane & Hamadi Redissi, Religion and politics: Islam and Muslim civilisation (Ashgate 2004), at 26.

54 Sankar Muthu, Enlightenment against empire (Princeton University Press 2003), at 259.

55 Stephen Neill, Colonialism and Christian missions (Lutterworth 1966), at 11.

56 Andrew F. Walls, 'The eighteenth century protestant missionary awakening in its European context', in Brian Stanley (ed), Christian missions and the Enlightenment (Eerdmans 2001), at 23.

57 Brian Stanley, 'Christianity and civilization in English evangelical mission thought, 1792–1857', in Brian Stanley (ed), Christian missions and the Enlightenment (Eerdmans 2001), at 176.

58 Brian Dolan, Exploring European frontiers: British travellers in the age of Enlightenment (Macmillan 2000), at 115.

59 Thomas J. Lawrence, The principles of international law (D.C. Heath 1895), at 136.

were degrees of civilisation among the "uncivilised".[60] Consequently, international law was only serving nation states. This legal regime would, according to Williams, legitimise the "genocidal conquest and colonization of the non-Western peoples of the New World";[61] for example as witnessed against the Indians by the Americans or against the Herero by the Germans. This law had a global reach and effectively established, as put by Onuma, an "unequal international society"[62] for the future. Against this setting, Haldar fairly depictes the function of colonial law to organise, rationalise and assimilate

> that which is, or those who are, initially outside its imperial jurisdiction. It exposes the manner in which the law weaves these historically hitherto unconnected peculiarities into its own theoretically all-encompassing textual order. It exposes a process of subjection and uncovers an interlacing range of mechanisms employed in justifying its universality and grip. What occurs in the specific context of colonialism, in other words, is indicative of the very structure of Occidental juridical thought.[63] [...] The spread of modern Occidental legal systems and their institutions over larger areas, and the administration of laws to greater numbers of people propound the gradual demise of local laws and crystallize the disregard for individual differences. [...] Indeed, the racism inherent within the legal process must be attributed to its structural blindness and impartiality that leaves open a means of engendering an emotional bias at the level of decisions.[64]

3.2.3 *The Standard of Civilisation*

Against the background of the colonisation of the "non-Western" Other by the "Western" Self, a Western standard of civilisation envisaged the ultimate goal of civilisational progress for this Other. When these "uncivilised" colonised peoples aspired this standard, they could finally belong to the international

---

60 John Westlake, Chapters on the principles of international law (Cambridge University Press 1894), at 141–155.

61 Robert A. Williams Jr., The American Indian in Western legal thought: the discourses of conquest (Oxford University Press 1990), at 6.

62 Yasuaki Onuma, 'When was the law of international society born? An inquiry of the history of international law from an intercivilizational perspective', (2000) 2 Journal of the History of International Law, 1, at 64.

63 Piyel Haldar, Law, orientalism and postcolonialism: the jurisdiction of the lotus eaters (Routledge-Cavendish 2007), at 2.

64 Id., at 5.

community of nation states.[65] Contrary to what Laski had claimed, this value system had enough roots in the renewal of another type of faith, not in the supernatural but in the civilisational.[66] Consequently, from a utilitarian point of view, the society was formed, according to Haldar, by a "civilizing process [...] which in turn colonizes and shapes the emotional range of existence as a means of inhabiting the legal subject".[67] The colonised subject had to correspond to the demands of the coloniser to achieve its standard of civilisation.[68] This sentimental compromise of a rather theological deterministic nature and a socio-economic immobilism[69] reinforced the idea that the essential differences of humanity were difficult to overcome. In particular, when the whole theorisation and rationalisation of humanity's identity used the Western universal standard of humanity against which other allegedly different categories of peoples had to be assessed.[70] If the primitive peoples did not meet the yardstick of civilisation, no access would be granted to the status of the sovereign.[71] They would remain excluded from the modern world of nation states.

In this respect, since the nineteenth century, international law and its theory of state recognition, built upon this standard of civilisation,[72] found its way into customary international law.[73] Hence, as the colonial subjects themselves were considered to lack a legal existence as individuals, their legal recognition as a people was missing as well. This assumption fitted with the understanding of the idea of conscience. This conscience was, according to Drury, "the symbol of the unnatural process by which man has been robbed of his wild and original self".[74] Universal applicable norms were used to attain the colonisers' ambition. However, the scope of international law brought the barbarians

65 Gerrit W. Gong, The standard of "civilization" in international society (Clarendon Press 1984), at 54–93.
66 Harold J. Laski, Faith, reason and civilisation: an essay in historical analysis (Gollancz 1944), at 36.
67 Haldar, at 15.
68 Crocker, at 364.
69 Hervouët, at 16.
70 Claudia Moscovici, Double dialectics: between universalism and relativism in Enlightenment and postmodern thought (Rowman & Littlefield 2002), at 113.
71 Gerry J. Simpson, Great powers and outlaw states: unequal sovereigns in the international legal order (Cambridge University Press 2004), at 243–44.
72 Jean Allain, 'Slavery and the League of Nations: Ethiopia as a civilised nation', (2006) 8 Journal of the History of International Law, 213, at 215.
73 Georg Schwarzenberger, 'The standard of civilisation in international law', (1955) 8 Current Legal Problems, 212, at 220.
74 Drury, at 126.

within its ambit but kept them outside its protection.[75] Full protection would only be guaranteed in case of complete membership.[76] Because the colonial subjects were not meeting the "civilised" conditions, this law was not applicable to them.[77] Only organised societies with stable governments[78] could benefit from the protection of international law. Only the sovereign state recognised by the family of "civilised" nations would benefit from the protection of international law which safeguarded their interdependence and equality.[79] In spite of the promises of international law to transcend "societies altogether, just as God transcends the world",[80] as put by Unger, the true agent on the international plane remained the white man and its organisation.[81] It seemed that the homogenising attempts of the international legal order were not fully cosmopolitan[82] as this order continued to give preference to the refined and sociable members of its community.[83]

Instead, the door was open for colonial subjugation and exploitation of those subhuman peoples.[84] Again, the acknowledgement for European harmonisation and cooperation among its states strongly contrasted with the lawlessness which was flourishing outside Europe with its intervention.[85] Given the narrowly defined concept of sovereignty, indigenous peoples were never

---

75 Antony Anghie, 'On critique and the other', in Anne Orford (ed), International law and its others (Cambridge University Press 2006), at 394.

76 Antony Anghie, 'Francisco de Vitoria and the colonial origins of international law', in Eve Darian-Smith & Peter Fitzpatrick (eds), Laws of the postcolonial (University of Michigan Press 1999), at 103–4.

77 Pasquale Fiore, International law codified and its legal sanction (Baker, Voorhis and Company 1918), at 45.

78 Alpheus Henry Snow, The question of aborigines in the law and practice of nations (G.P. Putnam's Sons: The Knickerbocker Press 1921), at 315–16.

79 Stéphane Beaulac, 'The Westphalian legal orthodoxy: myth or reality?' (2000) 2 Journal of the History of International Law, 148, at 149; Karen O'Brien, Narratives of Enlightenment: cosmopolitan history from Voltaire to Gibbon (Cambridge University Press 1997), at 139.

80 Roberto Mangabeira Unger, Law in modern society: toward a criticism of social theory (The Free Press 1976), at 79.

81 André Siegfried, La civilisation occidentale (Clarendon Press 1945), at 5.

82 David P. Fidler, 'Revolt against or from within the West? TWAIL, the developing world, and the future direction of international law', (2003) 2 Chinese Journal of International Law, 29, at 37.

83 Harold Mah, Enlightenment phantasies: cultural identity in France and Germany, 1750–1914 (Cornell University Press 2003), at 51.

84 Hobson, at 241.

85 F.S. Ruddy, 'International law and the Enlightenment: Vattel and the 18th century', (1968–1969) 3 International Lawyer, 839, at 856.

able to assume statehood and their lands were considered *terra nullius* before their colonisation.[86] The discovery of sophisticated cultures in those overseas territories brought feelings of insecurity to the Western civilisation itself.[87] Therefore, despite the West's so-called "narcissistic fascination"[88] for its mirrored Other, the Self and Other's relationship has been informed by violence. This was the case whenever the so-called "myth of the noble savage"[89] had been scattered. Violence was used when this reality did not correspond to its imagery. For those reasons, according to Frankel, "the use of primitive society to show the origin of contemporary institutions was a way of divesting these institutions of their sanctity, of showing the similarity between contemporary behavior and the unenlightened practices of savages".[90] Clearly, the "Western" Self did not only dehistorise and decontextualise its own rationality,[91] it also deterritorialised the Other. It took away the Other's natural rights and treated any deviations from its norms as abnormal. In particular, nineteenth century international law only served when its discipline was persuasive and rhetorical enough to obscure the actual practices of its modernist, pragmatic and progressive narrative.[92] According to Lawrence, these images of the ordered Self and the disordered Other would "instill faith in and hope for the development of international law".[93] Also de Vattel, for example, confirmed this tendency:

> The end of the natural society established among men in general is that they should mutually assist one another to advance their own perfection and that of their conditions; and Nations, too, since they may be regarded as so many free persons living together in a state of nature, are bound mutually to advance this human society. Hence the end of the great

86 S. James Anaya, Indigenous peoples in international law (Oxford University Press 2004), at 19 and 22.

87 John James Clarke, Oriental Enlightenment: the encounter between Asian and Western thought (Routledge 1997), at 33.

88 Dale, in, at 66.

89 Ann Thomson, Barbary and Enlightenment: European attitudes towards the Maghreb in the 18th century (E.J. Brill 1987), at 95.

90 Charles Frankel, The faith of reason: the idea of progress in the French Enlightenment (King's Crown Press 1948), at 88.

91 Muhammad Tavakkuli Tarqi, Refashioning Iran: orientalism, occidentalism, and historiography (Palgrave 2001), at 4.

92 David Kennedy, 'International law and the nineteenth century: history of an illusion', (1997–1998) 17 Quinnipiac Law Review, 99, at 104.

93 Annelise Riles, 'Aspiration and control: international legal rhetoric and the essentialization of culture', (1993) 106 Harvard Law Review, 723, at 725.

> society established by nature among all nations is likewise that of mutual assistance in order to perfect themselves and their condition.[94]

While celebrating order above anarchy,[95] international law was constructing a discriminatory system around the core principle of so-called "sovereign equality".[96] According to Nesiah, this concept of sovereignty was "posited as the natural and universal measure of territoriality".[97] After the destruction of the cultures of the primitive peoples, international law and its modern practices fulfilled their role to provide the necessary assistance to these primitive peoples.[98] As part of the duality of human nature, this so-called "civilizing therapy"[99] found its first institutionalised application under the Mandate System of the League of Nations and later under the Trusteeship System of the UN. The international territorial administrations in East-Timor and Kosovo are later examples thereof. Under the tutelage of an international regulatory body, i.e. the League of Nations, the Mandatories, from the beginning of the twentieth century, supported the gradual process of self-determination of the colonial peoples within their territories. In view of this interest of the international community of "civilised" states, the competing territorial claims between European powers over their overseas dominions had to be halted. However, no explicit provisions on such annexation were made to prevent conflicts to emerge.[100] In this respect, it seemed that twentieth century international law was on the verge of renewing[101] itself upon the ruins of the past failures of the

---

94 Emmerich de Vattel, Le droit des gens ou principes de la loi naturelle appliqués à la conduite et aux affaires des nations et des souverains (Carnegie Endowment for International Peace 1916), at 6.

95 Matthew Craven, 'Introduction: international law and its histories', in Matthew Craven, Malgosia Fitzmaurice & Maria Vogiatzi (eds), Time, history and international law (Martinus Nijhoff Publishers 2006), at 1.

96 Simpson, at 247; see also Heinhard Steiger, 'From the international law of Christianity to the international law of the world citizen: reflections on the formation of the epochs of the history of international law', (2001) 3 Journal of the History of International Law, 180, at 191.

97 Vasuki Nesiah, 'Placing international law: white spaces on a map', (2003) 16 Leiden Journal of International Law, 1, at 6.

98 Michel Henry, La barbarie (Presses universitaires de France 2004), at 13.

99 Antony Anghie, 'Colonialism and the birth of international institutions: sovereignty, economy, and the Mandate System of the League of Nations', (2001–2002) 34 New York University Journal of International Law and Politics, 513, at 547.

100 Ralph Wilde, International territorial administration: how trusteeship and the civilizing mission never went away (Oxford University Press 2008), at 371.

101 Kennedy, at 109.

civilising mission. This civilising mission appeared to remain inherently present throughout the reinvention of new concepts[102] seeking for support and recognition from the international community. The General Act of the Berlin Conference (on the scramble of Africa) and the Covenant of the League of Nations were particularly illustrative:

> All the Powers exercising sovereign rights or influence in the aforesaid territories bind themselves to watch over the preservation of the native tribes, and to care for the improvement of the conditions of their moral and material well-being, and to help in suppressing slavery, and especially the slave trade.[103]
>
> To those colonies and territories which as a consequence of the late war have ceased to be under the sovereignty of the States which formerly governed them and which are inhabited by peoples not yet able to stand by themselves under the strenuous conditions of the modern world, there should be applied the principle that the well-being and development of such peoples form a sacred trust of civilisation and that securities for the performance of this trust should be embodied in this Covenant.[104]

3.3 Capitalism versus Communism

3.3.1 *Imperialism*

Besides the allegedly altruistic intentions of those civilising efforts on behalf of the West, the Other was also the subject of competition between the capitalist and communist ideologies since the 1917 Russian Revolution onwards. Each bloc had its own imperialistic and expansionist tendencies and wanted to influence the Other in particular when the decolonisation of those territories started to take place after the Second World War and during the Cold War. Each empire had the prerogatives to control its periphery in accordance with its wishes to transform the traditional societies in modern capitalist and communist ones. Israel accurately described this trend: "Highly complex systems of imperial subjugation had developed across much of the world in the construction of which the colonizing powers utilized various blends of ideology and

102 Antony Anghie, 'Finding the peripheries: sovereignty and colonialism in nineteenth century international law', (1999) 40 Harvard International Law Journal, 1, at 80.

103 Article 6, 1885 General Act of the Berlin Conference.

104 Article 22, 1919 Covenant of the League of Nations.

institutions, exploiting to the full the mystiques of monarchy, aristocracy, and religious justification as well as newer notions of racial hierarchy and mercantilist doctrine of national prosperity."[105]

Ultimately it was the nation state which was the precursor of the whole industrial capitalist project. Predominantly Western capitalist powers had benefited from these modes of industrial production within their borders and their overseas colonial territories. The state was the guardian of the different classes and their struggles at home and the colonial administrator of the so-called "international division of labour" overseas.[106] Within those colonial territories, the vertical segregation between the colonisers and the colonised showed proof of this institutionalised division whose foundations for later competing economic claims were difficult to overcome.[107] All these hierarchies as endorsed by the colonial state determined the conditions for economic development: the colonised periphery remained subjected to the pre-capitalist mode of production, namely to deliver its raw materials to industrial Western markets. Hence, no prospects for independent manufacturing were allowed and true trade competition had been curtailed.[108] Initiated under the colonial regime, this unfair competition seemed to continue under the Bretton Woods agreements and those of the World Trade Organization (WTO).

Though, some regional economic integration projects as witnessed within the West started to live their own lives in the decolonised territories. Meanwhile, during the colonial era, Western powers, as put by Said, wanted to bring under control "virtually every space in the world".[109] The dismantlement of the natives from their cultural and territorial identity[110] was accompanied with their ethnicisation along the local political groups.[111] The imperial powers

105 Jonathan Irvine Israel, Enlightenment contested: philosophy, modernity, and the emancipation of man, 1670–1752 (Oxford University Press 2006), at 590–91.

106 Tony Spybey, Social change, development and dependency: modernity, colonialism and the development of the West (Polity 1992), at 74.

107 Frederick Cooper, Colonialism in question: theory, knowledge, history (University of California Press 2005), at 105.

108 Alexander Lyon Macfie, Orientalism: a reader (Longman 2002), at 94.

109 Edward W. Said, 'Yeats and decolonization', in Terry Eagleton, Fredric Jameson & Edward W. Said (eds), Nationalism, colonialism, and literature (University of Minnesota Press 1990), at 77.

110 T.K. Oommen, 'Introduction: conceptualizing the linkage between citizenship and national identity', in T.K. Oommen (ed), Citizenship and national identity: from colonialism to globalism (Sage 1997), at 34.

111 Mahmood Mamdani, When victims become killers: colonialism, nativism, and the genocide in Rwanda (Princeton University Press 2002), at 24.

used these new divisions to rule over them. In this respect, misreading the experience[112] of the natives' so-called "original state"[113] rationalised the Other from within the Western perspective and legalised their new subservient status as inseparable from the Western one.[114] Despite the Western anti-slavery and abolition movements from the eighteenth and nineteenth century onwards, Mowbray emphasised the extent to which these unequal practices continued to infringe upon the basic needs of survival of those underprivileged peoples until today:

> In this way the colonial period established a trading system which generally served to increase inequalities between North and South. This would not necessarily have affected the South's food situation, if the South had continued to grow its own food. But available land in the South was increasingly used for the production of commodities for export, rather than the production of food for domestic consumption.[115]

3.3.2 *Liberalism*

After the Cold War, the liberal political and economic order continued to prevail and impose the conditions of those inequalities, not only materially but also psychologically. The hypothesis that each individual was naturally driven by self-interest and profit formed the basis of pursuing the type of economic and commercial expansion which Edgeworth spoke about.[116] As with other scientific disciplines, these economic abstractions simplified the complexity of humanity's behaviour.[117] In this regard, even from the early days of Western

---

112 William Luis, 'Borges, the encounter, and the other: blacks and the monstrous races', in Fernando de Toro, Alfonso de Toro & Kathleen Quinn (eds), Borders and margins: post-colonialism and post-modernism (Vervuert 1995), at 67.

113 Anthony Pagden, 'The effacement of difference: colonialism and the origins of nationalism in Diderot and Herder', in Gyan Prakash (ed), After colonialism: imperial histories and postcolonial displacements (Princeton University Press 1995), at 141.

114 Colette Guillaumin, 'The idea of race and its elevation to autonomous scientific and legal status', in Marion O'Callaghan (ed), Sociological theories: race and colonialism (The Unesco Press 1980), at 48–50.

115 Jacqueline Mowbray, 'The right to food and the international economic system: an assessment of the rights-based approach to the problem of world hunger', (2007) 20 Leiden Journal of International Law, 545, at 550.

116 See Francis Ysidro Edgeworth, Mathematical psychics: an essay on the application of mathematics to the moral sciences (Kegan Paul 1881).

117 Michel Henry, C'est moi la vérité: pour une philosophie du christianisme (Seuil 1996), at 345.

colonialism, European trading companies were seeking to live up to those mercantilist ideals through indirect rule over the overseas territories. Only later, from the nineteenth century onwards, the European nation states were assuming the so-called "humanitarian and civilizing tasks"[118] which accompanied the economic exploitation of those regions. As mentioned earlier, the inhabitants of those overseas territories were envisaged inside the realm of international law but stayed outside its protection. Only sovereign states benefited from the laws created by them.

Beyond the law, from the mid-twentieth century onwards, the global economic liberalisation of market outlets was another way for the post-colonial enterprise to solidify its structural advantages across the globe:[119] surplus goods in the West flooded non-Western regions which in their turn were unable to truly compete with the West. Against this background, the impact of the laws of nature, as developed from the fifteenth century, seemed to confirm the dynamics of the market whose regulation favoured the privileged.[120] However, nowadays, international organisations, such as the WTO, increasingly determine the course of trade relationships beyond the initial competences of the nation state.[121] This would further deterritorialise the consecutive decision-making leading to other concerns of unaccountability. This liberal understanding of utilitarian behaviour itself created and reinforced its own reality where necessarily the Self took advantage of the available resources, including those of the Other. Resistance from the Other would lead to oppression on behalf of the Self. Therefore, having recourse to the normativity of human nature, i.e. the survival of the fittest, facilitated this to take place.

Moreover, according to Hervouët, "cette logique du profit poussée jusqu'en ses ultimes conséquences inspire des stratégies financières et industrielles à court terme, prédatrices et sacrificielles, aux conséquences suicidaires".[122] In particular, industrialisation changed social relationships and constructed them along the division of labour into a working class at the service of the

118 Martti Koskenniemi, The gentle civilizer of nations: the rise and fall of international law, 1870–1960 (Cambridge University Press 2002), at 145.

119 Tuck, at 234.

120 Oswaldo de Rivero, The myth of development: the non-viable economies of the 21st century (Zed Books 2001), at 81.

121 Antony Anghie, 'Time present and time past: globalization, international financial institutions, and the Third World', (1999–2000) 32 New York University Journal of International Law and Politics, 243, at 271.

122 Hervouët, at 196. Free translation: "The logic of profit pushed to its ultimate consequences inspires short term financial and industrial strategies with predatory, sacrifying and suicidal consequences."

establishment.[123] Paradoxically even, political liberalism which introduced human agency and legal status engendered another outcome, i.e. the desubjectivation and dehumanisation of the individual through its classification of economic belonging.[124] This belonging was useful to serve the Self from its Other. Nonetheless, in spite of the subject's alienation from its agency, the consumer would be given the impression that it could still pursue its happiness through materialism; upon the condition that the subject adhered to the expectations which this liberal ideology prescribed. Though, within Western societies, collective mobilisation had, at multiple occasions, challenged the social order and was equally suppressed by the establishment, such as during the 1960s. This so-called "strategy of containment"[125] and protectionism was vital to the (post-)colonial enterprise and the concept of sovereignty served to ensure loyalty to one or the other socio-economic regime.[126]

3.3.3 *Humanitarianism*

It appeared that throughout the colonial enterprise and the post-colonial order the West had deprived the colonial and post-colonial peoples from the privileged economic conditions it was benefiting from. Almost as a self-fulfilling prophecy, the West enhanced its missionary role and guaranteed future dependency of those unprivileged peoples. In this regard, economic interventions reinforced the inequalities which the liberal economic models were institutionalising. The nineteenth century's standard of civilisation and white racial supremacy which had served the Western colonial powers to justify their politics were replaced by another humanitarian narrative. After the Second World War, economic development was now at the foreground of the West's humanitarian efforts to assist developing countries to make progress on the economic level. In this regard, according to Leftwich, developing states in the Third World needed continuous assistance to "shape, pursue and encourage […] the conditions and direction of economic growth".[127]

123 Hervieu-Léger & Champion, at 198.

124 Hervouët, at 210–11.

125 Hobson, at 241.

126 Dan Sarooshi, 'Sovereignty, economic autonomy, the United States, and the international trading system: representations of a relationship', (2004) 15 European Journal of International Law, 651, at 653.

127 Adrian Leftwich, 'Bringing politics back in: towards a model of the developmental state', (1995) 31 Journal of Development Studies, 400, at 401.

Moreover, the neoliberal economic ideas on "structural adjustment",[128] privatisation[129] programmes started from the 1950s onwards. They were continuously adapted to the new challenges and conditionalities which the world economic order required, such as the Poverty Reduction Strategy Papers from the twentieth-first century onwards. These programmes were mapped out by the world's financial and economic institutions, such as the World Bank and the International Monetary Fund. However, they would seem to sustain the same economic dependency which was already present before their intervention. From this developmental perspective, failures to their implementation and the continuous underdevelopment were predominantly attributed to the internal characteristics of the developing states which were accused of not having strictly adhered to these programmes in the first place.[130] Developing states on the other hand, argued that the structure of the international economic system and the laws of economics impeded them to make such progress. In addition, stricter developmentalism would only close the emerging markets from foreign investment and hence exclude those markets from the global one.

Capitalism seemed to favour the developed Self and to deprive the underprivileged Other. This ambition of the capitalist industrial economy also went beyond this external division. Internally, the Western state had to produce economic surpluses in order to appease the growing unemployed proletariat and to make them benefit from its redistribution. Within this growing gap between the rich and the poor, this space became shaped by conflicting interests for scarce resources. In particular, and in addition to the economic marginalisation of the non-Western Other, this Other was also left behind with the racial and ethnic divisions as introduced by the former coloniser. In order to compete for the abundant resources, these programmed identities continued to be exploited through violence. In this regard, during the Cold War, the capitalist and communist blocs were supporting the warring parties in developing nations to fight their proxy wars. In this context and after the Cold War, state sovereignty once again remained a relative concept whose content was flexible for many subscriptions. Therefore, there was a lot to be done in order for the (de-)colonised peoples to ever provide for themselves economically

---

128 Christopher S. Clapham, Africa and the international system: the politics of state survival (Cambridge University Press 1996), at 169.

129 Jeswald W. Salacuse, 'From developing countries to emerging markets: a changing role for law in the Third World', (1999) 33 International Lawyer, 875, at 884.

130 Thomas J. Biersteker, 'The "triumph" of liberal economic ideas in the developing world', in Barbara Stallings (ed), Global change, global response: the new international context of development (Cambridge University Press 1995), at 176.

while other divisions were destroying them at the same time. The so-called *de jure* "sovereign equality"[131] appeared to be vain in reality. Though, natural law in particular, according to Maritain, one of the drafters of the 1948 Universal Declaration of Human Rights, did not necessarily have an enforceable character; it could have a substantial normative value instead;[132] at least, to decide upon and for one's own development.

3.4 From Decolonisation to Globalisation

3.4.1 *Self-Determination versus Sovereignty*

The present socio-economic conditions in some non-Western nations would still seem to be indicative of their colonial roots. Apparently, the path towards their independence has been influenced by external restraints. Hence, the decolonisation process has proven how the prerogatives of self-determination of those peoples were exercised in practice. In reality, international law was not equally applied for the protection of all peoples and nations.[133] Not only economic and political reasons explained its application,[134] its construction in the first place served to gratify the civilising mission as an ethic and aesthetic project. Built in this same tradition, the expansion of international law and its new principles, such as the one of self-determination, perpetuated to dismantle the Other.[135] The Other though, was limited to appropriate its new identity and responsibility within the realm of international law but outside its shelter. Only recognised states and governments could enter into relations with the other so-called "members of the family of nations".[136] This cosmopolitan democratic ideal has been restricted by the politics of recognition curtailing this ideal's revolutionary foundations to assume the universal right of

131 Fidler, at 42.

132 Andrew Woodcock, 'Jacques Maritain, natural law and the Universal Declaration of Human Rights', (2006) 8 Journal of the History of International Law, 245, at 248.

133 Jean Allain, 'Orientalism and international law: the Middle East as the underclass of the international legal order', (2004) 17 Leiden Journal of International Law, 391, at 395.

134 Clarke, at 206.

135 Malcolm N. Shaw, 'Peoples, territorialism and boundaries', (1997) 8 European Journal of International Law, 478, at 484.

136 Hans Kelsen, 'Recognition in international law: theoretical observations', (1941) 35 American Journal of International Law, 605, at 605.

self-determination of peoples.[137] As under the community of Christian and "civilised" states, this legal consciousness has once again robbed both the Self and the Other from its original natural rights. Lauterpacht, however, contended that such distinction cannot be made for reasons of recognition policies.[138]

The nationalistic ideologies which Western countries produced in the nineteenth century were useful for the colonial peoples in their revolt against the Western powers.[139] With their own sense of identity, their right of self-determination was thought to be fully realisable,[140] whilst the West considered the decolonisation, as put by Orford, as "the sense of the foreign as a threat".[141] For those reasons, the West also had to produce a future legal strategy which could ensure the division they once introduced in their overseas territories. In this respect, according to Summer, a "political doctrine about how States, and the international law based on them, should be structured".[142] Hence, the principle of *uti possidetis* served this end; namely, to restrict the exercise of this peoples' right of self-determination within the borders of the colonial state.[143] Once this right was consumed, it did not give any new incentives for self-determination to other groups within the newly independent state. Most likely, leaving such an emptied right of self-determination into the hand of other groups along racial and ethnic classifications, could lead to greater frustrations and endless violence. The 1990s' Balkan wars were striking examples thereof.

Therefore, after the decolonisation, international law accompanied the independence and safeguarded the existing interests of the West especially in terms

137 Louis-Philippe May, Esquisse d'un tableau des apports de la France à la civilisation (Michel 1951), at 588.

138 Hersch Lauterpacht, Recognition in international law (Cambridge University Press 1947), at 31.

139 Philip D. Curtin, The world and the West: the European challenge and the overseas response in the Age of Empire (Cambridge University Press 2000), at 196.

140 Terry Eagleton, 'Nationalism: irony and commitment', in Terry Eagleton, Fredric Jameson & Edward W. Said (eds), Nationalism, colonialism, and literature (University of Minnesota Press 1990), at 28.

141 Anne Orford, Reading humanitarian intervention: human rights and the use of force in international law (Cambridge University Press 2003), at 149.

142 James J. Summers, 'The rhetoric and practice of self-determination: a right of all peoples or political institutions?' (2004) 73 Nordic Journal of International Law, 325, at 343.

143 James A.R. Nafziger, 'Self-determination and humanitarian intervention in a community of power', (1991) 20 Denver Journal of International Law and Policy, 9, at 19.

of foreign investment after succession.[144] Despite these post-colonial guarantees, international law also started to be concerned with the protection of the human conditions all over the world. Though accused of a neo-imperialistic agenda, the human rights narrative would seem to enhance individual human rights for the sake of collective rights to be exercised, such as the right of self-determination of unprivileged groups.[145] The treatment of individuals within particular states could now be scrutinised by the international community of states assessing its respect and violation. This liberal human rights project as initiated by the West now found and justified its universal expansion to be achieved through the individual. Such communitarian aspirations, however, were competing with the core principle of international law, i.e. sovereignty both internally as externally.[146] Nonetheless, the peremptory nature of the right of self-determination imposed certain obligations upon the international community as a whole, namely the so-called *erga omnes* obligations.[147] In case of their violation, a humanitarian intervention on behalf of the whole of humanity could become mandatory. Still, this human rights strategy kept the Self in a "safely distanced contact with the certifiably barbaric", as Kennedy puts it.[148]

3.4.2 *Professionalism versus Anarchy*

Having acknowledged the universal validity of capitalism and liberal democracy, it remained to be determined how these values could be implemented.[149] Good governance, as seen by Gathii, was one of the methods to advance "economic recovery and political freedom".[150] This method could also assess the

144 See Matthew Craven, The decolonization of international law: state succession and the law of treaties (Oxford University Press 2007).

145 Anghie, 'On critique and the other', in, at 396.

146 Christopher Harding, 'Statist assumptions, normative individualism and new forms of personality: evolving a philosophy of international law for the twenty-first century', (2001) 1 Non-State Actors and International Law, 107, at 117.

147 2001 Draft Articles on Responsibility of States for Internationally Wrongful Acts, with Commentaries, 2001 Yearbook of the International Law Commission, Vol. II, Part II, at 85.

148 David Kennedy, 'Spring break', (1984–1985) 63 Texas Law Review, 1377, at 1386.

149 Jonathan R. Macey & Geoffrey P. Miller, 'The end of history and the new world order: the triumph of capitalism and the competition between liberalism and democracy', (1992) 25 Cornell Journal of International Law, 277, at 283–84.

150 James Thuo Gathii, 'Retelling good governance narratives on Africa's economic and political predicaments: continuities and discontinuities in legal outcomes between markets and states', (2000) 45 Villanova Law Review, 971, at 971.

ongoing corruption[151] and disorder in the countries of the South. It was time that those governments were fully adhering to the objectives of the West, i.e. to make true progress. However, their consent did not alter the hierarchical qualities of these conditionalities[152] as proposed by the institution-building efforts of the international community.[153] In addition, if the state were unable to provide these certainties, then the private sector would give a better answer to the demands of the global market. It is within this context, as Kennedy saw it, that a "private order builds itself naturally through the work of the economic market".[154] Finally, such global governance could overcome the degenerated approaches of local authorities and bring stability.[155] Some states, however, completely failed, became ungovernable and virtually disintegrated along warring factions. In such worst case scenarios, according to Forrest, only the "surviving elements of the state become immersed in or devoted to warfare while sectors of society ally with rebels or become inundated with social banditry".[156]

These failed states would have to be rehabilitated.[157] In this regard, the concept of earned sovereignty was developed to reconcile the humanitarian intervention and the state-building capacity of the Self with the lost political and territorial sovereignty and integrity of the Other.[158] Once more the victimised Other had to be saved by the benevolent West.[159] Not only the Other would be helped, these interventions had also served the geopolitical interests of

---

151 Mushtaq H. Khan, 'The new political economy of corruption', in Ben Fine, Costas Lapavitsas & Jonathan Pincus (eds), Development policy in the twenty-first century: beyond the post-Washington Consensus (Routledge 2001), at 113.

152 Chantal Thomas, 'Causes of inequality in the international economic order: critical race theory and postcolonial development', (1999) 9 Transnational Law and Contemporary Problems, 1, at 14.

153 James R. Hooper & Paul R. Williams, 'Earned sovereignty: the political dimension', (2003) 31 Denver Journal of International Law and Policy, 355, at 363.

154 David Kennedy, 'The forgotten politics of international governance', (2001) 2 European Human Rights Law Review, 117, at 118.

155 Anghie, Imperialism, sovereignty, and the making of international law, at 249.

156 Joshua Bernard Forrest, 'State inversion and nonstate politics', in Leonardo A. Villalón & Phillip A. Huxtable (eds), The African state at a critical juncture: between disintegration and reconfiguration (Lynne Rienner 1998), at 52.

157 Ruth Gordon, 'Saving failed states: sometimes a neocolonialist notion', (1997) 12 American University Journal of International Law and Policy, 904, at 967.

158 Michael P. Scharf, 'Earned sovereignty: juridical underpinnings', (2003) 31 Denver Journal of International Law and Policy, 373, at 374.

159 See Makau Mutua, 'Savages, victims, and saviors: the metaphor of human rights', (2001) 42 Harvard International Law Journal, 201.

the "Western" Self.[160] In particular their investments could be secured before and after the conflict.[161] According to Orford, this debate appeared to be "premised on the need to protect a boundary between self and other, national and international, sovereign autonomy and foreign control".[162] Against this light, Orford continued and gave an accurate account on the production of this imagery:

> The progress of the narrative, from crisis to resolution through the punishment, sacrifice or salvation of the target state, operates to reaffirm the order, position and ideals that were under threat at the start of the narrative. Narratives of crisis and redemption operate to reinsert the viewer into a discourse or symbolic order which heals the crisis revealed at the start of the narrative.[163] [...] The images of new threats of violence and instability serve to announce the attractiveness of such heroes as guarantors of stability, bearers of democracy and protectors of human rights and of the oppressed.[164]

3.4.3 *Moralism versus Terrorism*

Understandably, as formulated by Sartre, the "dehumanization of the oppressed turns against the oppressors and becomes their alienation".[165] In particular, the so-called "threat vacuum"[166] after the Cold War was considered to be filled by Islamic extremism, i.e. the West's new enemy.[167] This so-called "insurrectional violence",[168] both private and state-sponsored,[169] has been

160 William Russell Easterly, The white man's burden: why the West's efforts to aid the rest have done so much ill and so little good (Oxford University Press 2006), at 333.

161 Orford, at 47.

162 Id., at 149.

163 Id., at 177.

164 Id., at 166.

165 Jean-Paul Sartre, Colonialism and neocolonialism (Routledge 2001), at 53.

166 Douglas Little, American orientalism: the United States and the Middle East since 1945 (University of North Carolina Press 2002), at 36.

167 Azza M. Karam, 'Islamisms: globalisation, religion and power', in Ronaldo Munck & Purnaka L. de Silva (eds), Postmodern insurgencies: political violence, identity formation and peacemaking in comparative perspective (St. Martin's Press 2000), at 220.

168 Ariel Merari, 'Du terrorism comme stratégie d'insurrection', in Gérard Chaliand (ed), Les stratégies du terrorisme (Desclée de Brouwer 2002), at 78.

169 Thomas Weigend, 'The universal terrorist', (2006) 4 Journal of International Criminal Justice, 912, at 917.

classified under the rubric of terrorism though waged in a semantics of war.[170] Given the West's lasting moral engagement with these parts of the world, as a reaction, it tried to suppress[171] the destabilisation of its global authority.[172] It did so through humanitarian interventions and proxy wars to secure its lifestyle respectively after and during the Cold War.[173] It was not until 9/11, that under the command of the righteous authorities, counter-terrorist and stabilization operations were launched against this new enemy.[174] At its so-called "apex of civilizational hierarchy",[175] the Coalition of the Willing knew best how to wage this war against terror. As any other legal justification under international law, IHL kept the new savages outside their conventional and customary protection.[176] Hence, the Other's sovereignty was not a match for this renewal of Western militarism[177] which wanted to crush the Other's alleged aggression at and beyond its borders. Since the 2011 Arab Spring, the right for opposition that was once left for the Other gave a new incentive to the dynamic relationship between the "Western" Self and its Other who in most Middle Eastern countries continues to be violently repressed and denounced as terrorists by its own leadership and allies.

While Western countries were reluctant at first to intervene in the domestic affairs of those Middle Eastern countries, the increased popular resistance and violent oppression by the respective regimes in those countries such as

170 See Frédéric Mégret, '"War"? Legal semantics and the move to violence', (2002) 13 European Journal of International Law, 361.

171 Jörg Friedrichs, 'Defining the international public enemy: the political struggle behind the legal debate on international terrorism', (2006) 19 Leiden Journal of International Law, 69, at 87.

172 Nicholas Thomas, Colonialism's culture: anthropology, travel and government (Polity Press 1994), at 170.

173 Anthony Carty, 'The Iraq invasion as a recent United Kingdom "contribution to international law"', (2005) 16 European Journal of International Law, 143, at 150.

174 Jean Bethke Elshtain, Just war against terror: the burden of American power in a violent world (Basic Books 2003), at 54.

175 Brett Bowden, 'Civilization and savagery in the crucible of war', (2007) 19 Global Change, Peace & Security, 3, at 4.

176 Frédéric Mégret, 'From "savages" to "unlawful combatants": a postcolonial look at international humanitarian law's "other"', in Anne Orford (ed), International law and its others (Cambridge University Press 2006), at 310; see also Helen M. Kinsella, 'Discourses of difference: civilians, combatants and compliance with the laws of war', (2005) 31 Review of International Studies, 163.

177 Eyal Benvenisti, 'The US and the use of force: double-edged hegemony and the management of global emergencies', (2004) 15 European Journal of International Law, 677, at 691.

Egypt, Libya and Syria, the public opinion in the West soon advocated for intervention. In Libya, the doctrine of the responsibility to protect could be operationalized with the mandate to protect civilian populations against human suffering, but rather aimed at regime change in practice.[178] The "Western" Self however, did not succeed to be benevolent enough to counter the international pressures to facilitate peaceful change in other regimes and has been accused of using double standards in this regard;[179] nor has it fully defined its long-term political support to the transitional regimes in some countries after its past support to opposition groups against the dictatorial rule of the Other.[180] In addition, in such power vacuum, the "Western" Self has become more suspicious about the outcome of the democratic processes in the Middle East and the rise of Islamism[181] and the Islamic State in Syria and Iraq in particular. The latter struggle has also warranted an intervention on behalf of the West and its Middle Eastern allies since 2014 and might pave the way for future interventions in other countries where Islamic State is establishing its authority—most recently in Libya in the aftermath of its first Western intervention.

3.5 Conclusion

Throughout the Western history on the Self and the Other, these dichotomies have been reinvented so many times along different divisions, each having their specific characteristics. Religious, racial, civilisational, developmental and other standards have been produced to favour one particular side of the equation. While the communitarian respect has been curtailed by liberal ideologies whose creation of these identities on the Self are built upon the negation of the Other, it still depends on the gradually disintegrating Western societies. Hence, it appears that the renewal of knowledge is necessary in order to compete for the sake of the individual and public opinion and support to

178 Christian Henderson, 'International measures for the protection of civilians in Libya and Côte d'Ivoire', (2011) 60 International and Comparative Law Quarterly 767, at 773–777.

179 Marie-José Domestici-Met, 'Protecting Libya on behalf of the international community', (2011) 3 Goettingen Journal of International Law 861, at 881–882.

180 See also Olivier Corten & Vaios Koutroulis, 'The illegality of military support to rebels in the Libyan war: aspects of jus contra bellum and jus in bello', (2013) 18 Journal of Conflict and Security Law 59.

181 William McCants, 'Al Qaeda's challenge: the jihadists' war with Islamist democrats', (2011) 90 Foreign Affairs 20, at 32.

the Western authorities. Although international law and humanitarian law in particular have a universal reach, they are conveying another message rather limiting the scope of their protection. In this respect, as will be discussed in Chapter VI, the structure of the legal arguments in IHL seems to promote this division. In addition, as Nordstrom argued,

> there is a curious irony in the popular epistemologies that surround violence in the West. Violence is presented as something both integral to the human condition and as antithetical to it. This portrayal has led to a tendency to fetishize violence, fueling a fascination with the topic while banishing it to the outer margins of human life and everyday reality. It is cast as the excessive, the abnormal, the other, and yet as intrinsic. We are taught to ascribe tremendous power to violence, and then to fear that power to the extent that we seek to remove it from "our worlds," from those places where we live our lives.[182]

Humanity should no longer succumb to this senseless predisposition of its nature. The civilising process only reinforced the construction of such a societal order repressing its members for the sake of its survival. Furthermore, the institutionalisation of humanity's divisions necessarily puts the very survival of the human species at stake. Therefore, the "lost" human ethics need to find their roots again in the unity of humanity and experience the Self and Other from within, in the essence of the Self, in the conscience of each human being. Only in this manner, can human civilisation save itself from those forces which undermine the totality of its origin. Life is everything. Even Hobbes, proposed a way to reconcile the laws of nature with the societal imperatives of respect:

> Perhaps some man, who sees all these precepts of Nature deriv'd by a certain artifice from the single dictate of Reason advising us to look to the preservation, and safeguard of our serves, will say. That the deduction of these Lawes is so hard, that it is not to be expected they will be vulgarly known, oblige not, nay, indeed are not Lawes. To this I answer, it's true. That hope, fear, anger, ambition, covetousness, vain glory, and other perturbations of mind, doe hinder a man so, as he cannot attaine to the knowledge of these Lawes, whilst those passions prevail in him: But there is no man who is not sometimes in a quiet mind: At that time therefore

182 Carolyn Nordstrom, A different kind of war story (University of Pennsylvania Press 1997), at 16.

there is nothing easier for him to know, though he be never so rude and unlearn'd, than this only Rule, That when he doubts, whether what he is now doing to another, may be done by the Law of Nature, or not, he conceive himself to be in that that others stead. Here instantly those perturbations which perswaded him to the fact, being now cast into the other scale, disswade him as much: And this Rule is not only easie, but is Anciently celebrated in these words, Quod tibi fieri non vis, alteri ne feceris: Do not that to others, you would not have done to your self.[183]

183 Hobbes, at 37–8.

CHAPTER IV

The "Islamic" Self and the Other

4.1 Introduction

As pursued in Chapter III, the aim of this chapter is to trace back the historical evolution of the construction of the "Islamic" Self and its Other. In particular, the conflicts which have waged for centuries between Muslims and their external and internal opponents are illustrative of the apparent tension between the "Islamic" Self and its Other. The conflict between the "Islamic" Self and its Other can also be interpreted as a possible strategy to divide and rule over humanity. This historical approach will be particularly useful for the next Part III which juxtaposes the positivist and historical analysis of ILW. In this Part II, as will be submitted, it is also possible that the historical justifications and explanations as formulated from the Western perspective in the previous Chapter III are not that different from the Islamic perspective either. Consequently, when building upon these positivist and historical analyses of, respectively, the laws of armed conflict and the contexts in which these laws have applied and are still applicable, the next Chapters V and VI, respectively on the structure of the legal arguments in ILW and IHL, can actually also be similar.

From the period of Revelation onwards, the message of Islam faced opposition within the Arabian Peninsula. Nevertheless, the Prophet Muhammad was determined to defend the cause of God and spread His word around the world for the benefit of the whole of humanity. Islam united peoples and tribes across different borders and instituted tolerance for the non-Muslim inhabitants. Because the Islamic mission was not always embraced by all peoples, sooner or later, a doctrine of division of the world into the abode of Islam, i.e. *dar al-Islam*, and the abode of war, i.e. *dar al-harb*, served the new Islamic leadership. In particular after the time of the Prophet, when unification against such resistance raised Islam to one of the greatest civilisations humanity has ever witnessed.[1]

The division in order to rule was also often challenged by others from within the Islamic community, i.e. the *ummah*, when claiming their own legitimacy

1 Richard C. Martin, 'The religious foundations of war, peace, and statecraft in Islam', in James Turner Johnson & John Kelsay (eds), Just war and jihad: historical and theoretical perspectives on war and peace in Western and Islamic traditions (Greenwood Press 1991), at 97.

 DOI 10.1163/9789004298248_006

to control the believers.[2] Ultimately, the fragmentation of the abode of Islam into several Islamic sub-empires, such as the Ottomans, the Mughals, and the Safavids, along with other factors, such as corruption, led to its decline.[3] From the nineteenth century onwards, this oriental prey was soon subjected to Western colonialism and nationalism. Islam had to be responsive in order to survive from and compete with this modernist enterprise.[4] Different answers have been formulated to accommodate this external confrontation with internal challenges. Nationalist, modernist, revivalist, secessionist, and terrorist approaches were among those answers which, one could rationally argue, were serving particular agendas not necessarily reflecting the views of the Islamic community as a whole. This can possibly prove that the duality of human nature to advance its selfish interests is difficult to be moderated by the communitarian injunctions to truly help and know each other, both within and beyond one's religion.

4.2 From the Period of Revelation to Western Colonisation

4.2.1 *The Early Path to Justice*

Right from the beginning, it was hard for the early Muslim converts to survive in the Arabian societies without any opposition. The Bedouin Arabs, in particular, were noted to be a warring people.[5] Also in the few cities, *jahiliyyah*, i.e. the time of tribal chauvinism when tribes were defending their causes mostly with violence, prevailed instead of divine guidance. Thus, Islam needed to convince the Arabs to leave behind their anarchical primitive state of living and look for "civilised" unity among all Muslims instead. There are mixed views as to whether the Meccan trade and its so-called "mercantile economy",[6] on the one hand, or the religious desire of the newly established Islamic community to convert all souls to Islam, on the other hand, was crucial to the conquest of

---

2 Isam Kamel Salem, Islam und Völkerrecht: das Völkerrecht in der islamischen Weltanschauung (Express Edition 1984), at 69–73.

3 Majid Khadduri, 'The Islamic theory of international relations and its contemporary relevance', in J. Harris Proctor (ed), Islam and international relations (Pall Mall 1965), at 30.

4 Ann Elizabeth Mayer, 'War and peace in the Islamic tradition and international law', in James Turner Johnson & John Kelsay (eds), Just war and jihad: historical and theoretical perspectives on war and peace in Western and Islamic traditions (Greenwood Press 1991), at 198.

5 Anne-Claude Dero-Jacob, Société et institutions traditionnelles de l'islam: une introduction sociologique (Peeters 1995), at 153.

6 Patricia Crone, Meccan trade and the rise of Islam (Gorgias Press 2004), at 231.

tribal Arabia and the territory outside of it.[7] In this regard, the former rational and materialistic argument explains that the expansion of trade relations with other parts of the Middle East was necessary to fuel the expeditions and to sanction political power. Whereas the latter idealistic and spiritual argument shows proof of the rewards believers have to seek from God when fighting in His cause.[8]

Advancing the military objective view, Sharma observed that, "[t]he sword is said to have been used to increase the territorial and political spread of Islam where its creed could find fertile soil to flourish".[9] Hence, the Prophet necessarily had to lay down the foundations of some kind of organisation[10] if the newly established Islamic society wanted to survive and develop within this particular hostile environment.[11] Evidently, during His mission the Revelation was an essential guide to the establishment and consolidation of the *ummah*.[12] So if God's cause had to be rendered justice, then war and victory for this cause were permissible.[13] In particular those encounters with non-Muslims, such as the People of the Book, i.e. *ahl al-kitab* (Christians and Jews), or the Zorostrians, could have constituted a source of conflict. Nonetheless, with these peoples belonging to monotheistic religions, treaties of submission, i.e. *dhimma*, were concluded and put an end to their conflicts.[14] Though these peoples have been conquered by the Muslims, in return for the payment of a poll tax, i.e. *jizya*, they were tolerated and could continue to practice their own personal laws of religion upon the condition they respected the rules of the Islamic public order. Clearly, this protection of religious minority rights went hand in hand with the respect for the laws of the Islamic government.[15] Moreover, the

---

7 Id., at 243.
8 R. Stephen Humphreys, Islamic history: a framework for inquiry (Tauris 1991), at 210.
9 Shashi S. Sharma, Caliphs and sultans: religious ideology and political praxis (Rupa 2004), at 124–25.
10 I.M. Lapidus, 'The Arab conquests and the formation of Islamic society', in Wael B. Hallaq (ed), The formation of Islamic law (Ashgate Variorum 2004), at 18.
11 Id., in, at 18.
12 Wael B. Hallaq, The origins and evolution of Islamic law (Cambridge University Press 2006), at 31.
13 Ignáz Goldziher, Bernard Lewis, Andras Hamori & Ruth Hamori, Introduction to Islamic theology and law (Princeton University Press 1981), at 24.
14 Ye'or Bat, Islam and dhimmitude: where civilizations collide (Fairleigh Dickinson University Press 2002), at 42.
15 Mohamed Berween, 'Al-Wathiqa: the first Islamic state constitution', (2003) 23 Journal of Muslim Minority Affairs, 103, at 111 and 113.

Islamic state could not impose on those peoples to convert as indicated in the following Qur'anic verse:[16]

> Let there be no compulsion in religion: Truth stands out clear from Error: whoever rejects evil and believes in Allah hath grasped the most trustworthy hand-hold, that never breaks. And Allah heareth and knoweth all things. (Q2:256)

Despite these guarantees of tolerant and peaceful coexistence with the followers of other beliefs, the Islamic order was continuously under attack both ideologically and politically. As a matter of safeguarding its survival, as Kennedy put it, "the umma could not stand still, it had to expand or disintegrate".[17] From this realist perspective, there was no other choice than conquering the territories within and beyond the Arabian Peninsula. In addition, the prohibition of raiding and fighting within the *ummah* deprived the Arab tribes of their livelihood and, as Karsh continued, "drove them inexorably toward imperial expansion".[18] These internal dynamics within the *ummah* appeared not to be sufficient to support such imperial enterprise. Therefore, some kind of ideology justified the expansion and the subservience of the unbelievers who were conquered subsequently.[19] According to Sharma, "the advantage of belonging to the most correct and the most superior way of life, gives to the Muslim community a legitimate sense of puissance, which also translates in their craving for unqualified power".[20] Beyond this sense of superiority, institutional demands were necessary to accommodate the growing quest for power. In this respect, the surrounding civilisations have influenced the organisation of the early Islamic society. Particularly the Byzantine Empire inspired the early conquerors to unite their efforts and advance their triumphs.[21] For example, the shift from

---

16 Mohammed Talbi, 'Les structures et les caractéristiques de l'état islamique traditionnel', in Mohammad Arkoun (ed), L'islam, morale et politique (Desclée de Brouwer 1986), at 191; Aibek Ahmedov, 'Religious minorities and apostacy in early Islamic states: legal and historical analysis of sources', (2006) 2 Journal of Islamic State Practices in International Law 1, at 2.

17 Hugh Kennedy, The Prophet and the age of the Caliphates: the Islamic Near East from the sixth to the eleventh century (Longman 2004), at 48.

18 Efraim Karsh, Islamic imperialism: a history (Yale University Press 2006), at 19.

19 Id., at 22.

20 Sharma, at 54.

21 Michael McCormick, Eternal victory: triumphal rulership in late antiquity, Byzantium and the early medieval West (Cambridge University Press 1986), at 26.

the institution of the Prophet and Caliphs to the one of kingship[22] showed proof of this so-called "monarchization of the caliphdom",[23] as formulated by Bedhad. Grounding the predominantly religious leadership into a societal one, gave greater political and administrative prerogatives to the leadership. In this regard, the Sasanian Empire's bureaucratic management proved to be useful to lay the foundations for the upcoming Islamic leadership in order to pragmatically govern and protect its *ummah*.

Already since the seventh century, besides the continuation of the tradition of the Prophet and His righteous Caliphs, the Islamic leaderships were also developing their own laws of war and fiscal laws responding to the circumstances of their time. For example, the Umayyad dynasty (seventh–eighth century) wanted to regulate warfare against their external enemies. On the material side, the confiscation of war booty as well as the collection of taxes of the conquered populations were indicative of the dynasty's ambition to consolidate its administrative power and wealth.[24] On the spiritual side, the Byzantine Christian Empire lost a lot of its disciples to Islam in its North African territories and in the Middle East and also the Persian Empire was converted to Islam.[25] However, the remaining non-Muslim religious communities continued to live in peace under the new Islamic leadership.[26] Upon grounds of equality, these Islamic authorities enacted legislations welcoming the non-Muslims into the *ummah*.[27] Nevertheless, as Frye pointed out, these steps of equal treatment contrasted with the taxation regime imposed upon the non-Muslims. In this regard, the Umayyad dynasty discouraged conversion so they could continue to tax non-Muslims under the *dhimma* agreements.[28] Understandably, in order to carry out the historical religious mission,[29] only the Muslims enjoyed full membership. Still, according to the Prophet, Muslims had duties vis-à-vis the *dhimmies* (as stipulated in the *dhimma* agreements)

22 Sohrab Bedhad, 'Islam, revivalism and public policy', in Sohrab Behdad & Farhad Nomani (eds), Islam and public policy (JAI Press 1997), at 9.

23 Id., in, at 9.

24 Joseph Schacht, 'Pre-Islamic background and early development of jurisprudence', in Wael B. Hallaq (ed), The formation of Islamic law (Ashgate Variorum 2004), at 38.

25 Gai Eaton, Islam and the destiny of man (Islamic Texts Society 1994), at 29.

26 Sulayman Nyang, 'Religion and the maintenance of boundaries', in Sohail H. Hashmi (ed), Islamic political ethics: civil society, pluralism and conflict (Princeton University Press 2002), at 110.

27 Hallaq, at 22.

28 Richard N. Frye, The golden age of Persia (Phoenix Press 2003), at 75.

29 Marshall Goodwin Simms Hodgson, The venture of Islam: conscience and history in a world civilization (University of Chicago Press 1974), at 74.

and their violation would lead to God's punishment.[30] Living together in peace was a higher goal as illustrated in the Qur'an:

> Allah forbids you not, with regard to those who fight you not for (your) Faith nor drive you out of your homes, from dealing kindly and justly with them: for Allah loveth those who are just. (Q60:8)

Certainly, not all unbelievers were trustworthy as indicates the consecutive verse Q60:9 but so were Muslims who perverted the religion through their lack of adherence to it;[31] they were called *kafirs*. Against these internal enemies of Islam, i.e. the apostates, the Islamic authorities upheld the Islamic ideal. However, this claim of the allegedly legitimate Islamic leadership was, according to Karsh, only "a handy façade behind which they could fully enjoy the material fruits of imperial expansion".[32] In this respect, resistance by those illegitimate forces to the material interests of the central Islamic authorities was unacceptable.[33] As a justification for their struggle against the central Islamic regimes, the different schismatic (Sunni, Shi'i, Khariji) groups invoked the misappropriation of power by those central Islamic authorities and their non-adherence to the Islamic precepts as previously practiced by the Prophet.[34] It was not until the Abbasid dynasty (eighth-thirteenth century) that the Umayyad caliphate was taken over by the non-Arabian periphery who restored Islam for the whole *ummah*. Finally, as opposed to the Arab domination of their predecessors, this new Islamic leadership was truly representative of the multicultural character of the *ummah* which was already present from the beginning.[35] However, both in the religious and social sphere divisions continued to exist respectively between Muslims and non-Muslims as well as between the leadership and their Muslim populace.

---

30 Yusuf Qaradawi, M. Moinuddin Siddiqui, Syed Shukry & Kamal Helbawy, The lawful and the prohibited in Islam: al-Halal wal-haram fil Islam (American Trust Publications 1960), at 338.

31 Toshihiko Izutsu, The concept of belief in Islamic theology: a semantic analysis of îmân and islâm (The Keio Institute of Cultural and Linguistic Studies 1965), at 7–10.

32 Karsh, at 43.

33 Id., at 28.

34 Robert Anciaux, 'La guerre religieuse: le cas de l'islam et la chrétienté', in Jacques Lemaire (ed), La guerre et la paix (Editions de l'Université Libre de Bruxelles 1991), at 55–6.

35 Karsh, at 40–1.

4.2.2 *The Imperial Venture*

Though from the beginning of the early Islamic empires, social and religious differences between peoples continued to divide and rule, the message of Islam intended to bring salvation and liberation to all those oppressed peoples.[36] In particular in pre-Islamic Persia, the allegedly inegalitarian and misguided societies had to be freed by the Arab legions.[37] According to Crone, "Islam had come to move people from the service of servants (i.e. other humans) to the service of God".[38] Evidently, leaving behind the *jahiliyyah* in order to live peacefully in a growing *ummah* which provided the necessary security to practice Islam, was indeed very appealing for the territories around Arabia as well as in Africa.[39] No longer class-based societies of masters and slaves would resist the unifying force of Islam, as the submission to God only blurred those social boundaries. However, as mentioned earlier, the subjugation of non-Muslims remained of economic importance to the early conquerors which could then tax these peoples.[40] Also the slavery of non-Arab peoples both the whites, i.e. *mamluk*, and the blacks, i.e. *'abd*, confirmed the reluctance of the Arab aristocracy to give up their privileges. Both the economic exploitation of such slaves and the sense of social and ethnic superiority contrasted with the true content of the universal peaceful message of Islam.[41] Whatever the social, economic or ethnic divisions Muslims had imposed upon their subjects, the Qur'an stresses that piety is the ultimate quality which distinguishes peoples from each other:

> And among His Signs is the creation of the heavens and the earth, and the variations in your languages and your colours: verily in that are Signs for those who know. (Q30:22)

> O mankind! We created you from a single (pair) of a male and a female, and made you into nations and tribes, that ye may know each other (not that ye may despise (each other). Verily the most honoured of you in the sight of Allah is (he who is) the most righteous of you. And Allah has full knowledge and is well acquainted (with all things). (Q49:13)

---

36 Mian Mohammad Sharif, A history of Muslim philosophy: with short accounts of other disciplines and the modern renaissance in Muslim lands (Harrassowitz 1963), at 1390.

37 Rom Landau, Islam and the Arabs (George Allen & Unwin 1958), at 41.

38 Patricia Crone, Medieval Islamic political thought (Edinburgh University Press 2004), at 334.

39 Ustaz Yoonus Abdullah, Sharia in Africa (Shebiotimo Publications 1998), at 7.

40 Goldziher, Lewis, Hamori & Hamori, at 27.

41 Bernard Lewis, Race and color in Islam (Harper & Row 1971), at 19.

Of course, some believers, such as the Khariji, considered themselves to be more religious than the imperial establishment and created their own sects. In spite of these internal tensions within the *ummah*, generally the different Middle Eastern societies, such as the Byzantine, the Persian and the peripheral ones in Arabia, found unity and became integrated into a new comprehensive and more developed civilisation.[42] In addition, from the Abbasid dynasty onwards, no longer did the Arab superiority further institutionalise discrimination against the majority of non-Arabs found in the new lands.[43] These followers of the Abbasid dynasty settled in the garrison cities at the periphery of the Islamic territory. Irrespective of the social and economic differences among the Muslims, they formed, as put by Zubaida, a kind of "an urban bourgeoisie"[44] which wanted to profile itself as the guardian of piety and virtue. From then onwards, the Islamic political authorities were seeking legitimacy from their population and found this on the spiritual level.[45] Therefore, with the help of jurists they found such legitimacy within the primary sources of Islam, i.e. the Qur'an and the Sunnah. These sources gave authority to the Islamic leadership to pursue their mission. In exchange for the jurists' support, the political class assisted them financially in their elucidation of the Shari'a which regulated spiritual and worldly affairs. Nevertheless, the cooperation between the political and juristic class was quite exclusive. Not everybody had access to the juristic profession or could assume such political responsibilities within the *ummah*. Only learned men could discover and apply the truthful law of God[46] which guaranteed salvation for humanity in view of the Day of Judgment.[47]

This almost sacred nature of the Islamic leadership[48] and its divine attributes to rule as the vicegerent of God on earth[49] were not sufficient to face the other challenges of administering and safeguarding the expanding Islamic Empire. Besides the religious legitimacy as elucidated by legal scholars and their intellectual support granted to the Islamic authorities, the Islamic authorities also had to rely on a strong and efficient army. Not only to ensure

42 Lapidus, in, at 1–2.

43 Karsh, at 26.

44 Sami Zubaida, Law and power in the Islamic world (I.B. Tauris 2003), at 83.

45 Id., at 83.

46 Samuel D. Goitein, 'The birth-hour of Muslim law? An essay in exegesis', in Wael B. Hallaq (ed), The formation of Islamic law (Ashgate Variorum 2004), at 71.

47 Tilman Nagel & Thomas Thornton, The history of Islamic theology: from Muhammad to the present (Markus Wiener 2000), at 15.

48 Ernest Gellner, Culture, identity, and politics (Cambridge University Press 1987), at 138.

49 Deno John Geanakoplos, Medieval Western civilization and the Byzantine and Islamic worlds: interaction of three cultures (D.C. Heath 1979), at 151.

social order but to reassure their policy of centralisation. For example, Turkish slaves—as enrolled in the Islamic armies—provided the necessary resources for the military expeditions as well as for the maintenance of the rule of law within the Islamic Empire. In this regard, all these protagonists, i.e. the political leadership, the juristic scholarship and the army were complementary in their endeavours to reinforce the economic and spiritual growth of the Islamic empires. They kept each other in balance.[50] As a consequence, as opposed to the universal message of Islam distinguishing peoples along religious criteria, the once tribal (non-)Arab societies were breaking down in an Islamic society which became based again on social class and political power.[51] In spite of the unifying force of Islam, it almost seemed impossible for humanity to actually transcend the institutional and social divisions among the members of this growing religion.

However, such policies and divisions were not only present within the Islamic societies; they were also introduced beyond them. In particular, from the late eighth century onwards,[52] Muslim jurists divided the world in different spheres of influence, namely the abode of Islam (*dar al-Islam*) where justice reigned and the abode of war (*dar al-harb*) where violence dominated.[53] The complementary worldview of believers and unbelievers as found within the primary sources became replaced by military-political territorialities whose universal ambitions rather advocated political above religious submission.[54] As a self-fulfilling prophecy, such political theory reinforced this legal fiction which justified the political context where Muslims necessarily were facing resistance from non-Muslims. Instead of defending against such aggression, this legal fiction served as a legitimation to settle the conflict between both territories. Hence, only an aggressive *jihad* could overcome the oppression by the non-Muslims. Apparently, in reality, humanity's appropriation of religious duties distorted the tolerant vision of Islam and its defensive stance against

50 Clifford Edmund Bosworth, 'Barbarian incursions: the coming of the Turks into the Islamic world', in Donald Sydney Richards (ed), Islamic civilisation, 950–1150: a colloquium published under the auspices of the Near Eastern History Group, Oxford and the Near East Center, University of Pennsylvania (Cassirer 1973), at 6.

51 Lapidus, in, at 21–2.

52 Fred M. Donner, 'The sources of Islamic conceptions of war', in James Turner Johnson & John Kelsay (eds), Just war and jihad: historical and theoretical perspectives on war and peace in Western and Islamic traditions (Greenwood Press 1991), at 50.

53 Baber Johansen, Contingency in a sacred law: legal and ethical norms in the Muslim fiqh (Brill 1999), at 228.

54 Id., at 236–37.

attacks.[55] Needless to say, peoples had to be responsible for the fate and failures of the divisions they invented throughout their histories and societies as opposed to the unity of God's creation.[56] In this respect, the Qur'an makes reference to the rewards and punishments human beings deserve with respect to their behaviours:

> That was a people that hath passed away. They shall reap the fruit of what they did, and ye of what ye do! Of their merits there is no question in your case! (Q2:134)

> [...] Verily never will Allah change the condition of a people until they change it themselves (with their own souls). But when (once) Allah willeth a people's punishment, there can be no turning it back, nor will they find, besides Him, any to protect. (Q13:11)

Beyond the suspicion of the external enemies of Islam, the governing authorities were also facing internal rebellion whose agenda was to secede from the imperial core. These rebel forces felt frustrated about the growing corruption and exploitation caused by the Islamic leadership at the expense of their power and human dignity. Political autonomy on behalf of this periphery was initially not accepted by the central Islamic authorities. Accusations in terms of the lack of religious piety in the governance of the Islamic Empire constituted the apparent basis for divergence between the Islamic central authorities and the Islamic rebel forces. As a matter of survival, the Abbasid Caliphate had to give in to those centrifugal forces which had already started to develop their own political centres and cultural practices.[57] Although this redistribution of power established a greater balance between the political actors within the growing Islamic Empire, this fragmentation instead created only more divisions. For security reasons, different principalities were even forced to forge alliances to fight each other as well as against external enemies such as the Christian crusaders.[58] In addition to these centrifugal forces, internal

55 Shaheen Sardar Ali & Javaid Rehman, 'The concept of jihad in Islamic international law', (2005) 10 Journal of Conflict and Security Law, 321, at 329–330.

56 Ali Shariati, 'A new approach to understanding of Islam', in Harbans Singh Bhatia (ed), Studies in Islamic law, religion and society (Deep & Deep Publications 1996), at 208.

57 Kennedy, at 201–2.

58 Karsh, at 70–85.

competition for political power[59] brought the whole political and religious leadership into moral decline.[60] The initial legitimacy and authority which the Islamic leadership had found in collaboration with the jurists and the army was in fact neglecting the concerns of the whole *ummah*. In this regard, the Mongol invasion (d. 1258) in the Middle East was considered to be, as formulated by Jaques, "a manifestation of God's divine justice"[61] against the Islamic regimes which, apparently, were more preoccupied with their own interests. Based upon some verses in the Qur'an, Ibn Kahtir interpreted these events in analogy with the causes of destruction of the city of Jerusalem when the aggression of the Jewish people on its turn led to empower their enemies to strike at their hearts:[62]

> And We gave (Clear) Warning to the Children of Israel in the Book, that twice would they do mischief on the earth and be elated with mighty arrogance (and twice would they be punished) (Q17:4)
>
> When the first of the warnings came to pass, We sent against you Our servants given to terrible warfare: they entered the very inmost parts of your homes; and it was a warning (completely) fulfilled. (Q17:5)

After this manifestation of foreign destruction and division and before any resurrection with purified intentions, the inner *jihad* made Islamic rulers reflect upon their self-centred behaviour. No longer would the externalisation of the enemy be an excuse not to question their personal performances. No longer would the submission to the material interests and other desires accompanying the wealth of the Islamic empires replace the universal message of Islam, i.e. to submit to God only. Still, the Abbasid Caliphate stayed in power and had suzerainty over different sultanates[63] across the empire; until the Ottomans seized the opportunity to unify the abode of Islam again under the influence of one political authority (1517–1918).[64] This did not mean that internal rivalry disappeared. For the sake of maintaining optimal diplomatic and economic

59 R. Kevin Jaques, Authority, conflict, and the transmission of diversity in medieval Islamic law (Brill 2006), at 5.

60 Id., at 8.

61 Id., at 6.

62 Muhammad Saed Abdul-Rahman, Tafsir Ibn Kathir Juz' 15 (Part 15): Al-Israa (or Bani Isra'il) 1 to Al-Kahf 74 (MSA Publication Limited 2009), at 30–1.

63 Sharma, at 245.

64 Karsh, at 89.

relations with the upcoming European powers and economies, the Mughal Empire in northern India (1526–1858) and the Safavid dynasty (1501–1722) in Persia continued to compete for military and political power.[65] For those reasons, these different empires showed proof of tolerance towards their minorities in particular by granting privileges to Christian citizens and traders; as long as the latter did not challenge the dictatorial order of governance in the empires of their residence.[66] These signs of multicultural and multi-confessional societies only persisted at the height of these Islamic empires' existence.

4.2.3 *The Western Colonisation*

Against such background of growing moral and political decline, human nature seemed to slip again into its egocentric ambitions. The Ottoman establishment was not an exception to this rule. In this regard, the political authorities, the legal scholars and the army supported each others' cause to uphold the authoritarian system and their prerogatives. On the one hand, some *ulama*, i.e. Islamic religious scholars, favoured this form of governance, according to Umar, at the expense of a free "Islamic public order".[67] While on the other hand, other scholars rather advocated full submission to God alone regardless of the possible consequences of political anarchy. Another view on this religious duty of citizenship and obedience to the leadership was only owed as long as the commands of the leadership were not conflicting with the Shari'a.[68] As another form of *jahiliyyah*, Islamic history, however, proved that the Ottoman establishment laid the foundations for its own material and spiritual decline. And this while the Qur'an provides the necessary direction toward strict obedience to God:

> O ye who believe! Obey Allah, and obey the Messenger, and those charged with authority among you. If ye differ in anything among yourselves, refer it to Allah and His Messenger, if ye do believe in Allah and the Last Day: that is best, and most suitable for final determination. (Q4:59)

---

65 Id., at 90.

66 Javaid Rehman, Islamic state practices, international law and the threat from terrorism: a critique of the "clash of civilizations" in the new world order (Hart 2005), at 65.

67 Muhammad Sani Umar, Islam and colonialism: intellectual responses of Muslims of Northern Nigeria to British colonial rule (Brill 2006), at 160.

68 Nasim Hasan Shah, 'Islamic concept of state', in Harbans Singh Bhatia (ed), Studies in Islamic law, religion and society (Deep & Deep Publications 1996), at 80.

Nonetheless, the rhetoric of the Ottoman leadership asserted the opposite. The Ottomans were the true defenders of the Islamic orthodoxy[69] whereas the Persians were the enemies of Sunni Islam. In this conflict, the Ottoman armies went as far as allying with non-Muslim armies and foreign mercenaries.[70] For example, the military alliances with the German Harbourgs to fight against the Persian Safavid Empire. While the Ottomans were focusing on their own economic, political and military survival in the East, they ignored the other competition which took place in the West. Though the Ottoman Empire was clearly present during the sixteenth century on the European political scene, as it even possessed territories at the borders of Europe's capitals, this realisation however came centuries too late.[71] Despite some reforms, such as the sixteenth century Capitulations between the Ottoman Empire and European nations or the nineteenth century Tanzimat in the Ottoman Empire, Europe's renaissance was irreversible. In the hope of stimulating trade and the benefits for the corrupt and inefficient Ottoman Empire,[72] it granted the European residents privileges and other concessions. For example, the millet system was abolished but non-Muslims were still treated as secondary class people.[73] In spite of European pressures to foster equality on the religious level, the *dhimmis*—named *rayas*, were still discriminated in the Ottoman Empire.[74] Understandably, at moments of decline, the equal treatment of the non-Muslim Other decreased.

After the First World War, the European Mandate Powers set up another strategy of dismantling the relatively peaceful religious coexistence in the Middle East. Their classification of the Middle Eastern peoples along racial, religious, nationalistic lines highlighted those divisions to become appropriated by those peoples in future conflicts among them. Nationalism or rather Kemalism replaced Ottomanism and instilled fear unto non-Muslim peoples,

69 Colin Imber, Ebu's-su'ud: the Islamic legal tradition (Edinburgh University Press 1997), at 5.

70 Hamed Sultan, 'La conception islamique du droit international humanitaire dans les conflits armés', (1978) 34 Revue égyptienne de droit international, 13, at 14; Anciaux, in, at 58–9.

71 Yadh Ben Achour, Politique, religion et droit dans le monde arabe (Cérès productions 1992), at 110–11.

72 Haim Gerber, State, society, and law in Islam: Ottoman law in comparative perspective (State University of New York 1994), at 135.

73 David D. Grafton, The Christians of Lebanon: political rights in Islamic law (Tauris Academic Studies 2003), at 75.

74 Bat, at 42.

such as Armenians, Assyrians, Copts, Jews and Maronites.[75] Paradoxically, the modernisation of the Islamic world favoured certain members of religious minorities to play key roles in its transition.[76] In addition to the Mandate System, such redistribution of political power humiliated the occupied Muslim populations even more so.[77] Of course, also Muslim elites[78] were responsible for the growing frustrations among their populations. For example the incorporation of their reigns along capitalistic lines further marginalised the Muslims in an age of Western imperialism.[79] Therefore, across the Islamic world, from the Mediterranean to the Indian Ocean, the commercial exchange between European and Muslim powers altered as soon as the Europeans gained military superiority over those territories and the Muslim armies themselves became militarily inferior on land.[80] From that moment onwards, a colonial enterprise assumed the lost sovereignty over those Muslim lands and their peoples.[81] Though colonisation had not led to the conversion of Muslims to another faith, it did contribute to a lower self-esteem of the Muslims.

4.3 From Sovereignty to Emancipation

4.3.1 *Nationalism*

Against the background of colonial domination by Western powers over the Muslim world, *jihad* became the driving force behind the decolonisation wars against the colonial powers. No longer was colonialism tolerated and the Mahdist movements would, as Peters states, "restore justice on earth and put an end to corruption and oppression".[82] No longer were the newly independent Islamic nation states to be considered backwards[83] and they had to be

75 Id., at 155–58.

76 Id., at 162.

77 Id., at 164.

78 Mehmet Ozay, Islamic identity and development: studies of the Islamic periphery (Routledge 1990), at 38.

79 Id., at 38.

80 David Ayalon, 'Islam versus Christian Europe: the case of the Holy Land', in David Ayalon (ed), Islam and the abode of war (Variorum 1994), at 254.

81 Sohail H. Hashmi, 'Political perceptions in early Anglo-Indian relations', (2001) 12 Islam & Christian-Muslim Relations, 211, at 212 and 224.

82 Rudolph Peters, Islam and colonialism: the doctrine of jihad in modern history (Mouton 1979), at 42.

83 Mohammed Bedjaoui, 'Succession of states and governments: succession in respect of matters other than treaties', in International Law Commission (ed), Yearbook of the International Law Commission (International Law Commission 1969), at 88.

admitted to the international community of progressive states.[84] The Algerian war for independence in particular was very violent. In this regard, nationalism was the ultimate remedy for sovereign self-determination and created another consciousness beyond religious, ethnic and social identities. However, opposing claims for and within different Islamic nation states, fragmented the *ummah*—the ideal unity—even more.[85] In addition, these struggles have been supported by both the capitalist and communist blocs during the Cold War. Arab nationalism as conceived by Nasser was the precursor to fight foreign intervention in the Middle East that wanted to impose its divisive rhetoric along these economic ideologies. Pan-Islamism, as embodied in the Organisation of the Islamic Conference (OIC), provided a different answer which united the forces against the Western interests in the Islamic world. This endeavour was, as stated by the OIC Charter, "guided by the noble Islamic values of unity and fraternity, and affirming the essentiality of promoting and consolidating the unity and solidarity among the Member States in securing their common interests at the international arena".[86]

Hence, cooperation among Muslims was essential and in particular against the external enemies of Islam. Within the Palestinian struggle, both for Muslim and non-Muslim Arabs, Zionism was considered to be the imperial tool which, according to the Palestine National Covenant, stroke "at the hopes of the Arab nation for liberation, unity, and progress".[87] As for example in Afghanistan and Yemen, the godless communism in the heart of the Islamic lands also had to be eradicated. So was the domination of the former non-Muslim establishment within the decolonised territories, such as in Lebanon. Apparently, this ideology of liberation cut on both sides as demonstrated by the secessionist movements of non-Muslim populations such as in East-Timor, or even the partition between India and Pakistan. Clearly, the colonial legacies of division along such deep ethnic and religious lines were hard to overcome. Arabs were fighting Arabs. Muslims were fighting Muslims. No longer on theological grounds but on political ones; for example the secessionist war of Pakistan-Bangladesh, the Iran-Iraq war, the Turks against the Kurds and Morocco's invasion in Western Sahara. According to the Islamic doctrine, these wars among Muslims would be unacceptable as the unity of the Islamic community and

---

84 Ali Oumlil, 'L'islam et l'état-nation', in Mohammed Arkoun (ed), L'islam, morale et politique (Desclée de Brouwer 1986), at 217.

85 Riaz Hassan, 'Globalisation's challenge to the Islamic ummah', (2006) 34 Asian Journal of Social Science, 311, at 314 and 317.

86 Preamble, 1972 OIC Charter.

87 Article 22, 1968 Palestine National Covenant; see also in Yehuda Lukacs, Documents on the Israeli-Palestinian conflict, 1967–1983 (Cambridge University Press 1984), at 142.

the peaceful coexistence among Muslims had to be preserved[88] regardless of the territorial division into nation states.[89] More specifically, the Qur'an is a source of guidance to cope with this *jahiliyyah* under the form of nationalistic aspirations for power:

> If two parties among the Believers fall into a quarrel, make ye peace between them: but if one of them transgresses beyond bounds against the other then fight ye (all) against the one that transgresses until it complies with the command of Allah; but if it complies then make peace between them with justice and be fair: for Allah loves those who are fair (and just). (Q49:9)

4.3.2 *Modernism*

While wars of national liberation were waged in the Muslim world, some European educated Muslims, such as Jamal al-Din al-Afghani, reflected on the inherent Islamic nature of the Western modern value system. They tried to give voice to a Islamic political discourse. For them, there was no need to dissociate the *ummah* from the "colonial sector",[90] as understood by Malik, but to find its immanent presence within it. These modernists actually wanted to avoid the so-called "blind imitation of the past",[91] i.e. *taqlid*, and to restore the rational reinterpretation of the primary sources, i.e. *ijtihad*, in order to meet the needs of the present society. This "Islamic renaissance"[92] replaced the so-called "pseudo-religion of progress"[93] and could face, according to Khan, "the global threat of an imperialist, hypocritical and hostile West".[94] In their view, real unity was possible again among all Muslims of the worldwide *ummah*. Opposed to these integrationists, the traditionalists feared that the Islamic

---

88 Eric Corthay, 'Le régime juridique du recours à la force tel qu'interprété par les états membres de l'Organisation de la Conférence islamique', (2005) 7 Journal of the History of International Law, 211, at 236.

89 Khaled Abou El Fadl, Rebellion and violence in Islamic law (Cambridge University Press 2001), at 272.

90 Jamal Malik, Colonization of Islam: dissolution of traditional institutions in Pakistan (Manohar 1996), at 23.

91 Mohammad Muslehuddin, Philosophy of Islamic law and the orientalists: a comparative study of Islamic legal system (Islamic Publications 1977), at 82.

92 Hamid Algar, 'Islam and the intellectual challenge of modern civilization', in Altaf Gauhar (ed), The challenge of Islam (Islamic Council of Europe 1978), at 288.

93 Id., in, at 290.

94 M.A. Muqtedar Khan, 'The political philosophy of Islamic resurgence', (2001) 13 Cultural dynamics, 211, at 218.

traditions would get lost in this process towards emancipation.[95] According to them, the government could only be fully legitimate when it applied the Shari'a.[96] One could not simply set aside the history of Islam and its incredible civilisation. In order to be pragmatic, the richness of Islamic resources which were full of possibilities had to be addressed in the first place before even considering moulding the qualities of external regimes with the Islamic culture. In this ideological conflict, modernity was the antipode of authenticity.[97]

Although the West's introduction of modernity and its technological innovations in their colonial territories left traces of exploitation in the minds of the Muslims, they were also used by the Muslim populations themselves. Such technology enabled them to exchange ideas with their Muslim brothers and sisters around the world.[98] Modern transportation and communication bridged the distance between Muslims so they could find the unity to defend their common interests—even on the international plane. In addition to the technical support, Islamic associations[99] could take advantage of modern organisational practices to function properly and efficiently. Through a so-called "developmentalist agenda",[100] Islamists could easily reach their converts among the marginalised proletariat which had become the victim of rapid maldevelopment and cultural restructuration; precisely because colonialism and its aftermath adjusted these traditional societies along the capitalist secular model.[101] Therefore, modern Islamism undid the control of the modern secular state over the society and established "a virtual counter-state",[102] as named by Nasr, which could defend itself against its internal and external enemies. As opposed to the previously imported and appropriated deceiving systems of power which originated from the West, this awakened Islamic society could

95 Malik, at 24.

96 Ishtiaq Ahmed, The concept of an Islamic state: an analysis of the ideological controversy in Pakistan (Pinter 1987), at 176.

97 Yildiz Atasoy, Turkey, Islamists and democracy: transition and globalisation in a Muslim state (I.B. Tauris 2005), at 1–2.

98 R. Michael Feener, Muslim legal thought in modern Indonesia (Cambridge University Press 2007), at 2.

99 Id., at 19.

100 Id., at 118.

101 Ozay, at 41–2.

102 Seyyed Vali Reza Nasr, 'Ideology and institutions in Islamist approaches to public policy', in Sohrab Behdad & Farhad Nomani (eds), Islam and public policy (JAI Press 1997), at 46.

bring real democracy and progress along.[103] The Qur'an inspires that it is never too late to alter situations:

> Ye shall certainly be tried and tested in your possessions and in your personal selves; and ye shall certainly Hear much that will grieve you, from those who received the Book before you and from those who worship many gods. But if ye persevere patiently, and guard against evil,—then that will be a determining factor in all affairs. (Q3:186)

> Whoever works righteousness benefits his own soul; whoever works evil, it is against his own soul: nor is thy Lord ever unjust (in the least) to His Servants. (Q41:46)

4.3.3 *Revivalism*

With growing self-esteem, the Islamic rhetoric was now able to profile itself as an alternative for the Western liberal thought. Many former Muslim colonies considered the discourse of international human rights to be a new ideology which removed religiosity in its advocacy of human dignity. According to them, this corrupted the moral value system as prescribed by the Shari'a in Muslim societies.[104] By favouring the individual human rights perspective, one ignored the personal responsibility[105] toward the Muslim collectivity. This move to individualism was accused of being used as a pretext for intervention in the internal affairs of Muslim countries. These states, in fact, were rather confident that their "Islamic constitutional theory",[106] as put by Coulson, limited the authority of the state. In this regard, the Shari'a was the basis upon which public welfare was defined and derived from. Therefore, according to Said, it was the "state's duty to enhance human dignity and alleviate conditions that hinder individuals in their efforts to achieve happiness".[107] In practice, however, Islamic regimes used religion to justify their authoritarian practice which

103 Terenjit Sevea, '"Islamist" intellectual space: "true Islam" and the Ummah in the East', (2007) 35 Asian Journal of Social Science, 575, at 596.

104 Mashood A. Baderin, International human rights and Islamic law (Oxford University Press 2003), at 26 and 45.

105 Ayesha Jalal, Self and sovereignty: individual and community in South Asian Islam since 1850 (Routledge 2000), at 8.

106 Noel James Coulson, 'The state and the individual in Islamic law', (1957) 6 International and Comparative Law Quarterly, 49, at 49.

107 Abdul Aziz Said, 'Human rights in Islamic perspectives', in Adamantia Pollis & Peter Schwab (eds), Human rights: cultural and ideological perspectives (Praeger 1979), at 87.

satisfied their interests first above those of their populations.[108] Nonetheless, the intentions as professed in the Cairo Declaration on Human Rights in Islam stated the contrary; member states were instead

> reaffirming the civilizing and historical role of the Islamic Ummah which God made the best nation that has given mankind a universal and well-balanced civilization in which harmony is established between this life and the hereafter and knowledge is combined with faith; and the role that this Ummah should play to guide a humanity confused by competing trends and ideologies and to provide solutions to the chronic problems of this materialistic civilization. [And were] wishing to contribute to the efforts of mankind to assert human rights, to protect man from exploitation and persecution, and to affirm his freedom and right to a dignified life in accordance with the Islamic Shari'ah.[109]

Although spiritual self-realisation went beyond certain material conditions, the redistribution of wealth among the needy within the *ummah* had to be conducted in a spirit of solidarity.[110] A classless Islamic social order as advocated by some Islamic revivalists denounced the monopolies of fortunes[111] and based its social model on the primary sources of Islam, i.e. the Qur'an and the Sunnah. This nostalgia for the golden ages of Islam justified the advocacy for a morally and institutionally purified orthodoxy predating the Western colonisation. Moreover, in order to continue to carry out the historical mission toward universal Islam, Islamic revivalists did not allow their followers to borrow from inferior and infidel civilisations.[112] Such discrimination based on religious beliefs in combination with the so-called "doctrine of apostasy"[113] just reified the original claims of the establishment to demand obedience in the name of the perfect and superior Islam.

108 Javaid Rehman, 'Accommodating religious identities in an Islamic state: international law, freedom of religion and the rights of religious minorities', (2000) 7 International Journal on Minority and Group Rights, 139, at 156.

109 Preamble, 1990 Cairo Declaration on Human Rights in Islam.

110 Mouloud Kassim Nait-Belkacem, 'The concept of social justice in Islam', in Altaf Gauhar (ed), The challenge of Islam (Islamic Council of Europe 1978), at 137.

111 Bedhad, in, at 2.

112 Bat, at 199.

113 Ahmed, at 198.

4.4 From Decadence to Devotion

4.4.1 *Rebellious Fundamentalism*

In spite of these efforts to emancipate the Islamic world from colonial domination and to restore its values within the new economic order after the Second World War, the newly independent countries rather advanced the modern secular system which they inherited from the Western colonial powers. The political establishments were unable to truly free themselves from the material benefits which both the capitalist or communist blocs promised them. They were also unable to promote the spiritual submission to God instead. Although these leaders were Muslims and were living in the Muslim lands, they would now become the internal enemies of Islam. Their authority was challenged through a continuous revolutionary fight.[114] Only under such circumstances, against this appropriated "world of neo-jahiliyyah",[115] as called by Qutb, Islamic solidarity could be found again beyond the national boundaries. The disbelief as displayed by the political authorities in these Muslim nation states had to be eradicated.[116] Regime change as propagated by rebellious groups was the ultimate means to re-establish the religious Islamic public order. Only such order could finally give answers again to the real needs of Muslim societies. Gauhar fairly portrayed these frustrations whose presence is still experienced among today's deprived Muslims.

> Within the nation states our effort is to preserve the legacy of imperialism: corrupt systems of elections, alien modes of education, and outlandish procedures of administration. We allow ourselves to be divided along linguistic and racial lines, because such divisions appear to offer greater prospects of material gain.[117] [...] The trouble started when Muslims were an ascendant force in the world. While we claimed that Islam permitted no dichotomy or diarchy, the rulers started undermining the unity of the Islamic State when they asserted that the affairs of the state were

114 Richard Bonney, Jihad: from Qur'an to bin Laden (Palgrave Macmillan 2004), at 217.

115 Sayyid Qutb, Al-Islam wa mushiklat al-hadarah (Dar al-Shuruq 1988), at 195.

116 Dale F. Eickelman, 'The Middle East's democracy deficit and the expanding public sphere', in Peter van der Veer & Shoma Munshi (eds), Media, war, and terrorism: responses from the Middle East and Asia (RoutledgeCurzon 2004), at 64.

117 Altaf Gauhar, 'Islam and secularism', in Altaf Gauhar (ed), The challenge of Islam (Islamic Council of Europe 1978), at 305.

> their sole concern, though they would not claim authority in matters of religion.[118]

This moral decline has already been challenged in the nineteenth century. The Wahhabi inspired by Hanbali scholar Ibn Taymiyyah for example, initiated thorough reforms of the institutional and legislative practice within the Kingdom of Saudi-Arabia. There, Shari'a as grounded in the foundational sources of Islam, i.e. the Qur'an and the Sunnah, had to be fully applied again. Later in the early twentieth century, the Muslim Brotherhood and its leading ideologist Sayyid Qutb unsuccessfully advocated the transformation of the Egyptian state and religious policies as well. Whereas the Iranian revolution under the guidance of Ayatollah Khomeini did succeed in reinstating Shari'a and in privileging the former religious leadership, i.e. the *ulama*, to interpret and implement the Shari'a again. The path from decay to justice was difficult and often violent; for example as witnessed during the civil war in Algeria in the 1990s. In particular, martyrdom, seen by Alinejad, as "the most destructive Muslim weapon yet",[119] convinced some followers of such worldview to commit themselves to God's cause, even through death.[120] Although these types of rebellion against unjust Muslim rulers was justifiable, the methods of warfare still ought to respect certain provisions in the Qur'an:

> Let those fight in the cause of Allah Who sell the life of this world for the hereafter. To him who fighteth in the cause of Allah,—whether he is slain or gets victory—soon shall We give him a reward of great (value). (Q4:74)
>
> And do not kill (or destroy) yourselves: for verily Allah hath been to you Most Merciful! (Q4:29)
>
> If any do that in rancour and injustice,—soon shall We cast them into the Fire: and easy it is for Allah. (Q4:30)

---

118 Id., in, at 306.

119 Mahmoud Alinejad, 'Political Islam in Iran and the emergence of a religious public sphere: the impact of September 11', in Peter van der Veer & Shoma Munshi (eds), Media, war, and terrorism: responses from the Middle East and Asia (RoutledgeCurzon 2004), at 76.

120 Ahmad Shboul, 'Islam and globalization: Arab world perspectives', in Virginia Matheson Hooker & Amin Saikal (eds), Islamic perspectives on the new millennium (Institute of Southeast Asian Studies 2004), at 49.

In addition to these restrictions, only wars based on theological grounds could be fought against Islamic regimes, not for political or worldly interests.[121] In this respect, Muslims extremists claimed their legitimacy and piety to be greater than those of the existing leaderships within Muslim countries. According to them, the establishment was corrupted and acted as an agent of foreign occupiers;[122] in particular against the background of the Cold War. In addition, after the Cold War era, the Islamic faith continued to be deculturalised.[123] In the view of those Islamic extremists, globalisation only reinforced the prevailing Western values which continued to marginalise the Islamic faith for the sake of the idea of progress.[124] No longer should Muslims face such domination under the veil of an increasing cultural and political influence of the West.[125] No longer should Muslims have to obey the Islamic leadership which was backed by Western powers. These leaderships were attacked during the so-called "sacred jihad".[126] However, in Central Asia and the Caucasus, this defensive *jihad* as led by Islamic fundamentalists was crushed by the despotic leaderships which themselves were reluctant to give up their economic and political interests.[127] Conversely, these corrupted regimes were assisted by Western non-Muslim forces. The Gulf War was an example thereof and illustrated, as during the Ottoman Empire, the value of alliances between Islamic nation states and Western powers, in particular regarding issues of neutrality during warfare.[128] This also raised questions about the legitimacy of these coalitions in light of certain Qur'anic provisions which acknowledge on the

121 Abou El Fadl, at 272.

122 Quintan Wiktorowicz, 'The Salafi movement: violence and the fragmentation of community', in Miriam Cooke & Bruce B. Lawrence (eds), Muslim networks from Hajj to hip hop (University of North Carolina Press 2005), at 221–22.

123 Mohamad Abu Bakar, 'Managing the future: Islam in the post-Cold War era', in Syed Othman Alhabshi & Nik Mustapha Nik Hassan (eds), Islamic civilization: present and future challenges (Institute of Islamic Understanding Malaysia 1997), at 56.

124 Mustapha Chérif, L'islam et l'occident: rencontre avec Jacques Derrida (Odile Jacob 2006), at 121.

125 Ruud Peters, 'The enforcement of God's law: the Shari'ah in the present world of Islam', in Philip Ostien, Jamila M. Nasir & Franz Kogelmann (eds), Comparative perspectives on Shari'ah in Nigeria (Spectrum Books 2005), at 123.

126 Ruh Allah ibn Mustafa Khumayni & Hamid Algar, Islam and revolution: writings and declarations of Imam Khomeini (Mizan Press 1981), at 116.

127 Mohammad Karim, 'Globalization and post-Soviet revival of Islam in Central Asia and the Caucasus', (2005) 25 Journal of Muslim Minority Affairs, 439, at 443.

128 Muhammad Hamidullah, Muslim conduct of state (Sh. Muhammed Ashraf 1961), at 283–304.

one hand the enmities between Muslims and non-Muslims and on the other hand the justness by which Muslims have to treat non-Muslims.[129] The first Medina Constitution (d. 622) also stressed the importance of cooperation between different religious groups living on the territory of the Islamic state in case of an attack against it.[130]

> O ye who believe! Take not the Jews and the Christians for your friends and protectors: They are but friends and protectors to each other. And he amongst you that turns to them (for friendship) is of them. Verily Allah guideth not a people unjust. (Q5:51)

> Allah forbids you not, with regard to those who fight you not for (your) Faith nor drive you out of your homes, from dealing kindly and justly with them: for Allah loveth those who are just. (Q60:8)

> Allah only forbids you, with regard to those who fight you for (your) Faith, and drive you out of your homes, and support (others) in driving you out, from turning to them (for friendship and protection). It is such as turn to them (in these circumstances), that do wrong. (Q60:9)

Understandably, the suspicion among Muslim dissidents to their traitor regimes directed their claims toward authenticity instead of toward the modern concept of "cultural hybridity"[131] that was accused of eroding the Islamic identity. For these traditionalists, the imposition of a legal system which was alleged to be completely alien to the historical experience of the Islamic world[132] only further instigated new breading grounds of resistance and insurrection in the newly independent Muslim nation states. They ignored, however, the fact that the *ummah*, throughout its history, was a product of cultural diversity and a symbol of coexistence of different cultures. Paradoxically enough, secularisation had pushed Islamic fundamentalism to adjust the current modern needs of the Islamic societies with the precepts of tradition. In this regard, the concept of *maslaha*, i.e. public welfare, justified this process of

---

129 Yvonne Yazbeck Haddad, 'Operation Desert Storm and the war of fatwas', in Muhammad Khalid Masud, Brinkley Morris Messick & David Stephan Powers (eds), Islamic legal interpretation: muftis and their fatwas (Harvard University Press 1996), at 300.

130 Berween, at 117.

131 Hassan, at 319.

132 Sayid Mujtaba Rukni Musawi Lari, Western civilisation through Muslim eyes (FIL Inc 1979), at 62.

permissiveness.[133] Nonetheless, in spite of the efforts of this new leadership, according to Gauhar, "there is nothing but power at the summit. Morality is for the bushes and the slopes, and principles for barren valleys. These are but symptoms."[134] Consequently, Islamic doctrines justifying the legitimate exercise of authority and control on Muslim subjects were the pretexts for the rulers to advance their own interests before those of their subjects.[135] Within this conflict between the political and religious establishment and the rebellious insurgency, their respective competing claims had to be truly grounded on theological instead of material arguments. In case of the victory of one over the other party, humanity had to be reminded that it only had limited sovereignty under God's suzerainty.[136]

4.4.2 *Local Secessionism*

The dynamics which emerged after the end of the Cold War led to a violent competition for filling the power vacuum. Within this conflict of so-called "balkanisation", not only states but also non-state actors were expressing their views on the international plane. Moreover, globalisation made it easier for Islamic secessionist movements to bring their cause into the limelight of public attention. They received greater sympathy in their struggle for freedom from the systematic violation of human rights against their peoples. For those peoples, secession was a last resort for external self-determination. Within this fight for independence, special humanitarian networks of so-called "nomadic jihadis"[137] dispatched Muslim fighters to any corner of the world—wherever Muslim populations were suffering from attack, such as in Bosnia, Chechnya, China, Kashmir, Kosovo, Lebanon, Macedonia, Israel-Palestine, the Philippines, Tajikistan, Uzbekistan, etc. In addition, the legacy of colonial borders and ethnic divisions made it impossible to establish peaceful coexistence within these areas of dispute.[138] However, instead of having recourse to violence, Iqbal's advice was to consult the Qur'an which, according to him, acted as "a catalyst

---

133 Sami Zubaida, 'Islam and secularization', (2005) 33 Asian Journal of Social Science, 438, at 445.

134 Gauhar, in, at 305–6.

135 Abdallah Cheriet, 'Problématique du pouvoir en islam: l'état de l'émir Abd el-Kader et la théorie du cheikh Ben Badis', in Mohammed Arkoun (ed), L'islam, morale et politique (Desclée de Brouwer 1986), at 216.

136 Ghulam Sarwar, 'State and religion: the Islamic perspective', in Harbans Singh Bhatia (ed), Studies in Islamic law, religion and society (Deep & Deep Publications 1996), at 99.

137 Wiktorowicz, in, at 219.

138 Lari, at 137.

to awaken persons to a wider sense of reality".[139] In this respect, the following Qur'anic verse might bring solace:

> To thee We sent the Scripture in truth, confirming the scripture that came before it, and guarding it in safety: so judge between them by what Allah hath revealed, and follow not their vain desires, diverging from the Truth that hath come to thee. To each among you have we prescribed a law and an open way. If Allah had so willed, He would have made you a single people, but (His plan is) to test you in what He hath given you: so strive as in a race in all virtues. The goal of you all is to Allah. It is He that will show you the truth of the matters in which ye. (Q5:48)

Muslims living in the West did not remain indifferent to these struggles for self-determination and human dignity by their Muslim brothers and sisters in other parts of the world. These Western Muslims themselves might have been deprived of basic human conditions in the countries of their residence. The world had never been this intertwined and what happened in one place resonated elsewhere. Their status of illegality and consecutive discrimination on racial and religious grounds called also for reassessing the immigration situation in those states whose fear for the Other has turned them inwards.[140] Modernist Islamic scholarship reassured that the accommodation of Muslims in Western societies could take place peacefully because their universal value system was initially grounded on Islamic principles.[141] However, this tolerant attitude might frustrate the Muslim populations as it seemed to depict Muslim affirmative (and perhaps violent) action as exceptional and unacceptable. In this regard, also Muslims, as any other people, had the right to fight for integrity and acceptance.[142] The equivocal stance of Western governments regarding Muslim minorities at home and their policies abroad with respect to the Muslim world only further fed into the frustrations which all Muslims over the world felt.

---

139 Sheila McDonough, Muslim ethics and modernity: a comparative study of the ethical thought of Sayyid Ahmad Khan and Mawlana Mawdudi (Wilfrid Laurier University Press 1984), at 82.

140 Daniel Riot & Driss Ajbali, Ben Laden n'est pas dans l'ascenseur... L'immigration, miroir des peurs de la société (Desmaret 2002), at 22.

141 Hisham A. Hellyer, 'Minorities, Muslims and Shari'a: some reflections on Islamic law and Muslims without political power', (2007) 18 Islam & Christian-Muslim Relations, 85, at 100.

142 Sherman A. Jackson, 'Jihad and the modern world', (2002) 7 Journal of Islamic Law & Culture, 1, at 21.

4.4.3 *Global Terrorism*

All over the world, Islamic communities experienced the terrifying threats of secular globalisation. The market and its invisible hand tied down their governments' policies to Western interests. Such *jahiliyyah*, i.e. the intervention and occupation of the Islamic lands and minds, was defied by Islamic terrorists. With regard to the object of their attacks, their use of terror against innocent civilians was justified as it would only equate with the heinous suffering inflicted upon the Muslims.[143] This eternal struggle[144] would be won when the abode of Islam had taken over the abode of disbelievers. Within such Islamic territory, Islamic law representing the right values and truths[145] could be again fully applied. Though persuasion and patience would be a means to achieve this goal, the current state of world affairs had caused so much daily despair that only violence was the way out.[146] Apparently, the market had deprived the human dimension of human interaction and had replaced it with it a monetary value instead.

As opposed to the rebellious or secessionist movements respectively fighting for internal or external self-determination, terrorist networks were fighting their external and internal enemies, both in the *dar al-harb* and *dar al-Islam*. While the status and obligations of rebels were regulated by the Islamic laws related to rebellion, i.e. *ahkam al-bughat*,[147] or by IHL for non-international armed conflicts, the terrorists' actions were judged by the criminal law of the national jurisdiction where their targeting took place. Issues of state-sponsored terrorism raised questions of other types of accountability, in particular during the wars in Iraq and Afghanistan. Nonetheless, according to Lari, the world was facing much greater concerns of responsibility:

---

143 Glenn E. Robinson, 'The battle for Iraq: Islamic insurgencies in comparative perspective', (2007) 28 Third World Quarterly, 261, at 268.

144 Bonney, at 217.

145 Ali K. Khan, A theory of international terrorism: understanding Islamic militancy (Martinus Nijhoff Publishers 2006), at 129.

146 Ahmad bin Hamad Al-Khalîli, 'Elements of the nation's renaissance', in Qatar Ministry of Awqâf and Islamic Affairs, Research and Studies Center & American Open University (eds), Civilizational role of the Muslim nation in the world of tomorrow: a selection of scholars and authors (Ministry of Awqâf and Islamic Affairs 2000), at 54.

147 Khaled Abou El Fadl, 'Ahkam al-bughat: irregular warfare and the law of rebellion in Islam', in James Turner Johnson & John Kelsay (eds), Cross, crescent, and sword: the justification and limitation of war in Western and Islamic tradition (Greenwood Press 1990), at 80.

> The more progress technology and the material side of civilisation makes, the more men quote the maxim "Si vis pacem para bellum" ["If you wish for peace, prepare for war"] as a pretext for an arms race not merely in quantities but also in destructiveness, the more obvious is the truth made that humanity stands at a crossroads of choice between mass suicide or salvation by faith, annihilation or acceptance of ethical principles, the brutal dictatorship of a man or the merciful government of God. When man wakes up to this situation—and the very horrors which face him may themselves open his eyes—we pray that the light of reason and of heavenly wisdom will lead him onto "the good road, the road of those to whom God is gracious, not the road of those who continue to grope in darkness."[148]

The recent and unprecedented uprisings in the Middle East ever since 2011 have further challenged the leadership in those countries.[149] Due to decades of oppression and social and economic hardship, the regimes across the Middle East were losing their legitimacy vis-à-vis their own populace. Peaceful and popular resistance and violent rebellion were possible answers to such human suffering. These struggles have been denounced by several regimes as illegitimate interferences of Western powers and the Arab League in their domestic affairs and as terrorist actions against their legitimate national rule. Libya in particular was one of those battlefields where responsibilities to protect have put the civilian population under even greater pressure. Syria is a more recent example where the international community and the Arab League are struggling to pave the path towards a peaceful resolution of the conflict between rebellious factions and the central government.[150] Though these fights have altered the power relations in those countries, they have also exposed the diverse religious and political factions, tribes and social and economic divisions within those societies. A lot of uncertainties remain as to prospects of real change that can accommodate these differences into a unified and new democratic mode of governance.

---

148 Lari, at 138.

149 F. Gregory Gause III, 'Why Middle East studies missed the Arab Spring: the myth of authoritarian stability', (2011) 90 Foreign Affairs, 81.

150 Matthias Vanhullebusch, 'The Arab League and military operations: prospects and challenges in Syria', (2015) 22 International Peacekeeping, 151.

4.5 Conclusion

Throughout the history of Islam, the Muslim leaderships and their opponents have found different methods to claim legitimacy over each other.[151] In order to eliminate their internal and external enemies, they accused each other of ignorance and lack of religious piety.[152] Moreover, the construction of the image of their enemies,[153] namely of the excluded Other as opposed to the all-encompassing "Islamic" Self, has to be analysed within a context of division in order to rule. Sooner or later these fictions started to live their own realities, became institutionalised and informed the structure of the legal arguments limiting or expanding the protection to their enemies. From this utilitarian perspective, the nature of one's rival can justify the (non-)application of one's own advanced principles of proportionality and distinction as will be looked upon in the following Chapter V. Apparently, the unambiguous universal message of Islam which required the respect for the life of all human beings at all times and everywhere, was set aside by such a discriminatory discourse which dehumanised the opponents of the acclaimed righteous leadership.

Understandably, no Muslim is immune to the duality of human nature. Because a Muslim has a "God-given potential for good as well as evil",[154] as noted by Zaman, he/she shall see both ways; namely through the advancement of his/her own sovereign happiness and through the communitarian respect for the aspirations of others. However, these human struggles for Islamic self-realisation have too often been marked by disbelief on its own behalf and not necessarily by its other.[155] The division of the "Islamic" Self and its Other necessarily has only found its legitimation within the conflict and violence upon which it is premised. From a complementary worldview, humanity should be reminded of its spiritual "superiority over other beings",[156] as Zaman

151 Daveed Gartenstein-Ross, 'No other Gods before me: spheres of influence in the relationship between Christianity and Islam', (2004–2005) 33 Denver Journal of International Law and Policy, 223, at 281.

152 Thomas Scheffler, 'West-Eastern cultures of fear: violence and terrorism in Islam', in Kai Hafez & Mary Ann Kenny (eds), The Islamic world and the West: an introduction to political cultures and international relations (Brill 2000), at 76.

153 Kai Hafez, 'Islam and the West: the clash of politicised perceptions', in see id., at 8.

154 Syed Muhammad Zaman, 'Place of man in the universe in the world: view of Islam', in Harbans Singh Bhatia (ed), Studies in Islamic law, religion and society (Deep & Deep Publications 1996), at 258.

155 Tilman Nagel, 'La théorie islamique de l'état: aspects politiques et éthiques', in Mohammed Arkoun (ed), L'islam, morale et politique (Desclée de Brouwer 1986), at 200.

156 Zaman, in, at 258.

continued, and should believe in its abilities to overcome the distinctions and discriminations it created in its material existence. In particular with reference to armed conflicts, humanity's salvation lies in the recognition and respect for the life and unity of humanity, i.e. God's creation which precedes everything,[157] and in the acceptance of humanity's diversity as stated in the Qur'an in the following verses:

> Mankind was one single nation, and Allah sent Messengers with glad tidings and warnings; and with them He sent the Book in truth, to judge between people in matters wherein they differed. (Q2:213)

> O mankind! We created you from a single (pair) of a male and a female, and made you into nations and tribes, that ye may know each other (not that ye may despise (each other). (Q49:13)

---

157 Jacques Berque, L'islam au temps du monde (Sindbad 1984), at 254.

PART III

Toward a Naturalist Legal Analysis of the Laws of War

CHAPTER V

The Structure of the Legal Arguments in Islamic Law of War

5.1 Introduction

The aim of this chapter is to examine how historical identities on the "Islamic" Self and its Other—as discussed in the previous Chapter V in Part II—have informed the creation and application of the universal principles of distinction and proportionality in ILW. Combining the positivist analysis of those rules applicable in armed conflicts—as examined in Chapter I in Part I—with the historical analysis of the context in which the laws of war have evolved over time and in space, can reveal how the structure of the laws of war in theory and in practice have been formulated against those different historical backgrounds. From the period of Revelation and the subsequent Muslim conquests onwards, a shift can be witnessed in the way the jurisdictional scope of ILW has been portrayed. The introduction, by Islamic jurists from the late eighth century, of different abodes, i.e. abode of peace (*dar al-Islam*) and abode of war (*dar al-harb*) respectively, avoided the original placatory principles against warfare such as demonstration of patience, persuasion and tolerance as promoted in the primary sources of Islamic law, i.e. the Qur'an and the Sunnah.

From a utilitarian perspective, these legal fictions have served the Islamic leaderships and their empires over the centuries to deal with their enemies at home and abroad. The determination of who can challenge the Islamic authorities and who cannot remains in the hands of the prevailing establishments at a given moment in the history of Islam. Evidently, only the Islamic rulers had the righteous authority to implement Islamic law as opposed to those rebels who were perceived not to understand the correct interpretation to establish the Islamic state and to implement its laws. This same state had to be protected against the Western infidels who have continuously attacked the Islamic community and who have imposed their own Western values since their colonisation of the Muslim lands and minds. In such environment it was justified to use all necessary means to fight internal resistance and external oppression. Hence, the principles of protection could be set aside by such requirements of military necessity. This however, distorted the true application of the sacred texts.

 | DOI 10.1163/9789004298248_007

Although, from a realist perspective, it would be impossible to outlaw war in this world, but from a (religious) humanist perspective, the survival of the human species remains at risk. Respect for all members of humanity—despite their differences—is one of the hallmarks of God's creation. No distinction between peoples whatsoever should be legitimised during peace but in particular during wartime. However, Islamic history has shown that such divisions have primarily served the rulers and the legal authorities, which have benefited from this in order to rule over their divided subjects. The universal message of Islam instead has always favoured the protection of life and human beings above all sorts of divisions introduced by humanity upon itself. Prohibiting the evil and commanding the good within ILW can actually redress the indiscriminate invocation of military necessity to serve the interests of the leaderships at the expense of innocent civilian casualties. The necessity to treat the Other with justice necessarily can lead to a more just world for all members of humanity.

5.2 Jurisdiction and Distinction

5.2.1 *Authority in Warfare*

The jurisdictional regimes of ILW are closely connected with the issue of legitimate belligerency and the authority or agency to define such legitimate belligerency. Depending on the nature of the enemies to Islam, i.e. internal or external, the protection granted to them relies on the definition of the conflict and its associated legal regime. Wars of internal resistance to Islam, i.e. rebellion, are regulated by the laws on rebellion (*ahkam al-bughat*).[1] Whereas armed conflicts waged between Muslims and non-Muslims, i.e. external *jihad*, are subject to rules addressing such conflicts of external nature.[2] The primary sources of Islamic law, however, do not refer to such dichotomous formulation of armed conflicts. Instead, those legal and juristic terms were formulated to meet the needs of the changing context since the Revelation and at the time of the Prophet Muhammad. The political and military context throughout Islam's history has informed the interpretation and application of the initial stipulations in the relevant revealed texts. Rationalising such context in conflicting terms from a political theory perspective permits, within the Islamic world, to set aside the complementary nature of the world as revealed within

1 See Khaled Abou El Fadl, Rebellion and violence in Islamic law (Cambridge University Press 2001).

2 See Chapter I: 1.2.2, 1.3.2, 1.4.2.

sacred texts. According to Zubaida, "there is a tension between the theoretical sovereignty of the sacred law, and the reality of its co-existence with profane law, and often its confinement in relation to it".[3] Thus, instrumentalising the context for the creation of legal fictions itself can legitimise the context to live its own reality as fabricated by those legal fictions. In this regard, the dependency on juristic authorities to justify certain political actions recognised the authoritative doctrines as universally applied by the political authorities at a given moment in Islamic history.[4]

For those reasons, the Islamic leadership claimed that obedience to its command was a prerequisite to guarantee the survival of the Islamic faith within a hostile environment in which—at least in the beginning—found support with only a few. In this respect, *jihad* has been understood by jurists to mean the actual fighting, i.e. *qital*, against non-Muslims and soon these jurists developed their own doctrine on permanent war with the aggressors of Islam.[5] *Jihad* would be the instrument to fulfil God's promise, i.e. the ultimate goal of the Islamic faith.[6] Throughout many stages of Islamic history, violence was the main instrument to safeguard the Islamic order. Generally, force was the societal norm at the very beginning of and even before the Revelation. Such normalisation and legitimation through the laws of armed conflict reflected the inevitable violent context in which Islam emerged and had to survive. Nonetheless, within this doctrine, until the entire world has been brought under the Islamic religious order, coexistence, which necessarily would accommodate the natural differences amongst peoples across the globe, imposed certain territorial and personal constraints on the use of force. Respectively, ILW had jurisdiction *ratione loci* (territorial jurisdiction), i.e. in the *dar al-Islam* and the *dar al-harb*, as well as jurisdiction *ratione personae* (personal jurisdiction), i.e. on Muslim believers.

In this respect, the Qur'an does make reference to a world where belief, i.e. *iman*, and disbelief, i.e. *kufr*, were naturally and complementarily present in humanity's existence.[7] The later juristic inferences from this dichotomy within

3 Sami Zubaida, Law and power in the Islamic world (I.B. Tauris 2003), at 79.

4 Wael B. Hallaq, Authority, continuity and change in Islamic law (Cambridge University Press 2001), at 61 and 85.

5 Bassam Tibi, 'War and peace in Islam', in Sohail H. Hashmi (ed), Islamic political ethics: civil society, pluralism, and conflict (Princeton University Press 2002), at 178.

6 Abdulaziz A. Sachedina, 'The development of jihad in Islamic revelation and history', in James Turner Johnson & John Kelsay (eds), Cross, cresent, and sword: the justification and limitation of war in Western and Islamic tradition (Greenwood Press 1990), at 36–7.

7 The Qur'an provides many references to the world of belief and disbelief, for example: Q2:108, Q3:167, Q3:176, Q3:177, Q16:106.

the Qur'an favoured a rather divisive understanding of the world in conflicting terms instead. Therefore, such interpretation necessarily advocated a doctrine of eternal conflict between these two worlds of belief and of disbelief. This legal fiction started to live its own reality. The jurists' perception of the enemies, whether internal (apostates) or external (polytheists, Peoples of the Book), has clearly influenced the development of different jurisdictional regimes within ILW and the different standards of protection provided for them. Of course, the legal classification of an armed conflict was and still is an issue of authority. Regarding the war against non-Muslims, the legal status of such state of war is a matter of recognition in relation to the religious obligation to defend against this aggression as non-Muslims attack and threaten the essence of the Islamic faith (to continue) to exist.[8] Only the legitimate Islamic authority can go to war against the internal and external enemies of Islam. These authorities would choose those legal regimes which necessarily advanced what they perceived to be the Islamic interest to wage and to win such wars against their enemies. One of the *hadiths* refers to this authority of Muslim rulers to call for Muslims to fight in the cause of God:

> Allah's Apostle said, "There is no Hijra (i.e. migration) (from Mecca to Medina) after the Conquest (of Mecca), but Jihad and good intention remain; and if you are called (by the Muslim ruler) for fighting, go forth immediately."[9]

Having determined the actual application of the laws of war at a particular time, such juristic contributions have not remained untouched by continuous criticism and resistance of other parties. These opponents were necessarily not involved in the previous process which controlled their thoughts and modes of reasoning. Moreover, the struggle between competing ideologies and their methodologies were usually settled at the expense of the weaker party to this conflict; though, each school of law would like to have seen its own logic/rationalisation to the Revelation to be favoured above other interpretations and applications of ILW.[10] There was little room for the other parties to the conflict to challenge their (limited) protection as formulated by the juristic authorities. Rebels in particular were considered to disrupt the stability and order within

8 Majid Khadduri & Herbert J. Liebesny, Law in the Middle East / Vol. 1, Origin and development of Islamic law (Middle East Institute 1955), at 359.

9 Al-Bukhari, Vol. 4, Book 52, Number 42. (Narrated by Ibn 'Abbas)

10 Norman Calder, Jawid A. Mojaddedi & Andrew Rippin, Interpretation and jurisprudence in medieval Islam (Ashgate 2007), at Part III (at 981).

the Islamic community and should be crushed for their ambitions to defy the just and religious leadership of the *ummah*. Such conflicts within the Islamic community, amounting to exclusion of participation and citizenship within it,[11] have been criticised by many jurists. Ibn Taymiyya, for example, argued that the invention of *ahkam al-bughat*, i.e. the laws on rebellion, has been introduced to take away the legitimate belligerent status of rebels fighting the unjust leadership. He found support in the primary sources as no *hadith* provided for the fighting against rebels but only the fighting against apostates and the Khariji.[12]

The juristic tradition of ILW, however, through its language and modes of interpretation has neutralised the inherent biases and personal preferences it established from its creation onwards.[13] Such legal formalism conceals its ideological commitment to a divisive worldview by hiding behind the sources of Islamic law. Their interpretations and rationalisations gain legitimacy as they were alleged to be supported by those primary sources.[14] Apparently, the juristic authorities rather advocated a strict observance to the letter of ILW rather than its spirit.[15] Vogel continued by stating that the *ijtihad* can give access to the transcendental knowledge of the divine law, "by offering a broad and final human authority for law, the constitutive compromise supports the horizontal aspiration of a determinate universal divine paradigm for human life. It pays respect to the vertical aspiration of transcendence only by somewhat roundabout technique of delegation, of constructive divine authority."[16] Evidently, the rules present within the Qur'an and the Sunnah preceded their man-made implementations as they came straight from God or from the practice of the Prophet Muhammad. However, the rationalists, such as the Mu'tazalis, as opposed to the traditionalists, argued that human reason and agency could extract what the divine justice was about: whether something was good or bad; whereas the traditionalists said that God only could dictate whether some actions were inherently good or bad and believers had to implement such

11 John Kelsay, 'Civil society and government in Islam', in Sohail H. Hashmi (ed), Islamic political ethics: civil society, pluralism, and conflict (Princeton University Press 2002), at 25.

12 Abou El Fadl, at 62.

13 Lawrence Rosen, The anthropology of justice: law as culture in Islamic society (Cambridge University Press 1989), at 42.

14 Sherman A. Jackson, 'Fiction and formalism: toward a functional analysis of usul al-fiqh', in Bernard G. Weiss (ed), Studies in Islamic legal theory (Brill 2002), at 194.

15 Joseph Schacht, An introduction to Islamic law (Clarendon Press 1965), at 204.

16 Frank E. Vogel, Islamic law and legal system: studies of Saudi Arabia (Brill 2000), at 39.

divine law.[17] The latter literalist/traditionalist position, according to Vogel, "lends itself well to the vertical aspiration, since its operation emphasizes the divide between the divine and the human. But it satisfies the horizontal aspiration rather poorly, because it offers no firm, stable, and determinate rules for human life, but only a host of personal guesses at God's law, liable to constant divergences of opinion."[18] Despite God's absolute sovereignty as opposed to humanity's relative authority to elucidate the divine commands, both perspectives, however, can be perfectly complementary to each other. According to Hallaq, "for revelation cannot be understood without the intervention of human reason, just as human reason cannot, without the aid of revelation, comprehend the divine intention".[19]

For more than three centuries after the Revelation, the tension between juristic and political authorities caused major divisions and gaps which were exploited by leaders on both sides to advance their authority at the expense of the other, both in relation to the Muslim population as well as to the non-Muslim inhabitants and foreigners. It was the Abbasid dynasty which reconciled the juristic and political prerogatives within the Islamic state[20] and it were the jurists who were the guardians of Islamic law.[21] It is this technical legal language as created and used by juristic authorities that served as a primary instrument for jurists to assert and legitimise their power over the normative arguments within ILW. With respect to the conduct of warfare, these arguments had to be guided by the jurists' preferences. They also determined how and who could challenge their authority both doctrinally as well as on the battlefield.[22] Jurists did not only claim interpretative authority over the revealed texts, they also set up a sophisticated methodology to access the text from the human context. From their professional juristic guilds they had recourse to abrogation, i.e. *naskh*, which repeals one legal provision by another one.[23] This legal technique, as applied by classical jurists in relation to the

---

17 Norman Anderson, Islamic law in the modern world (New York University Press 1959), at 9.

18 Vogel, at 39.

19 Wael B. Hallaq, A history of Islamic legal theories: an introduction to Sunni usul al-fiqh (Cambridge University Press 1999), at 225.

20 David F. Forte, Studies in Islamic law: classical and contemporary application (Austin & Winfield 1999), at 11–25.

21 Colin Imber, Ebu's-su'ud: the Islamic legal tradition (Edinburgh University Press 1997), at 65.

22 Abou El Fadl, at 106 and 321.

23 Aqil Ahmad & Iqbal Ali Khan, Text book of Mohammedan law (Central Law Agency 2004), at 20.

different verses on warfare, had mostly ignored the principles of tolerance and peace, which the primary sources of Islamic law stand for and whose message would be convincing enough to persuade non-Muslims in their relations with the Muslims.[24] Hence, the so-called "sword verses" were favoured at the expense of the "peace" ones.[25]

Such attitudes necessarily promote even greater tension between the warring parties and their causes to go to war and in particular regarding their respect of the laws of war during the actual hostilities. One party or the other will always be more excluded than the other; in spite of the reciprocal character of warfare, such marginalisation can lead to even more violations of the laws of war knowing that the unprivileged legal position of such party to the conflict creates a gap within the law between the legitimate warring party and the disadvantaged one. Such asymmetrical situation and sharp distinction in ILW reinforces the asymmetrical conditions on the battlefield; while the primary sources of ILW would have been put in place to avoid such unequal treatment of belligerency and to provide protection during warfare in the first place. Nonetheless, also as a matter of reciprocity, treating the enemy well would lead to the same courtesy on behalf of the opponent. In addition, the dehumanisation of the Other in the conflict justified not to take or apply the principles of distinction and proportionality strictly. If the *ummah* had to be preserved and protected for the coming generation of Muslims, a humanitarian cost could not be avoided. In this respect, wars would be the necessary means to achieve this goal and to implement God's command to serve humanity in this manner. That is why many Muslim rulers over time have claimed that wars were a necessary evil to establish ultimate peace on earth. The second caliph Umar Ibn Al-Kattab, however, was convinced that Islam would prevail not because of its force but instead because of the respect it imposes for the values it is sharing with other peoples.[26] Again, reciprocity, as a matter of natural law, would bring the warring parties to act justly with each other both for the good and the bad. For example the Qur'an states the following:

24 M. Raquibuz Zaman, 'Islamic perspectives on territorial boundaries and autonomy', in Sohail H. Hashmi (ed), Islamic political ethics: civil society, pluralism, and conflict (Princeton University Press 2002), at 92.

25 See Chapter I, 1.2.1, Footnotes 13 and 15.

26 Sheikh Wahbeh al-Zuhili, 'Islam and international law', (2005) 87 International Review of the Red Cross, 269, at 274.

> Allah commands justice, the doing of good, and liberality to kith and kin, and He forbids all shameful deeds, and injustice and rebellion: He instructs you, that ye may receive admonition. (Q16:90)

All empires having emerged ever since the creation of the major schools of Islamic law within Sunni Islam, remained faithful to the doctrines framed by that school as it limited and justified their actions and authority by those doctrines and methodologies.[27] Any further development by juristic authorities working for the political authorities within those empires attributed their interpretations and findings to one or the other school of thought.[28] Such doctrinal and juristic authority, however, as opposed to the authority residing in the primary sources of Islamic law, has only a relative meaning which remains subject to change and mediation.[29] Within such environment of legal pluralism, changing contexts over time would give rise to other interpretations of the laws of war.[30] This doctrinal diversity has been severely put at risk by the Western colonial presence in the Muslim lands where the juristic conscience was detached from its doctrinal foundations and replaced by a positivist Western classification and codification of the legal system.[31] This of course caused major tensions between traditionalists and modernists respectively wanting to protect/re-Islamise[32] the past legal pluralism and advance toward a more predictable nature of a uniform rationalised doctrine on the sources of law of the country in question. Hallaq mitigated and found that this latest trend had similar evolutions already from the early beginning of Islam's history:

---

27 Bernard G. Weiss, 'The madhhab in Islamic legal theory', in P.J. Bearman, Rudolph Peters & Frank E. Vogel (eds), The Islamic school of law: evolution, devolution, and progress (Harvard University Press 2005), at 1–2; Gudrun Krämer & Sabine Schmidtke, 'Introduction: religious authority and religious authorities in Muslim societies: a critical overview', in Gudrun Krämer & Sabine Schmidtke (eds), Speaking for Islam: religious authorities in Muslim societies (Brill 2006), at 5.

28 Wael B. Hallaq, 'Takhrij and the construction of juristic authority', in Bernard G. Weiss (ed), Studies in Islamic legal theory (Brill 2002), at 333.

29 Weiss, in, at 4.

30 Ihsan Yilmaz, 'Inter-madhhab surfing, neo-ijtihad, and faith-based movement leader', in Peri J. Bearman, Rudolph Peters & Frank E. Vogel (eds), see id., at 192.

31 Yadh Ben Achour, Politique, religion et droit dans le monde arabe (Cérès productions 1992), at 7.

32 Bernard Botiveau, Loi islamique et droit dans les sociétés arabes: mutations des systèmes juridiques du Moyen-Orient (Karthala 1993), at 277.

> The search for a legal identity in twentieth-century Islam and the crises that are associated with reformulating both a legal theory and a general concept of law represent the latest historical stage in which humanistic and positivist tendencies have collided with the imperatives of revelation. True, this collision is unprecedented in the profound impact and the havoc it wreaked upon the intellectual and structural make-up of the traditional Islamic legal systems. But the tension between reason and revelation—that is, between human considerations of man's own welfare in this life, on the one hand, and divine intervention and decree, on the other—has been consistently present since Muhammad migrated to Medina.[33]

5.2.2 *On Jurisdiction*

Besides the divisive policies of the juristic and political authorities, their presence proved to be complementary and crucial in the endeavours to administer the growing Islamic empires ever since the death of the Prophet. A united Islamic community was the ultimate prerequisite to survive in a hostile environment and to safeguard its expansion. Most Muslim emigrants were Arabs having left their homeland to serve their religion in the new Muslim lands in the Middle East.[34] Other non-religious motives had also pushed these first settlers of the garrison cities out of the Arabian Peninsula, such as hunger, poverty, and demographic expansion.[35] The early Umayyad dynasty did favour the position of Arab tribes above non-Arab peoples and the departure from the egalitarian norms which the sacred texts provided.[36] Since the end of the Umayyad dynasty where primarily Arab interests had been served, the tribal differences among Muslims blurred and an undivided Islamic community established itself in juxtaposition to the other great empires at that time.[37] This unity found its political representation through, in the first place the Caliphate, and later onwards under the Ottomans, through the sultanate. Especially from the Abbasid dynasty, transcending the Arab privileges of the previous leaderships

---

33 Hallaq, A history of Islamic legal theories: an introduction to Sunni usul al-fiqh, at 255.

34 Patricia Crone, 'The early Islamic world', in Kurt Raaflaub & Nathan Rosenstein (eds), War and society in the ancient and medieval worlds: Asia, the Mediterranean, Europe, and Mesoamerica (Harvard University Press 1999), at 312.

35 Edward Hotaling, Islam without illusions: its past, its present, and its challenges for the future (Syracuse University Press 2003), at 100.

36 Wael B. Hallaq, The origins and evolution of Islamic law (Cambridge University Press 2006), at 180.

37 Gerasimos P. Makris, Islam in the Middle East: a living tradition (Blackwell Publishing 2007), at 45.

restored the initial doctrine of Islam having rather a communitarian aspiration to assemble all peoples through its faith.[38] Therefore, the establishment of an Islamic community was necessary to clearly differentiate the outside chaotic world of lawlessness from the Islamic world where the Islamic community and its leaders could implement the divine laws peacefully.[39]

However, only some interpretations of the Islamic laws have been authoritative enough to claim their universality.[40] Strictly speaking, the universal nature of Islamic law only has a personal character and binds all Muslims, including the leaderships of those territories under Muslim sovereignty.[41] Such Islamic conscience creates duties and rights for Muslims, not only vertically between God and the Muslims as revealed within the sacred texts but also in its horizontal application among the Muslims themselves.[42] As an ideal unity[43] represented in the oneness of God and its creation, the harmony reached through the *ummah's* consciousness integrated people's conscience and the textual conscience. In terms of salvation, the nurturing force of the *ummah* had to spread so it could transcend the natural differences that have been exploited by humanity.[44] Nevertheless, the intention to assemble peoples under the same Islamic religion, changed into disunity whenever the invitation to embrace the truth of Islam has been rejected by other religions.[45] Within such world order, it was necessary to profile the Islamic religion as distinctive from other faiths,[46] as the other faiths did also profile themselves as being distinctive from Islam.

---

38 Edward Mortimer, Faith and power: the politics of Islam (Faber and Faber 1982), at 40.

39 Muhammad Mumtaz Ali, The concepts of Islamic Ummah & Shariah (Pelanduk Publications 1992), at 4.

40 Fred Halliday, Islam and the myth of confrontation: religion and politics in the Middle East (I.B. Tauris 2003), at 115.

41 Aharon Layish, Islamic law in the contemporary Middle East (Centre of Near & Middle Eastern Studies, School of Oriental and African Studies, University of London 1989), at 1.

42 Mahmoud M. Ayoub, Islam: faith and history (Oneworld 2004), at 220.

43 W. Montgomery Watt, Islam and the integration of society (Routledge & Kegan Paul 1966), at 90.

44 Frederick M. Denny, 'The problem of salvation in the Quran: key terms and concepts', in Arnold H. Green (ed), In quest of an Islamic humanism: Arabic and Islamic studies in memory of Mohamed al-Nowaihi (The American University in Cairo Press 1986), at 207.

45 Peter Antes, 'Relations with the unbelievers in Islamic theology', in Annemarie Schimmel & Abdoldjavad Falaturi (eds), We believe in one God: the experience of God in Christianity and Islam (Burns & Oates 1979), at 103.

46 W. Montgomery Watt, Islamic revelation in the modern world (Edinburgh University Press 1969), at 99–100.

In this respect, the Qur'an is particularly illustrative of this privileged belonging as well as the rights and responsibilities to preserve the *ummah*:

> And hold fast, all together, by the rope which Allah (stretches out for you), and be not divided among yourselves; and remember with gratitude Allah's favour on you; for ye were enemies and He joined your hearts in love, so that by His Grace, ye became brethren; and ye were on the brink of the pit of Fire, and He saved you from it. Thus doth Allah make His Signs clear to you: that ye may be guided. (Q3:103)

> Be not like those who are divided amongst themselves and fall into disputations after receiving Clear Signs: for them is a dreadful penalty. (Q3:105)

> Ye are the best of peoples, evolved for mankind, enjoining what is right, forbidding what is wrong, and believing in Allah. If only the People of the Book had faith, it were best for them: among them are some who have faith, but most of them are perverted transgressors. (Q3:110)

This Islamic conscience defined any opposition against it as part of a strategy to destroy their Islamic community both from within as from outside. This conscience was particularly raised whenever conflicts occurred and where the Islamic leadership and authority had been challenged. In this respect, from its early establishment, non-Muslims, such as the Jews and the Byzantine Christians feared the Islamic community and launched first attacks against their new neighbours. As a matter of self-defence, Muslims took those necessary measures against the aggressors. Also from the Middle Ages, Western crusades[47] in and the later Western colonisation of the Muslim lands from the nineteenth century onwards, created further tensions between the Muslims and the West.[48] The frustration felt ever since by Muslims which were divided by the West's intervention and occupation in their territories continued to manifest itself through the establishment of secular nation states.[49] Those modernisation projects were considered as other attempts to continue to divide both

47 Françoise Micheau, 'Les croisades vue par les historiens arabes d'hier et d'aujourd'hui', in Françoise Micheau (ed), Les relations des pays d'islam avec le monde latin: du milieu du Xe siècle au milieu du XIIIe siècle (Editions Jacques Marseille 2000), at 67.

48 John L. Esposito, The Islamic threat: myth or reality? (Oxford University Press 1999), at 17.

49 John L. Esposito, Unholy war: terror in the name of Islam (Oxford University Press 2002), at 40.

the territory and identity of Muslim peoples.[50] Although the sacred texts have always acknowledged the natural division between humanity as a whole and the privileged community of Muslims, the territorial fiction as produced by the early Islamic jurists continued to serve its purpose to defend Islam against any aggression or even to expand Islam according to today's Islamic extremists.[51] Instead, the complementary reality of God's creation,[52] i.e. a world of belief and a world of disbelief, has been translated into a divisive political and legal ideology as coined during the Islamic conquests and thereby projected the Muslim world to be at war with the non-Muslims.[53] Although these non-Muslims necessarily have not found the complete truth which God revealed to the Prophet or have not come under the Islamic sovereignty yet,[54] the Qur'an remains strict in regulating the waging of *jihad* against them. As part of the higher objectives of the Shari'a, i.e. *maqasid al-Shariah*, namely to command the good and forbid the evil, Muslims are encouraged not to attack first:

> Fight in the cause of Allah those who fight you, but do not transgress limits; for Allah loveth not transgressors. (Q2:190)

> To those against whom war is made, permission is given (to fight), because they are wronged;—and verily, Allah is most powerful for their aid. (Q22:39)

According to that divisive doctrine, the *dar al-harb* where non-Muslims reside and where the Islamic authority does not yet prevail, war would be a necessary means to protect the Islamic conscience from aggression. However, war could never be a moral end in itself.[55] Moreover, the Islamic faith has always acknowledged the complementarity of the tension between war and peace in the material world and more importantly also the obligation to struggle for

---

50 David Zeidan, The resurgence of religion: a comparative study of selected themes in Christian and Islamic fundamentalist discourses (Brill 2003), at 256.

51 James P. Piscatori, Islam in a world of nation-states (Cambridge University Press 1991), at 46.

52 Hamadi Redissi & Jan-Erik Lane, 'Does Islam provide a theory of violence?' in Amélie Blom, Laetitia Bucaille & Luis Martinez (eds), The enigma of Islamist violence (Hurst & Company 2007), at 27–8.

53 Bassam Tibi, 'War and peace in Islam', in Andrew G. Bostom (ed), The legacy of jihad: Islamic holy war and the fate of non-Muslims (Prometheus Books 2005), at 328.

54 Riaz Hassan, Inside Muslim minds (Melbourne University Press 2008), at 110.

55 Khaled Abou El Fadl, The great theft: wrestling Islam from the extremists (HarperCollins Publishers 2005), at 223.

a peaceful world on the spiritual level, i.e. the inner *jihad*.[56] If external *jihad* against non-Muslims was supposed to open all of humanity to Islam,[57] then how would the Qur'anic prohibition of compulsion in religion (Q2:256) continue to be respected? Also since the decolonisation of the Muslim lands, the fight led by those Islamic extremists against the secularisation of the Muslim states is considered to be waged against Muslim leaders who are viewed as stooges and foreigners corrupted by Western governments.[58] Consequently, ILW regulating armed conflicts against non-Muslims also apply to them; though, technically speaking, these political establishments are still Muslims under Islamic law. Nonetheless, from the perspective of natural law, the principles of distinction and proportionality have to be respected by all warring parties to the conflict regardless whether they are Muslims or not. The same thing can be said of the global *jihad* as a technique to externalise their allegedly internal enemies of Islam within the Muslim states in order to avoid the protection given to Muslims for wars conducted among Muslims.[59] In spite of the fragmentation of the Islamic world into nation states, the liberation of the several national *ummahs* from Western imperialism as already witnessed in the early encounters with the Byzantine Empire,[60] would find a transnational support among all *ummahs* sharing the same experiences of oppression and corruption.[61] Undeniably, the recourse to the doctrine of *dar al-Islam* and *dar al-harb* has served to legitimise such actions against the perceived infidels.[62] This Other, according to Sharma, "would be a constant ontological irritant to

56 Mary R. Habeck, Knowing the enemy: jihadist ideology and the war on terror (Yale University Press 2006), at 53.

57 Bassam Tibi, The challenge of fundamentalism: political Islam and the new world disorder (University of California Press 1998), at 54.

58 Thomas Scheffler, 'West-Eastern cultures of fear: violence and terrorism in Islam', in Kai Hafez & Mary Ann Kenny (eds), The Islamic world and the West: an introduction to political cultures and international relations (Brill 2000), at 77; Gilles Kepel, The war for Muslim minds: Islam and the West (The Belknap Press of Harvard University Press 2004), at 74.

59 Fawaz A. Gerges, The far enemy: why jihad went global (Cambridge University Press 2005), at 160.

60 Anthony Pagden, Worlds at war: the 2500-year struggle between East and West (Oxford University Press 2008), at 202.

61 Stephen Vertigans, Militant Islam: a sociology of characteristics, causes and consequences (Routledge 2009), at 71–5.

62 Andrew Wheatcroft, Infidels: the conflict between Christendom and Islam, 638–2002 (Viking 2003), at 323.

the faithful".[63] Within this purview, the Islamic conscience could again prevail against the Western globalizing and materialistic values;[64] in spite of the ethnic lines along which Muslims have started to identify themselves with, as seen in the conflicts in Afghanistan, Pakistan and the former Yugoslavia.[65]

With respect to the later modern internal armed conflicts among Muslims, it appears that the fragmentation introduced by the West through its colonisation of the Muslim lands has left a deep division along ethnic and racial lines, beyond the common religious identity of Muslims;[66] something which Muslims have already witnessed before the Umayyad dynasty whose leadership initially has been assumed by Arabs. Only later in the political history of Islam, has the leadership been shared by other peoples within the Islamic world, such as the Mughals, Persians and Turks. The real division, however, among Muslims throughout their history has rather been of a social nature where juristic, political and military establishments were dictating ordinary people.[67] The former needed to make sure that all Muslims abide by their extrapolation of rules which were derived from the sacred texts. Therefore, obedience was crucial to capitalise the universal message of Islam.[68] Any resistance from within the Islamic community against the unity of the Islamic state had to be suppressed both physically and psychologically. Under the doctrine of predestination, the Muslim masses could be controlled as the social hierarchy in which they found themselves had been determined by God.[69] Although there exists social inequality, a greater bound of solidarity would unite the Muslims and bring social change in this world, for example through *zakat*.[70] Despite these common aspirations, Islamic leaderships throughout their history have suffered from opposition and inversely have accused and oppressed

---

63 Shashi S. Sharma, Caliphs and sultans: religious ideology and political praxis (Rupa 2004), at 39.

64 Alan G. Jamieson, Faith and sword: a short history of Christian-Muslim conflict (Reaktion Books 2006), at 208.

65 Tibi, The challenge of fundamentalism: political Islam and the new world disorder, at 131.

66 Zubair Murshed, 'Power and identity in the discourse of jihad', (2003) 7 Gender Technology and Development, 399, at 412.

67 Patricia Crone, Medieval Islamic political thought (Edinburgh University Press 2004), at 355.

68 Tilman Nagel & Thomas Thornton, The history of Islamic theology: from Muhammad to the present (Markus Wiener 2000), at 35 and 57.

69 Ignáz Goldziher, Bernard Lewis, Andras Hamori & Ruth Hamori, Introduction to Islamic theology and law (Princeton University Press 1981), at 84.

70 Khurram Murad & Abdur Rashid Siddiqui, Inter-personal relations: an Islamic perspective (Islamic Foundation 2005), at 2.

violently their opponents under the guise of the defence of their own vision of Islamic values.[71] Technically, ILW remained applicable for those armed conflicts among Muslims. However, based on the claimed sovereign legitimacy of the Islamic leadership, it could determine the rebellious Other as brigands, i.e. *muharibun*, and consequently circumvent the protection which ILW guaranteed for those Muslims fighting its rule.

> And fight them on until there is no more tumult or oppression, and there prevail justice and faith in Allah. But if they cease, let there be no hostility except to those who practise oppression. (Q2:193)

> Allah's Apostle said, "A Muslim is a brother of another Muslim, so he should not oppress him, nor should he hand him over to an oppressor. Whoever fulfilled the needs of his brother, Allah will fulfill his needs; whoever brought his (Muslim) brother out of a discomfort, Allah will bring him out of the discomforts of the Day of Resurrection, and whoever screened a Muslim, Allah will screen him on the Day of Resurrection."[72]

> The Prophet said, "It is obligatory for one to listen to and obey (the ruler's orders) unless these orders involve one disobedience (to Allah); but if an act of disobedience (to Allah) is imposed, he should not listen to or obey it."[73]

In today's conflicts across the Islamic world in general and the Middle East in particular, one witnesses strong oppositions between the central authorities and local constituencies. The brutality of the autocratic regimes suppresses the voices of its political and religious opponents. Ethnic and racial divisions, as once introduced by Western colonialism, have even further highlighted the polarisation between different groups in those societies. In Afghanistan and Pakistan, rebellious forces challenge the Western interventionist forces as well as the central governments because of their corruption and lack of piety or even apostacy. Such opposition has been violently crushed as for example in 2009 in the Swat valley of Pakistan. The transnational nature of the conflict in South Asia makes its even more difficult to have recourse to IHL and ILW instead offers an unique opportunity to regulate the conduct of hostilities not

71 Javaid Rehman, Islamic state practices, international law and the threat from terrorism: a critique of the "clash of civilizations" in the new world order (Hart 2005), at 59.

72 Al-Bukhari, Vol. 3, Book 43, Number 622. (Narrated by 'Abdullah bin Umar)

73 Al-Bukhari, Vol. 4, Book 52, Number 203. (Narrated by Ibn 'Umar)

on the basis of territoriality, i.e. international and non-international armed conflicts, but rather on the basis of personal jurisdiction, i.e. war between Muslim believers and non-Muslims. Also the 2011 Arab Spring exposed the unsustainability of dictatorial rule upon the general populace. Although their existence relied in part on the international support especially from Western countries, popular resistance has questioned the legitimacy of its rule. As a response, those voices have been undermined and denounced as terrorist attempts to destabilise the respective countries and their regimes, such as in Libya and Syria. The continued violence in the Horn of Africa equally shows proof of the conflict between rebellions and central authorities in Somalia. All Muslims are bound by Islamic law and certain protective measures are imposed during warfare. However, the qualification of such conflict largely depends on the strongest party to the conflict, namely to recognise the cause of its opponents and afford them the necessary protection under the jurisdictional regimes of the laws of war.

5.2.3 *On Distinction*

All human beings are equal before God and no distinction in treatment during warfare can be made;[74] except between combatants, i.e. those participating in the armed hostilities, and non-combatants.[75] Both in external and internal *jihad*, this communitarian and naturalist principle of distinction between combatants and civilians has been sanctioned by several *hadiths*[76] but can be set aside whenever dictated by military necessity. This is the case when the enemy violates this same principle; then Islamic fighters can as a matter of reciprocity violate likewise yet proportionate to the violation by the enemy. This sovereignty argument of necessity has also been guided by ideological motivations and classifications of the enemy. The Other necessarily has threatened the Islamic community from outside or even from within. Most asymmetrical conflicts, such as the Israeli-Palestinian one, translate the frustration of the oppressed peoples both internally and externally and justify the violation of principles of protection such as distinction/discrimination by shifting the responsibility of collateral damage of innocent civilians upon

74 M. Kheir Ereksoussi, 'Le Coran et les conventions humanitaires', (1960) 503 International Review of the Red Cross, 641, at 644.

75 James J. Busuttil, '"Slay them wherever you find them": humanitarian law in Islam', (1991) 30 Revue de Droit Militaire et de Droit de la Guerre, 111, at 122.

76 For example: Al-Bukhari, Vol. 4, Book 52, Number 257. (Narrated by 'Abdullah) and Al-Bukhari, Vol. 4, Book 52, Number 280. (Narrated by Abu Sa'id Al-Khudri)

the enemy's fault to have involved its populace within such conflict.[77] Others, however, like the Persian (Isma'ili) Nizaris, launched discriminatory targetted killings or assassinations against their enemies, consequently avoiding a lot of bloodshed.[78] The Qur'an also prescribes this very issue where the Muslims can punish the enemy who has been aggressive against the Islamic community but within the limits of proportionality.

> The prohibited month for the prohibited month,—and so for all things prohibited,—there is the law of equality. If then any one transgresses the prohibition against you, transgress ye likewise against him. But fear Allah, and know that Allah is with those who restrain themselves. (Q2:194)

However, as part of commanding the good and forbidding the evil, Muslim fighters should spare those who are not participating in the armed conflict and use only force against other combatants.[79] Performing this main objective by adhering to the principle of distinction during external and internal *jihad*, the enemy necessarily can be persuaded of the communitarian and naturalist values of Islam to honour life and of the moral conduct of Muslim fighters who are defending the Islamic community against aggressors from outside and inside the *ummah*. On the other hand, the Revelation is not blind to the threats posed against the Islamic faith and consequently accepts belligerent reprisals against the enemies of Islam as a just cause.[80] Because *jihad* is, ideally, aimed at opening the whole of humanity to the goodness of Islam, the Qur'an necessarily recognises reciprocity and apparently expects the Other, the enemy of Islam, as a matter of natural law recognised by all peoples and civilisations of the world, to respect ILW although, *in sensu stricto*, Islamic law is only applicable to Muslims. This is also the case where the central Islamic authorities considered their Muslim enemies inside the *ummah* to be no longer Muslims and to have fallen outside the scope of protection of ILW. Nonetheless, in view of demonstrating tolerance and patience towards the external and internal Other

---

77 John Kelsay, 'Islam and the distinction between combatants and noncombatants', in James Turner Johnson & John Kelsay (eds), Cross, crescent, and sword: the justification and limitation of war in Western and Islamic tradition (Greenwood Press 1990), at 208–9.

78 Marshall Goodwin Simms Hodgson, The venture of Islam: conscience and history in a world civilization (The University of Chicago Press 1974), at 137.

79 Seyyed Hossein Nasr, 'Islam and the question of violence', in Aftab Ahmad Malik (ed), With God on our side: politics and theology of the war on terrorism (Amal Press 2005), at 274–75.

80 Maimul Ahsan Khan, Human rights in the Muslim world: fundamentalism, constitutionalism, and international politics (Carolina Academic Press 2003), at 133.

which has become externalised, the Qur'an calls for a balanced and proportional attitude in warfare instead of justifying dehumanising discourses that curtail those objectives.

> Invite (all) to the Way of thy Lord with wisdom and beautiful preaching; and argue with them in ways that are best and most gracious: for thy Lord knoweth best, who have strayed from His Path, and who receive guidance. (Q16:125)
>
> And if ye do catch them out, catch them out no worse than they catch you out: But if ye show patience, that is indeed the best (course) for those who are patient. (Q16:126)

Some *hadiths* as well as recorded orders of the early Caliphs explicitly call for the respect of the principle of distinction, for example:

> During some of the Ghazawat of the Prophet a woman was found killed. Allah's Apostle disapproved the killing of women and children.[81]
>
> Do not kill a minor child or an old man of advanced age or a woman.[82]
>
> Do not kill an old man or a woman or a minor.[83]

5.3 Necessity and Proportionality

5.3.1 *Actions of Warfare*

From the analysis of the application of the different jurisdictional regimes of ILW which regulate the conduct of armed hostilities in the external and internal *jihad*, it is clear that throughout the history of Islam the authority to choose and to call for the observation of these legal regimes which provide the necessary protection, in particular towards non-combatants, has been subject to the classification and dehumanisation of the enemy to Islam. Given the continuous threats the Islamic empires faced from outside and within the Islamic community, violence became normalised and the doctrines on the laws of war

81 Al-Bukhari, Vol. 4, Book 52, Number 257. (Narrated by 'Abdullah)

82 Abu Bakr cited in Muhammad Hamidullah, Muslim conduct of state (Sh. Muhammed Ashraf 1961), at 307.

83 Umar cited in Id., at 309.

reflected the divisions which the practice has created. Although this division of the world into the abode of Islam and abode of war, as introduced by the jurists under the Abbasid dynasty, had no textual support whatsoever within the sacred texts, it started to live its own reality serving the leadership at a given moment to divide and rule over peoples across both abodes.[84] At the discretion of the Islamic leadership, the conflicts against their opponents both internally and externally could be classified as threats against the religion and trigger the application of the laws of war regulating respectively the internal and external *jihad*.

On the one hand, given the necessities of warfare and as a matter of reciprocity, the principle of distinction is difficult to be observed in particular when the Other has violated this same principle of discrimination against the Muslim population. In fact, the Qur'an permits reciprocity in warfare.[85] On the other hand, Islam, in order to convince non-Muslims or those who have renounced Islam such as the apostates, wants to promote the good and forbid the evil. Such Islamic conscience would necessarily attract many new (and old) members to follow the straight path (again). For the sake of demonstrating this balance which Islam stands for, during armed conflicts, Islam allows the lifting of a prohibition to attack non-combatants as a matter of revenge but would limit its fighters in their reprisals.[86] It is against this background that it becomes clear that Islam restrains fighting and wants to avoid a vicious circle of violence against its enemies, especially while it is being faced with the challenges to protect its community of followers. Though there seems to be a conflict between the protection of the *ummah* and the avoidance of endless reprisals, the task, however, of Islam is to approximate the ultimate objective to command the good and to forbid the evil. In this respect, violence necessarily would not be the ultimate means to achieve this end or to settle this tension at the expense of a balanced approach during armed hostilities.

In addition, as with the actual application of the rules of the different jurisdictional regimes, the proportionate or balanced conduct of warfare necessarily will be affected by the image of the "Islamic" Self and its neglected Other; even if this Other violates ILW and hence calls for retaliation on behalf of the Muslim fighters. If in the first place the fictional division of the world in conflicting terms already departs from the complementary reality of the world of belief and disbelief as revealed in the Qur'an, then such legal justification outside the sacred text would give voice again to the interests of the rulers

84 Marcel A. Boisard, L'humanisme de l'islam (Albin Michel 1979), at 214.

85 See for example Q2:191.

86 See Q2:190.

to divide and dominate their Others. In this regard, under the guise of a continuously changing public interest, i.e. *maslaha*, and on the basis of military necessity, prevalence can be given to the Islamic cause which is alleged to be under threat by the enemy. Consequently, disproportionate violence has always taken place throughout the history of Islam; from the Arab conquests, the Mongol invasions, the World Wars until the present Global War on Terror and Arab Spring.[87] And obedience to the (Islamic) leadership would prevent any criticism to challenge such indiscriminate and disproportionate actions in warfare.

5.3.2 *On Necessity*

In case of emergency, the prohibition of disproportionate actions against the enemy can be overridden, i.e. *al-darura tubih al-mahzurat.*[88] *Darura*, i.e. necessity, has been developed, based on Qur'anic principles,[89] by jurists to allow for certain actions which are normally prohibited.[90] When this urgent and public need, such as the defence of Muslims, has not been met, then the *ummah* might even face worse consequences instead.[91] Military necessity is usually invoked to protect the public good of the *ummah*, i.e. *maslaha*, and to justify reprisals in case of violations of the laws of war by the enemy as a matter of reciprocity.[92] In warfare, the conditions under which such military necessity is allowed is unclear and subject to discussion. In this discussion, from the doctrinal point of view, it is possible that a changed custom itself can set aside the prevailing authoritative doctrines.[93] The particularity of a custom as developed by the diverse communities within the *ummah* can advance a contextualised answer to the universalising opinions of the central juristic authorities. From the practical point of view, on the battlefield, the asymmetrical position of the Muslim fighters can push them into having recourse to less conventional

87 Ye'or Bat, Islam and dhimmitude: where civilizations collide (Fairleigh Dickinson University Press 2002), at 48–9.

88 Tibi, 'War and peace in Islam', in, at 331.

89 See for example Q2:173.

90 Ihsan Yilmaz, 'Inter-madhhab surfing, neo-ijtihad, and faith-based movement leader', in Peri J. Bearman, Rudolph Peters & Frank E. Vogel (eds), The Islamic school of law: evolution, devolution, and progress (Harvard University Press 2005), at 193.

91 Mohammad Muslehuddin, Islamic jurisprudence and the rule of necessity and need (Islamic Research Institute 1975), at 62.

92 Sohail H. Hashmi, 'Saving and taking life in war: three modern Muslim views', in Jonathan E. Brockopp (ed), Islamic ethics of life: abortion, war, and euthanasia (University of South Carolina Press 2003), at 146–47.

93 Hallaq, Authority, continuity and change in Islamic law, at 231.

means and methods of warfare such as indiscriminate weaponry or terrorist actions. The use of fire weapons in urban combat in the early Islamic military campaigns, is an illustration thereof;[94] despite its prohibition based on the belief that only God has the prerogative to punish with fire, as indicated in the following *hadith*:

> Allah's Apostle sent us in a mission (i.e. an army-unit) and said, "If you find so-and-so and so-and-so, burn both of them with fire." When we intended to depart, Allah's Apostle said, "I have ordered you to burn so-and-so and so-and-so, and it is none but Allah Who punishes with fire, so, if you find them, kill them."[95]

Moreover, the symbolic value of such warfare—deemed to be necessary for the Muslims to challenge and to defend the enemy—inflicts fear upon this aggressive Other and rallies the support of all members of the Islamic community for its religious cause. In particular, Islamic extremists have exploited this dichotomy between the Self and the Other[96] and attracted many foreign fighters to confront Western intervention in their peripheries, such as in Afghanistan, Iraq and the former Yugoslavia.[97] For example, according to al-Zarqawi, one of the former leaders of al-Qaeda, those infidels who are unwilling to conclude peace with the Muslims can not be protected against targeting unless for the most vulnerable such as children and women.[98] Likewise for armed conflicts among Muslims, if the enemy violates the commands of God, then, as a matter of belligerent reprisal, Muslim fighters have to ensure that their Muslim enemies comply again with God's commands.[99] Within such internal or even external *jihad* it is possible that innocent believers get killed by other Muslims. For example when Muslim captives used as human shields have been killed.[100] Their death, as part of the doctrine of predestination, would be justified to

94 Hugh Kennedy, The armies of the caliphs: military and society in the early Islamic state (Routledge 2005), at 177.

95 Al-Buhkari, Vol. 4, Book 52, Number 259. (Narrated by Abu Huraira)

96 Amélie Blom, Laetitia Bucaille & Luis Martinez, 'Introduction: imaginaires of Islamist violence', in Amélie Blom, Laetitia Bucaille & Luis Martinez (eds), The enigma of Islamist violence (Hurst & Company 2007), at 16–17.

97 Jean-Pierre Filiu, Les frontières du jihad (Fayard 2006), at 283.

98 Devin R. Springer, James L. Regens & David N. Edger, Islamic radicalism and global jihad (Georgetown University Press 2009), at 176.

99 Q49:9.

100 Mawil Izzi Dien, Islamic law: from historical foundations to contemporary practice (Edinburgh University Press 2004), at 89.

protect Islam and achieve the military victory over the Other who threatened the Islamic religion.[101] Also, the destruction of property is permissible if it could not be avoided in the conduct of the hostilities.[102] Beyond the killing and destruction of the Other, throughout the history of Islam, Muslim fighters themselves have wilfully used their bodies as means/weapons of warfare and have killed themselves for God's cause.[103] Islamic extremists, such as Hasan al-Banna, one of the founding fathers of the Muslim Brotherhood (al-Ikhwan al-Muslimun) in Egypt, glorified the death of suicidal terrorist action and allegedly found a legal justification within the Qur'anic text,[104] such as:

> Let those fight in the cause of Allah Who sell the life of this world for the hereafter. To him who fighteth in the cause of Allah,—whether he is slain or gets victory—soon shall We give him a reward of great (value). (Q4:74)

Man thus becomes a weapon for the cause of God and should be awarded in heaven. It remains to be seen whether as a method of warfare under ILW, suicide missions are really permissible or treacherous as they would also violate the principle to distinguish civilian from combatant status and also goes against the general prohibition of suicide under Islamic law. In this regard, according to Munir, suicide bombers commit at least five crimes under Islamic law, namely, "killing civilians, mutilating their bodies, violating the trust of enemy soldiers and civilians, committing suicide and destroying civilian objects or properties".[105] Indeed, the Qur'an adds that:

> Whether open or secret; take not life, which Allah hath made sacred, except by way of justice and law: thus doth He command you, that ye may learn wisdom. (Q6:151)

5.3.3 *On Proportionality*

The higher objective of Islam is to command the good and to forbid the evil. Even within the context of warfare, the Qur'an desires to make peace above

---

101 Monte Palmer & Princess Palmer, At the heart of terror: Islam, jihadists, and America's war on terrorism (Rowman & Littlefield Publishers 2004), at 142.

102 Muhammad Zafrulla Khan, Islam: its meaning for modern man (Routledge & Kegan Paul 1980), at 178.

103 See Bernard K. Freamon, 'Martyrdom, suicide, and the Islamic law of war: a short legal history', (2003–2004) 27 Fordham International Law Journal, 299.

104 Towqueer Alam Falahi, The Quranic concept of war and peace (Kanishka Publishers 2004), at 68.

105 Muhammed Munir, 'Suicide attacks and Islamic law', (2008) 90 International Review of the Red Cross, 71, at 71.

killing and bloodshed.[106] In view of persuading new (and old) followers to join the Islamic community (again), from the early Islamic conquests onwards, Islamic warfare necessarily had its limitation to achieve its religious cause, i.e. to protect the Islamic religion from aggression. Therefore, deliberate destruction and massacres were generally excluded[107] as well as the extension of the conflict when peace could be concluded. In spite of the unavoidable calamities of warfare suffered by all parties to the conflict as witnessed for example by the extensive number of Arab casualties during the early Islamic age,[108] the peaceful and egalitarian message as carried out by Islamic conquerors, in particular under the Ottomans, has helped in extending the abode of peace and in spreading the Islamic religion beyond its initial boundaries.[109] During warfare, it is believed that God is watching and approving His fighters' steadfastness to this higher objective of self-restraint and justice.[110] Muslim fighters who on their own initiative have persevered in their just conduct towards their enemies will be rewarded by God. The same attitude is required in their reaction to the enemies' violation of their self-imposed natural law principles of protection; belligerent reprisals have to be proportionate to the crimes inflicted upon the Muslims. Muslim fighters are personally responsible for their actions and intentions before God.[111] Only God can see whether their conduct has been righteous toward the enemies. This principle of proportionality is well reflected in the following Qur'anic provisions:

> And if ye do catch them out, catch them out no worse than they catch you out: But if ye show patience, that is indeed the best (course) for those who are patient. (Q16:126)

> Help ye one another in righteousness and piety, but help ye not one another in sin and rancour: fear Allah. For Allah is strict in punishment. (Q5:2)

106 Rudolph Peters, Jihad in medieval and modern Islam: the chapter on jihad from Averroes' legal handbook "Bidayat al-mudjtahid" and the treatise "Koran and fighting" by the late Shaykh al-Azhar Mahmud Shaltut (Brill 1977), at 27.

107 Hugh Kennedy, The great Arab conquests: how the spread of Islam changed the world we live in (Weidenfeld & Nicolson 2007), at 372–73.

108 Michael Lecker, 'On the burial of martyrs in Islam', in Hiroyuki Yanagihashi (ed), The concept of territory in Islamic law and thought (Kegal Paul International 2000), at 37.

109 Dankwart A. Rustow, 'Political ends and military means in the late Ottoman and post-Ottoman Middle East', in Vernon John Parry & Malcolm E. Yapp (eds), War, technology and society in the Middle East (Oxford University Press 1975), at 386–87.

110 Khan, Islam: its meaning for modern man, at 179.

111 John Kelsay, Arguing the just war in Islam (Harvard University Press 2007), at 193.

> Every soul will be (held) in pledge for its deeds. (Q74:38)

> For Allah is with those who restrain themselves, and those who do good. (Q16:128)

Advocating human dignity during armed hostilities as part of adhering to this higher objective to command the good and to forbid the evil, has in reality not always been that successful. Again, the normative construction of the Other along different jurisdictional regimes has influenced the application of the principle of proportionality. Clearly, beyond the doctrinal and textual promises to respect the Other lies a more cruel reality where the interests to wage war against the enemies have determined, from the outset, the attitude towards the enemies of Islam. In this regard, invoking military necessity as a legal excuse can overcome the primary obligations to respect innocent life for the sake of defending the *ummah*. In Sunni Islam, such determination of public interest, i.e. *maslaha*, remains at the discretion of juristic and political authorities; in Shi'i Islam, similar recourse to the argument of preserving the Islamic state is usually raised by the political authority.[112] The legal indeterminacy of the necessity and/or public interest is a powerful tool to divide and rule which at any time can be used by the leaders within the Islamic community to deny the protection which the sacred texts provide to all members of humanity who are involved in armed conflicts with the believers.

5.4 Back to Tradition

5.4.1 *Confronting the Evil*

Throughout the history of Islam, the identity politics, which divided the "Islamic" Self from its Other, have always been manipulated by many establishments whether they were of juristic, military, political, or religious nature. In order to divide and rule over their opponents and even their own subjects, these authorities became authoritarian in their reading of the authoritative sacred texts. They used their reason to extract the meaning of those texts in such a manner that the text became constructed according to their benefit; while the text only is supposed to have the sole authority given its Revelation

112 Sohrab Bedhad, 'Islam, revivalism and public policy', in Sohrab Behdad & Farhad Nomani (eds), Islam and public policy (JAI Press 1997), at 14.

by the God, who, to Muslims, is the only sovereign in this world.[113] Again the tension between the rationalist and the traditionalists emerged in this extraction of the rules from the Qur'an and the Sunnah as respectively translated in the doctrine of acquisition and of creation. *In sensu largo*, the utilitarian attitude of the establishments to serve their own interests before those of the community and those of others confirms, somehow, their interpretation of the texts in order to realise their own understanding of justice; while according to the traditionalists such prerogatives only belong to God.[114] Hence, in practice as understood from the dominant rationalist perspective, the whole process of establishing Islamic law, i.e. *ijtihad*, can merely be the approximation of the actual revealed laws.[115] The authority attributed to the law as extracted by the jurists from the sacred texts not only sanctioned those texts, but transferred the original sovereignty which resides in God alone into the human world where the revealed law instead, as interpreted by the jurists, became representative of that sovereignty. Thus, it has been argued that the Islamic community has become a nomocracy.[116] In this view, jurists only have intended to approximate the higher objective to command the good and to forbid the evil. But the jurist also introduced new legal concepts, such as the *dar al-Islam* and *dar al-harb*, which allegedly were sanctioned by the scriptures.[117] Their interpretation of the sacred instead of the texts themselves became authoritative and has, *de facto*, put the jurists at the source of the laws they have created. If in theory the jurists stand above the laws they have created, then, from an egalitarian perspective, they also lack the authority to impose them upon others.[118]

The juristic interpretations started to live their own reality as in their turn they would be reflective of the situation on the battlefield which has found its justification/legitimation in their divisive doctrines. Such hermeneutic rationalisations created a new reality alleged to be sanctioned by the sacred texts and were understood to be necessary to face the challenges the Islamic

113 Khaled Abou El Fadl, The authoritative and authoritarian in Islamic discourses: a contemporary study (Al-Saadawi Publications 2002), at 56.

114 Majid Khadduri, The Islamic conception of justice (Johns Hopkins University Press 1984), at 54–9.

115 Bernard G. Weiss, 'Interpretation in Islamic law: the theory of ijtihad', (1977–1978) 26 American Journal of Comparative Law, 199, at 205.

116 Wael B. Hallaq, '"Muslim rage" and Islamic law', (2003) 54 Hastings Law Journal, 1705, at 1707.

117 Norman Calder, Studies in early Muslim jurisprudence (Clarendon Press 1993), at 218.

118 Ahmad Atif Ahmad, Structural interrelations of theory and practice in Islamic law: a study of six works of medieval Islamic jurisprudence (Brill 2006), at 14.

empires met from within and outside their boundaries.[119] In warfare, *darura*, i.e. military necessity, and *maslaha*, i.e. the public good, were examples of such seemingly objective concepts which could bypass the tolerant attitude towards the internal and external enemies of Islam and which could serve the particular subjective preferences of only a few.[120] Also the methodologies by which the jurists linked the text with the context and vice versa have given them enormous power to create and change realities within and beyond the text. For example, *istishab*, is a method to rationalise the (non-)existence of certain rules which allows for, or prevents, new ones to be created. Such permissibility is central to Islamic law: everything is allowed unless forbidden.[121] Clearly, reason can possibly justify and create any law unless already explicitly forbidden. Hence, the law and reason are closely connected.[122]

Within the Islamic legal sciences, the relative and limited power of rationality[123] seems to be equated with the absolute truth it wants to extract.[124] Because of its authoritativeness, the dangers of utilitarianism can lead to the realisation of interests of the "Islamic" Self alone at the expense of the other members of humanity.[125] From the early beginnings of the history of Islam, the appeal to rationalise one's personal wishes through analogical reasoning was part of an open attitude stimulating the access to knowledge.[126] Later onwards, however, when the compilation of the Sunnah came into existence, reference to scriptures somehow limited the unbound exercise of *ijtihad*.[127] Although

119 Ebrahim Moosa, 'Languages of change in Islamic law: redefining death in modernity', in Ravindra S. Khare (ed), Perspectives on Islamic law, justice, and society (Rowman & Littlefield 1999), at 163.

120 M. Cherif Bassiouni & Gamal M. Badr, 'The Sharia'h: sources, interpretation, and rule-making', (2002) 1 UCLA Journal of Islamic and Near Eastern Law, 135, at 158.

121 Mohammad Hashim Kamali, Principles of Islamic jurisprudence (Islamic Texts Society 2003), at 395–96.

122 Abu al-Fazl Izzati, An introduction to Shi'i Islamic law and jurisprudence with an emphasis on the authority of human reason as a source of law according to Shi'i law (Ashraf Press 1976), at 15.

123 Muhammad Mumtaz Ali, Islam and the Western philosophy of knowledge: reflections on some aspects (Pelanduk Publications 1994), at 89–90.

124 Noel James Coulson, Conflicts and tensions in Islamic jurisprudence (University of Chicago Press 1969), at 6.

125 Murtada Mutahhari, Understanding Islamic sciences: philosophy, theology, mysticism, morality, jurisprudence (ICAS Press 2002), at 198.

126 Faruqi al-Isma'il, 'Islam as culture and civilization', in Salem Azzam (ed), Islam and contemporary society (Longman 1982), at 150.

127 Ahmad Hasan, Analogical reasoning in Islamic jurisprudence: a study of the juridical principle of qiyas (Adam 1994), at 27.

people make the law, the Qur'an remains the constitution. The function of the juristic authorities to elaborate on the law necessarily has transferred the sovereignty of the law upon them. They would represent the *ijma*, i.e. the will of the community.[128] It is accepted that such contextualisation of Islamic law in its elaboration is useful to accommodate the revealed text to the changing circumstances; however, it can never be fully free from the selfish interests of those establishments who are giving their own interpretations.[129] It remains difficult to entirely change this selfish human condition for the benefit of humanity as a whole. Though, the reality of warfare necessarily demonstrates such tension in the duality of human nature, namely to know one another, as indicates Q49:13, is a pedagogical task.[130]

Not only has the juristic division of the world into the abode of war and abode of peace been an example of denying the need for solidarity between all members of humanity, the practical violation of the principles of protection such as distinction and proportionality during armed hostilities is another illustration where identity politics have continued to have their effects within this legal fiction. Within this context of war, it would be justifiable that those principles could be set aside upon the basis of military necessity. The perceived irrational aggressiveness of the internal and external enemies of Islam[131] can rationally necessitate, as a matter of self-defence, a response on behalf of the Muslims. If the enemy only understands a language of violence, then a likewise and reciprocal violent answer would be reasonable and hence legitimate. While this may conform with natural law, over-rationalising such violent Other justifies any legitimate action and this remains at the discretion of the authorities in place at a given moment in the history of Islam.[132] In addition, being convinced of the superiority of the "Islamic" Self towards its inferior Other contributed to such worldview whose confines need to be protected at all (humanitarian) costs. As a self-fulfilling prophecy, the relationship between the practice and the doctrine can be established by the juristic authorities whose role was to reconcile both ends for the sake of justifying warfare against their enemies under the banner of implementing the divine commands to establish world peace. Within this juristic exercise, the intention/consciousness

---

128 Ahmad Hasan, The doctrine of ijma in Islam (Islamic Research Institute 1976), at 22.

129 Yusuf Qaradawi & Al-Hadi A. Khalifa, Islamic law in the modern world (King Faisal Center for Research and Islamic Studies 2000), at 23.

130 Mohammed Arkoun, Islam: to reform or to subvert? (Saqi 2006), at 129.

131 Amyn B. Sajoo, Muslim ethics: emerging vistas (I.B. Tauris 2004), at 50.

132 Mohammed Arkoun, Pour une critique de la raison islamique (Maisonneuve et Larose 1984), at 79.

to divide the world in conflicting terms as opposed to the complementary ones of the Qur'an shows that the jurists had exclusivist agendas denying the real potential of pluralist coexistence from the outset.[133] Or as put by Tibi in the following words:

> In this sense, Muslims believe that expansion through war is not aggression but a fulfilment of the Qur'anic command to spread Islam as a way to peace. The resort to force to disseminate Islam is not war (*harb*), a word that is used only to describe the use of force by non-Muslims. Islamic wars are not *hurub* (the plural of *harb*) but rather *futuhat*, acts of "opening" the world to Islam and expressing Islamic jihad.[134]

5.4.2 *Fighting the Inner Jihad*

In spite of the natural differences between the members of humanity, the challenge of humanity is to embrace this richness and diversity.[135] What distinguishes Islam from other religions or even secularist worldviews, is the belief that God is the Creator of the universe and that His creation serves to experience the diversity as a blessing from Him. Therefore, in their relationship with all these other peoples, Muslims would see this interconnectedness of all human beings as well as their inherent solidarity between their spirits. Given this pluralistic world, some members of humanity do not believe in this blessing and rather resist it. This could lead to conflicts between Muslims and non-Muslims and also between Muslims themselves when they differ upon the path to be followed within their own belief. The legal fictions have only contributed to this tension and denied the complementarity of the creation to flourish in all its diversity. This conflict is and has been rather exploited for personal ends which violently destroys the community of humanity. In this respect, according to Nasr,

> Islam, in controlling the use of force in the direction of creating equilibrium and harmony, limits it and opposes violence as aggression to the rights of both God and His creatures as defined by the divine Law. The goal of Islam is the attainment of peace, but this peace can only be experienced through ourselves and leads to living in the world in accordance with the dicta of the Sharia. Islam seeks to enable man to live according

---

133 Ayoub, at 220–22.

134 Tibi, 'War and peace in Islam', in, at 328.

135 Nathan C. Funk & Abdul Aziz Said, Islam and peacemaking in the Middle East (Lynne Rienner Publishers 2009), at 218.

> to his theomorphic nature and not to violate that nature. Islam condones the use of force only to the extent of opposing that centripetal tendency which turns man against what he is in his inner reality. The use of force can only be condoned in the sense of undoing the violation of our own nature and the chaos which has resulted from the loss of equilibrium. But such a use of force is not in reality violence as usually understood. It is the exertion of human will and effort in the direction of conforming to the Will of God and in surrendering the human will to the divine Will. From this surrender (taslim) comes peace (salam), hence Islam, and only through this Islam can the violence inbred within the nature of fallen man be controlled and the beast within subdued so that man lives at peace with himself and the world because he lives at peace with God.[136]

Thus, God has mandated the *ummah* to be tolerant vis-à-vis and live in solidary with the other members of humanity.[137] Such communitarian and naturalist approach requires an individual and spiritual effort, i.e. an inner *jihad* to open the "Islamic" Self up to its Other;[138] namely to witness the diversity around oneself and to realise that one is part of this creation blessed with this diversity to know one another better through it. Such peaceful mindset starts with the Self first which accepts the roots of its creation, i.e. God. It has to submit to His commands to do good and to forbid the evil. It is the Qur'an which is the link between the divine and the human[139] and which convinces Muslims of the unity between God and them. This harmonious complementarity of the creation is another feature of the unity emanating from God.[140] The conscience which unites God with human beings functions as spiritual control on humanity's actions in its relations with Others, namely to treat them justly.[141] Once God has breathed His spirit into Adam,[142] i.e. the father of the human species, this spiritual conscience has its purpose to be fulfilled in the material world

136 Nasr, in, at 276.

137 Abou El Fadl, The great theft: wrestling Islam from the extremists, at 208; Ahmet Alibasic, 'The place for others in Islam', (2007) 3 Comparative Islamic Studies 98, at 101.

138 John L. Esposito, 'Struggle in Islam', in Joshua Cohen & Ian Lague (eds), The place of tolerance in Islam (Beacon Press 2002), at 76.

139 Ziauddin Sardar & Merryl Wyn Davies, Distorted imagination: lessons from the Rushdie affair (London 1990), at 88.

140 Boisard, at 84.

141 Afif Abdulfattah Tabbarah, The spirit of Islam: an interpretive survey of the foundations, graces and teachings of Islam as seen in the light of science and philosophy (Abdel-Hafiz Bsat 1978), at 199 and 353.

142 See Q15:29.

where human beings live together.[143] According to Christmann, this "'spirit of God' (memory) enabled nations to write their history self-reflectively and use historiography to enhance humankind's historical consciousness. By giving human beings knowledge and legislation, Allah initiated a qualitative jump in history: creatures turned into human beings through the acquisition of God's spirit."[144]

Such internal struggle to liberate one's heart from the material desires in the human world is a tremendous task and responsibility towards God and His creation.[145] Directing this personal trial toward the oneness of God might link the human experience again with the love for God and consequently also for other human beings which are part of His creation.[146] The search for internal peace with oneself and externally with others goes hand in hand with a lot of tensions which are complementary to this whole process of inward seeking. God shall reward those who have made the effort to find the right balance when meeting the internal and external challenges of human existence. But, as human history has shown, this internal tension to feel good with oneself and in its relationships with others has not always been that successful. Through their description of the world in conflicting terms, some Islamic jurists and theologians have somehow broken the potential solidarity between human beings. The consecutive disruption of this horizontal transcendentalism among human beings gave more authority to the jurists-theologians as they profiled themselves as the sole interlocutors between God and the believers. Moreover, their interpretation of the Qur'an is accompanied with an exclusivist rhetoric which blurs the reality of this unity of the creation. The required obedience to their rationalisation of the divine text is confused with the authority given to the Qur'an itself which constitutes the direct link between the divine and the human. Hence, the need to restore both the vertical and horizontal direct conscience/link between God and human beings respectively and among human beings themselves; so they are able to follow the righteous path/truth again, i.e. the divine will to learn from the diversity which is at the heart of human-

143 Abdur Razzaque, Prayer: for progress (Sh. Muhammad Ashraf 1967), at 48–9.

144 Andreas Christmann (ed), The Qur'an, morality and critical reason: the essential Muhammad Shahrur (Brill 2009), at 165.

145 Tariq Ramadan, Western Muslims and the future of Islam (Oxford University Press 2004), at 120.

146 Tariq Ramadan, Islam, the West and the challenges of modernity (Islamic Foundation 2001), at 61–2.

ity's existence.[147] The Golden Rule, according to Schweiker, is also another "religious expression to the imperative of responsibility, just as the symbols of creation signal the complexity of goods that constitute the moral space of life".[148]

> And among His Signs is the creation of the heavens and the earth, and the variations in your languages and your colours: verily in that are Signs for those who know. (Q30:22)

Having found inner peace, human beings are able to live in peace with the unity of creation and the other members of humanity.[149] The Qur'an teaches about the unity in diversity and not about the division of the world in artificial abodes of peace and war.[150] Accepting the membership to this spiritual and material unity does not entail to give up the existence of material diversity. However, the effort is required to give up at least those selfish attributes which prevent to find the right balance to accept oneself within the greater whole of the creation. In fact, God has bestowed the creation with a natural equilibrium which human beings simply have to live up to again and have to avoid the domination of the personal preferences above the communitarian ones from which all human beings spiritually and materially benefit.[151] Only such purified heart can witness the unity of God as lodged in His creation.[152] In this respect, not only reason could convince humanity of the unity in diversity having a divine source, but intuition as followed by the heart, as observed by Rahman, "establishes the unity of the self as an abiding reality in the midst of multiplicity".[153] Evidently, as the Qur'an realistically reveals, there will always

147 Mohammed Arkoun, Essais sur la pensée islamique (Maisonneuve et Larose 1973), at 188–91.

148 William Schweiker, Theological ethics and global dynamics: in the time of many worlds (Blackwell 2004), at 213.

149 Jacques Berque, L'islam au temps du monde (Sindbad 1984), at 254.

150 Israfil Balci, 'An Islamic approach toward international peace', in J. Dudley Woodberry, Osman Zümrüt & Mustafa Köylü (eds), Muslim and Christian reflections on peace: divine and human dimensions (University Press of America 2005), at 120.

151 Muhammad Qutb, 'What Islam can give to humanity today', in Altaf Gauhar & Islamic Council of Europe (eds), The challenge of Islam (Islamic Council of Europe 1978), at 319–20.

152 'Abdul-Qadir al-Jilani & Shaikh Tosun Bayrak al-Jerrahi al-Halveti, The secret of secrets (Islamic Texts Society 1992), at 56 and 76.

153 Syedur Rahman, An introduction to Islamic culture and philosophy (Mullick Brothers 1963), at 149.

be a world of belief and disbelief that is part of His creation and that have to live together peacefully side by side:

> To each among you have we prescribed a law and an open way. If Allah had so willed, He would have made you a single people, but (His plan is) to test you in what He hath given you: so strive as in a race in all virtues. The goal of you all is to Allah. It is He that will show you the truth of the matters in which ye dispute. (Q5:48)

> If thy Lord had so willed, He could have made mankind one people: but they will not cease to dispute. Except those on whom thy Lord hath bestowed His Mercy: and for this did He create them: and the Word of thy Lord shall be fulfilled: "I will fill Hell with jinns and men all together." (Q11:118–119)

5.4.3 *Respecting God's Creation*

Understandably, the Revelation reflects the dichotomy between the world of belief and disbelief but not necessarily in conflicting terms. The creation reflects such duality which is also found in human nature. In this respect, the tension between the sovereign Self and the community on the level of the individual is also taking place on the global level between the believers and non-believers. As with the inner spiritual *jihad*, such tension is not supposed to be settled by violence but by transcending selfishness and aligning it with the communitarian aspects of life. A freed ego necessarily unfolds creativity to peacefully accommodate the interests of the Self with those of the Others.[154] Whereas, the external and internal *jihad* against the so-called enemies of Islam, is settled through warfare. If humanity finds its inner peace, embraces the love of God and shares this love with all other members of humanity, then war will no longer be a means to achieve a world of inner and external peace. In this respect, violence becomes meaningless as it destroys the peace people have found in themselves and through each other as God has endowed them with such capability to find this peace both internally and externally. Persevering in these spiritual efforts can lead to positive results in the material world. Nonetheless, the Qur'an is aware of the duality to do good and bad things but urges humanity to develop itself for the good by following the path of God:

> And those who strive in Our (cause),—We will certainly guide them to our Paths: for verily Allah is with those who do right. (Q29:69)

154 Allama Muhammad Iqbal, The reconstruction of religious thought in Islam (Sh. Muhammad Ashraf 1968), at 123.

> Repel evil with that which is best: We are well acquainted with the things they say. (Q23:96)

Fulfilling God's promise, i.e. the text/Revelation, within the universe, i.e. context, should not be reconciled through violence/*jihad* even though violence has always been part of human history until now.[155] War would be a necessary evil as long as people are not convinced of the unity of existence created by God.[156] The struggle to balance between the two complementary ends of the duality of human nature, i.e. to do good and evil, and the world, i.e. of belief and disbelief, have to be accompanied with political and social action instead.[157] However, this struggle has been led by those authorities who found more benefits to portray the world in unbridgeable conflicting terms which could only be settled through violence with their promise that at the end of time peace would be found. Such division in order to rule has put the survival of the entire human species at stake for the benefit of those in power. Juristic authorities in particular have blurred the line between the Revelation and their human elucidations of the divine laws.[158] As self-proclaimed guardians of the sacred texts,[159] the jurists' authority on the legal traditions of warfare could not be challenged and was materialised in *ijma*, i.e. the will of Islamic community. Of course, as a community, the Muslims, throughout their history, have been the object of aggression. This historical context necessarily justified such a juristic elaboration of the divine rules which, however, went beyond the distinction of a complementary world of belief and disbelief as revealed by the Qur'an. Their legal fictions of a conflicting world of peace and of war did not bring justice to the revealed text. Despite their external facade to provide the *ummah* with such legal and political tools to defend itself against the aggressors, the authorities' intentions rather reveal a strategy to divide and rule through this permanent conflict. According to Esack, such exegetical and linguistic casuistry compels "inclusivist texts to produce exclusivist meanings".[160]

Those rationalisations of the Islamic jurisprudence only focus on the horizontal and external relationship among the members of humanity and not

155 Fazl-I-Ahmad Kuraishi, Islam: the religion of humanity (Kitab Manzil 1956), at 309.

156 Clement Huart, 'The law of war', in Andrew G. Bostom (ed), The legacy of jihad: Islamic holy war and the fate of non-Muslims (Prometheus Books 2005), at 284.

157 Mohammed Arkoun, Rethinking Islam: common questions, uncommon answers (Westview Press 1994), at 13.

158 John L. Esposito, Islam: the straight path (Oxford University Press 2005), at 227.

159 Daniel W. Brown, Rethinking tradition in modern Islamic thought (Cambridge University Press 1996), at 133.

160 Farid Esack, Qur'an, liberation and pluralism: an Islamic perspective of interreligious solidarity against oppression (Oneworld 1997), at 147.

on the vertical and internal relationship between human beings and God.[161] Instead, the jurists' interpretation of the divine law stands between the divine law and its application by the believers and prevents believers to have direct access to the truth and justice which the Qur'an has revealed to this world. The jurists' introduction of legal fictions dividing the world in conflicting terms, as influenced by the historical narrative on the "Islamic" Self and its Other, has distorted the true meaning of the Qur'an, as revealed at this particular moment in Arab history.[162] And reason portrayed as the ultimate means to access the truth of the divine commands would attribute the sole authority of jurists to actually do so. Nevertheless, all human beings can also access God not through reason only but through the heart as well. Therefore, the jurists' intermediary between God and the believers only has its anticipated effects within a paradigm which puts reason central in the endeavours to access the sacred texts and where historical data confirm the lived realities of their legal fictions. While, from the "life paradigm" which puts human conscience central in these efforts to witness the love of God in and for His creation, the relationship between God and the believers enables to transcend the artificial divisions which humanity, as part of its human nature, has introduced upon itself in order to divide and rule.

Going beyond the legal discourse as dominated by reason and juristic authorities is essential to give voice again to the human conscience, both vertically and horizontally, which is already present but which is deafened by such legal formalism. Such solidarity among all human beings can awaken humanity of the risks it has endured during its human history where it continuously has put the survival of its very kind at stake. The life bestowed by God upon His creation is a blessing. Therefore, the higher objective to command the good and to forbid the evil has to bring together human beings as true agents of their existence in this world for which they remain accountable toward their others in the here and toward God in the hereafter. Warfare and destruction, though they have been part of humanity's history, no longer have any place in the paradise on earth which God has created for the benefit of all humanity. Though God acknowledges the duality of human nature in its last Revelation, i.e. to make peace and to wage war, its last Revelation was also a reminder of the potential He has put in His creation and in human beings to find the right

161 Baber Johansen, Contingency in a sacred law: legal and ethical norms in the Muslim fiqh (Brill 1999), at 24.

162 Allahbukhsh K. Brohi, 'Islam: its political and legal principles: a proglomena to the theory and practice of politics and law', in Salem Azzam (ed), Islam and contemporary society (Longman 1982), at 97.

balance and to act with justice between the interests of the Self and the Other so they can find inner peace with the Self and the Other. The fruits of this potential lie in the human conscience to find Him and all other human beings through Him; and humanity is the bearer of those fruits. Such conscience ultimately bounds all human beings in their shared material existence and most importantly in the spiritual world where their spirit originates. Or as Ramadan concludes:

> This initial positive outlook, associated with the invitation to human conscience to remember and be thankful, is of foremost importance. It affects all the areas of human knowledge about the created Universe: a Universe that is both a gift and a "sign" fraught with meaning and its Creator.[163] [...] Humankind must, through the ethics of their actions in the world, try to remain faithful to what they have received in the very nature of their being in the world. One should therefore act faithfully and not forget to be thankful.[164]

5.5 Conclusion

This chapter has tried to establish that the identities on the "Islamic" Self and its Other have informed the creation and application of the legal fictions which jurists have constructed in order to justify and legitimatise the use of violence against the internal and external enemies of Islam. The creation of the jurisdictional regimes regulating warfare within the abode of peace, i.e. *dar al-Islam*, and the abode of war, i.e. *dar al-harb*, did provide for the universal principles of protection, i.e. those of distinction and proportionality. As almost a matter of natural law these communitarian principles had to be safeguarded against the calamities of warfare. However, these same principles are set aside by the sovereignty argument of military necessity only in those situations where the enemy has violated one of those principles first. As a response to that, Muslim fighters can retaliate but only likewise without transgressing in their actions.

Within this legal framework, jurists have attributed themselves the authority to establish the laws of war and indirectly affect the conduct of hostilities. Such power enabled them and the other interest groups in Islamic societies to divide and rule over their subjects and deny them the access to challenge

163 Tariq Ramadan, Radical reform. Islamic ethics and liberation (Oxford University Press 2009), at 104.

164 Id., at 90.

their sophisticated modes of reasoning. They have put themselves between the revealed divine texts and the Muslim populace. By inserting conflicting divisions within the interpretation of Islamic law, the jurists, albeit unintentionally, appear to have distorted the true meaning of the Qur'an which describes the world in complementary terms. The interconnectedness of all human beings necessarily was blurred through those legal fictions and humanity was made a passive receiver of them and their lived realities. Believing again in the unity of the world and its diversity as created by God is a possible avenue to see this complementarity of human existence. As freed agents, human beings can embrace God's blessing and life again for the sake of the survival of the entire species through a more naturalist reading and application of ILW.

CHAPTER VI

The Structure of the Legal Arguments in International Humanitarian Law

6.1 Introduction

The aim of this chapter is to demonstrate that the discourses on the "Western" Self and its excluded Other—as discussed in Chapter III in Part II—continue to be present in the structure of the legal arguments in IHL. Throughout the history of the West's encounter with the Other within Europe and beyond, the very dichotomies between, generally, the Christian/"civilised" and non-Christian/"barbarian", capitalist and communist, moralist and terrorist, continue to affect the interpretation and application of IHL—as examined in Chapter II of Part I. In particular, today's battlefield is marked with unbridgeable asymmetries which have perpetuated in the Western populace's mind and in its military campaigns. All over the world, such a worldview necessarily affects how the laws of armed conflict are to be interpreted and applied and how much room the laws actually give to manoeuvre between two opposing values, namely of sovereignty, i.e. necessity, and community, i.e. protection.

Although IHL seems to advocate universal values of protection by and for all peoples, its creation and application did not remain untouched by the strongest party's interest, i.e. sovereignty. The weaker parties to the conflict did manage to give voice to their more communitarian approach, i.e. to get themselves a legitimate belligerent status. In addition, their commitment for adherence to the principle of distinction and proportionality is central to their cause. However, stronger and weaker belligerent parties change over time and without hesitation man's nature soon alters its position so it can continue to divide and rule over the weaker Others. Illegitimate combatancy excludes the enemies from the protection of the jurisdictional regimes of the laws of war and military necessity justifies setting aside the principles of distinction and proportionality in the fight against these Others.

With the help of the primary sources of IHL and relevant jurisprudence, this chapter will demonstrate that the indeterminacy of the law actually favours the stronger party in armed hostilities. This chapter will also submit that those legal arguments as formulated in conflicting terms are only settled through violence. As a result, within such conflictual paradigm, the relativism between necessity and humanity threatens the very existence of human life. Instead,

 | DOI 10.1163/9789004298248_008

from the “life paradigm” one can offer a possible way to accept the complementarity of the duality of human nature, i.e. sovereignty and community oriented interests, to be put at the service of life itself, i.e. the nature of things. Therefore, this chapter will try to point out how humanity’s conscience got lost through those impersonal utilitarian discourses. Perhaps humanity can again experience the unity of its human coexistence and safeguard its survival in particular in light of the on-going armed conflicts all around the world and across the Islamic one in particular.

6.2 Jurisdiction and Distinction

6.2.1 *Agency in Warfare*

Legitimate belligerency and the principle of distinction are closely related to each other. Whenever arguments of jurisdictional regimes under IHL are raised to define or delimitate the application of the laws of armed conflict, whether it is of an international or non-international character, these legal arguments are necessarily formulated within a particular political context. Relying on this situation, policy makers, jurists and military strategists, are inclined to assess such situation which favours the course of their action against their opponents. On the one hand, international armed conflicts are regulated by the 1899–1907 Hague Regulations, the 1949 Geneva Conventions, and AP I. These conflicts have clearly defined actors, i.e. states and their militaries. These states have to act in compliance with these legal sources in as far as they have ratified them. On the other hand, it becomes more difficult when establishing the application of the laws of war for non-international armed conflict as codified by common Article 3 to the 1949 Geneva Conventions and AP II. Not all non-state belligerent parties to the conflict are necessarily recognised as belligerents legitimately fighting the central government. Nonetheless, customary international law remains applicable regardless of states’ signatory status to these conventional norms.

Attitudes towards the antagonists in conflict situations are of a rather utilitarian nature. In this regard, the overarching discourse on the Self and the enemy Other continue to play a role in influencing the actual application of the protection provided by the laws of armed conflict. As long as the identification of the conflict and of the opponent, along the legal criteria of armed hostilities, as laid out in the primary sources of IHL and as applied in (inter) national jurisprudence, favours one or the other’s political, socio-economic and humanitarian position, each protagonist can use either a sovereignty or a community based approach to reach its several objectives. As a consequence, the possibility to use violence against one's enemies, both within and outside its territory, finds its legal authority within the laws of armed conflict permitting to do so upon the condition of certain restrictions. In the case where the distinction between international and non-international armed conflicts and its participants is less clearly identified and formulated by one or the other protagonists, the conduct of the hostilities are necessarily affected by the extent to which each party regards its enemy and the latter's population. The dehumanisation which is presented discursively legitimises violent actions against the enemy Other.[1] Kennedy recognised this strategic importance of the use of IHL and in particular found that "the law of armed conflict has so often been a vocabulary used by the rich to judge the poor".[2] Apparently, the violent discourses do legitimise agency on behalf of the violent actors. According to Porter, these discourses change over the course of time but they tend to be structured along the same idea, i.e. one of a "Primordial East driven by visceral or pre-modern urges, against the West, rational and modern".[3]

In this respect, the legal arguments raised by the conflicting parties are subjected to their personal motivations and to the expectations of their social environment. This environment is supposed to have fostered some kind of group identity that contrasts with the threats of their enemies.[4] Necessarily, such positions can only be formulated within the boundaries of the laws of armed conflict. IHL itself allows such discourse to take place and to determine its application. Against the background of the emergence of Western nationalism since the nineteenth century, Western nations rationalised and used state identities for the purpose of their aggrandisement within and outside Europe; and this at the exclusion of non-state actors.[5] When these sovereign states were endangered by internal and external threats, they had the sole prerogative to treat these threats in accordance with their own national laws.[6] Particularly, when these threats were coming from non-state actors and were alleged to be supported by foreign governments, it became easier for these threatened states to set aside the possible application of international law and deal with these non-state actors under their national laws. From the nation

1 Vivienne Jabri, Discourses on violence: conflict analysis reconsidered (Manchester University Press 1996), at 127.
2 David Kennedy, Of war and law (Princeton University Press 2006), at 136.
3 Patrick Porter, Military orientalism: Eastern war through Western eyes (Hurst & Company 2009), at 192.
4 Ken Booth, Strategy and ethnocentrism (Croom Helm 1979), at 94–5.
5 Jeremy Black, Why wars happen (New York University Press 1998), at 139.
6 David Rodin, War and self-defense (Oxford University Press 2002), at 182.

state perspective, the privilege to kill as dictated by the laws of armed conflict can only be attributed to legitimate belligerent parties. In addition, violence as used by the stronger party to the conflict determines and sets aside this privilege. Hence, to be part of one or the other community of the warring parties and to be represented through one or the other's impersonal discourse on group identification enable a community to separate itself from the Other; though, the law of armed conflict allows (only legitimate) belligerent parties to regulate their status and their conduct towards each other upon the condition that all warring parties involved have signed up to those rules—yet customary IHL remains applicable. IHL, however, cannot bridge the distance when warring parties deny each others' legitimate status to participate in international or non-international armed conflicts, especially in today's asymmetrical and even transnational conflicts.[7] Or as Wilson put it: "For all their apparent incompatibility, there is a fragile partnership between humanity and warfare, the result of which is the humanitarian law of armed conflict, or jus in bello."[8]

Both the apologetic and idealistic stance which parties to the conflict assume, in fact influences their behaviour on the battlefield as well as their aspiration to adhere to the norms of armed conflict.[9] The relativity of the degree of discrepancy between state practices and normative principles[10] undermines the actual role of IHL to possibly reconcile both ends of the equation. Therefore, laws of armed conflict and their jurisdictional regimes, including and excluding belligerent parties (depending on their definition by the stronger one), do affect the application of the principle of distinction; because illegitimate combatants can only be treated inside the laws of war as either combatants or civilians. Outside the laws of war, those illegitimate combatants are subjected to the national laws. Conversely, their illegal status blurs the distinction with non-combatants which on their turn can be accused of being fighters as well; this leads to even more indiscriminate action against populations, especially when they are being associated with the enemies' perfidious strategies. Kennedy continued that "the law of sharp distinctions can

---

7 See Eyal Benvenisti, 'The legal battle to define the law on transnational asymmetric warfare', (2009–2010) 20 Duke Journal of Comparative and International Law 339.

8 Heather A. Wilson, International law and the use of force by national liberation movements (Clarendon Press 1988), at 36.

9 Mika Nishimura Hayashi, 'The principle of civilian protection and contemporary armed conflict', in Howard M. Hensel (ed), The law of armed conflict: constraints on the contemporary use of military force (Ashgate 2007), at 105.

10 Martti Koskenniemi, 'Politics of international law', (1990) 1 European Journal of International Law, 3, at 8.

still facilitate the identification of appropriate targets, or prevent the enemy's civilian resources from blurring into the war effort. It can define and delegitimate enemy perfidy."[11]

In the latter case, treating the armed hostilities under national laws possibly associates the populations with the allegedly illegitimate fighters. In this regard, police or military operations put these populations at greater risk for the arbitrary recourse to violence as conducted by the central state authorities. As opposed to international and non-international armed conflicts with more clearly defined belligerent actors, these conflicts fall outside the protection of the laws of war. Consequently, states do not longer need to comply with international norms. They can simply invoke the exceptional nature of the on-going conflict within its boundaries or can also deny the existence of such norms regulating these particular situations,[12] especially in light of the fight against terrorism and counterinsurgency operations.[13] The past and today's Western discourses on the Self and the Other have influenced the present legal paradigm and its demarcation of jurisdictional regimes into international and non-international armed conflicts. These discourses are not entirely different from the nineteenth century narrative of "civilised" and "barbarian" peoples. In particular, the non-Europeans were easily subdued to the authorities of Western countries because the technological gap within this encounter facilitated the colonial enterprise.[14] Von Clausewitz, for example, detected how the political, socio-economic and humanitarian contexts affected the way that wars had been fought between and among the Self and the Other:

> If the wars of civilised people are less cruel and destructive than those of the savages, the difference arises from the social condition both of states in themselves and in their relations to each other. Out of this social conditions and its relations war arises, and by it war is subjected to conditions, is controlled and modified. But these things do not belong to war

11 Kennedy, at 103.

12 Theodor Meron, War crimes law comes of age: essays (Oxford University Press 1998), at 172; see also Jason Ralph, 'The laws of war and the state of the American exception', (2009) 35 Review of International Studies, 631.

13 See Ganesh Sitaraman, 'Counterinsurgency, the war on terror, and the laws of war', (2009) 95 Virginia Law Review 1745; Matthew C. Waxman, 'The structure of terrorism threats and the laws of war', (2009–2010) 20 Duke Journal of Comparative and International Law 429.

14 David Killingray, 'Guardians of empire', in David Killingray & David Omissi (eds), Guardians of empire: the armed forces of the colonial powers c. 1700–1964 (Manchester University Press 1999), at 5–6.

> itself; they are only given conditions; and to introduce into the philosophy of war itself a principle of moderation would be an absurdity.[15]

In spite of the changes of those conditions throughout the West's history with respect to the legitimacy of combatancy and the correlative jurisdictional regimes of protection IHL provides, IHL has remained culturally constructed by the divisive rhetoric on the "Western" Self and the Other.[16] Both the rationalisation of such natural differences, as embodied in those discourses, zooms out of the actual human experience of suffering of the excluded Other. The legalistic view of warfare as witnessed in the interbellum made it easier for states to avoid fitting their conflicts into the precise definition of the laws of war. Instead, states argued that their actions fall in some other non-war category.[17] Nonetheless, throughout the years, the Western mind-set did become more sensitive to the civilian and military casualties in armed hostilities. In this regard, the developments of IHL reflected this growing awareness to reduce human suffering while at the same time the international legal order was trying to advocate world peace on a larger scale.[18] In this view, war remained instrumental for a greater peace.[19] As far as the jurisdictional regimes and the principle of distinction are concerned, this utilitarian approach is not unbiased. Because, IHL in its creation and application faced challenges to actually reconcile an apologetic practice and utopian ideal. Hence, violations are the natural outcome of the current legal paradigm which cannot be settled peacefully. Today's humanitarian interventions and the Global War on Terror further illustrate the extent of this approach where diplomatic and other peaceful means have lost their meaning and ability to address conflicts differently and where the laws of peace or jus contra bellum have failed.

---

15 Carl von Clausewitz, On war (Wordsworth Editions Limited 1997), at 6.

16 See Jeremy Black, Rethinking military history (Routledge 2004), at 235.

17 Stephen C. Neff, War and the law of nations: a general history (Cambridge University Press 2005), at 286.

18 Hilaire McCoubrey, International humanitarian law: modern developments in the limitation of warfare (Ashgate 1998), at 5.

19 Michael Howard, 'Temperamenta belli: can war be controlled?' in Michael Howard (ed), Restraints on war: studies in the limitation of armed conflict (Oxford University Press 1979), at 14.

6.2.2 *On Jurisdiction*

Despite the mid-nineteenth century early conventional efforts to establish a legal tradition regulating the conduct of warfare,[20] the allegedly universal application of those norms were limited to armed conflicts between equal sovereigns, i.e. Western nations. These colonial powers, until the decolonisation process, deliberately excluded the wars fought in their overseas territories to be classified as armed conflicts. Mégret recognised this exclusionary nature of IHL and found that the Other "of international humanitarian law is every individual, concrete or imagined, every state of affairs that the laws of war aim to keep at bay".[21] During this colonial period, "uncivilised" peoples were predominantly considered to be unworthy to fall under the protection of the laws of armed conflict to which only European peoples had access. By the end of the nineteenth century, Europeans found that the "savage" Other had not yet reached their civilisational standard of warfare. European states were very clear about this; the 1914 British Military Manual for example "emphasized that the rules of International Law apply only to warfare between civilized nations [...] They do not apply in wars with uncivilized States and tribes".[22] While at the same time, as said by Martens, "de plus, on est d'accord que la mission des nations européennes est précisément d'inculquer aux tribus et peuples de l'Orient les idées du droit, et de les initier aux principes éternels et bienfaisants qui ont mis l'Europe à la tête de la civilisation et de l'humanité".[23]

IHL also adopted this equivocal worldview existing at those times. The 1863 Lieber Code delimitated the application of the laws of war to wars among states. In this regard, only states showed proof, according to the Lieber Code, of "civilized existence that men live in political, continuous societies, forming organized units, called states or nations, whose constituents bear, enjoy, suffer,

20 See Chapter III.

21 Frédéric Mégret, 'From "savages" to "unlawful combatants": a postcolonial look at international humanitarian law's "other"', in Anne Orford (ed), International law and its others (Cambridge University Press 2006), at 267.

22 James Edward Edmonds & Lassa Oppenheim, Land warfare: an exposition of the laws and usages of war on land, for the guidance of officers of His Majesty's Army (His Majesty's Stationary Office 1912), at para. 7.

23 Fyodor Fyodorovich Martens, La Russie et l'Angleterre dans l'Asie centrale (Van Doosselaere 1879), at 8. Free translation: "Moreover, one agrees that the mission of European nations is exactly to instil the ideas of law in the tribes and peoples of the Orient and to initiate them into the eternal and beneficial principles which have put Europe at the head of civilisation and of humanity."

advance and retrograde together, in peace and in war".[24] General international law and its doctrine of the sources explicitly pronounced itself about the idea of the superiority of the Western legal principles. For example, the 1920 Statute of the Permanent Court of International Justice in its Article 38 which has been taken over by the 1945 Statute of the ICJ in the same Article 38 provides that "1. The Court, whose function is to decide in accordance with international law such disputes as are submitted to it, shall apply: [...] c. the general principles of law recognized by civilized nations [...]."[25] In particular those European states which had participated in the 1899–1907 Hague Peace Conferences remained confident about their humanitarian conscience. This conscience was inherently present in the Western civilisation and would alert European nations to diligently manage those situations which the conventions had not explicitly dealt with. The so-called Martens clause embodied this attitude:

> Until a more complete code of the laws of war has been issued, the High Contracting Parties deem it expedient to declare that, in cases not included in the Regulations adopted by them, the inhabitants and the belligerents remain under the protection and the rule of the principles of the law of nations, as they result from the usages established among civilized peoples, from the laws of humanity, and the dictates of the public conscience.[26]

This civilisational progress and consciousness prevented "civilised" nations to have recourse to "barbarian" warfare. From this humanitarian perspective, according to the 1863 Lieber Code, wars principally ought to bring a "renewed state of peace".[27] In this regard, peace was the normal condition of interstate relationships. Of course, the High Contracting Parties to such humanitarian conventions were only bound to follow the laws of war they signed up to. However, such sovereignty argument was somehow narrowed down by the communitarian proposition that higher goals could possibly be pursued. In this regard, also the 1868 St. Petersburg Declaration had the ambition to recognise the communitarian spirit among Europe's sovereign nations to restrict their conduct of warfare to a minimum. Despite the atrocities of the World Wars, the Allied Forces after the Second World War did seem to pursue

---

24 Article 20, 1863 Instructions for the Government of Armies of the United States in the Field (Lieber Code).

25 Article 38, ICJ Statute.

26 Preamble, 1907 Hague IV.

27 Article 29, 1863 Lieber Code.

a prosecution of these war crimes under the existing laws of war at that time. The indictment before the International Military Tribunal of Nuremberg stipulated that "these methods and crimes constituted violations of international conventions, of internal penal laws and of the general principles of criminal law as derived from the criminal law of all civilized nations, and were involved in and part of a systematic course of conduct".[28] Already from the mid-nineteenth century, such common agreement to regulate warfare existed among European nations. However, in the aftermath of the Second World War, the Nuremberg Trials demonstrated the vulnerability of these legal and rational restraints on warfare. Irrational behaviour toppled the laws of war and on its turn was defined again in terms of the everlasting dichotomy between the "civilised" Self and the "barbarian" Other—even among European nations:

> For in this conception of "total war", the moral ideas underlying the conventions which seek to make war more humane are no longer regarded as having force or validity. Everything is made subordinate to the overmastering dictates of war. Rules, regulations, assurances and treaties all alike are of no moment, and so, freed from the restraining influence of international law, the aggressive war is conducted by the Nazi leaders in the most barbaric way. Accordingly, war crimes were committed when and wherever the Fuehrer and his close associates thought them to be advantageous. They were for the most part the result of cold and criminal calculation.[29]

As a response to such intolerable human suffering, the international community of states, through the forum of the ICRC, decided to proceed with the progressive development of the laws of armed conflict integrating the previous 1899–1907 Hague Regulations into the 1949 Geneva Conventions.[30] These conventions, however, limited their jurisdictional scope to international armed conflicts where "two or more of the High Contracting Parties"[31] were involved.

---

28 Nuremberg Trial Proceedings, Vol. 1, Indictment: Count Three: War Crimes: VIII. Statement of the Offence.

29 *Judgment of the International Military Tribunal for the Trial of German Major War Criminals*, International Military Tribunal of Nuremberg, War Crimes and Crimes against Humanity, General, 30 September–1 October 1946, at http://avalon.law.yale.edu/imt/judwarcr.asp#general (Last accessed on 15 February 2015)

30 Dietrich Schindler, 'International humanitarian law: its remarkable development and its persistent violation', (2003) 5 Journal of the History of International Law, 165, at 181.

31 Article 2, GC I; Article 2, GC II; Article 2, GC III; Article 2, GC IV.

This implicit reference to state armies was reflected accordingly in these conventions. In this respect, the provisions on prisoners of war revealed a strict adherence to lawful belligerent status and its correlative protection.[32] The requirements that resistance movements had to respect, i.e. command responsibility, distinctive signs, openly carrying arms and conduct in accordance with IHL,[33] caused much ambiguity as to their practical feasibility. Instead, their communitarian aim to encompass a large group of fighters remained subject to the sovereign discretion of each belligerent state party which had captured such alleged persons. In this regard, states were still free to limit the scope of protection to such fighters under the respective jurisdictional regime of international armed conflicts. Clearly, the principle of distinction between combatants and civilians is intimately related with the question of jurisdiction and legitimate belligerency.

In spite of this state-centred and sovereignty-based worldview after the Second World War, there was much less reference to the "civilised" status of actors on the international plane. With respect to non-state actors, in their common Article 3, the 1949 Geneva Conventions did stipulate a minimum standard of protection applicable in conflicts of a non-international character. After the Second World War, this protection proved to be particularly important to impose a minimum of humanitarian requirements in those newly independent territories which on their turn had become proxies in the armed conflicts between the capitalist and communist blocs. During the fights for decolonisation where colonial peoples were *de jure* and *de facto* still within the territory of one single colonial power, common Article 3 also served to provide those minimum safeguards. These peoples struggling for national liberation had to wait until AP I to have their armed conflict to resort under the ambit of the protection of the rules regulating an international armed conflict. Also in the non-international armed conflicts, insurgents or dissident armed forces had to cope with similar claims of their legitimate belligerency against central (decolonised) governmental armed forces. They too had to wait until AP II for more humanitarian safeguards. In particular during the Cold War, both national liberation movements and insurgents were divided and ruled along a new dichotomy of capitalist versus communist signature. The asymmetrical conflict in Afghanistan was an example thereof. Hence, these fighters had more difficulties to fight their cause within the legal parameters of IHL and had easier recourse to less conventional military tactics curtailing the boundaries which the laws of war initially prescribed within those armed

32 See Article 4, GC III.

33 See Article 4 A.(2), GC III.

conflicts.[34] It empowered the weaker parties to the conflict to have the privilege of the initiative. While the stronger antagonist still had the legal authority to claim its agency and privilege to kill, both under its national laws and under IHL.

It was only at the end of the Cold War that AP I and AP II have principally become adopted.[35] Understandably, the proxies of the capitalist and communist blocs had postponed their commitment to safeguard the rights of all warring parties during the non-international armed conflicts within their territories. Already soon after the collapse of the communist regimes all around the world, these countries became subject to internal strives along ethnic and racial lines. Wars amongst the peoples themselves succeeded the previous threats of interstate industrial warfare during the World Wars and during the proxy wars of the Cold War era.[36] The protection afforded by AP II however remained elusive and subject to the ratification of sovereign states. Hence, the greater need to provide protection beyond the laws of armed conflict and to have recourse to other international legal regimes. In this regard, the ICTY in the *Tadić* case stated that "a sovereignty-oriented approach has been gradually supplanted by a human being-oriented approach".[37] Indeed, even Part II on Humane Treatment of AP II has a human rights law orientation. Moreover, the rigid distinction between jurisdictional regimes on international and non-international armed conflict, according to this international jurisprudence, was out-dated.[38] No longer should it be possible to waive the accountability for violations in both types of conflict. No longer should warring parties shield their responsibility behind such dichotomy both in legal and political terms:

> Whenever armed violence erupted in the international community, in traditional international law the legal response was based on a stark dichotomy: belligerency or insurgency. The former category applied to armed conflicts between sovereign States (unless there was recognition

34 Ivan Arreguin-Toft, 'How the weak win wars: a theory of asymmetric conflict', (2001) 26 International Security, 93, at 107.

35 See website of the ICRC: ICRC, at http://www.icrc.org/IHL.nsf/%28SPF%29/party_main_treaties/$File/IHL_and_other_related_Treaties.pdf. (Last accessed on 15 February 2015)

36 Kalevi Jaakko Holsti, The state, war, and the state of war (Cambridge University Press 1996), at 16.

37 *Prosecutor v. Tadić*, ICTY, Appeals Chamber, Decision on the Defence Motion for Interlocutory Appeal on Jurisdiction, 2 October 1995, Case No. IT-94-1-AR72, at www.icty.org, para. 97. (Last accessed on 15 February 2015)

38 Sandesh Sivakumaran, 'Re-envisaging the international law of internal armed conflict', (2011) 22 European Journal of International Law 219, at 232.

> of belligerency in a civil war), while the latter applied to armed violence breaking out in the territory of a sovereign State. Correspondingly, international law treated the two classes of conflict in a markedly different way: interstate wars were regulated by a whole body of international legal rules, governing both the conduct of hostilities and the protection of persons not participating (or no longer participating) in armed violence (civilians, the wounded, the sick, shipwrecked, prisoners of war). By contrast, there were very few international rules governing civil commotion, for States preferred to regard internal strife as rebellion, mutiny and treason coming within the purview of national criminal law and, by the same token, to exclude any possible intrusion by other States into their own domestic jurisdiction. This dichotomy was clearly sovereignty-oriented and reflected the traditional configuration of the international community, based on the coexistence of sovereign States more inclined to look after their own interests than community concerns or humanitarian demands.[39]

Along with such decentralisation of violence as reflected in those non-international armed conflicts after the Cold War, humanitarian intervention under the auspices of the international community was another striking example of the responsibility to protect.[40] From the 1990s onwards, the interventions in East-Timor, Haiti, Ivory Coast, Kosovo, Somalia, etc. are examples thereof. Whenever sovereign governments failed to address a humanitarian situation in such non-international armed conflicts, the instrumentalisation of such communitarian human rights approach was mandatory.[41] Here jus in bello intervenes as it needs to find its justification in the existing law on the use of force. The law, however, as practiced by the UN collective security system, only gives authority to have recourse to armed force in case of an armed attack by another state.[42] It is only based on a logic of war not on one of intervention.[43]

---

39 *Prosecutor v. Tadić*, ICTY, Appeals Chamber, Decision on the Defence Motion for Interlocutory Appeal on Jurisdiction, 2 October 1995, Case No. IT-94-1-AR72, at www.icty.org, para. 96. (Last accessed on 15 February 2015)

40 See David M. Mednicoff, 'Humane wars? International law, just war theory and contemporary armed humanitarian intervention', (2006) 2 Law, Culture and the Humanities, 373.

41 Mary Kaldor, New and old wars: organized violence in a global era (Stanford University Press 1999), at 138–139.

42 See Article 51, UN Charter.

43 J. Bryan Hehir, 'Intervention militaire et souveraineté nationale: une relation à repenser', in Jonathan Moore (ed), Des choix difficiles: les dilemmes moraux de l'humanitaire (Gallimard 1999), at 54.

In addition, the UN Charter in its Article 2(4) forbids any intervention into the sovereign affairs of a state regardless whether this intervention is communitarian or state-related. Consequently, when the law did not provide a right for humanitarian intervention, an appeal was made on morality. Such responsibility to protect was already reflected in the International Law Commission's work on state responsibility,[44] and recently operationalized through the mandate of civilian protection on behalf of the international community of states in Libya in 2011.[45] Clearly, the jus in bello had to inscribe itself within the legal regime on the use of force, i.e. jus ad bellum;[46] though IHL's application remained completely independent of the reasons to intervene or go to war.[47]

Related to this discussion on the presence of international actors during armed conflicts, was the issue of transnational terrorism and counterterrorist operations. The Global War on Terror was characterised in terms of military action in overseas countries such as Afghanistan, Iraq, Pakistan, Yemen, etc. where state armies were fighting non-state actors. Or as Byman and Waxman described it: "International terrorist organizations, most notably, share important attributes with the types of militia groups and other hostile actors common to coercive humanitarian operations: lack of a decision-making hierarchy, indistinguishability of civilians from combatants, lack of territorial control, and so on."[48] Such identification of the enemies could be easily invoked whenever to avoid the protections which IHL granted to the treatment of prisoners of war in international armed conflicts. The laws of war on non-international armed conflicts, however, did not provide these safeguards but promised a humane treatment instead. As mentioned earlier, this shift towards a human rights approach brought human rights law back into the picture and found itself to be applicable during armed conflicts; regardless how the protagonists

---

44 Article 48, 2001 Draft Articles on Responsibility of States for Internationally Wrongful Acts, International Law Commission.

45 See Marie-José Domestici-Met, 'Protecting Libya on behalf of the international community', (2011) 3 Goettingen Journal of International Law, 861; Hitoshi Nasu, 'Operationalising the "responsibility to protect" and conflict prevention: dilemmas of civilian protection in armed conflict', (2009) 14 Journal of Conflict and Security Law, 209.

46 Bernard Kouchner, Les guerriers de la paix: du Kosovo à l'Irak (Bernard Grasset 2004), at 461.

47 Olivier Corten, Eric David & François Dubuisson, 'Droit humanitaire et légalité du recours à la force: deux logiques essentiellement différentes', in Bernard Adam (ed), Militaires humanitaires: à chacun son rôle: cohérence et incohérences des opérations militaro-humanitaires (Editions GRIP 2002), at 36.

48 Daniel Byman & Matthew C. Waxman, The dynamics of coercion: American foreign policy and the limits of military might (Cambridge University Press 2002), at 199.

would like to define the armed hostilities. The same thing counted for peace situations where no warring party liked to call their conflict to be armed.[49] Once again the law could be set aside by both parties to the conflict wanting to defend their interests and to find as much as possible leverage to reach their objectives beyond the communitarian humanitarian and human rights constraints.

Moreover, in both humanitarian interventions and military counter-terrorist operations, the law of occupation as Article 42 of the 1899–1907 Hague Regulations prescribed, can be circumvented. Such military actions were claimed not to assume authority over the territory in question. Hence, attempts were made to advance an accountability strategy outside the existing laws of war. For example, in the *Banković* case, the European Court of Human Rights had to assess the effective control requirement the NATO forces were alleged to have during the extra-territorial bombing campaigns in the former Yugoslavia related to the 1999 Kosovo conflict. The Court declared the application inadmissible given the lack of effective control of the NATO forces over the territory in question. Consequently, no human rights remedies under the European conventional human rights regime could be invoked by the victims of these NATO actions.[50] From such positivist reading, neither IHL nor human rights law could bring solace or provide remedies to the suffering inflicted upon these populations. The intimate link between international accountability and the jurisdictional regimes of the laws of war was undermined. By invoking a rather non-legal standard of the humanitarian and just causes, these actions were supposed to be guided by, but were rather putting *de facto* the armed conflict outside the reach of the laws of war. This also applied for the UN peacekeeping operations. These sovereignty-oriented justifications were probably balanced with the humanitarian aid provided during and after the conflict. In this regard, the discourse of the benevolent "Western" Self and the Other in need of the former continued to have a role in these humanitarian crises, especially in light of the current crisis in Middle East since the popular uprising in 2011. In particular, the rhetoric on good governance to restore the rule of law,

49 See Noam Lubell, 'Challenges in applying human rights law to armed conflict', (2005) International Review of the Red Cross, 737.

50 *Banković and Others v. Belgium and 16 Others Contracting States*, ECHR, Grand Chamber, Decision as to the Admissibility of Application No. 52207/99, 12 December 2001, Application No. 52207/99, at www.echr.coe.int, para. 82. (Last accessed on 15 February 2015)

i.e. jus post bellum, further advanced, according to Rajagopal, the "structurally violent and divisive nature of development interventions"[51] after the conflict.

6.2.3 *On Distinction*

After having determined the jurisdictional regimes of the international and non-international armed conflicts, the principle of distinction between civilian and military targets, both objects and persons, will be looked upon. The evolution of the principle of distinction, as with the development of jurisdictional regimes, did not remain untouched by the leaderships' strategy to divide and rule over their Other. This happened both in the legal argument and in practice. Though one of the first humanitarian conventions, such as the 1863 Lieber Code, wanted to accredit the Western civilisation for having developed such humanitarian principle, it remained inapplicable toward other "uncivilised" peoples which had not yet made sufficient progress.[52] In this regard, as the 1868 St. Petersburg Declaration reiterated, the primary military goal was to disable the enemies' forces and to leave the civilian population alone. Also the 1899–1907 Hague Regulations in their Preambles underscored this very ambition to serve humanity and to improve the relationship among the warring parties and their populations. The initial focus of these early conventions was not so much on the objects of attack but rather on the persons who were the target of attack.[53] Understandably, this has got to do with the military industrial innovations which could attack larger objects and not necessarily military personnel only. Moreover, the technological innovations created an even greater emotional distance between the perpetrator and the actual target. The loss of personhood of the target affected the application of the principle of distinction.

Hence, at the time of attack, the nature of the object would have to be assessed rather than the actual persons behind it; though precautionary measures would have to be taken when there were risks of incidental damage to civilians or civilian objects.[54] The World Wars in particular gave proof of manifest disregard of this principle of distinction as if this principle could not be complied with. The actual conduct of the belligerent parties advanced

---

51 Balakrishnan Rajagopal, 'Invoking the rule of law: international discourses', in Agnès Hurwitz & Reyko Huang (eds), Civil war and the rule of law: security, development, and human rights (Lynne Rienner Publishers 2008), at 48.

52 Article 22, 24 and 25, 1863 Lieber Code.

53 A.P.V. Rogers, Law on the battlefield (Juris Publishing 2004), at 12.

54 See Article 57, AP I.

a rather apologetic point of view as to the binding nature of this customary principle. In addition, for belligerent reprisals to prior violations by the other party to the conflict, this principle of distinction was set aside[55] and the impersonal masses had become the object of attack. With respect to non-international armed conflicts, when reading common Article 3 of the 1949 Geneva Conventions in conjunction with Article 13(3) of AP II, there was a combination of focus on respectively the status (cf. "members of armed forces") and the behaviour (cf. "direct part in hostilities"). One the one hand, this ambiguity associated dissident armed groups with the population. On the other hand, it favoured those groups to hide among the civilian population. Thus, in non-international armed conflicts, the factual distinction between fighters and civilian population was oblique and was used to disregard as much as possible the legal principle of distinction. Again, sovereign interests as supported by the image-building of one's enemy further guided the concrete application of this communitarian principle.[56] Its violation, as Kissinger called it, was simply based on "inherent bad faith".[57] Instead, Hayashi urged to balance between the normative prescriptions and the realities of warfare, though it was not clear whether this could happen within the law:

> Principles that constitute the cornerstones of the law of armed conflict, such as the principle of civilian protection, are, by nature, aspirational and utopian. Indeed, precisely because reality is far from utopia, the principle of civilian protection is needed in situations of armed conflict. At the same time, a complete shift from the apologetic view to the utopian view would be harmful. A law of armed conflict which is purely aspirational and is not supported by the actors concerned would exert no influence on the parties to the armed conflicts, and would serve no purpose.[58]

Though the law intended to legitimise violence by sovereign states and dissident armed forces within their respective jurisdictional regimes, it also imposed legal constraints upon the conduct of warfare. Like the principle of distinction, the manifest failure of its observance as justified by the military necessity, did not leave much of authority to this principle. Maybe the law's adherence

55 Hayashi, in, at 109–114.

56 Booth, at 99.

57 Henry Kissinger, Necessity for choice: prospects for American foreign policy (Chatto and Windus 1960), at 194.

58 Hayashi, in, at 119.

should come rather from man's conscience instead. Such human(itarian) conscience would probably not be as easily used in function of the polarising and dehumanising discourses on the enemy Other. A call for this conscience could prove particularly important in light of the negative definition of a civilian as stated by the ICTY in the *Galić* case.[59] Moreover, according to Article 50(1) of AP I, "in case of doubt a person is a civilian, that person shall be considered to be a civilian". Related to this, where combatants were present among the civilian population, the nature of the object of attack did not loose its civilian character as pointed out by the ICTY in its *Strugar* case.[60] However, using the civilian population as a human shield remained prohibited under IHL.[61] The real difficulty lies with the establishment of the actual criminal responsibility of violations against this principle. In this regard, the ICTY in the *Kordić* and *Čerkez* case confirmed that "the burden of proof as to whether a person is a civilian rests on the Prosecution".[62] Thus, at the time of attack, a member of the (dissident) armed forces would not need to feel reluctant to attack civilians per se, as the risk of prosecution might be ephemeral; though as the United States Naval Handbook pointed out, precaution has to be made on a case-by-case basis: "Combatants in the field must make an honest determination as to whether a particular civilian is or is not subject to deliberate attack based on the person's behavior, location and attire, and other information available at the time."[63]

Besides such legal assessment at the time of attack, the sovereign choice of weaponry, however, particularly deployed since the Second World War, unavoidably challenged the communitarian principle of distinction. These weapons' capacity to destroy and to produce "casualties at an industrial rate",[64] as formulated by Smith, could not avoid collateral civilian damage. In the *Galić* case, the ICTY considered that "apparently disproportionate attacks may give

59 *Prosecutor v. Galić*, ICTY, Trial Chamber, Judgment, 5 December 2003, Case No. IT-98-29-T, at www.icty.org, at 47. (Last accessed on 15 February 2015)

60 *Prosecutor v. Strugar*, ICTY, Trial Chamber, Judgment, 31 January 2005, Case No. IT-01-42-T, at www.icty.org, para. 282. (Last accessed on 15 February 2015)

61 See Michael N. Schmitt, 'Human shield in international humanitarian law', (2008–2009) 47 Columbia Journal of Transnational Law 292.

62 *Prosecutor v. Kordić and Čerkez*, ICTY, Appeals Chamber, Judgment, 17 December 2004, Case No. IT-95-14/2-A, at www.icty.org, para. 48. (Last accessed on 15 February 2015)

63 United States Naval Handbook, para. 830 cited in Jean-Marie Henckaerts & Louise Doswald-Beck, Customary international humanitarian law (Cambridge University Press 2005), at 24.

64 Rupert Smith, The utility of force: the art of war in the modern world (Allen Lane 2005), at 114.

rise to the inference that civilians were actually the object of attack".[65] In the *Halilović* case, the ICTY reaffirmed that "in case of doubt as to the status of a person, that person shall be considered to be a civilian". The Tribunal continued that, "however, in such cases, the Prosecution must show that in the given circumstances a reasonable person could not have believed that the individual he or she attacked was a combatant".[66] Hence, precautionary measures at the time of attack were linked with the question of burden of proof beyond reasonable doubt, as practiced retroactively under international criminal law. Clearly, there is a contradiction when it comes to making an honest determination at the time of the attack. Such determination is to anticipate the benefit of hindsight already at that time of attack and even beyond reasonable doubt; though, Article 57 (2)b) of AP I as a rule of customary law, was particularly important during asymmetrical armed conflicts waged in the era of "balkanisation" after the Cold War and the Global War on Terror. It was framed in a communitarian spirit to avoid incidental human suffering during military operations. Considerations of military necessity had to be balanced against the principles of distinction and proportionality as will be discussed in the following subsection:

> An attack shall be cancelled or suspended if it becomes apparent that the objective is not a military one or is subject to special protection or that the attack may be expected to cause incidental loss of civilian life, injury to civilians, damage to civilian objects, or a combination thereof, which would be excessive in relation to the concrete and direct military advantage anticipated.[67]

6.3 Necessity and Proportionality

6.3.1 *Actions of Warfare*

After having assessed the influence of the divisive discourses on the "Western" Self and the Other on the interpretation and on the application of jurisdictional regimes and their correlative principle of distinction, both in theory and practice, a closer look upon the actual military actions will prove that they are

---

65 *Prosecutor v. Galić*, ICTY, Trial Chamber, Judgment, 5 December 2003, Case No. IT-98-29-T, at www.icty.org, paras. 59–60. (Last accessed on 15 February 2015)

66 *Prosecutor v. Halilović*, ICTY, Trial Chamber, Judgment, 16 November 2005, Case No. IT-01-48-T, at www.icty.org, para. 36. (Last accessed on 15 February 2015)

67 Article 57 (2)b), AP I.

subjected to the same discourses. From the inception of IHL, the first humanitarian conventions aimed at limiting the cruelties of warfare. They took on a rule-utilitarian approach where every rational human being was guided by some kind of conscience to respect life and to bring long-term peace along with war.[68] Hence, the laws of armed conflict put constraints on the Lotus doctrine,[69] i.e. the prevailing universal legal morality where everything is permissible unless prohibited. Thus, the introduction of concepts such as military necessity and proportionality or humanity had tried to rationalise this natural legal order of Lotus. Nonetheless, beyond this rationalisation, there was an appeal to some kind of communitarian and humanitarian conscience. In this respect, Article 68 of the 1863 Lieber Code was particularly illustrative: "Modern wars are not internecine wars, in which the killing of the enemy is the object. The destruction of the enemy in modern war, and, indeed, modern war itself, are means to obtain that object of the belligerent which lies beyond the war. Unnecessary or revengeful destruction of life is not lawful." Moreover, the 1868 St. Petersburg Declaration linked this humanitarian endeavour to diminish unnecessary suffering and to ban the use of weaponry inflicting such suffering to the progress which Western civilisation has already gone through. This Declaration's scope was, however, limited to primary objects of targeting, namely the enemies' armed forces. Also the 1899–1907 Hague Regulations were primarily focusing on the conduct of warfare between the belligerent states' armies.

It was not until the end of the Second World War that GC IV raised a greater consciousness for the treatment of civilians under international occupation especially after having witnessed the mass atrocities against them. In addition, in light of the Lotus doctrine, every incidental civilian casualty and every deliberate targeting of the civilian population would have been permissible. If the laws of war before the outbreak of the Second World War did not forbid this explicitly then it remained at the sovereign discretion of the warring parties to act otherwise. In order to win their hearts and minds of the civilian population, state armies and non-state actors were rather utilitarian in

---

68 Richard B. Brandt, Morality, utilitarianism, and rights (Cambridge University Press 1992), at 351.

69 See *The Case of the S.S. "Lotus"*, PCIJ, Judgment, 7 September 1927, PCIJ Series A, Case No. 10, 1927, at http://www.icj-cij.org/pcij/serie_A/A_10/30_Lotus_Arret.pdf, 63 (Last accessed on 15 February 2015) Dissenting Opinion of Judge M. Nyholm: "There is a kind of international law which amounts to this: that the absence of a rule prohibiting an action suffices to render that actions permissible, for not only is it in most cases inadmissible of thus to deduce permission from the absence of a prohibition."

their approach to make the population whether an object of their attacks or not.[70] This belligerents' attitude was necessarily affected by group identities and discourses which dehumanised their enemies' armed forces and civilian populations. In this regard, it was very difficult to apply the customary rule of distinction and its correlative prohibition of disproportionate military actions in relation to the anticipated military gain as assessed at the time of attack; particularly during the non-international armed conflicts which waged during the Cold War, between capitalist and communist supporters, and after the Cold War, between ethnic and racial groups. Both sides to the conflict had used civilian populations in order to win the struggle for their minds.[71] As with the Global War on Terror, intentionally harming innocent civilians became part of the strategy to reach the higher goal for better peace.[72] This justification and rationalisation in terms of military necessity fell into the trap of endless violence and destruction. The initial projection of the laws of war's moral standards, though based on a Western-centric worldview, was ousted by the very use of force. Within such battle of ideologies, the enemies', as formulated by Wells, "moral standard are less than civilized, and they do not deserve, thus, the protection which decent ideologies have a right to".[73]

Thus, if war is about winning it, pragmatism with respect to the conduct of warfare and its means does no longer have to reason in moral terms. A pragmatist approach can try to find its interests served within the existing legal framework of IHL or to argue outside of it. Respecting the Other was not necessarily part of such military campaign. In this regard, utilitarian arguments for on the one hand military necessity and proportionality on the other hand, can hardly be settled within the existing laws of war. IHL's creation and application was already accused to be Western-centric and state-centric. Moreover, even bringing the Others back into the legal picture and taking them into consideration did not automatically confer a positive obligation upon the warring parties to respect the communitarian principle of proportionality within the existing conflictual legal paradigm. Especially, the technological developments in weaponry had literally distanced the very legal assessment of the situation prior to the attack from the possible emotional backlash of the human suffering witnessed after the attack.[74] Such impersonalised

70 David Galula, Counterinsurgency warfare: theory and practice (Praeger Security International 2006), at 52.

71 Smith, at 20.

72 James P. Sterba, Justice for here and now (Cambridge University Press 1998), at 156.

73 Donald A. Wells, War crimes and laws of war (University Press of America 1984), at 100.

74 Dave Grossman, On killing (Back Bay Books 1996), at 106.

industrial warfare started already in the late nineteenth century. According to Coker, such warfare "locked the warrior into a system in which his performance was increasingly evaluated in industrial terms: productivity and predictability".[75] Consequently, the combatants' agency and subjectivity had been taken over by such a desubjectivising discourse which had started to live its own life. Also military discipline prevented the combatants to listen to their own humanitarian conscience. The proportionality of their actions were already rationalised within this legal paradigm in particular in light of the anticipated military advantage at the time of attack. The laws of war rationalised and legitimised this gap in time.[76] In addition, both the law and the technology, which the combatant respectively had to apply and was using, were not value-free. Or as Douzinas and Warrington put it:

> Choices must be made but the only guidance offered is a not very useful reference to respect for the various conflicting interpretations and to the need for principles as guiding lights. Merely hearing all sides is precisely what positivism offers; likewise not "theoretically" (as distinct from practically […]) reducing disfavoured perspectives to inferior positions. And again the principles envisaged are not different from those offered by hermeneutical jurisprudence, nor is it clear how the commitment to the ethics of alterity will affect their constitution and application.[77]

6.3.2 *On Necessity*

Though the Western states wanted to limit the calamities of warfare, they remained realistic about the necessities of warfare as well. From the beginning, IHL subordinated the limitation to the cruelties of war to the military requirements whose determination remained at the discretion of the sovereign. The 1863 Lieber Code understood military necessity to consist of "those measures which are indispensable for securing the ends of war, and which are lawful according to the modern law and usages of war".[78] To take the latter's lawfulness into consideration referred to the common decency among "civilised" nations. In view of bringing back peace through war, these states wanted to

---

75 Christopher Coker, The future of war: the re-enchantment of war in the twenty-first century (Blackwell Publishing 2004), at 85.

76 Gabriella Blum, 'The laws of war and the "lesser evil"', (2010) 35 Yale Journal of International Law 1, at 45–46.

77 Costas Douzinas & Ronnie Warrington, Justice miscarried: ethics and aesthetics in law (Harvester Wheatsheaf 1994), at 209.

78 Article 14, 1863 Lieber Code.

prevent irresponsible suffering in their road to victory. Moreover, during the armed hostilities, the 1863 Lieber Code continued, that not the law but some kind of conscience would bring combatants to act humanely: "Men who take up arms against one another in public war do not cease on this account to be moral beings, responsible to one another and to God."[79] In their Preambles, the 1899–1907 Hague Regulations were advocating the same "desire to diminish the evils of war as far as military necessities permit" though "within such limits as would mitigate their severity as far as possible". The latter obligation of proportionality was not a duty to achieve a given result. Instead, proportionality was formulated as an obligation to perform to the best of one's abilities and hence became conditional upon the military capacity to comply with such humanitarian requirements.[80]

Related to this obligation was the customary rule stating that "all feasible precautions must be taken to avoid, and in any event to minimise, incidental loss of civilian life, injury to civilians and damage to civilian objects".[81] Collecting the best military intelligence was mandatory in order to fully assess the situation at the time of attack. The use of particular weapons and their technological developments, such as precision-guided weaponry, could have contributed to this same capacity to live up to this duty of best efforts; though their industrial character rather revealed a focus upon technological superiority which itself was supposed to guarantee a military success instead.[82] However, already in 1856, Bernard, argued that this "quickest road to victory is not always the best, and even in a certain saving in the sum-total of bloodshed and suffering may be too dearly bought, by the use of means which shock the instincts of humanity".[83] Though it kept the door open for future scientific improvements, the 1868 St. Petersburg Declaration wanted to reconcile these new technologies with the principles of protection, i.e. distinction and proportionality. In this regard, it banned the use of indiscriminate weapons. Later weapons conventions banned such weaponry which caused unnecessary and superfluous suffering. Depending on the terms of agreement of those weapons conventions, signatory parties intended to subject the conduct of warfare to the communitarian obligation to achieve a specific result. The ICJ in the *Nuclear*

79 Article 15, 1863 Lieber Code.

80 Geoffrey Francis Andrew Best, Humanity in warfare: the modern history of the international law of armed conflict (Methuen 1983), at 177.

81 Henckaerts & Doswald-Beck, at 51.

82 Robert L. O'Connell, Of arms and men: a history of war, weapons, and aggression (Oxford University Press 1989), at 4.

83 Montague Bernard, 'The growth of laws and usages of war', in X. (ed), Oxford essays (John W. Parker and Son 1856), at 117.

Weapons case found that this customary rule as codified by treaty law limited the ultimate freedom of states to choose their means of warfare; for example in inflicting unnecessary suffering upon combatants.[84] Judge Shahabuddeen further elaborated upon this suffering which was disproportionate to military necessity and warned about the dangers of a vicious circle of unlimited violence:

> Suffering is superfluous or unnecessary if it is materially in excess of the degree of suffering which is justified by the military advantage sought to be achieved. A mechanical or absolute test is excluded: a balance has to be struck between the degree of suffering inflicted and the military advantage in view. The greater the military advantage, the greater will be the willingness to tolerate higher levels of suffering.[85]

Clearly, the concept of military necessity touched upon many aspects of the conduct of warfare. In first instance, it affected how far suffering could be inflicted upon the combatant community. In this respect, the customary prohibition of unnecessary and superfluous suffering intended to limit the choice of weaponry causing such suffering. Given its codification, this customary rule brought military necessity back into the realm of public conscience. In second instance, the requirement of military necessity could not be invoked to violate the principle of distinction. In this regard, in the *Strugar* case, the ICTY, "rejected any exemption on the grounds of military necessity and underscored that there is an absolute prohibition on targeting of civilians and civilians objects in customary international law".[86] In third instance, the targeting of combatants and military objects as necessitated by the military requirements, could have incidental collateral damage upon civilians and civilian objects in spite of the latter's non-combatant immunity.[87] Consequently, the sovereign exercise of military necessity had to balance the anticipated military advantage against the humanitarian cost at the time of attack by taking precautionary measures and by adopting proportionate actions. On the one hand, this

---

84 Vincent Chetail, 'The contribution of the International Court of Justice to international humanitarian law', (2003) 85 International Review of the Red Cross, 235, at 256.

85 *Legality of the Threat or Use of Nuclear Weapons in Armed Conflict*, ICJ, Advisory Opinion, 8 July 1996, I.C.J. Reports 1996, at http://www.icj-cij.org/docket/files/95/7495.pdf, 402. (Dissenting Opinion of Judge M. Shahabuddeen) (Last accessed on 15 February 2015)

86 *Prosecutor v. Strugar*, ICTY, Trial Chamber, Judgment, 31 January 2005, Case No. IT-01-42-T, at www.icty.org, para. 280. (Last accessed on 15 February 2015)

87 Judith Gail Gardam, 'Proportionality and force in international law', (1993) 87 American Journal of International Law, 391, at 398.

relative test is necessarily influenced by the depiction of the enemy and its population, causing the communitarian principle of proportionality to be subordinated to the military necessity of the sovereign as will be discussed below. On the other hand, Western public opinion has played an important role to denounce collateral damage and disproportionate civilian losses.[88]

6.3.3 *On Proportionality*

During armed conflicts the belligerent parties deploy unlimited force in order to win against their opponents.[89] The laws of war, however, put some restraints on the actual behaviour of armed forces during combat in order to avoid unnecessary suffering against combatants and to avoid incidental damage to civilians. With respect to the protection of the unarmed civilians, the 1863 Lieber Code, in its Article 22, linked the principle of distinction to the principle of proportionality. Despite the West's civilisational progress, this regulation continued that protection could only be guaranteed "as much as the exigencies of war will admit". Conversely, as reiterated by the Martens clause, the West's public conscience still has an influence on the conduct of the belligerent parties. In particular, in relation to air warfare, the 1923 Rules concerning the Control of Wireless Telegraphy in Time of War and Air Warfare as drafted by a Commission of Jurists, advanced the same principle in its Article 24.[90] However, these early restatements of this fundamental principle regulating the conduct of warfare, had little or few implications on the battlefield; especially against a background of aerial bombardment during the First World War and of the horrifying bombings of Guernica during the Spanish Civil War (1936–1939). Precaution was unlikely to redress the discourse on the Self and the Other. Such discourse wanted to divide and destroy the enemy and it did so by invoking military necessity at its will. Moreover, the Second World War did scatter all hopes to implement this humanitarian conscience whose meaning did not translate into real actions. Nonetheless, though only retrospectively, the International Military Tribunal of Nuremberg in its *Krupp* case, did find some optimism as to the binding and legal nature of the principle of proportionality:

88 Joseph Holland, 'Military objective and collateral damage: their relationship and dynamics', (2004) 7 Yearbook of International Humanitarian Law 35, at 56.

89 Martin Van Creveld, The transformation of war: the most radical reinterpretation of armed conflict since Clausewitz (The Free Press 1991), at 218.

90 Article 24, 1922–1923 Rules concerning the Control of Wireless Telegraphy in Time of War and Air Warfare, Commission of Jurists at the Hague, December 1922–February 1923.

> [The Martens clause] is much more than a pious declaration. It is a general clause, making the usages established among civilized nations, the laws of humanity and the dictates of the public conscience into the legal yardstick to be applied if and when the specific provisions of the Convention [...] do not cover specific cases occurring in warfare, or concomitant to warfare.[91]

However, it was still not clear how much humanitarian care would have to be exercised in order to balance the military requirements at the time of attack. Nor was it clear how much sovereignty would have to be given in.[92] In spite of the Articles 51 (5)b) and 57 (2)b) of AP I which referred respectively to possible attacks causing incidental civilian damages disproportionate to "the concrete and direct military advantage anticipated" and to their cancellation or suspension, the degree of "excessiveness" remained dependent upon the military necessity of the situation at the time of attack. The principle of proportionality's self-referential character prevented it from relying on an independent meaning. True enough, from the ICRC Commentary it appeared that it wanted to give an autonomous meaning to the principle of proportionality which no longer had to be assessed in relation to military necessity: "The Protocol does not provide any justification for attacks which cause *extensive* civilian losses and damage. Incidental losses and damages should never be *extensive*."[93] Consequently, this "extensiveness" would make it possible for proportionality to stand on its own. The ICTY, however, in its *Galić* case, did not follow this interpretation and instead put forward a standard of reasonableness (cf. *paterfamilias*). Hence, the assessment of precautionary measures for proportionate action set aside any independent appeal for humanitarian conscience on behalf of the armed forces: "In determining whether an attack was proportionate it is necessary to examine whether a reasonably well-informed person in the circumstances of the actual perpetrator, making reasonable use of the

91 *USA v. Krupp et al.*, International Military Tribunal of Nuremberg, Tribunal III, Judgment, 31 July 1948, Case No. 10, at http://www.loc.gov/rr/frd/Military_Law/pdf/NT_war-criminals_Vol-IX.pdf, 1341. (Last accessed on 15 February 2015)

92 William R. Smyser, The humanitarian conscience: caring for others in the age of terror (Palgrave Macmillan 2003), at 279.

93 Yves Sandoz, Christophe Swinarski & Bruno Zimmermann (eds), Commentary on the Additional Protocols of 8 June 1977 to the Geneva Conventions of 12 August 1949 (International Committee of the Red Cross 1987), para. 1980. (Emphasis added)

information available to him or her, could have expected excessive casualties to result from the attack."[94]

In the end, the assessment of proportionality at the time of attack remained an exercise which tried to bridge the distance between the armed forces and the objects of attack. This same remoteness favoured other influences to approach the enemy. This would be determinative in the ultimate decision whether to attack or not. Besides the impact of the discourses on the Self and the Other which desubjectivised the Other, utilitarian motivations to safeguard the own troops were present as well. These motivations necessarily gave more leverage to the personal safety of those troops and even to the just cause of their actions. Especially, the cause of war, such as humanitarian interventions, restoring peace and democracy, or the Global War on Terror, greatly determined how far jus in bello had to be respected against enemies which disregarded jus ad bellum in the first place; whereas the Preamble of AP I called for an adherence to the 1949 Geneva Conventions and AP I itself "without any adverse distinction based on the nature or origin of the armed conflict or on the causes espoused by or attributed to the Parties to the conflict"; though, understandably, the laws of armed conflict kept favouring the supremacy of military necessity over humanitarian expectations and demands. If only these military requirements were more flexible and took into consideration the principle of proportionality.[95] The application of the latter principle in practice, showed rather proof of privileging a minimum of casualties of one's own combatants instead of advancing the protection of the enemy population.[96] Evidently, urban combat and counterinsurgency operations put all belligerent parties at risk and in particular the more conventional armed forces to the conflict. The United States Counterinsurgency Manual is particularly illustrative of the everlasting attempt to accommodate the personal safety of the forces and military necessity with the protection of civilians:

> Limiting the misery caused by war requires combatants to consider certain rules, principles, and consequences that restrain the amount of force they may apply. At the same time, combatants are not required to take so much risk that they fail in their mission or forfeit their lives. As long as

94 *Prosecutor v. Galić*, ICTY, Trial Chamber, Judgment, 5 December 2003, Case No. IT-98-29-T, at www.icty.org, para. 58. (Last accessed on 15 February 2015)

95 Eric S. Krauss & Mike O. Lacey, 'Utilitarian vs. humanitarian: the battle over the law of war', (2002) Parameters, 73, at 75–76.

96 Gardam, at 409.

> their use of force is proportional to the gain to be achieved and discriminates in distinguishing between combatants and noncombatants. Soldiers and Marines may take actions where they knowingly risk, but do not intend, harm to noncombatants.[97]

6.4 Towards Progress

6.4.1 *Facing Human Selfishness*

Despite the potential impact of a unifying humanitarian conscience upon the principles of distinction and proportionality, the presence of identity politics in the interpretation and application of the laws of war provided a powerful tool for leaders to divide and rule over their peoples. Namely they wanted to formulate the legal arguments on military necessity and proportionality in utilitarian and thus in conflicting terms. For example, a more sovereign view would advance military requirements to be given preference over the communitarian position advocating the former to be balanced against humanitarian considerations. Linking these arguments with the underlying divisive discourses of the Self and Other demonstrated the dynamism of the positions which belligerent parties could assume. Identities transformed themselves in accordance with the needs and benefits of the parties to the conflict. In particular through means of propaganda, these identities served the selfish interests of one or the other warring party to the conflict.[98] Hence, the dehumanisation of the Other justified dehumanising conduct of warfare by the Self against its Other. Such allegedly legitimate action on behalf of the Self became very questionable. In this regard, Ricoeur brought this ever-returning inhuman egoism back to mythical proportions which made alternative altruistic actions even less plausible. Simply because, according to him, human beings "are confronted by that alternative every time we skirt the enigma of a non-human, perhaps pre-human, evil; and we renew that enigma every time we manifest evil in ourselves and among ourselves".[99] This worldview *de facto* found its way in social reality and war was simply the normal state of affairs in the human

---

97 Article 7–23, 2006 Counterinsurgency Manual, United States Government Interagency Counterinsurgency Initiative, at http://www.usgcoin.org/library/doctrine/COIN-FM3-24.pdf (Last accessed on 15 February 2015)

98 Robert A. Hinde, Bending the rules: morality in the modern world: from relationships to politics and war (Oxford University Press 2007), at 220.

99 Paul Ricoeur, The symbolism of evil (Beacon Press 1969), at 329–30.

world. The laws of war were just another illustration re-affirming this appropriated reality. Mégret underscored this very instrumentalisation and manifestation of Western powers but ignored today's universality of the 1949 Geneva Conventions:

> The laws of war are *also* and unmistakably a project of Western expansion and even imperialism, one that carries its own violence even as it seeks to regulate violence. To the extent that the laws of war project a fantasy about what it means to make war, they are also part of the dissemination and realization of that fantasy—one which, inevitably, is not initially shared universally.[100]

Against this background of the general creation and dissimenation of the usages and laws of war, the Lotus doctrine, as a self-fulfilling prophecy, proved to play an important role in the natural international legal order which was based on a utilitarian morality. Consequently, all military actions were permissible when they were not explicitly prohibited. On the one hand, military necessity imposed an obligation on behalf of the armed forces to achieve the specific results which the military operations prescribed. On the other hand, besides the stricter prohibition of attacking civilian persons and targets, proportionality did not impose an absolute prohibition but rather was an obligation of best efforts to avoid as much as possible incidental civilian damages. From this military practical perspective, settling one or the other obligation, led most likely to a recourse of violence in order to achieve the military requirements. Such exercise of violence—as informed by identity politics on the Self and the Other—decided upon the relativity of the legal arguments. Hence, the sovereign position held the discretionary powers to give or deny the principle of humanity an independent meaning. It almost looked as if this unbridgeable structure of the legal arguments in IHL could only be settled through force instead. Ultimately, military necessity prevails given the absence of the laws of war to settle the conflicting legal arguments peacefully. From the theoretical perspective, the relativity of the structure of the legal arguments in IHL was interpreted in conflicting terms, i.e. necessity versus humanity. When rationalising such conflicting arguments along questions of jurisdiction and legitimate belligerency, it trivialised the actual personal experience of human suffering which took place outside the law and outside the legal discussion. Realistically speaking, given the inherent contradictions, the laws of war are limited in

100 Mégret, in, at 308. (Emphasis added by Mégret)

their endeavour to give actual agency to a humanitarian conscience. Evidently, according to Watkin, "the protection of human life during armed conflict depends not only on the direct application of norms written in humanitarian law treaties but also on the culture and command climate developed within armed groups. If much depends on 'the heart of men', the law can only provide one means by which to limit collateral injury and death."[101] This humanitarian conscience can transcend this divisive structure of the legal arguments so it can hopefully redress the calamities of war. In its early attempts to regulate warfare, the Institute of International Law already recognised these challenges and limitations of human nature:

> Une semblable réglementation ne saurait sans doute avoir pour effet la suppression complète des maux et des dangers que la guerre entraîne, mais elle peut les atténuer dans une mesure considérable, soit en déterminant les limites que la conscience juridique des peuples civilisés impose à l'emploi de la force, soit en mettant le faible sous la protection d'un droit positif.[102]

Moreover, the rationalisation of violence and its justification through a legal platform such as the laws of armed conflict has limited the scope of the actual agency that warring parties can assume in order to access their humanitarian conscience. In this respect, the influence of the discourses on the Self and the Other had brought the rationalisation and/or theorisation of violence into an impersonal rhetoric of warfare. Despite idealistic normative conceptions of how war should be waged, the actual actors of warfare have lost their autonomy to act beyond these laws of war. The influence of those discourses upon the creation and application of IHL, left little room for the dissident and regular armed forces to manoeuvre within those boundaries of IHL. In particular when IHL was on its turn already rationally structured upon the conflicting interests of necessity and humanity. Reason actually prevents to have access to

---

101 Kenneth Watkin, 'Assessing proportionality: moral complexity and legal rules', (2005) 8 Yearbook of International Humanitarian Law 3, at 52.

102 Examen de la Déclaration de Bruxelles de 1874, Institut de Droit International, Session de la Haye 1875, Rapporteur M. Gustave Rolin-Jaequemyns. Free translation: "Without doubt, a similar regulation could not be able to suppress completely the evils and dangers the war brings along, but it can reduce them to a considerable extent by determining the limits the judicial conscience of civilised peoples imposes upon the use of force or by putting the vulnerable under the protection of a positive law."

a humanitarian conscience which is situated outside the law and whose binding force is supposed to depend on the nature of the law itself. Hence, belligerent parties are prevented to find this conscience if they have wanted to give the communitarian argument of the law at least some voice. Such rationalisation of violence as reflected in the laws of war desubjectivises the actors of warfare and has been further accentuated by those discourses on the Self and the Other. According to Winfield, this leaves "freedom without any reality, for the individuality of self-determination is nowhere achieved".[103] Consequently, any possibilities to humanise warfare ever again seems lost as, according to Coates, "war is seen as an industrial and mechanical process in which the distinction between the human and the material element is systematically suppressed".[104]

Moreover, technical reason which led to the development of missile guided weaponry, widened the gap between the impersonal (legal) discourses and the possible personal suffering of the victims of warfare even further. Moreover, these victims have already lost their individuality/subjectivity/personhood through the essentialising discourses on the Self and the Other. Such theorisation or rational production of knowledge legitimises and justifies violence. It alienates the very architects of these rationalisations from the other members of the human species. This leads to an existential crisis which can only be redressed through violence against the Other. In this regard, the construction and destruction of the Other by the Self for the sake of exercising power over this Other possibly centres the Self again. Obviously, such worldview and its associated anthropocentric, rationalised and objectified production of knowledge have dissociated itself from the nature it wanted to control and master. This could be one of the causes why humanity had become des-enchanted and had lost its roots in nature and its faith in humanity.[105] Within this gap, humanity has found another place where it could justify the conduct of warfare against the very survival of its own kind. At the zenith of this existential crisis which started in the mid-nineteenth century, the first conventions on the laws of war were created and were showing proof of this self-fulfilling but in the end auto-destructive process of identity-seeking. In this respect, Tillich and Thomas continued by saying that:

> The basic idea, namely, man's self lost in his own production, in the production that he calls the world of objects, has two sides: he became an object amongst the world of objects produced by his own cognitive

103 Richard Dien Winfield, Reason and justice (State University of New York Press 1999), at 102.

104 Anthony J. Coates, The ethics of war (Manchester University Press 1997), at 220.

105 Paul Tillich, The courage to be (Collins Clear-Type Press 1962), at 93–4.

> approach, losing the power in which he produced it, namely, his own centered selfhood, his own subjectivity. And the other side, as we found, was that man was divided into different spheres within this world. He lost not only his self, his subjectivity, he lost also his unity. And taking both sides together, he became deprived of his centered self, in theory as well as in practice.[106]

6.4.2 *Awakening the Human(itarian) Conscience*

The production of knowledge in conflicting terms on the behaviour, both psychologically and sociologically, of this decentred and disoriented Self led to an endless struggle of relative truths. Necessarily, the competition between those views on human nature, primarily an egoistic and an altruistic one, introduced a view on the duality of human nature which was derived from man's own experience and relationship with others.[107] Moreover, humanity's alienation of nature made it even more difficult to find the qualities of this duality in nature itself. Such disharmony and detachment of the Western mind-set respectively in and from nature, affected the human realities which the Western man wanted to mould to its own decentred image. Having lost its roots, the Western man's impersonal and rationalised discourses could not guarantee to trace back its existence. These discourses on the Self and the Other created another paradigm which removed the autonomy or agency of man to challenge the divide and rule from within this paradigm. This conflictual paradigm served the powerful to divide and conquer over their lost subjects. This could actually take place when violence was given a function to resolve the conflict between sovereignty and communitarian positions as they were not meant to be settled peacefully from the outset. In this respect, the exercise of violence gave man the impression to have found its agency back again and settle the everlasting conflict between sovereignty and community arguments. Even with such impression, violence never brought man back again to its roots because man was already decentred from nature in the first place. The conflictual legal paradigm was just another manifestation of the illusion to give agency back to humanity to settle the disputes presented before it. However, humanity's subjectivity was limited by the law instead and in particular in the laws of war where questions of legitimate belligerency and protection could only be determined by the stronger party to the conflict. The relativist position simply

---

106 Paul Tillich & J. Mark Thomas, The spiritual situation in our technical society (Mercer University Press 1988), at 112.

107 Lydia Voigt & William E. Thornton, The limits of justice: a sociological analysis (University Press of America 1984), at 81.

endorsed and banalised the existence of human suffering as humanity could be equally good and evil within this worldview.[108]

Hence, the need to formulate a way out of this conflictual world paradigm where the impersonal discourses produced exclusionary ideas and practices under the veil of a benevolent Western progress narrative. In particular, it appears that the interconnectedness and human conscience of peoples as found in nature had been broken and had been decentred from nature in order to favour the interests of only a few instead. The laws of war justify settling with violence this created disharmony of relativism on the duality of human nature. Seeing the world in complementary terms instead is another possibility to mediate the allegedly opposing ends of the sovereign and the community. These ends are inherently present in and complementary to human existence and human nature.[109] These propositions are not necessarily conflicting but were rather meeting both on the personal level and the communitarian level. Accepting this complementarity on the duality of human nature can potentially make humanity more resilient to the impersonal divisive discourses. These discourses wanted to undermine humanity's unity whose human interconnectedness was at the root of its evolution. Such acceptance is not just an idealistic formulation which re-enchants the common bounds of human beings as they existed in nature and as they developed through human civilisation. It is an effort to challenge the existing man-made world paradigm which subdues the life-centred paradigm for the whole of humanity.[110] There is a possibility to step outside the appropriated reality of struggles between relativist arguments and of divisions between human beings. According to Sorokin, "the cessation of warfare between partial truths [...] will lead to a replacement of our attitude of uncertainty by one of certitude. In its turn this will bring genuine peace of mind to a humanity now lost in the jungle of relative hypotheses and contradictory half-truths".[111] No longer shall relativism dictate humanity's destiny and divide and rule its members. Life instead is absolute as it is the nature of things. In this respect, human beings can transcend the divisive orders when focusing on their interconnectedness and human conscience instead. Such intersubjectivity reconciles the personal sovereignty

---

108 John Kekes, Facing evil (Princeton University Press 1990), at 235.

109 Leonard C. Feldstein, 'Toward integrity and wisdom: justice as grounding personal harmony', in Charles A. Kelbley (ed), The value of justice: essays on the theory and practice of social virtue (Fordham University Press 1979), at 62.

110 Nicholas Rescher, Ethical idealism: an inquiry into the nature and functions of ideals (University of California Press 1987), at 83.

111 Pitirim A. Sorokin, The reconstruction of humanity (The Beacon Press 1949), at 112–13.

with communitarian views as the interaction/interconnectedness between both complementary levels are taking place through the human conscience. The humanitarian conscience in particular is central to this horizontal transcendental experience. These bounds between the members of humanity can free themselves from the discourses on the Self and the Other because humanity is centred again in nature, where the human race originates from.[112] Within this natural realm, humanity becomes more considerate again about the value of life. Humanity then protects itself for the sake of its very survival. Also Farber touched upon this step to possible naturalist endeavours:

> The production of ideal fictions surely requires the activities of a material body. Hence the question of human finitude is bound with the fate of the human organism. Unless one is prepared to rest his case with speculative assumptions or an empty noumenal realm, he must center his aims, hopes, and efforts on the intranatural realm, and seek to improve his condition as a finite being. There is room for endless progress here; moreover there is no other choice, as a matter of fact.[113]

Such interconnectedness between human beings acknowledges a so-called horizontal transcendentalism that can give the laws of war a binding force which necessarily lies outside the divisive legal interpretations and applications of their structure. This humanitarian conscience, which is somehow already present within the preambulary clauses of the humanitarian conventions, transcends the discourses on the Self and the Other. This conscience circumvents the discourses' conflicting formulations as read within the current laws of war, i.e. between necessity versus humanity, as well as the indeterminacy of this inward-looking struggle of the law. It can be a powerful mitigating force upon the actual conduct of warfare as it realises that humanity and every life stand above the exercise of sovereignty and community positions. In addition, as opposed to the outside violence which the law favours to settle its indeterminacy, this conscience gives from outside this divisive project a non-violent voice. In this respect, Dunant acknowledged the need to be proactive in redressing the human suffering which war had inflicted upon the whole of humanity: "In an age when we hear so much of progress and civilization, is it not a matter of urgency, since unhappily we cannot always avoid wars, to press forward in a human and truly civilized spirit the attempt to prevent, or

112 Luc Ferry, Qu'est-ce qu'une vie réussie? (Grasset 2002), at 447.

113 Marvin Farber, Phenomenology and existence: toward a philosophy within nature (Harper Torchbooks 1967), at 53.

at least to alleviate, the horrors of war?"[114] This feeling of common ground can prevent the warring parties to inflict suffering to their own kind.[115] According to Westlake, such feeling of belonging "to a larger whole than their respective tribes or states, a whole in which the enemy too is comprised, so that duties arising out of that larger citizenship are owed even to him".[116] Giving meaning to life as the root of humanity's common existence, gives humanity's orientation back again which it has lost through reason. This reason had blurred the origins of humanity's shared nature as it naturalises its diversity in conflictual terms. Therefore, the premise not to kill its own species both in armed conflicts or during humanitarian interventions has to be represented in warfare.[117] Casualties can not simply be incidental to this human conscience.[118] All human suffering violates the whole unity of humanity,[119] not only in its conscience/spirit but also in its flesh. Mumford not only accepted the duality of human nature, he also saw the potential of humanity to find its unity again beyond the impersonal discourses. For the sake of the survival of the human species, humanity has to take into account that human conscience both on the personal as well as community level.

> If we keep this standard constantly in mind, we shall have both a measure for what must be rejected and a goal for what must be achieved. In time, we shall create the institutions and the habits of life, the rituals, the laws, the arts, the morals that are essential to the development of the whole personality and the balanced community: the possibilities of progress will become real again once we lose our blind faith in the external improvements of the machine alone. But the first step is a personal one: a change in direction of interest *towards* the person. Without that change,

114 Henry Dunant, A memory of Solferino (International Committee of the Red Cross 1986), at 127.

115 Adam Roberts, 'Land warfare: from Hague to Nuremberg', in Michael Howard, George J. Andreopoulos & Mark R. Shulman (eds), The laws of war: constraints on warfare in the Western world (Yale University Press 1994), at 136.

116 Lassa Oppenheim (ed), The collected papers of John Westlake on public international law (Cambridge University Press 1914), at 274.

117 James F. Childress, Moral responsibility in conflicts: essays on nonviolence, war, and conscience (Louisiana State University Press 1982), at 68.

118 Richard Norman, 'War, humanitarian intervention and human rights', in Richard Sorabji & David Rodin (eds), The ethics of war: shared problems in different traditions (Ashgate 2006), at 202.

119 Smyser, at 279.

> no great betterment will take place in the social order. Once that change begins, everything is possible.[120]

6.4.3 *Surviving Humanity*

The alleged contradictions between sovereignty and community values have been historical productions of the man-made paradigm which was created in order to divide and rule over human beings.[121] Once this is accepted, it is still not enough to see the world rather in complementary terms from within the current man-made paradigm. If humanity refuses to accept these facts and continues to believe that this struggle can be settled violently instead of peacefully within this paradigm, in all probability, it might solicit the very destiny of auto-destruction.[122] To refer to exclusion or inclusion reinforces the same worldview because the membership to one or the other group would still remain at the discretion of the most powerful. Here, and contrary to what Jodoin intended, deconstruction was used to demonstrate the exclusionary nature of the discourses on the Self and the Other. However, this study does not wish to give "alterity"/Otherness a platform in order to change the hierarchies within the existing conflictual paradigm.[123] Here, deconstruction serves to expose these hierarchies and the violent dynamics of self-destructiveness of this man-made paradigm. It also levels the path to argue outside this man-made paradigm from the life one instead. Though there exists a unity of humanity, this study remains realistic about humanity's dual nature which can threaten the very existence of its life. Within the unity of humanity, each human being as part of the whole has the agency and responsibility to respect the life of the whole and its parts.[124] Rationalising this responsibility is not sufficient to raise such consciousness.[125] Feeling re-enchanted again about the interconnectedness of all human beings can put humanity's evolutionary nature back into the

---

120 Lewis Mumford, The condition of man (Secker & Warburg 1944), at 423. (Emphasis added by Mumford)

121 Duncan Kennedy, 'The structure of the Blackstone's Commentaries', (1979) 28 Buffalo Law Review, 205, at 221.

122 Richard Falk, 'Janus tormented: the international law of internal war', in James N. Rosenau (ed), International aspects of civil strife (Princeton University Press 1964), at 193.

123 Sébastien Jodoin, 'International law and alterity: the state and the other', (2008) 21 Leiden Journal of International Law, 1, at 26.

124 Thomas M. Scanlon, What we owe to each other (The Belknap Press of Harvard University Press 1999), at 104.

125 John Kekes, Pluralism in philosophy: changing the subject (Cornell University Press 2000), at 202.

picture and it accepts life to be central again to the being and existence of everything. Hopefully, this "life paradigm" will be strong enough to challenge the historical illusion and disorientation of the dehumanising discourses which erased humanity's common identity and conscience. Therefore, beyond the superficiality of rationalised differences and collectivities, human beings can truly value their lives again instead of their lives' attributes. Human beings can act again as agents which are responsible for their own lives and those of others.[126] Especially against the background of human suffering as rationalised and legitimised within the laws of armed conflict, such values have lost their importance. Mandelstam argued that this very rationalisation lacked the sense of empathy which is inherently present amongst human beings:

> We have seen the triumph of evil after the values of humanism have been vilified and trampled on. The reason these values succumbed was probably that they were based on nothing except boundless confidence in the human intellect. I think we may now find a better foundation for them, if only because of the lessons we have drawn from our experience.[127]

Hence, reason alone is not the only tool which human beings possess in order to recognise this unity of humanity. Article 1 of the 1948 Universal Declaration of Human Rights endorsed that all human beings "are endowed with reason and conscience and should act towards one another in a spirit of brotherhood". Even such formal recognition tends to give meaning again to the interconnectedness between human beings both in terms of their belonging and their suffering. This human conscience transcends the impersonal discourses on the Self and the Other and can give the laws of armed conflict a binding humanitarian force after all. Despite the threats to the very existence of the human species, such horizontal transcendentalism can possibly reconnect human beings with each other. It can make humanity realise again what is at stake in wars, i.e. life, the source of everything and not only of human life. Through this intersubjective process between human beings, the completeness of this fundamental value can be cherished again in the present. Humanity lives now, not in the past nor in the future. Or as Tillich and Thomas put it, such "fulfilment is going on in every moment here and now beyond history, not some time in the future, but here and now above ourselves. [...] Something might happen that

126 Raimond Gaita, A common humanity: thinking about love and truth and justice (Routledge 2000), at 261.

127 Nadezhda Mandelstam, Hope against hope (The Harvill Press 1989) cited in Jonathan Glover, Humanity: a moral history of the twentieth century (Jonathan Cape 1999), at 405.

is elevated out of time into eternity. This then is a nonutopian and a true fulfilment of the meaning of history and of our own individual life".[128] Living the fullness of life can elevate humanity's state of mind, which wants to control life and nature, into a state of being where life, which given its completeness, gives meaning to humanity and not the other way around. In this respect, within the context of armed conflicts, one can notice that "the dictates of public conscience" of the Martens clause impose this very preference for life. Wars made the whole of humanity suffer from their destruction. Therefore, the humanisation of the laws of war necessarily has to ban all armed conflicts if it intends to save humanity from its self-destruction. Nonetheless, facing the history of humanity and awakening the human conscience are another way to safeguard humanity's existence. As Meron continues:

> The gap between the norms and the reality in human rights and humanitarian law has always been wide. Today the visibility and immensity of violations of international humanitarian law highlight issues of compliance that raise cynicism and doubt. In the long run, humanitarian norms must become a part of public consciousness everywhere. Education, training, persuasion, and emphasis on values that lie *outside the law*, such as ethics, honor, mercy, and shame, must be vigorously pursued. This job cannot be left to the law alone. Public opinion and the social consensus that proved so effective in the development of the law should be geared to transforming practice as well. For that, the creation of a culture of values is indispensable.[129]

6.5 Conclusion

In this chapter, one has tried to demonstrate the utilitarian nature of the dichotomies of the divisive discourses between the Self and the Other as reflected within the structure of the legal arguments in IHL. Questions of jurisdiction and distinction, necessity and proportionality, were affected by the indeterminacy of the laws of war within this conflictual man-made paradigm. In order to favour one or the other argument as advocated by one or the other warring party, the relativity between one or the other conflicting argument necessarily sees itself settled by having recourse to the use of violence. Throughout this

128 Tillich & Thomas, The spiritual situation in our technical society, at 95.

129 Theodor Meron, 'The humanization of humanitarian law', (2000) 94 American Journal of International Law, 239, at 278. (Emphasis added)

process whose settlement should be guided by good faith instead, the stronger party to the conflict can safeguard its sovereign interests above the communitarian ones. This party imposes its will through violent means. This division in order to rule as being present throughout the West's encounter with its Other within and beyond its borders, both in theory and in practice, had only led to more slaughter and bloodshed which on the long run puts the very survival of humanity at stake.

Therefore, the humanitarian considerations, as reflective within communitarian principles such as distinction and proportionality, need to find another way to transcend the inertia of the structure of the legal arguments in IHL. The suffering of human beings affected by warfare became subordinated to military requirements. Humanity's conscience as the manifestation of humanity's unity and interconnectedness in nature are possibly an independent force. It challenges the conflictual paradigm and defends the life one instead. Regardless of the appropriated reality of the dehumanising discourses and of the indeterminacy of the laws of war, this conscience gives full meaning again to good faith. Such good faith assesses the allegedly conflicting principles in the conflictual legal paradigm and takes into account the survival of the human species to which all warring parties biologically belong. Such humanitarian conscience awakens humanity about the suffering it is inflicting upon its own kind. In this regard, humanity should respect all forms of life. This humanitarian conscience can transcend the power which had driven the divisive discourses on the Self and the Other. The power of life instead can transcend the influence of those discourses upon the interpretation and application of the laws of armed conflict.

Conclusion

1 On Identity, Knowledge, and Morality

In this study, the deconstructivist analysis has provided some new insights on the impact of the discourses on the Self and the enemy Other on the creation, interpretation and application of the legal arguments within the Western and Islamic traditions on warfare. It has given an account of those historical events and mind-sets which have influenced the laws of armed conflict. This historical analysis has proved particularly useful to demonstrate the strategy of leaderships to divide and rule over their subjects. By creating certain dehumanising narratives on the Other, the Self was necessarily entitled to give only respect to the members of its own kind.[1] This analysis clearly emphasises the dichotomies which have been created to divide and rule over humanity. On the one hand, there is inclusive discourse on the Self, while on the other hand, there is an exclusive discourse on the Other. As seen by the deconstructivist approach, both discourses rely on each others' existence, but their deconstruction itself does not necessarily want to give voice to realities behind the textual discourses. It only gives a platform for the excluded Other. Hence, it reinforces the structure of the dichotomies, namely between inclusion and exclusion. Moreover, the only manner to settle this conflict is through violence. Violence becomes functional in resolving dichotomies and differences and reinforces the solution to be at the expense of one or the other position. Peace, compromise and dialogue in such conflictual paradigm are completely lost.

This study, however, tries to go beyond the unsustainability of these dichotomies which have been introduced and which have started to live their own appropriated realities. It attempts to transcend such approach which analyses and defines the social world in conflictual terms, namely in dichotomies, in order to explain the tensions between different peoples and which have been exploited by the powerful accordingly. However, this exposure of the unsustainability of the discriminatory narratives, according to this study, is not sufficient to bring actual justice beyond those textual realities. The impossibility of reading justice into those textual realities is an obstacle to foster any form of justice after deconstruction. Within this reasoning there is no justice possible beyond the text as the text is the only reality where deconstruction, i.e. justice, can take place. From this perspective, any reconstruction again favours

1 Marc Pilisuk & Jennifer Achord Rountree, Who benefits from global violence and war: uncovering a destructive system (Praeger Security International 2008), at 35.

 | DOI 10.1163/9789004298248_009

the interests of power to be reflected within the text. Instead, this study asserts that there is also another reality beyond the text as well, namely the world as such in which human beings live. This world necessarily can never be fully captured or represented by the text though it can control the knowledge of how one looks at this world, namely in conflictual terms.[2] In this way, it is possible to transcend the divisions which the texts have produced and which have started to live their own violent realities within this human world. As a scientific method of producing such knowledge, reason is limited in its capacity to grasp reality. It only gives a paradoxical account of it. As Zulaika noted:

> The goal of knowledge is only more knowledge, and reason becomes its most compelling argument, whereas the kind of puzzlement that forces ultimate questions about the paradoxes of violence demands movement beyond reason: the rational justification for killing, either in warfare or capital punishment, is all too banal for such perplexity.[3]

Therefore, this book observes and defines this world in rather complementary terms. No longer must different interests between human beings be seen as dichotomous or conflictual. No longer must such determination reinforce the project of a divided world with conflicting interests between peoples. Instead, this study aims at transcending such divisive knowledge of the world as witnessed through the text and their appropriated violent realities.[4] Beyond the dichotomies of inclusion and exclusion there is another option, namely to highlight the roots of humanity's common belonging whether it originates in nature or is found in God's creation. From these common roots, there also exists a human conscience which has evolved throughout the existence of human civilisations and human coexistence; and which according to Lockley and Morimoto, "repeatedly stress[es] the importance of loving communion between self and other".[5] Having agreed upon the origin of humanity and the development of its conscience, one can no longer see anything which emerges from its behaviour as being conflictual. Every opposition turns out to be complementary to the very existence of humanity. It is a matter of finding the

2 Barry Barnes, The nature of power (Polity Press 1988), at 98.

3 Joseba Zulaika, 'The anthropologist as terrorist', in Nancy Scheper-Hughes & Philippe Bourgois (eds), Violence in war and peace (Blackwell Publishing 2004), at 419.

4 See also John Paul Lederach, The moral imagination: the art and soul of building peace (Oxford University Press 2005), at 61.

5 Martin Lockley & Ryo Morimoto, How humanity came into being: the evolution of consciousness (Floris Books 2010), at 311.

right balance between several identities and interests.[6] Such commitment to a more sustainable worldview fosters the interconnectedness and dialogue between all members of the human race and the responsibility of shared human existence.[7] Levinas in particular endorsed this complementary view: "This idea of human refers back to the approach of the Other in the face, in a dimension of height, in responsibility for oneself and for the Other."[8]

In this discussion on the philosophy of science, issues of morality influence the examination of this debate. Such morality has to be complementary in its endeavours to remind humanity of its origins and of its responsibility towards its kind, namely to give a realistic account of its idealistic ambitions.[9] Within this discussion, a humanistic worldview has to take into consideration the language available to promote its ideals, namely to argue in rational terms. Nonetheless, scientific reason still continues to problematise the object of its study and continues to see the world in conflictual terms. Consequently, the debate on the philosophy of science itself remains divided. Within this division, both rationalists and relativists agree that there are two opposing and hence conflictual ends of each argument. The rationalists, however, argue that one can only be rationally and distinctively true, while the relativists submit that there is a plurality of truths in the first place.[10] Despite the belief in relative truths and the idea of diversity of views, the relativist approach threatens the very existence of one humanity which lies at the roots of the social diversity in this world. By focusing in particular on the textual realities of such diversity, it is impossible for a deconstructivist to reconcile the diversity whose history has become incommensurable within its parts. Such rationalisation further reinforces strategies to divide and rule and polarise. In this case, within the philosophy of science, methodologies and objects of scientific knowledge and studies deny the reality of the unity of humanity.[11] The only way to safeguard the unity of humanity in its origins lies in the acceptance of the complementarity of its diversity. This, of course, necessarily has implications on the existing philosophy of science and its methodologies which until now have divided humanity in its worldview. Or as Strauss argued:

---

6 Kwame Anthony Appiah, The ethics of identity (Princeton University Press 2005), at 212.

7 See Stuart Rees, Passion for peace: exercising power creatively (University of New South Wales Press 2003), at 281.

8 Emmanuel Levinas, Totality and infinity: an essay on exteriority (Kluwer Academic Publishers 1991), at 214.

9 Iris Murdoch, The sovereignty of good (Routledge 1991), at 78.

10 Barry Barnes & David Bloor, 'Relativism, rationalism and the sociology of knowledge', in Martin Hollis & Steven Lukes (eds), Rationality and relativism (Basil Blackwell 1990), at 25–28.

11 See Ernest Gellner, 'Relativism and universals', in see id., at 183.

> Under certain social conditions a man may undergo so many or such critical experiences for which conventional explanations seem inadequate, that he begins to question large segments of the explanatory terminology that has been taught him. In the internal rhetorical battle that ensues, his opponents may be conceived as lying or manipulating events to their own advantage, as wrong, or as duped. But a man cannot question his own basic terminology without questioning his own purposes. If in large measure he rejects the explanations he once believed, then he has been alienated and has lost a world. He has been "spiritually dispossessed". If he embraces a set of counter-explanations or invents a set of his own, then he has regained the world, for the world is not merely "out there" but is also what he makes of it.[12]

Clearly, there are possibilities to reason from another perspective which questions the role of scientific reason itself which has made humanity to become decentred from its existence in nature or in the creation. Reason instead has become instrumentalised to justify the existence of the divisive discourses on the Self and the enemy Other. In this manner, such "*fragmentary* logic"[13] stands between humanity and nature or the creation and prevents humanity to become centred again within nature or the creation. In addition, reason has contextualised and rationalised those divisions and treated them to be part of the almost natural course of human condition and history. Linked with the debates on the role and content of reason, Emon observed that questions of legitimacy in the law too often obfuscate other issues of authority in the following words:

> The challenge for researchers today is to recognize and understand the presumptions about what constitutes legitimate authority in the law, and how those presumptions contribute to a regulatory system that often obscures the distances between experience and expectation. In other words, future research may want to address how much of the distance between expectation and experience is actually hidden from view by the legal methods designed to account for that distance in the first place.[14]

---

12 Anselm L. Strauss, Mirrors and masks: the search for identity (Free Press 1959), at 38.

13 Amartya Sen, Identity and violence: the illusion of destiny (Allen Lane 2006), at 176. (Emphasis added by Sen)

14 Anver M. Emon, Islamic natural law theories (Oxford University Press 2010), at 205.

Lorenz in particular warned about the risks of those rationalised assumptions and stated that "all the great dangers threatening humanity with extinction are direct consequences of conceptual thought and verbal speech. They drove man out of the paradise in which he could follow his instincts with impunity and do or not do whatever he pleased."[15] Understandably, scientific reason and the worldview it adopts inherently reinforces, through its conflictual reasoning, the division between the members of humanity and the alienation from nature or the creation. Though the discussion on the philosophy of science is predominantly based on reason, this study questions the morality and responsibility of such scientific efforts. In this respect, Lorenz continued:

> True morality, in the highest human sense of the word, presupposes a mental capacity which no animal possesses, and conversely, human responsibility would itself be impossible without a definite foundation of sentiment. Even in man, the feeling of responsibility has its roots in the deep, instinctive "layers" of his mind and he may not do with impunity all that cold reason affirms.[16]

2 On War, Division, and Conscience

While positivists and deconstructivists respectively look at the letter and the power behind the law and are accusing each other for lacking respectively agency and contextualisation in their interpretation of the law, this study gives also the spirit of the laws of war and in particular of the principles of protection a voice. Instead, the study proposes to foster a human(itarian) conscience to have an impact on the existing rules of armed conflict and in particular on their interpretation and application. Though the laws of war necessarily legitimate the use of force but constrain the actual conduct during warfare through the principles of protection, i.e. distinction and proportionality, at the same time military necessity justifies any violation of those principles.[17] The inherent contradiction within the laws of war, as seen by deconstructivists, are an outcome of the influence of the discourse on the Self and the excluded Other.

---

15 Konrad Lorenz, On aggression (Routledge 1996), at 204–5.

16 Konrad Lorenz, Man meets dog (Methuen 1977), at 184.

17 See Nobuo Hayashi, 'Requirements of military necessity in international humanitarian law and international criminal law', (2010) 28 Boston University International Law Journal, 39; Michael N. Schmitt, 'Military necessity and humanity in international humanitarian law: preserving the delicate balance', (2010) 50 Virginia Journal of International Law, 795.

The only way to settle this actual contradiction is through the use of violence itself. Such analysis necessarily reinforces its worldview in conflictual terms. It rationalises the use of violence and gives it a function, namely to settle the tension between sovereignty- and community-based arguments. Also the positivist analysis of the laws of war ignores how such conflictual worldview affects the operation of the laws of war which themselves have been formulated in conflictual terms, namely between humanity and military necessity. Moreover, this approach retroactively gives violence a function in particular after the violations of the principles of protection. On a case-by-case basis, positivists forget about the impact of human suffering beyond the actual actions and violations in a particular context. In this respect, Mangabeira Unger questioned the very act of given meaning to those actions, necessarily retroactively:

> To view action through the prism of meaning is to regard it as an event in history. There is a superficial sense in which historical knowledge is retrospective. But in fact all understanding is based upon what has been learned from the past even when it is concerned with the prediction of the future. What distinguishes historical knowledge is its effort to grasp, and to assume, the position of the actor. The actor may know some of the consequences of his actions, but he cannot know all of them, nor can he avoid the experience of choosing among different possible purposes and courses of conduct.[18]

Within the context of warfare, military necessity which envisages an anticipated military advantage in the future is already given meaning at the moment of attack. It cannot possibly capture what human suffering will take place in the future. Principles of protection deserve to be applied at any time regardless of any future action which is advantageous for one or other party to the conflict. This anticipated rationalisation and hence future justification of violence sets aside the protection in the present. Clearly, military necessity disregards humanitarian necessity to protect life. War necessarily gives up life in its definition to be human.[19] Because violence is given a function initially in view of settling the conflict between humanitarian and sovereignty arguments both within the text and on the battlefield, this worldview in conflictual terms as understood by deconstructivists also finds its place within the positivist analysis. History necessarily repeats itself, as the analysis of that violent history itself

18 Roberto Mangabeira Unger, Law in modern society: toward a criticism of social theory (The Free Press 1976), at 248.

19 Daniel Pick, War machine: the rationalisation of slaughter in the modern age (Yale University Press 1993), at 15.

is rationalised in almost natural terms. Violence has always occurred during human history and consequently is considered to be part of human nature. When human beings have associated themselves along different identities, in this worldview it is understood that there always will be a tension between those different groups. Violence is a means to settle the conflict between the Self and the enemy Other and the laws of war legitimise its use. Clearly, the law is not the so-called "antithesis of violence",[20] as Brooks puts it. Under this conflictual paradigm, such repeated history of violence by and against the human species has an apocalyptic outcome, namely that the survival of the human species is at stake. Though humanity has invented war it can invent peace as well.[21] According to Fry, "*[i]f war is seen as natural, then there is little point in trying to prevent, reduce, or abolish it. Consequently, the acceptance of war as a social institution facilitates its continuance.*"[22] By retrospectively giving such meaning to violence, one not only justifies its presence on the battlefield alone but also within the discourses on the Self and Other which had already started to live their own appropriated realities. While reason can never fully grasp why human beings have recourse to such auto-destructive means both discursively and physically,[23] such rationalising attempts in fact contribute to the very destruction of the human species itself.

Because the determination of military necessity is an anticipated exercise which takes into account the military advantage belligerents can gain in the future, it cannot fully assess the human suffering which will take place in the future as well. In this regard, there is a temporal division between the future gain of an attack and the present avoidance of suffering during an attack. Military necessity operates in the future while principles of protection apply in the present. Within this gap, there is even more room for polarising and dehumanising discourses to inform the decision-making of any military advantageous operation on the battlefield. Humanitarian requirements become subservient to the military ones instead. The formulation of the laws of war in both the Western and Islamic tradition makes this possible. Hence, within the temporal

---

20 Rosa Ehrenreich Brooks, 'The new imperialism: violence, norms, and the "rule of law"', (2002–2003) 101 Michigan Law Review, 2275, at 2306.

21 Santiago Genovés, Is peace inevitable? Aggression, evolution, and human destiny (George Allen and Unwin 1972), at 178. Even the Preamble of the UNESCO Constitution refers to this in the following words: "Since wars begin in the minds of men, it is in the minds of men that the defenses of peace must be constructed."

22 Douglas P. Fry, The human potential for peace: an anthropological challenge to assumptions about war and violence (Oxford University Press 2006), at 2. (Emphasis added by Fry)

23 See James Gilligan, Violence: reflections on our deadliest epidemic (Jessica Kingsley Publishers 2000), at 102.

void, only agency is given to the belligerents which contextualise their enemies through dehumanising and abstract narratives of the enemy[24] and which attribute functions to violence to defeat them. The victims of violence instead have never had the agency to call for their protection within this temporal gap. Such treatment of human suffering simply cannot be rationalised. Reason cannot be criticised on those grounds given its inability to do so. However, reason creates the illusion that the use of violence through it is justifiable. Or as Lamprecht argued:

> Reason is able, even in the state of nature and in the midst of war, to perceive the moral desirability of peace and honesty and mutual kindness. But reason itself cannot make conditions prevail in which reasonable man can reasonably perform reasonable acts. The laws of nature do not require a man to expose his innocence to the brutal aggression of others.[25]

Instead of giving meaning to violence or rationalising violence by giving it meaning in the causal relationship between military necessity and anticipated military advantage, this study exposes the auto-destructive nature and reasoning of this very process. It is submitted that this rationalisation, justification and legitimation of violence through the laws of war reinforce the function given to violence to settle a worldview full of paradoxes and polarisations. Such approaches necessarily look at the perpetrators' perspective to find out whether they have actually respected the principles of protection (positivism) and how discourses on the Self and Other have informed those actions with regard to the obedience of those principles of protection (deconstructivism). No voice has been given to the actual victims of such violations of the principles of protection which themselves are excused on grounds of military necessity. Albeit unintentionally, both the positivists and the deconstructivists contribute to the silencing of human suffering through the examination of the violent agent only and by giving meaning to its violence.[26] Any theory on violence has difficulties in rationalising, justifying and legitimising the individual

24 Caroline Holmqvist-Jonsäter, 'War as perpetual policing', in Caroline Holmqvist-Jonsäter & Christopher Coker (eds), The character of war in the 21st century (Routledge 2010), at 117–18.

25 Sterling P. Lamprecht, Our philosophical traditions (Appleton Century-Crofts 1955), at 280.

26 Anton Blok, 'The enigma of senseless violence', in Göran Aijmer & Jon Abbink (eds), Meanings of violence: a cross cultural perspective (Berg 2000), at 33.

experience of suffering by the victims of violence. For those victims, violence is simply meaningless and cannot be given any function or a meaning which rationalises, justifies and legitimises their suffering. At this point in history and in the Islamic and Middle Eastern world, humanity, as Holmes argued, "can no longer hope, as it may once have, to muddle interminably through war after war. The potential destructiveness of war has progressed too far for that."[27]

Within these vicious circles of violence, the survival of the human species remains at risk. Because the violent law, which reinforces the use of violence to settle conflicts between the Self and the Other, prevents human beings to have access to their conscience, this study intends to remind them about it again. This human(itarian) conscience respects the interconnectedness of all human beings beyond their differences and urges for a solidarity which can safeguard the survival of its kind. While leaders have always divided humanity through their rule, namely through the divisive narratives on the Self and the Other and their impact upon the interpretation and application of laws of war legitimising violence, a human(itarian) conscience transcends this division and promotes the life of all members of humanity instead. The binding force of this conscience does not necessarily stem from legal or moral codes, but rather from the intersubjective relationships between human beings beyond the alienating narratives of the Self and the Other in order to see human dignity to be fulfilled.[28] This same conscience, however, does not want to abolish the existing principles of protection which have become subservient to auto-destructive military necessity. Instead this conscience gives a binding force to those principles from outside the laws of war which are formulated in conflictual terms, namely between protection and necessity. This drive for the survival of the whole of humanity can affect the interpretation and application of the laws of war. According to Rapoport, "even though the immediate pragmatic value of a conscience-driven act may not be demonstrable, in historical perspective it appears that great, irreversible changes in the human condition have been brought about by accumulations of such acts".[29] It transcends the division which they have reproduced within the text by reviving the humanitarian spirit of the laws of war.

---

27 Robert L. Holmes, On war and morality (Princeton University Press 1989), at 294.

28 See Christopher Coker, Ethics and war in the 21st century (Routledge 2008), at 126.

29 Anatol Rapoport, Strategy and conscience (Schocken Books 1969), at 288.

3 On Unity, Protection, and Life

While the narratives of the Self and the enemy Other have divided humanity and whose fictions have started to become appropriated in reality, this study highlights the existence of another reality outside the textual realities and their divisive discourses. This reality is premised on the evolutionary or creationary unity of humanity. This very unity of humanity constitutes the basis upon which the human(itarian) conscience is formulated. It stresses the interconnectedness of human beings which is found in nature or which is found in the creation of God. From this unity and interconnectedness, a greater solidarity and cooperation is the expression of humanity's common fate between all of its members beyond the discourses which fear the Other.[30] This common fate exists in the very life which is shared by all human beings in this world. No longer division will find fertile ground in a world which is shared by all of humanity and where life is put central to it. Or as Arends noted, "as its only point of reference [it could] unfold its entire fertility".[31] No longer is it acceptable that a worldview thriving on conflict and violence finds legitimacy to destroy the very life which lies at the basis of its existence. Life simply consists of everything, even conflict. But the objective is to safeguard the very life of humanity without which no human civilisations can exist. Handy, vividly described this need to transcend the problematisation of contradictions which themselves are strategies to divide and rule over humanity:

> Life is full of contradictions and surprises, that it is, in fact, full of paradoxes. But if we can learn to understand and accept these paradoxes, then I believe that we can eventually find pathways through them. We can live with them and manage them. This is especially necessary as times become more turbulent, because at such times the world becomes even more complex and difficult to understand. [...] Life is like a seesaw, a game where the movement and the excitement come from a balance of opposites, because it will always inevitably be full of paradoxes. I believe that the key to progress and even to survival in life and work is to be aware that contradictions can coexist, and to learn to live with them.[32]

---

30 See Bertrand Russell, Common sense and nuclear warfare (Routledge 2001), at 70.

31 Hannah Arendt, The human condition (The University of Chicago Press 1958), at 320.

32 Charles Handy, 'Finding sense in uncertainty', in Rowan Gibson (ed), Rethinking the future (Nicholas Brealey Publishing 1999), at 18–9.

Because humanity throughout its history has decentred itself from nature (where humanity lives), it forgets about its life which is rooted in nature—from a secular perspective—and/or its creation—from a religious perspective. Within nature contradictions exist but within nature violence is not always given a function to settle a conflict at the expense of its survival. Still, human nature itself is reflective of such dualism. Where, according to Fromm, "the enormous power of the will for destruction which we see in the history of man, and which we have witnessed so frightfully in our own time, is rooted in the nature of man, just as the drive to create is rooted in it".[33] Both potentialities to create and destroy life are indeed complementary in humanity's nature; however, their formulation in conflictual terms always gives violence a function to settle this natural tension. Consequently, it rationalises, justifies and legitimises violence to take place and set up laws of war contributing to these ends. When humanity realises that its life is rooted in nature and/or its creation, it will care much more about that life which it shares with all members of humanity. Hence, the need to become centred again in nature and/or the creation, to acknowledge the duality of human nature in complementary terms, and to respect life as it is present. When life is put central again to human coexistence, humanity itself has to make those efforts and assume its responsibility to protect it in absolute terms for the sake of humanity itself.[34] Any violence against the life of a human being, is, because of its shared existence by other human beings, an act of violence against the whole of humanity. In this respect, if the selfish side of a human being wants to survive, it can only do so with the human community it belongs to and where life is central to the existence of both. This realisation, however, requires responsibility as Lorenz pointed out:

> Originally sympathy was most certainly present only when one individual was bonded to another by love. Love for what lives is an important, indispensable emotion. This emotion is what places the burden of responsibility for all life on our planet squarely upon humans who are sovereign over all of it. The responsible human being may not push aside or repress awareness of the suffering endured by other creatures and least of all the suffering sustained by fellow humans. With this responsibility the human is confronted by a most difficult task. [...] As important as it is to awaken in humans their sympathy for all living beings dwelling

33 Erich Fromm, The sane society (Routledge & K. Paul 1956), at 37.

34 Christopher Coker, Waging war without warriors? The changing culture of military conflict (Lynne Rienner Publishers 2002), at 181.

> together with us on the earth, and as indispensable as an understanding of that love for what lives may be, we must still make an incisive separation between our feelings for animals and those we have for our fellow humans.[35] [...] Humans who are capable of seeing how beautiful the world is cannot help but face the world with optimism. The knowledge they acquire about the grandeur and the beauty of creation will help them resist the methods and the messages of today's propaganda and the pressures of indoctrination. The truth inherent in the real world will teach them to bear no false witness against any neighbor. Their perceptibilities for the grand harmonies will become so deeply seated and skilled that they will be capable of differentiating what is sick from what is healthy and not be in despair about the great harmony of organic creation when they experience the tragedies of suffering and death of individual beings. Those are all things that are self-evident for every human near to nature. [...] All those who share this kind of world view perceive, unerringly, compassion for their fellow creatures and for the fate of the individual being; together with this compassion love is born for all that is alive and living, and with this love comes the realization of responsibility.[36]

For those reasons, life has to be protected by all means; not only within the real world but also through the textual realities. The laws of armed conflict in particular are one of those means to protect life. While, according to Brooks, "the law is an important part of how people come to terms with suffering and violence",[37] its present content has repeatedly continued to be informed by polarisation and dehumanisation. The power of life transcends such conflictual paradigm and gives the existing laws of war a binding character which is extra-legal. In this regard, the human(itarian) conscience is one of those means to foster adherence to the principles of protection. This conscience reminds humanity about its interconnectedness and shared life so necessity can no longer threaten the survival of the human species at all costs. Both positivists and deconstructivists can use this spirit beside their textual and contextual interpretations to advance the same ends of justice for and equality of humanity. Because humanity has direct access to this conscience, the law and the structure of the legal arguments in IHL and the ILW no longer prevent it to have access to it. No longer will those privileges of man be served but the

35 Konrad Lorenz, The waning of humaneness (Unwin Hyman 1988), 220–21.

36 Id., at 230.

37 Ehrenreich Brooks, at 2314.

privilege of life instead and the law can become truly humanitarian again. In this respect, according to Reiman, "war can never be justified as anything but a necessary evil, and even when justified, it stays an evil. It must above all be carried out with an eye to minimizing harm."[38] Ultimately, as Fromm argued, the outcome of this book and its "critical and radical thought will only bear fruit when it is blended with the most precious quality man is endowed with—the love of life".[39]

---

38 Jeffrey Reiman, 'Ethics for calamities: how strict is the moral rule against targeting noncombatants?' in Roger Wertheimer (ed), Empowering our military conscience: transforming just war theory and military moral education (Ashgate 2010), at 106.

39 Erich Fromm, The anatomy of human destructiveness (Henry Holt and Company 1992), at 485.

Bibliography

Abdul-Rahman, Muhammad Saed, Tafsir Ibn Kathir Juz' 15 (Part 15): Al-Israa (or Bani Isra'il) 1 to Al-Kahf 74 (MSA Publication Limited 2009).

Abdullah, Ustaz Yoonus, Sharia in Africa (Shebiotimo Publications 1998).

Abou El Fadl, Khaled, The great theft: wrestling Islam from the extremists (HarperCollins Publishers 2005).

———, 'Between functionalism and morality: the juristic debates on the conduct of war', in Jonathan E. Brockopp (ed), Islamic ethics of life: abortion, war, and euthanasia (University of South Carolina Press 2003).

———, The authoritative and authoritarian in Islamic discourses: a contemporary study (Al-Saadawi Publications 2002).

———, Rebellion and violence in Islamic law (Cambridge University Press 2001).

———, 'Ahkam al-bughat: irregular warfare and the law of rebellion in Islam', in James Turner Johnson & John Kelsay (eds), Cross, crescent, and sword: the justification and limitation of war in Western and Islamic tradition (Greenwood Press 1990).

Abu Bakar, Mohamad, 'Managing the future: Islam in the post-Cold War era', in Syed Othman Alhabshi & Nik Mustapha Nik Hassan (eds), Islamic civilization: present and future challenges (Institute of Islamic Understanding Malaysia 1997).

Abu Sulayman, Abdul Hamid Ahmad, Towards an Islamic theory of international relations: new directions for methodology and thought (International Institute of Islamic Thought, University of Pennsylvania, 1973).

Afsah, Ebrahim, 'Contested universalities of international law: Islam's struggle with modernity', (2008) 10 Journal of the History of International Law, 259.

Ahmad, Ahmad Atif, Structural interrelations of theory and practice in Islamic law: a study of six works of medieval Islamic jurisprudence (Brill 2006).

Ahmad, Aqil & Khan, Iqbal Ali, Text book of Mohammedan law (Central Law Agency 2004).

Ahmed, Ishtiaq, The concept of an Islamic state: an analysis of the ideological controversy in Pakistan (Pinter 1987).

Ahmedov, Aibek, 'Religious minorities and apostacy in early Islamic states: legal and historical analysis of sources', (2006) 2 Journal of Islamic State Practices in International Law 1.

al-Ghunaimi, Mohammad Tal'at, The Muslim conception of international law and the Western approach (Martinus Nijhoff Publishers 1968).

Alibasic, Ahmet, 'The place for others in Islam', (2007) 3 Comparative Islamic Studies 98.

al-Isma'il, Faruqi, 'Islam as culture and civilization', in Salem Azzam (ed), Islam and contemporary society (Longman 1982).

al-Jilani, 'Abdul-Qadir & Bayrak al-Jerrahi al-Halveti, Shaikh Tosun, The secret of secrets (Islamic Texts Society 1992).

Al-Khalîli, Ahmad bin Hamad, 'Elements of the nation's renaissance', in Qatar Ministry of Awqâf and Islamic Affairs, Research and Studies Center & American Open University (eds), Civilizational role of the Muslim nation in the world of tomorrow: a selection of scholars and authors (Ministry of Awqâf and Islamic Affairs 2000).

al-Zuhili, Sheikh Wahbeh, 'Islam and international law', (2005) 87 International Review of the Red Cross, 269.

Alexander, Amanda, 'The genesis of the civilian', (2007) 20 Leiden Journal of International Law, 359.

Algar, Hamid, 'Islam and the intellectual challenge of modern civilization', in Altaf Gauhar (ed), The challenge of Islam (Islamic Council of Europe 1978).

Ali, Maulana Muhammad, A manual of hadith (Curzon Press 1988).

Ali, Muhammad Mumtaz, Islam and the Western philosophy of knowledge: reflections on some aspects (Pelanduk Publications 1994).

———, The concepts of Islamic Ummah & Shariah (Pelanduk Publications 1992).

Ali, Yusuf, The Holy Quran, at http://www.harunyahya.com/Quran_translation/Quran_translation_index.php. (Last accessed on 15 February 2015)

Alinejad, Mahmoud, 'Political Islam in Iran and the emergence of a religious public sphere: the impact of September 11', in Peter van der Veer & Shoma Munshi (eds), Media, war, and terrorism: responses from the Middle East and Asia (RoutledgeCurzon 2004).

Allain, Jean, 'Slavery and the League of Nations: Ethiopia as a civilised nation', (2006) 8 Journal of the History of International Law, 213.

———, 'Orientalism and international law: the Middle East as the underclass of the international legal order', (2004) 17 Leiden Journal of International Law, 391.

Alonzo-Maizlish, David, 'When does it end? Problems in the law of occupation', in Roberta Arnold (ed), International humanitarian law and the 21st century's conflicts: changes and challenges (Editions universitaires suisses 2005).

al-Zuhili, Sheikh Wahbeh, 'Islam and international law', (2005) 87 International Review of the Red Cross, 269.

An-Na'im, Abdullahi Ahmed, Toward an Islamic reformation: civil liberties, human rights, and international law (Syracuse University Press 1996).

Anaya, S. James, Indigenous peoples in international law (Oxford University Press 2004).

Anciaux, Robert, 'La guerre religieuse: le cas de l'islam et la chrétienté', in Jacques Lemaire (ed), La guerre et la paix (Editions de l'Université Libre de Bruxelles 1991).

Anderson, Benedict, Imagined communities: reflections on the origin and spread of nationalism (Verso 1991).

Anderson, Norman, Islamic law in the modern world (New York University Press 1959).

Anghie, Antony, 'On critique and the other', in Anne Orford (ed), International law and its others (Cambridge University Press 2006).

———, Imperialism, sovereignty, and the making of international law (Cambridge University Press 2005).

———, 'Colonialism and the birth of international institutions: sovereignty, economy, and the Mandate System of the League of Nations', (2001–2002) 34 New York University Journal of International Law and Politics, 513.

———, 'Time present and time past: globalization, international financial institutions, and the Third World', (1999–2000) 32 New York University Journal of International Law and Politics, 243.

———, 'Finding the peripheries: sovereignty and colonialism in nineteenth century international law', (1999) 40 Harvard International Law Journal, 1.

———, 'Francisco de Vitoria and the colonial origins of international law', in Eve Darian-Smith & Peter Fitzpatrick (eds), Laws of the postcolonial (University of Michigan Press 1999).

Ankersmit, Frank R., Historical representation (Stanford University Press 2001).

Antes, Peter, 'Relations with the unbelievers in Islamic theology', in Annemarie Schimmel & Abdoldjavad Falaturi (eds), We believe in one God: the experience of God in Christianity and Islam (Burns & Oates 1979).

Appiah, Kwame Anthony, The ethics of identity (Princeton University Press 2005).

Archard, David, Gifford, Paul, Rapport, Nigel & Hart, Trevor A. (eds), 2000 years and beyond: faith, identity, and the common era (Routledge 2003).

Arendt, Hannah, The human condition (The University of Chicago Press 1958).

Arkoun, Mohammed, Islam: to reform or to subvert? (Saqi 2006).

———, Rethinking Islam: common questions, uncommon answers (Westview Press 1994).

———, Essais sur la pensée islamique (Maisonneuve et Larose 1984).

———, Pour une critique de la raison islamique (Maisonneuve et Larose 1984).

Arreguin-Toft, Ivan, 'How the weak win wars: a theory of asymmetric conflict', (2001) 26 International Security, 93.

Atasoy, Yildiz, Turkey, Islamists and democracy: transition and globalisation in a Muslim state (I.B. Tauris 2005).

Averroes, Nyazee, Imran Ahsan Khan & Abdul-Rauf, Muhammad, The distinguished jurist's primer: a translation of Bidayat al-mujtahid (Garnet Publishing 1994).

Ayalon, David, 'Islam versus Christian Europe: the case of the Holy Land', in David Ayalon (ed), Islam and the abode of war (Variorum 1994).

Ayoub, Mahmoud M., Islam: faith and history (Oneworld 2004).

Badar, Mohamed Elewa, 'Jus in bello under Islamic international law', (2013) International Criminal Law Review, 593.

Baderin, Mashood A., International human rights and Islamic law (Oxford University Press 2003).

———, 'The evolution of Islamic law of nations and the modern international order: universal peace through mutuality and co-operation', (2000) 17 American Journal of Islamic Social Sciences, 57.

Badr, Gamal M., 'A survey of Islamic international law', (1982) 76 American Society of International Law Proceedings, 56.

Balci, Israfil, 'An Islamic approach toward international peace', in J. Dudley Woodberry, Osman Zümrüt & Mustafa Köylü (eds), Muslim and Christian reflections on peace: divine and human dimensions (University Press of America 2005).

Bannelier, Karine, 'L'influence de la guerre asymétrique sur les règles du jus in bello', in Karine Bannelier (ed), L'intervention en Irak et le droit international (Pedone 2004).

Barnes, Barry & Bloor, David, 'Relativism, rationalism and the sociology of knowledge', in Martin Hollis & Steven Lukes (eds), Rationality and relativism (Basil Blackwell 1990).

Barnes, Barry, The nature of power (Polity Press 1988).

Bassiouni, M. Cheriff, 'The new wars and the crisis of compliance with the law of armed conflict by non-state actors', (2008) 98 Journal of Criminal Law and Criminology, 711.

Bassiouni, M. Cherif & Badr, Gamal M., 'The Sharia'h: sources, interpretation, and rule-making', (2002) 1 UCLA Journal of Islamic and Near Eastern Law, 135.

Bat, Ye'or, Islam and dhimmitude: where civilizations collide (Fairleigh Dickinson University Press 2002).

Baxter, Richard R., 'So-called "unprivileged belligerency": spies, guerrillas, and saboteurs', (1951) 28 British Yearbook of International Law, 321.

Beauchamp, Tom L. (ed), An enquiry concerning the principles of morals: a critical edition / David Hume (Clarendon Press 2006).

Beaulac, Stéphane, 'The Westphalian legal orthodoxy: myth or reality?' (2000) 2 Journal of the History of International Law, 148.

Bedhad, Sohrab, 'Islam, revivalism and public policy', in Sohrab Behdad & Farhad Nomani (eds), Islam and public policy (JAI Press 1997).

Bedjaoui, Mohammed, 'Succession of states and governments: succession in respect of matters other than treaties', in International Law Commission (ed), Yearbook of the International Law Commission (International Law Commission 1969).

Ben Achour, Yadh, Politique, religion et droit dans le monde arabe (Cérès productions 1992).

Bennoune, Karima, '"As-Salamu Alaykum" humanitarian law in Islamic jurisprudence', (1993–1994) 15 Michigan Journal of International Law, 605.

Benvenisti, Eyal, 'The legal battle to define the law on transnational asymmetric warfare', (2009–2010) 20 Duke Journal of Comparative and International Law 339.

———, 'The US and the use of force: double-edged hegemony and the management of global emergencies', (2004) 15 European Journal of International Law, 677.

———, The international law of occupation (Princeton University Press 1993).

Berman, Nathaniel, 'Privileging combat? Contemporary conflict and the legal construction of war', (2004–2005) 43 Columbia Journal of Transnational Law, 1.

Bernard, Montague, 'The growth of laws and usages of war', in X. (ed), Oxford essays (John W. Parker and Son 1856).

Bernard, Vincent (ed), 'Humanitarian debate: law, policy, action. Conflict in Afghanistan II—Part 2: Law and humanitarian action', (2011) 93 International Review of the Red Cross, 1.

Berque, Jacques, L'islam au temps du monde (Sindbad 1984).

Berween, Mohamed, 'Al-Wathiqa: the first Islamic state constitution', (2003) 23 Journal of Muslim Minority Affairs, 103.

Best, Geoffrey Francis Andrew, War and law since 1945 (Oxford University Press 1994).

———, Humanity in warfare: the modern history of the international law of armed conflict (Methuen 1983).

———, 'Restraints on war by land before 1945', in Michael Howard (ed), Restraints on war (Clarendon Press 1977).

Biersteker, Thomas J., 'The "triumph" of liberal economic ideas in the developing world', in Barbara Stallings (ed), Global change, global response: the new international context of development (Cambridge University Press 1995).

Black, Jeremy, Rethinking military history (Routledge 2004).

———, Why wars happen (New York University Press 1998).

Blom, Amélie, Bucaille, Laetitia & Martinez, Luis, 'Introduction: imaginaires of Islamist violence', in Amélie Blom, Laetitia Bucaille & Luis Martinez (eds), The enigma of Islamist violence (Hurst & Company 2007).

Blum, Gabriella, 'On a differential law of war', (2011) 52 Harvard International Law Journal, 163.

———, 'The laws of war and the "lesser evil"', (2010) 35 Yale Journal of International Law 1.

Boisard, Marcel A., L'humanisme de l'islam (Albin Michel 1979).

Bonney, Richard, Jihad: from Qur'an to bin Laden (Palgrave Macmillan 2004).

Booth, Ken, 'Human wrongs and international relations', (1995) 71 International Affairs, 103.

———, Strategy and ethnocentrism (Croom Helm 1979).

Borelli, Silvia, 'The treatment of terrorist suspects captured abroad: human rights and humanitarian law', in Andrea Bianchi & Yasmin Naqvi (eds), Enforcing international law norms against terrorism (Hart Publishing 2004).

Bosworth, Clifford Edmund, 'Barbarian incursions: the coming of the Turks into the Islamic world', in Donald Sydney Richards (ed), Islamic civilisation, 950–1150: a colloquium published under the auspices of the Near Eastern History Group, Oxford and the Near East Center, University of Pennsylvania (Cassirer 1973).

Bothe, Michael, Partsch, Karl Josef & Solf, Waldemar A., New rules for victims of armed conflicts: commentary on the two 1977 protocols additional to the Geneva Conventions of 1949 (Martinus Nijhoff Publishers 1982).

Botiveau, Bernard, Loi islamique et droit dans les sociétés arabes: mutations des systèmes juridiques du Moyen-Orient (Karthala 1993).

Bowden, Brett, 'Civilization and savagery in the crucible of war', (2007) 19 Global Change, Peace & Security, 3.

———, 'The colonial origins of international law, European expansion and the classical standard of civilization', (2005) 7 Journal of the History of International Law, 1.

Brandt, Richard B., Morality, utilitarianism, and rights (Cambridge University Press 1992).

Breckenridge, Carol A. & Veer, Peter van der, 'Orientalism and the postcolonial predicament', in Carol A. Breckenridge & Peter van der Veer (eds), Orientalism and the postcolonial predicament: perspectives on South Asia (University of Pennsylvania Press 1993).

Bredvold, Louis I., The brave new world of the enlightenment (University of Michigan Press 1961).

Brohi, Allahbukhsh K., 'Islam: its political and legal principles: a proglomena to the theory and practice of politics and law', in Salem Azzam (ed), Islam and contemporary society (Longman 1982).

Brown, Daniel W., Rethinking tradition in modern Islamic thought (Cambridge University Press 1996).

Brown, Jonathan A.C., Hadith: Muhammad's legacy in the medieval and modern world (Oneworld Publications 2009).

Brunner, Emil, Christianity and civilisation (Ams Press 1948).

Buber, Martin & Friedman, Maurice Stanley, The knowledge of man (George Allen & Unwin 1965).

Bugnion, François, 'Jus ad bellum, jus in bello and non-international armed conflicts', (2003) 6 Yearbook of International Humanitarian Law, 167.

Bukay, David, 'Peace or jihad? Abrogation in Islam', (2007) 14 Middle East Quarterly, 3.

Burton, John, The sources of Islamic law: Islamic theories of abrogation (Edinburgh University Press 1990).

Busuttil, James J., '"Slay them wherever you find them": humanitarian law in Islam', (1991) 30 Revue de Droit Militaire et de Droit de la Guerre, 111.

Butterworth, Charles E., 'Al-Fârâbî's statecraft: war and the well-ordered regime', in James Turner Johnson & John Kelsay (eds), Cross, crescent, and sword: the justification and limitation of war in Western and Islamic tradition (Greenwood Press 1990).

Byman, Daniel & Waxman, Matthew C., The dynamics of coercion: American foreign policy and the limits of military might (Cambridge University Press 2002).

Calder, Norman, Studies in early Muslim jurisprudence (Clarendon Press 1993).

Calder, Norman, Mojaddedi, Jawid A. & Rippin, Andrew, Interpretation and jurisprudence in medieval Islam (Ashgate 2007).

Camara, Helder, The Church and colonialism: the betrayal of the Third World (Dimension Books 1969).

Cardona Llorens, Jorge, 'Libération ou occupation? Les droits et devoirs de l'état vainqueur', in Karine Bannelier (ed), L'intervention en Irak et le droit international (Pedone 2004).

Carty, Anthony, 'The Iraq invasion as a recent United Kingdom "contribution to international law"', (2005) 16 European Journal of International Law, 143.

Cassese, Antonio, 'The Martens clause: half a loaf or simply pie in the sky?' (2000) 11 European Journal of International Law, 187.

———, 'Status of rebels under the 1977 Geneva Protocol on non-international armed conflict', (1981) 30 International and Comparative Law Quarterly, 416.

Chadwick, Elisabeth, Self-determination, terrorism and the international humanitarian law of armed conflict (Martinus Nijhoff Publishers 1996).

Cheriet, Abdallah, 'Problématique du pouvoir en islam: l'état de l'émir Abd el-Kader et la théorie du cheikh Ben Badis', in Mohammed Arkoun (ed), L'islam, morale et politique (Desclée de Brouwer 1986).

Chetail, Vincent, 'The contribution of the International Court of Justice to international humanitarian law', (2003) 85 International Review of the Red Cross, 235.

Childress, James F., Moral responsibility in conflicts: essays on nonviolence, war, and conscience (Louisiana State University Press 1982).

Christmann, Andreas (ed), The Qur'an, morality and critical reason: the essential Muhammad Shahrur (Brill 2009).

Chérif, Mustapha, L'islam et l'occident: rencontre avec Jacques Derrida (Odile Jacob 2006).

Clapham, Christopher S., Africa and the international system: the politics of state survival (Cambridge University Press 1996).

Clarke, John James, Oriental Enlightenment: the encounter between Asian and Western thought (Routledge 1997).

Coates, Anthony J., The ethics of war (Manchester University Press 1997).

Cobban, Alfred, In search of humanity: the role of the Enlightenment in modern history (George Braziller 1960).

Cohen, Amichai & Shany, Yuval, 'A development of modest proportions: the application of the principle of proportionality in the Targeted Killings case', (2007) 5 Journal of International Criminal Justice, 310.

Cohen, Marshall, 'Morality and the laws of war', in Virginia Held, Sidney Morgenbesser & Thomas Nagel (eds), Philosophy, morality, and international affairs (Oxford University Press 1974).

Coker, Christopher, Ethics and war in the 21st century (Routledge 2008).

———, The future of war: the re-enchantment of war in the twenty-first century (Blackwell Publishing 2004).

———, Waging war without warriors? The changing culture of military conflict (Lynne Rienner Publishers 2002).

Condorelli, Luigi & Naqvi, Yasmin, 'The war against terrorism and jus in bello: are the Geneva Conventions out of date?' in Andrea Bianchi & Yasmin Naqvi (eds), Enforcing international law norms against terrorism (Hart Publishing 2004).

Cooper, Frederick, Colonialism in question: theory, knowledge, history (University of California Press 2005).

Cornell, Drucilla, 'The violence of masquerade: law dressed up as justice', (1990) 11 Cardozo Law Review, 1047.

Corten, Olivier & Koutroulis, Vaios, 'The illegality of military support to rebels in the Libyan war: aspects of jus contra bellum and jus in bello', (2013) 18 Journal of Conflict and Security Law, 59.

Corten, Olivier, David, Eric & Dubuisson, François, 'Droit humanitaire et légalité du recours à la force: deux logiques essentiellement différentes', in Bernard Adam (ed), Militaires humanitaires: à chacun son rôle: cohérence et incohérences des opérations militaro-humanitaires (Editions GRIP 2002).

Corthay, Eric, 'Le régime juridique du recours à la force tel qu'interprété par les états membres de l'Organisation de la Conférence islamique', (2005) 7 Journal of the History of International Law, 211.

Coulson, Noel James, Conflicts and tensions in Islamic jurisprudence (University of Chicago Press 1969).

———, 'The state and the individual in Islamic law', (1957) 6 International and Comparative Law Quarterly, 49.

Coupland, Robin M., 'The SIrUS Project: towards a determination of which weapons cause "superfluous injury or unnecessary suffering"', in Helen Durham & Timothy L.H. McCormack (eds), The changing face of conflict and the efficacy of international humanitarian law (Martinus Nijhoff Publishers 1999).

Craven, Matthew, The decolonization of international law: state succession and the law of treaties (Oxford University Press 2007).

———, 'Introduction: international law and its histories', in Matthew Craven, Malgosia Fitzmaurice & Maria Vogiatzi (eds), Time, history and international law (Martinus Nijhoff Publishers 2006).

Crawford, Emily, 'Unequal before the law: the case for the elimination of the distinction between international and non-international armed conflicts', (2007) 20 Leiden Journal of International Law, 441.

Crocker, Lester Gilbert, Nature and culture: ethical thought in the French Enlightenment (Johns Hopkins University Press 1963).
Crone, Patricia, Meccan trade and the rise of Islam (Gorgias Press 2004).
———, Medieval Islamic political thought (Edinburgh University Press 2004).
———, 'The early Islamic world', in Kurt Raaflaub & Nathan Rosenstein (eds), War and society in the ancient and medieval worlds: Asia, the Mediterranean, Europe, and Mesoamerica (Harvard University Press 1999).
Cryer, Robert, 'The interplay of human rights and humanitarian law: the approach of the ICTY', (2009) 14 Journal of Conflict and Security Law, 511.
———, Prosecuting international crimes: selectivity and the international criminal law regime (Cambridge University Press 2005).
Curtin, Philip D., The world and the West: the European challenge and the overseas response in the Age of Empire (Cambridge University Press 2000).
Dale, Joshua Paul, 'Cross-cultural encounters through a lateral gaze', in Inge E. Boer (ed), After orientalism: critical entanglements, productive looks (Rodopi 2003).
Delavignette, Robert, Christianisme et colonialisme (Fayard 1960).
de Montesqieu, Charles-Louis de Secondat, De l'esprit des lois (Librairie de Paris 1777).
Denny, Frederick M., 'The problem of salvation in the Quran: key terms and concepts', in Arnold H. Green (ed), In quest of an Islamic humanism: Arabic and Islamic studies in memory of Mohamed al-Nowaihi (The American University in Cairo Press 1986).
de Rivero, Oswaldo, The myth of development: the non-viable economies of the 21st century (Zed Books 2001).
Dero-Jacob, Anne-Claude, Société et institutions traditionnelles de l'islam: une introduction sociologique (Peeters 1995).
Derrida, Jacques, 'Force de la loi: le "fondement mystique de l'autorité"', (1990) 11 Cardozo Law Review, 920.
Detter De Lupis, Ingrid, The law of war (Cambridge University Press 1987).
de Vattel, Emmerich, Le droit des gens ou principes de la loi naturelle appliqués à la conduite et aux affaires des nations et des souverains (Carnegie Endowment for International Peace 1916).
———, The law of nations or the principles of natural law (J. Chitty 1839).
de Vitoria, Franciscus, De Indis et de ivre belli (Carnegie Institution of Washington 1917).
Dien, Mawil Izzi, Islamic law: from historical foundations to contemporary practice (Edinburgh University Press 2004).
Dinstein, Yoram, The conduct of hostilities under the law of international armed conflict (Cambridge University Press 2004).
Dolan, Brian, Exploring European frontiers: British travellers in the age of Enlightenment (Macmillan 2000).

Domestici-Met, Marie-José, 'Protecting Libya on behalf of the international community', (2011) 3 Goettingen Journal of International Law 861.

Donner, Fred M., 'The sources of Islamic conceptions of war', in James Turner Johnson & John Kelsay (eds), Just war and jihad: historical and theoretical perspectives on war and peace in Western and Islamic traditions (Greenwood Press 1991).

Dorf, Michael C., 'The Orwellian Military Commissions Act of 2006', (2007) 5 Journal of International Criminal Justice, 10.

Douzinas, Costas & Warrington, Ronnie, Justice miscarried: ethics and aesthetics in law (Harvester Wheatsheaf 1994).

Drury, Shadia B., Terror and civilization: Christianity, politics, and the Western psyche (Palgrave Macmillian 2004).

Duffy, Helen, The "war on terror" and the framework of international law (Cambridge University Press 2005).

Dunant, Henry, A memory of Solferino (International Committee of the Red Cross 1986).

Dunn, L.C., 'Race and biology', in Leo Kuper (ed), Race, science and society (The Unesco Press 1975).

Duquoc, Christian & Floristán, Casiano (eds), Christian identity (T. & T. Clark 1988).

Dörmann, Knut, 'The legal situation of "unlawful/unprivileged combatants"', (2003) 85 International Review of the Red Cross, 45.

Eagleton, Terry, 'Nationalism: irony and commitment', in Terry Eagleton, Fredric Jameson & Edward W. Said (eds), Nationalism, colonialism, and literature (University of Minnesota Press 1990).

Easterly, William Russell, The white man's burden: why the West's efforts to aid the rest have done so much ill and so little good (Oxford University Press 2006).

Eaton, Gai, Islam and the destiny of man (Islamic Texts Society 1994).

Edgeworth, Francis Ysidro, Mathematical psychics: an essay on the application of mathematics to the moral sciences (Kegan Paul 1881).

Edmonds, James Edward & Oppenheim, Lassa, Land warfare: an exposition of the laws and usages of war on land, for the guidance of officers of His Majesty's Army (His Majesty's Stationary Office 1912).

Ehrenreich Brooks, Rosa, 'The new imperialism: violence, norms, and the "rule of law"', (2002–2003) 101 Michigan Law Review, 2275.

Eickelman, Dale F., 'The Middle East's democracy deficit and the expanding public sphere', in Peter van der Veer & Shoma Munshi (eds), Media, war, and terrorism: responses from the Middle East and Asia (RoutledgeCurzon 2004).

Ellul, Jacques, La subversion du christianisme (Seuil 1984).

Elshtain, Jean Bethke, Just war against terror: the burden of American power in a violent world (Basic Books 2003).

Emon, Anver M., Islamic natural law theories (Oxford University Press 2010).

Ereksoussi, M. Kheir, 'Le Coran et les conventions humanitaires', (1960) 503 International Review of the Red Cross, 641.

Esack, Farid, Qur'an, liberation and pluralism: an Islamic perspective of interreligious solidarity against oppression (Oneworld 1997).

Esposito, John L., Islam: the straight path (Oxford University Press 2005).

———, 'Struggle in Islam', in Joshua Cohen & Ian Lague (eds), The place of tolerance in Islam (Beacon Press 2002).

———, Unholy war: terror in the name of Islam (Oxford University Press 2002).

———, The Islamic threat: myth or reality? (Oxford University Press 1999).

Essien-Udom, Essien Udosen, 'Tribalism and racism', in Leo Kuper (ed), Race, science and society (The Unesco Press 1975).

Evans, Carolyn, 'The double-edged sword: religious influences on international humanitarian law', (2005) 6 Melbourne Journal of International Law, 1.

Falahi, Towqueer Alam, The Quranic concept of war and peace (Kanishka Publishers 2004).

Falk, Richard, 'Janus tormented: the international law of internal war', in James N. Rosenau (ed), International aspects of civil strife (Princeton University Press 1964).

Farber, Marvin, Phenomenology and existence: toward a philosophy within nature (Harper Torchbooks 1967).

Feener, R. Michael, Muslim legal thought in modern Indonesia (Cambridge University Press 2007).

Feldstein, Leonard C., 'Toward integrity and wisdom: justice as grounding personal harmony', in Charles A. Kelbley (ed), The value of justice: essays on the theory and practice of social virtue (Fordham University Press 1979).

Ferry, Luc, Qu'est-ce qu'une vie réussie? (Grasset 2002).

Fidler, David P., 'Revolt against or from within the West? TWAIL, the developing world, and the future direction of international law', (2003) 2 Chinese Journal of International Law, 29.

Filiu, Jean-Pierre, Les frontières du jihad (Fayard 2006).

Fiore, Pasquale, International law codified and its legal sanction (Baker, Voorhis and Company 1918).

Fischer, Horst, 'Protection of prisoners of war', in Dieter Fleck (ed), The handbook of international humanitarian law (Oxford University Press 2008).

Forrest, Joshua Bernard, 'State inversion and nonstate politics', in Leonardo A. Villalón & Phillip A. Huxtable (eds), The African state at a critical juncture: between disintegration and reconfiguration (Lynne Rienner 1998).

Forte, David F., Studies in Islamic law: classical and contemporary application (Austin & Winfield 1999).

Frankel, Charles, The faith of reason: the idea of progress in the French Enlightenment (King's Crown Press 1948).

Freamon, Bernard K., 'Martyrdom, suicide, and the Islamic law of war: a short legal history', (2003–2004) 27 Fordham International Law Journal, 299.

Friedrichs, Jörg, 'Defining the international public enemy: the political struggle behind the legal debate on international terrorism', (2006) 19 Leiden Journal of International Law, 69.

Fromm, Erich, The anatomy of human destructiveness (Henry Holt and Company 1992).

———, The sane society (Routledge & K. Paul 1956).

Fry, Douglas P., The human potential for peace: an anthropological challenge to assumptions about war and violence (Oxford University Press 2006).

Frye, Richard N., The golden age of Persia (Phoenix Press 2003).

Funk, Nathan C. & Said, Abdul Aziz, Islam and peacemaking in the Middle East (Lynne Rienner Publishers 2009).

Gaita, Raimond, A common humanity: thinking about love and truth and justice (Routledge 2000).

Gal, Tom, 'Unexplored outcomes of Tadić: applicability of the law of occupation to war by proxy', (2014) 12 Journal of International Criminal Justice, 1.

Galula, David, Counterinsurgency warfare: theory and practice (Praeger Security International 2006).

Gardam, Judith Gail, Non-combatant immunity as a norm of international humanitarian law (Martinus Nijhoff Publishers 1993).

———, 'Proportionality and force in international law', (1993) 87 American Journal of International Law, 391.

Garraway, Charles H.B., '"Combatants": substance or semantics?' in Michael N. Schmitt & Jelena Pejic (eds), International law and armed conflict: exploring the faultlines: essays in honour of Yoram Dinstein (Martinus Nijhoff Publishers 2007).

Gartenstein-Ross, Daveed, 'No other Gods before me: spheres of influence in the relationship between Christianity and Islam', (2004–2005) 33 Denver Journal of International Law and Policy, 223.

Gathii, James Thuo, 'Retelling good governance narratives on Africa's economic and political predicaments: continuities and discontinuities in legal outcomes between markets and states', (2000) 45 Villanova Law Review, 971.

Gauhar, Altaf, 'Islam and secularism', in Altaf Gauhar (ed), The challenge of Islam (Islamic Council of Europe 1978).

Gause III, F. Gregory, 'Why Middle East studies missed the Arab Spring: the myth of authoritarian stability', (2011) 90 Foreign Affairs 81.

Geanakoplos, Deno John, Medieval Western civilization and the Byzantine and Islamic worlds: interaction of three cultures (D.C. Heath 1979).

Gellner, Ernest, 'Relativism and universals', in Martin Hollis & Steven Lukes (eds), Rationality and relativism (Basil Blackwell 1990).

———, Culture, identity, and politics (Cambridge University Press 1987).

Genovés, Santiago, Is peace inevitable? Aggression, evolution, and human destiny (George Allen and Unwin 1972).
George, Robert P., In defense of natural law (Oxford University Press 2004).
Gerber, Haim, State, society, and law in Islam: Ottoman law in comparative perspective (State University of New York 1994).
Gerges, Fawaz A., The far enemy: why jihad went global (Cambridge University Press 2005).
Gilligan, James, Violence: reflections on our deadliest epidemic (Jessica Kingsley Publishers 2000).
Glover, Jonathan, Humanity: a moral history of the twentieth century (Jonathan Cape 1999).
Goitein, Samuel D., 'The birth-hour of Muslim law? An essay in exegesis', in Wael B. Hallaq (ed), The formation of Islamic law (Ashgate Variorum 2004).
Goldziher, Ignáz, Lewis, Bernard, Hamori, Andras & Hamori, Ruth, Introduction to Islamic theology and law (Princeton University Press 1981).
Gong, Gerrit W., The standard of "civilization" in international society (Clarendon Press 1984).
Goodman, Ryan, 'Controlling the recourse to war by modifying jus in bello', (2009) 12 Yearbook of International Humanitarian Law, 53.
Gordon, Ruth, 'Saving failed states: sometimes a neocolonialist notion', (1997) 12 American University Journal of International Law and Policy, 904.
Grafton, David D., The Christians of Lebanon: political rights in Islamic law (Tauris Academic Studies 2003).
Gray, John, Enlightenment's wake: politics and culture at the close of the modern age (Routledge 1995).
Greenwood, Christopher, 'Scope of application of humanitarian law', in Dieter Fleck (ed), The handbook of international humanitarian law (Oxford University Press 2010).
———, 'Human rights and humanitarian law: conflict or convergence', (2010) 43 Case Western Reserve Journal of International Law, 491.
———, Essays on war in international law (Cameron May 2007).
Griffel, Frank, 'The harmony of natural law and Shari'a in Islamist theology', in Abbas Amanat & Frank Griffel (eds), Shari'a: Islamic law in the contemporary context (Stanford University Press 2007).
Grossman, Dave, On killing (Back Bay Books 1996).
Guillaumin, Colette, 'The idea of race and its elevation to autonomous scientific and legal status', in Marion O'Callaghan (ed), Sociological theories: race and colonialism (The Unesco Press 1980).
Gunton, Colin, Enlightenment and alienation: an essay towards a Trinitarian theology (Marshall Morgan & Scott 1985).

Gutierrez Posse, Hortensia D.T., 'The relationship between international humanitarian law and the international criminal tribunals', (2006) 88 International Review of the Red Cross, 65.

Habeck, Mary R., Knowing the enemy: jihadist ideology and the war on terror (Yale University Press 2006).

Haddad, Yvonne Yazbeck, 'Operation Desert Storm and the war of fatwas', in Muhammad Khalid Masud, Brinkley Morris Messick & David Stephan Powers (eds), Islamic legal interpretation: muftis and their fatwas (Harvard University Press 1996).

Hafez, Kai, 'Islam and the West: the clash of politicised perceptions', in Kai Hafez & Mary Ann Kenny (eds), The Islamic world and the West: an introduction to political cultures and international relations (Brill 2000).

Hafez, Kai & Kenny, Mary Ann, The Islamic world and the West: an introduction to political cultures and international relations (Brill 2000).

Haldar, Piyel, Law, orientalism and postcolonialism: the jurisdiction of the lotus eaters (Routledge-Cavendish 2007).

Hallaq, Wael B., An introduction to Islamic law (Cambridge University Press 2009).

———, Shari'a: theory, practice, transformations (Cambridge University Press 2009).

———, The origins and evolution of Islamic law (Cambridge University Press 2006).

———, '"Muslim rage" and Islamic law', (2003) 54 Hastings Law Journal, 1705.

———, 'Takhrij and the construction of juristic authority', in Bernard G. Weiss (ed), Studies in Islamic legal theory (Brill 2002).

———, Authority, continuity and change in Islamic law (Cambridge University Press 2001).

———, A history of Islamic legal theories: an introduction to Sunni usul al-fiqh (Cambridge University Press 1999).

Halliday, Fred, Islam and the myth of confrontation: religion and politics in the Middle East (I.B. Tauris 2003).

Hamidullah, Muhammad, Muslim conduct of state (Sh. Muhammed Ashraf 1961).

Handel, Michael I., 'War termination: a critical survey', in Nissan Oren (ed), Termination of wars: processes, procedures and aftermaths (The Magnes Press 1982).

Handy, Charles, 'Finding sense in uncertainty', in Rowan Gibson (ed), Rethinking the future (Nicholas Brealey Publishing 1999).

Harding, Christopher, 'Statist assumptions, normative individualism and new forms of personality: evolving a philosophy of international law for the twenty-first century', (2001) 1 Non-State Actors and International Law, 107.

Hart, Herbert L.A., The concept of law (Clarendon 1994).

Hasan, Ahmad, Analogical reasoning in Islamic jurisprudence: a study of the juridical principle of qiyas (Adam 1994).

———, The doctrine of ijma in Islam (Islamic Research Institute 1976).

Hashmi, Sohail H., 'Saving and taking life in war: three modern Muslim views', in Jonathan E. Brockopp (ed), Islamic ethics of life: abortion, war, and euthanasia (University of South Carolina Press 2003).

———, 'Interpreting the Islamic ethics of war and peace', in Sohail H. Hashmi (ed), Islamic political ethics: civil society, pluralism, and conflict (Princeton University Press 2002).

———, 'Political perceptions in early Anglo-Indian relations', (2001) 12 Islam & Christian-Muslim Relations, 211.

Hassan, Riaz, Inside Muslim minds (Melbourne University Press 2008).

———, 'Globalisation's challenge to the Islamic ummah', (2006) 34 Asian Journal of Social Science, 311.

Hassan, Syed Riazul, The reconstruction of legal thought in Islam: a comparative study of the Islamic and the Western systems of law in the latter's terminology with particular reference to the Islamic laws suspended by the British rule in the sub-continent (Law Publishing Company 1974).

Hayashi, Mika Nishimura, 'The Martens clause and military necessity', in Howard M. Hensel (ed), The legitimate use of military force: the just war tradition and the customary law of armed conflict (Ashgate 2009).

———, 'The principle of civilian protection and contemporary armed conflict', in Howard M. Hensel (ed), The law of armed conflict: constraints on the contemporary use of military force (Ashgate 2007).

Hayashi, Nobuo, 'Requirements of military necessity in international humanitarian law and international criminal law', (2010) 28 Boston University International Law Journal, 39.

Hehir, J. Bryan, 'Intervention militaire et souveraineté nationale: une relation à repenser', in Jonathan Moore (ed), Des choix difficiles: les dilemmes moraux de l'humanitaire (Gallimard 1999).

Heintze, Hans-Joachim, 'On the relationship between human rights law protection and international humanitarian law', (2004) 86 International Review of the Red Cross, 789.

Hellyer, Hisham A., 'Minorities, Muslims and Shari'a: some reflections on Islamic law and Muslims without political power', (2007) 18 Islam & Christian-Muslim Relations, 85.

Henckaerts, Jean-Marie, 'Concurrent application of international human rights law and international humanitarian law: victims in search of a forum', (2007) 1 Human Rights and International Legal Discourse, 95.

Henckaerts, Jean-Marie & Doswald-Beck, Louise, Customary international humanitarian law (Cambridge University Press 2005).

Henderson, Christian, 'International measures for the protection of civilians in Libya and Côte d'Ivoire', (2011) 60 International and Comparative Law Quarterly, 767.

Henry, Michel, La barbarie (Presses universitaires de France 2004).

———, C'est moi la vérité: pour une philosophie du christianisme (Seuil 1996).

Hervieu-Léger, Danièle & Champion, Françoise, Vers un nouveau christianisme? Introduction à la sociologie du christianisme occidental (Cerf 1986).

Hervouët, Véronique, L'enjeu symbolique: islam, christianisme, modernité: interprétation psychanalytique des fondements religieux et idéologiques et de leurs conflits (L'Harmattan 2004).

Hinde, Robert A., Bending the rules: morality in the modern world: from relationships to politics and war (Oxford University Press 2007).

Hobbes, Thomas, De Cive (Kessinger Publishing 2004).

Hobsbawn, Eric J., Nations and nationalism since 1780: programme, myth, reality (Cambridge University Press 1993).

Hobson, John M., The Eastern origins of Western civilization (Cambridge University Press 2004).

Hodgson, Marshall Goodwin Simms, The venture of Islam: conscience and history in a world civilization (University of Chicago Press 1974).

Holland, Joseph, 'Military objective and collateral damage: their relationship and dynamics', (2004) 7 Yearbook of International Humanitarian Law 35.

Holmes, Robert L., On war and morality (Princeton University Press 1989).

Holmqvist-Jonsäter, Caroline, 'War as perpetual policing', in Caroline Holmqvist-Jonsäter & Christopher Coker (eds), The character of war in the 21st century (Routledge 2010).

Holsti, Kalevi Jaakko, The state, war, and the state of war (Cambridge University Press 1996).

Hooper, James R. & Williams, Paul R., 'Earned sovereignty: the political dimension', (2003) 31 Denver Journal of International Law and Policy, 355.

Hotaling, Edward, Islam without illusions: its past, its present, and its challenges for the future (Syracuse University Press 2003).

Howard, Michael, 'Temperamenta belli: can war be controlled?' in Michael Howard (ed), Restraints on war: studies in the limitation of armed conflict (Oxford University Press 1979).

Howse, Robert, 'Europe and the New World Order: lessons from Alexandre Kojève's engagement with Schmitt's "Nomos der Erde"', (2006) 19 Leiden Journal of International Law, 93.

Huart, Clement, 'The law of war', in Andrew G. Bostom (ed), The legacy of jihad: Islamic holy war and the fate of non-Muslims (Prometheus Books 2005).

Hulme, Karen, War torn environment: interpreting the legal threshold (Martinus Nijhoff Publishers 2004).

Humphreys, R. Stephen, Islamic history: a framework for inquiry (Tauris 1991).

Ibn Hayyun, Numan ibn Muhammad, Poonawala, Ismail Kurbanhusien & Fyzee, Asaf Ali Asghar, The pillars of Islam: Da'a'Im al-Islam of al-Qadi al-Nu'man (Oxford University Press 2002).

ICRC, at http://www.icrc.org/IHL.nsf/%28SPF%29/party_main_treaties/$File/IHL_and_other_related_Treaties.pdf. (Last accessed on 15 February 2015)

———, Interpretive Guidance on the Notion of Direct Participation in Hostilities under International Humanitarian Law (ICRC 2009).

Imber, Colin, Ebu's-su'ud: the Islamic legal tradition (Edinburgh University Press 1997).

Iqbal, Allama Muhammad, The reconstruction of religious thought in Islam (Sh. Muhammad Ashraf 1968).

Israel, Jonathan Irvine, Enlightenment contested: philosophy, modernity, and the emancipation of man, 1670–1752 (Oxford University Press 2006).

Izutsu, Toshihiko, The concept of belief in Islamic theology: a semantic analysis of îmân and islâm (The Keio Institute of Cultural and Linguistic Studies 1965).

Izzati, Abu al-Fazl, An introduction to Shi'i Islamic law and jurisprudence with an emphasis on the authority of human reason as a source of law according to Shi'i law (Ashraf Press 1976).

Jabri, Vivienne, Discourses on violence: conflict analysis reconsidered (Manchester University Press 1996).

Jackson, Sherman A., 'Fiction and formalism: toward a functional analysis of usul al-fiqh', in Bernard G. Weiss (ed), Studies in Islamic legal theory (Brill 2002).

———, 'Jihad and the modern world', (2002) 7 Journal of Islamic Law & Culture, 1.

Jacoby, Tim, Understanding conflict and violence: theoretical and interdisciplinary approaches (Routledge 2008).

Jalal, Ayesha, Self and sovereignty: individual and community in South Asian Islam since 1850 (Routledge 2000).

Jamieson, Alan G., Faith and sword: a short history of Christian-Muslim conflict (Reaktion Books 2006).

Jaques, R. Kevin, Authority, conflict, and the transmission of diversity in medieval Islamic law (Brill 2006).

Jodoin, Sébastien, 'International law and alterity: the state and the other', (2008) 21 Leiden Journal of International Law, 1.

Johansen, Baber, Contingency in a sacred law: legal and ethical norms in the Muslim fiqh (Brill 1999).

Johnson, James Turner, 'Maintaining the protection of non-combatants (part 1)', in David Kinsella & Craig L. Carr (eds), The morality of war: a reader (Lynne Rienner Publishers 2007).

———, The holy war idea in Western and Islamic traditions (Pennsylvania State University Press 1997).

Johnson, James Turner & Kelsay, John, Cross, crescent, and sword: the justification and limitation of war in Western and Islamic tradition (Greenwood Press 1990).

Kaldor, Mary, New and old wars: organized violence in a global era (Stanford University Press 1999).

Kalshoven, Frits, 'Reaffirmation and development of international humanitarian law applicable in armed conflicts: the Diplomatic Conference, Geneva, 1974–1977, Part I: combatants and civilians', (1977) 8 Netherlands Yearbook of International Law, 106.

———, The law of warfare: a summary of its recent history and trends in development (Henry Dunant Institute 1973).

Kamali, Muhammad H., Principles of Islamic jurisprudence (The Islamic Texts Society 2003).

Kant, Immanuel, Perpetual peace (Filiquarian Publishing, LLC 2007).

Karam, Azza M., 'Islamisms: globalisation, religion and power', in Ronaldo Munck & Purnaka L. de Silva (eds), Postmodern insurgencies: political violence, identity formation and peacemaking in comparative perspective (St. Martin's Press 2000).

Karim, Mohammad, 'Globalization and post-Soviet revival of Islam in Central Asia and the Caucasus', (2005) 25 Journal of Muslim Minority Affairs, 439.

Karsh, Efraim, Islamic imperialism: a history (Yale University Press 2006).

Kavolis, Vytautas, 'Histories of selfhood, maps and sociability', in Vytautas Kavolis (ed), Designs of selfhood (Associated University Press 1984).

Keefer, Scott Andrew, 'Building the palace of peace: The Hague Conference of 1907 and arms control before the World War', (2007) 9 Journal of the History of International Law, 35.

———, 'Building the palace of peace: The Hague Conference of 1899 and arms control in the progressive era', (2006) 8 Journal of the History of International Law, 1.

Kekes, John, Pluralism in philosophy: changing the subject (Cornell University Press 2000).

———, Facing evil (Princeton University Press 1990).

Kelsay, John, 'Al-Shaybani and the Islamic law of war', (2003) 2 Journal of Military Ethics, 63.

———, Arguing the just war in Islam (Harvard University Press 2007).

———, 'Civil society and government in Islam', in Sohail H. Hashmi (ed), Islamic political ethics: civil society, pluralism, and conflict (Princeton University Press 2002).

———, 'Islam and the distinction between combatants and noncombatants', in James Turner Johnson & John Kelsay (eds), Cross, crescent, and sword: the justification and limitation of war in Western and Islamic tradition (Greenwood Press 1990).

Kelsen, Hans, 'Recognition in international law: theoretical observations', (1941) 35 American Journal of International Law, 605.

Kennedy, David, Of war and law (Princeton University Press 2006).

———, 'Reassessing international humanitarianism', in Anne Orford (ed), International law and its others (Cambridge University Press 2006).
———, 'The forgotten politics of international governance', (2001) 2 European Human Rights Law Review, 117.
———, 'International law and the nineteenth century: history of an illusion', (1997–1998) 17 Quinnipiac Law Review, 99.
———, 'Spring break', (1984–1985) 63 Texas Law Review, 1377.
Kennedy, Duncan, 'The structure of the Blackstone's Commentaries', (1979) 28 Buffalo Law Review, 205.
Kennedy, Hugh, The great Arab conquests: how the spread of Islam changed the world we live in (Weidenfeld & Nicolson 2007).
———, The armies of the caliphs: military and society in the early Islamic state (Routledge 2005).
———, The Prophet and the age of the Caliphates: the Islamic Near East from the sixth to the eleventh century (Longman 2004).
Kepel, Gilles, The war for Muslim minds: Islam and the West (The Belknap Press of Harvard University Press 2004).
Khadduri, Majid, The Islamic conception of justice (Johns Hopkins University Press 1984).
———, The Islamic law of nations: Shaybani's Siyar (John Hopkins Press 1966).
———, 'The Islamic theory of international relations and its contemporary relevance', in J. Harris Proctor (ed), Islam and international relations (Pall Mall 1965).
———, War and peace in the law of Islam (Johns Hopkins Press 1955).
Khadduri, Majid & Liebesny, Herbert J., Law in the Middle East / Vol. 1, Origin and development of Islamic law (Middle East Institute 1955).
Khan, Ali K., A theory of international terrorism: understanding Islamic militancy (Martinus Nijhoff Publishers 2006).
Khan, Arif Ali & Syed, M.H., Concept of Islamic law (Pentagon Press 2007).
Khan, M.A. Muqtedar, 'The political philosophy of Islamic resurgence', (2001) 13 Cultural dynamics, 211.
Khan, M. Muhsin, Translation of Sahih Bukhari, at http://www.iiu.edu.my/deed/hadith/bukhari/index.html. (Last accessed on 15 February 2015)
Khan, Maimul Ahsan, Human rights in the Muslim world: fundamentalism, constitutionalism, and international politics (Carolina Academic Press 2003).
Khan, Muhammad Zafrulla, Islam: its meaning for modern man (Routledge & Kegan Paul 1980).
Khan, Mushtaq H., 'The new political economy of corruption', in Ben Fine, Costas Lapavitsas & Jonathan Pincus (eds), Development policy in the twenty-first century: beyond the post-Washington Consensus (Routledge 2001).

Khan, Saghir Ahmad & Rahim, Abdur, Islamic jurisprudence (Mansoor 1986).

Khoury, Adel Théodor, Toleranz im Islam (Kaiser; Grünewald 1980).

Khoury, Paul, Islam et christianisme: dialogue religieux et deïfie de la modernitè (Heidelberg Press-Lebanon 1973).

Khumayni, Ruh Allah ibn Mustafa & Algar, Hamid, Islam and revolution: writings and declarations of Imam Khomeini (Mizan Press 1981).

Killingray, David, 'Guardians of empire', in David Killingray & David Omissi (eds), Guardians of empire: the armed forces of the colonial powers c. 1700–1964 (Manchester University Press 1999).

Kinsella, Helen M., 'Discourses of difference: civilians, combatants and compliance with the laws of war', (2005) 31 Review of International Studies, 163.

Kissinger, Henry, Necessity for choice: prospects for American foreign policy (Chatto and Windus 1960).

Koskenniemi, Martti, From apology to utopia: the structure of international legal argument (Cambridge University Press 2005).

———, The gentle civilizer of nations: the rise and fall of international law, 1870–1960 (Cambridge University Press 2002).

———, 'Politics of international law', (1990) 1 European Journal of International Law, 3.

Kouchner, Bernard, Les guerriers de la paix: du Kosovo à l'Irak (Bernard Grasset 2004).

Krauss, Eric S. & Lacey, Mike O., 'Utilitarian vs. humanitarian: the battle over the law of war', (2002) Parameters, 73.

Krämer, Gudrun & Schmidtke, Sabine, 'Introduction: religious authority and religious authorities in Muslim societies: a critical overview', in Gudrun Krämer & Sabine Schmidtke (eds), Speaking for Islam: religious authorities in Muslim societies (Brill 2006).

Krüger, Hilmar, Fetwa und Siyar: zur internationalrechtlichen Gutachtenpraxis der osmanischen Seyh ül-Islâm vom 17. bis 19. Jahrhundert unter besonderer Berücksichtigung des "Behcet ül-Fetâvâ" (Harrassowitz 1978).

Kuraishi, Fazl-I-Ahmad, Islam: the religion of humanity (Kitab Manzil 1956).

Kwakwa, Edward K., The international law of armed conflict: personal and material fields of application (Kluwer Academic Publishers 1992).

Küng, Hans, Christianity: its essence and history (SCM Press 1995).

Lamp, Nicolas, 'Conceptions of war and paradigms of compliance: the "new war" challenge to international humanitarian law', (2011) 16 Journal of Conflict and Security Law, 225.

Lamprecht, Sterling P., Our philosophical traditions (Appleton Century-Crofts 1955).

Landau, Rom, Islam and the Arabs (George Allen & Unwin 1958).

Landau-Tasseron, Ella, "Non-combatants" in Muslim legal thought, at http://www.futureofmuslimworld.com/research/pubID.60/pub_detail.asp. (Last accessed on 15 February 2015)

Lane, Jan-Erik & Redissi, Hamadi, Religion and politics: Islam and Muslim civilisation (Ashgate 2004).
Langins, Janis, Conserving the Enlightenment: French military engineering from Vauban to the Revolution (MIT Press 2004).
Lapidus, Ira M., 'The Arab conquests and the formation of Islamic society', in Wael B. Hallaq (ed), The formation of Islamic law (Ashgate Variorum 2004).
Lari, Sayid Mujtaba Rukni Musawi, Western civilisation through Muslim eyes (FIL Inc. 1979).
Laski, Harold J., Faith, reason and civilisation: an essay in historical analysis (Gollancz 1944).
Lauterpacht, Hersch, Recognition in international law (Cambridge University Press 1947).
Lawrence, Thomas J., The principles of international law (D.C. Heath 1895).
Layish, Aharon, Islamic law in the contemporary Middle East (Centre of Near & Middle Eastern Studies, School of Oriental and African Studies, University of London 1989).
Lecker, Michael, 'On the burial of martyrs in Islam', in Hiroyuki Yanagihashi (ed), The concept of territory in Islamic law and thought (Kegal Paul International 2000).
Lederach, John Paul, The moral imagination: the art and soul of building peace (Oxford University Press 2005).
Leftwich, Adrian, 'Bringing politics back in: towards a model of the developmental state', (1995) 31 Journal of Development Studies, 400.
Levinas, Emmanuel, Totality and infinity: an essay on exteriority (Kluwer Academic Publishers 1991).
Lewis, Bernard, Race and color in Islam (Harper & Row 1971).
Little, Douglas, American orientalism: the United States and the Middle East since 1945 (University of North Carolina Press 2002).
Lockley, Martin & Morimoto, Ryo, How humanity came into being: the evolution of consciousness (Floris Books 2010).
Lorenz, Konrad, On aggression (Routledge 1996).
———, The waning of humaneness (Unwin Hyman 1988).
———, Man meets dog (Methuen 1977).
Lorimer, James, The institutes of the law of nations (William Blackwood and Sons 1883).
Lubell, Noam, 'Challenges in applying human rights law to armed conflict', (2005) International Review of the Red Cross, 737.
Luis, William, 'Borges, the encounter, and the other: blacks and the monstrous races', in Fernando de Toro, Alfonso de Toro & Kathleen Quinn (eds), Borders and margins: post-colonialism and post-modernism (Vervuert 1995).
Lukacs, Yehuda, Documents on the Israeli-Palestinian conflict, 1967–1983 (Cambridge University Press 1984).

Macey, Jonathan R. & Miller, Geoffrey P., 'The end of history and the new world order: the triumph of capitalism and the competition between liberalism and democracy', (1992) 25 Cornell Journal of International Law, 277.

Macfie, Alexander Lyon, Orientalism: a reader (Longman 2002).

Mah, Harold, Enlightenment phantasies: cultural identity in France and Germany, 1750–1914 (Cornell University Press 2003).

Mahmassani, S., Les principes du droit international à la lumière de la doctrine islamique (Recueil des Cours. Académie de Droit International 1966).

Makris, Gerasimos P., Islam in the Middle East: a living tradition (Blackwell Publishing 2007).

Malik, Jamal, Colonization of Islam: dissolution of traditional institutions in Pakistan (Manohar 1996).

Mamdani, Mahmood, When victims become killers: colonialism, nativism, and the genocide in Rwanda (Princeton University Press 2002).

Mandelstam, Nadezhda, Hope against hope (The Harvill Press 1989).

Mangabeira Unger, Roberto, Law in modern society: toward a criticism of social theory (The Free Press 1976).

Martens, Fyodor Fyodorovich, La Russie et l'Angleterre dans l'Asie centrale (Van Doosselaere 1879).

Martin, Richard C., 'The religious foundations of war, peace, and statecraft in Islam', in James Turner Johnson & John Kelsay (eds), Just war and jihad: historical and theoretical perspectives on war and peace in Western and Islamic traditions (Greenwood Press 1991).

Mathews, Robert J. & McCormack, Timothy L.H., 'The relationship between international humanitarian law and arms control', in Helen Durham & Timothy L.H. McCormack (eds), The changing face of conflict and the efficacy of international humanitarian law (Martinus Nijhoff Publishers 1999).

Mawardi, Ali ibn Muhammad & Yate, Asadullah, al-Ahkam as-Sultaniyyah: the laws of Islamic governance (Ta-Ha Publishers 1996).

Maxwell, Mark David & Watts, Sean M., '"Unlawful enemy combatant": status, theory of culpability, or neither?' (2007) 5 Journal of International Criminal Justice, 19.

May, Larry, War crimes and just war (Cambridge University Press 2007).

May, Louis-Philippe, Esquisse d'un tableau des apports de la France aÃ la civilisation (Michel 1951).

Mayer, Ann Elizabeth, 'The Islam and human rights nexus: shifting dimensions', (2007) 4 Muslim World Journal of Human Rights, 1.

Mayer, Ann Elizabeth, 'War and peace in the Islamic tradition and international law', in James Turner Johnson & John Kelsay (eds), Just war and jihad: historical and theoretical perspectives on war and peace in Western and Islamic traditions (Greenwood Press 1991).

McCants, William, 'Al Qaeda's challenge: the jihadists' war with Islamist democrats', (2011) 90 Foreign Affairs 20.

McCormick, Michael, Eternal victory: triumphal rulership in late antiquity, Byzantium and the early medieval West (Cambridge University Press 1986).

McCoubrey, Hilaire, International humanitarian law: modern developments in the limitation of warfare (Ashgate 1998).

McCoubrey, Hilaire & White, Nigel D., International law and armed conflict (Dartmouth 1992).

McDonough, Sheila, Muslim ethics and modernity: a comparative study of the ethical thought of Sayyid Ahmad Khan and Mawlana Mawdudi (Wilfrid Laurier University Press 1984).

McLaughlin, Robert, 'The law of armed conflict and international human rights law: some paradigmatic differences and operational implications', (2010) 13 Yearbook of International Humanitarian Law, 213.

McMahan, Jeff, Killing in war (Oxford University Press 2009).

Mednicoff, David M., 'Humane wars? International law, just war theory and contemporary armed humanitarian intervention', (2006) 2 Law, Culture and the Humanities, 373.

Mégret, Frédéric, 'From "savages" to "unlawful combatants": a postcolonial look at international humanitarian law's "other"', in Anne Orford (ed), International law and its others (Cambridge University Press 2006).

———, '"War"? Legal semantics and the move to violence', (2002) 13 European Journal of International Law, 361.

Merari, Ariel, 'Du terrorism comme stratégie d'insurrection', in Gérard Chaliand (ed), Les stratégies du terrorisme (Desclée de Brouwer 2002).

Meron, Theodor, 'The humanization of humanitarian law', (2000) 94 American Journal of International Law, 239.

———, War crimes law comes of age: essays (Oxford University Press 1998).

Micheau, Françoise, 'Les croisades vue par les historiens arabes d'hier et d'aujourd'hui', in Françoise Micheau (ed), Les relations des pays d'islam avec le monde latin: du milieu du Xe siècle au milieu du XIIIe siècle (Editions Jacques Marseille 2000).

Mignolo, Walter D. & Schiwy, Freya, 'Beyond dichotomies: translation/transculturation and the colonial difference', in Elisabeth Mudimbe-Boyi (ed), Beyond dichotomies: histories, identities, cultures, and the challenge of globalization (State University of New York Press 2002).

Moir, Lindsay, The law of internal armed conflict (Cambridge University Press 2002).

Moosa, Ebrahim, 'Languages of change in Islamic law: redefining death in modernity', in Ravindra S. Khare (ed), Perspectives on Islamic law, justice, and society (Rowman & Littlefield 1999).

Morrison, Heidi, 'Beyond universalism', (2004) 1 Muslim World Journal of Human Rights, 1.

Morrison, Wayne, Criminology, civilisation and the new world order: rethinking criminology in a global context (Routledge Cavendish 2006).

Mortimer, Edward, Faith and power: the politics of Islam (Faber and Faber 1982).

Moscovici, Claudia, Double dialectics: between universalism and relativism in Enlightenment and postmodern thought (Rowman & Littlefield 2002).

Mowbray, Jacqueline, 'The right to food and the international economic system: an assessment of the rights-based approach to the problem of world hunger', (2007) 20 Leiden Journal of International Law, 545.

Mumford, Lewis, The condition of man (Secker & Warburg 1944).

Munir, Muhammed, 'Suicide attacks and Islamic law', (2008) 90 International Review of the Red Cross, 71.

Murad, Khurram & Siddiqui, Abdur Rashid, Inter-personal relations: an Islamic perspective (Islamic Foundation 2005).

Murdoch, Iris, The sovereignty of good (Routledge 1991).

Murshed, Zubair, 'Power and identity in the discourse of jihad', (2003) 7 Gender Technology and Development, 399.

Muslehuddin, Mohammad, Philosophy of Islamic law and the orientalists: a comparative study of Islamic legal system (Islamic Publications 1977).

———, Islamic jurisprudence and the rule of necessity and need (Islamic Research Institute 1975).

Mutahhari, Murtada, Understanding Islamic sciences: philosophy, theology, mysticism, morality, jurisprudence (ICAS Press 2002).

Muthu, Sankar, Enlightenment against empire (Princeton University Press 2003).

Mutua, Makau, 'Savages, victims, and saviors: the metaphor of human rights', (2001) 42 Harvard International Law Journal, 201.

Nabulsi, Karma, Traditions of war: occupation, resistance, and the law (Oxford University Press 2005).

Nafziger, James A.R., 'Self-determination and humanitarian intervention in a community of power', (1991) 20 Denver Journal of International Law and Policy, 9.

Nagel, Tilman, 'La théorie islamique de l'état: aspects politiques et éthiques', in Mohammed Arkoun (ed), L'islam, morale et politique (Desclée de Brouwer 1986).

Nagel, Tilman & Thornton, Thomas, The history of Islamic theology: from Muhammad to the present (Markus Wiener 2000).

Nait-Belkacem, Mouloud Kassim, 'The concept of social justice in Islam', in Altaf Gauhar (ed), The challenge of Islam (Islamic Council of Europe 1978).

Nandy, Ashis, The intimate enemy: loss and recovery of self under colonialism (Oxford University Press 1988).

Naqvi, Yasmin, 'Doubtful prisoner-of-war status', (2002) 84 International Review of the Red Cross, 571.

Nasr, Seyyed Hossein, 'Islam and the question of violence', in Aftab Ahmad Malik (ed), With God on our side: politics and theology of the war on terrorism (Amal Press 2005).

Nasr, Seyyed Vali Reza, 'Ideology and institutions in Islamist approaches to public policy', in Sohrab Behdad & Farhad Nomani (eds), Islam and public policy (JAI Press 1997).

Nasu, Hitoshi, 'Operationalising the "responsibility to protect" and conflict prevention: dilemmas of civilian protection in armed conflict', (2009) 14 Journal of Conflict and Security Law, 209.

Neff, Stephen C., War and the law of nations: a general history (Cambridge University Press 2005).

Neill, Stephen, Colonialism and Christian missions (Lutterworth 1966).

Nesiah, Vasuki, 'Placing international law: white spaces on a map', (2003) 16 Leiden Journal of International Law, 1.

Neusner, Jacob (ed), Religious foundations of Western civilization: Judaism, Christianity, Islam (Abingdon Press 2006).

Nicholson, Michael, Rationality and the analysis of international conflict (Cambridge University Press 1992).

Nordstrom, Carolyn, A different kind of war story (University of Pennsylvania Press 1997).

Norman, Richard, 'War, humanitarian intervention and human rights', in Richard Sorabji & David Rodin (eds), The ethics of war: shared problems in different traditions (Ashgate 2006).

Nyang, Sulayman, 'Religion and the maintenance of boundaries', in Sohail H. Hashmi (ed), Islamic political ethics: civil society, pluralism and conflict (Princeton University Press 2002).

O'Brien, Karen, Narratives of Enlightenment: cosmopolitan history from Voltaire to Gibbon (Cambridge University Press 1997).

O'Connell, Robert L., Of arms and men: a history of war, weapons, and aggression (Oxford University Press 1989).

Onuma, Yasuaki, 'When was the law of international society born? An inquiry of the history of international law from an intercivilizational perspective', (2000) 2 Journal of the History of International Law, 1.

Oommen, T.K., 'Introduction: conceptualizing the linkage between citizenship and national identity', in T.K. Oommen (ed), Citizenship and national identity: from colonialism to globalism (Sage 1997).

Oppenheim, Lassa (ed), The collected papers of John Westlake on public international law (Cambridge University Press 1914).

Orakhelashvili, Alexander, 'The interaction between human rights and humanitarian law: fragmentation, conflict, parallelism or convergence?', (2008) 19 European Journal of International Law, 161.

Orford, Anne, Reading humanitarian intervention: human rights and the use of force in international law (Cambridge University Press 2003).

Oumlil, Ali, 'L'islam et l'état-nation', in Mohammed Arkoun (ed), L'islam, morale et politique (Desclée de Brouwer 1986).

Ozay, Mehmet, Islamic identity and development: studies of the Islamic periphery (Routledge 1990).

Özel, Soli, 'The inevitability of violence?', (2004) 9 Journal of Islamic Law and Culture, 27.

Pagden, Anthony, Worlds at war: the 2500-year struggle between East and West (Oxford University Press 2008).

———, 'The effacement of difference: colonialism and the origins of nationalism in Diderot and Herder', in Gyan Prakash (ed), After colonialism: imperial histories and postcolonial displacements (Princeton University Press 1995).

Palmer, Monte & Palmer, Princess, At the heart of terror: Islam, jihadists, and America's war on terrorism (Rowman & Littlefield Publishers 2004).

Pejic, Jelena, '"Unlawful/Enemy combatants": interpretations and consequences', in Michael N. Schmitt & Jelena Pejic (eds), International law and armed conflict: exploring the faultlines: essays in honour of Yoram Dinstein (Martinus Nijhoff Publishers 2007).

Peters, Rudolph, Jihad in classical and modern Islam (Markus Wiener 1996).

———, Islam and colonialism: the doctrine of Jihad in modern history (Mouton 1979).

———, Jihad in medieval and modern Islam: the chapter on jihad from Averroes' legal handbook "Bidayat al-mudjtahid" and the treatise "Koran and fighting" by the late Shaykh al-Azhar Mahmud Shaltut (E.J. Brill 1977).

Peters, Ruud, 'The enforcement of God's law: the Shari'ah in the present world of Islam', in Philip Ostien, Jamila M. Nasir & Franz Kogelmann (eds), Comparative perspectives on Shari'ah in Nigeria (Spectrum Books 2005).

Pfanner, Toni, 'Military uniforms and the law of war', (2004) 86 International Review of the Red Cross, 93.

Pick, Daniel, War machine: the rationalisation of slaughter in the modern age (Yale University Press 1993).

Pictet, Jean, Development and principles of international humanitarian law: course given in July 1982 at the University of Strasbourg as part of the courses organized by the International Institute of Human Rights (Martinus Nijhoff Publishers 1985).

Pilisuk, Marc & Achord Rountree, Jennifer, Who benefits from global violence and war: uncovering a destructive system (Praeger Security International 2008).

Piscatori, James P., Islam in a world of nation states (Cambridge University Press 1991).

Porter, Patrick, Military orientalism: Eastern war through Western eyes (Hurst & Company 2009).

Prakash, Gyan, 'Writing post-orientalist histories of the Third World: Indian historiography is good to think', in Nicholas B. Dirks (ed), Colonialism and culture (University of Michigan Press 1992).

Prins, Gwyn, 'Civil and uncivil wars', in Gwyn Prins & Hylke Tromp (eds), The future of war (Kluwer Law International 2000).

Pufendorf, Samuel, Of the law of nature and nations: eight books (The Lawbook Exchange, Ltd. 2005).

Putnam, Hilary, Enlightenment and pragmatism (Koninklijke Van Gorcum 2001).

Qaradawi, Yusuf & Khalifa, Al-Hadi A., Islamic law in the modern world (King Faisal Center for Research and Islamic Studies 2000).

Qaradawi, Yusuf, Siddiqui, M. Moinuddin, Shukry, Syed & Helbawy, Kamal, The lawful and the prohibited in Islam: al-Halal wal-haram fil Islam (American Trust Publications 1960).

Qutb, Muhammad, 'What Islam can give to humanity today', in Altaf Gauhar & Islamic Council of Europe (eds), The challenge of Islam (Islamic Council of Europe 1978).

Qutb, Sayyid, Al-Islam wa mushiklat al-hadarah (Dar al-Shuruq 1988).

Quénivet, Noëlle, 'The applicability of international humanitarian law to situations of a (counter-)terrorist nature', in Roberta Arnold (ed), International humanitarian law and the 21st century's conflicts: changes and challenges (Editions universitaires suisses 2005).

Rahim, Abdur, The principles of Islamic jurisprudence, according to the Hanafi, Maliki, Shafi'i and Hanbali schools (Kitab Bhavan 1994).

Rahman, Syedur, An introduction to Islamic culture and philosophy (Mullick Brothers 1963).

Rajagopal, Balakrishnan, 'Invoking the rule of law: international discourses', in Agnès Hurwitz & Reyko Huang (eds), Civil war and the rule of law: security, development, and human rights (Lynne Rienner Publishers 2008).

Ralph, Jason, 'The laws of war and the state of the American exception', (2009) 35 Review of International Studies, 631.

Ramadan, Tariq, Radical reform. Islamic ethics and liberation (Oxford University Press 2009).

———, Western Muslims and the future of Islam (Oxford University Press 2004).

———, Islam, the West and the challenges of modernity (Islamic Foundation 2001).

Rapoport, Anatol, Strategy and conscience (Schocken Books 1969).

Razzaque, Abdur, Prayer: for progress (Sh. Muhammad Ashraf 1967).

Redissi, Hamadi & Lane, Jan-Erik, 'Does Islam provide a theory of violence?' in Amélie Blom, Laetitia Bucaille & Luis Martinez (eds), The enigma of Islamist violence (Hurst & Company 2007).

Rees, Stuart, Passion for peace: exercising power creatively (University of New South Wales Press 2003).

Rehman, Javaid, Islamic state practices, international law and the threat from terrorism: a critique of the "clash of civilizations" in the new world order (Hart 2005).

———, 'Accommodating religious identities in an Islamic state: international law, freedom of religion and the rights of religious minorities', (2000) 7 International Journal on Minority and Group Rights, 139.

Reiman, Jeffrey, 'Ethics for calamities: how strict is the moral rule against targeting non-combatants?' in Roger Wertheimer (ed), Empowering our military conscience: transforming just war theory and military moral education (Ashgate 2010).

Rescher, Nicholas, Ethical idealism: an inquiry into the nature and functions of ideals (University of California Press 1987).

Ricoeur, Paul, The symbolism of evil (Beacon Press 1969).

Riles, Annelise, 'Aspiration and control: international legal rhetoric and the essentialization of culture', (1993) 106 Harvard Law Review, 723.

Riot, Daniel & Ajbali, Driss, Ben Laden n'est pas dans l'ascenseur … L'immigration, miroir des peurs de la société (Desmaret 2002).

Roberts, Adam, 'Land warfare: from Hague to Nuremberg', in Michael Howard, George J. Andreopoulos & Mark R. Shulman (eds), The laws of war: constraints on warfare in the Western world (Yale University Press 1994).

Robinson, Glenn E., 'The battle for Iraq: Islamic insurgencies in comparative perspective', (2007) 28 Third World Quaterly, 261.

Rodin, David, War and self-defense (Oxford University Press 2002).

Rodríguez-Villasante y Prieto, José Luis, 'Terrorist acts, armed conflicts and international humanitarian law', in P.A. Fernández-Sánchez (ed), The new challenges of humanitarian law in armed conflicts: in honour of professor Juan Antonio Carrillo-Salcedo (Martinus Nijhoff Publishers 2005).

Rogers, A.P.V., Law on the battlefield (Juris Publishing 2004).

Ronzitti, Natalino, 'The legality of covert operations against terrorism in foreign states', in Andrea Bianchi & Yasmin Naqvi (eds), Enforcing international law norms against terrorism (Hart Publishing 2004).

Rosen, Lawrence, The anthropology of justice: law as culture in Islamic society (Cambridge University Press 1989).

Rosenthal, Franz, 'On suicide in Islam', (1946) 66 Journal of the American Oriental Society, 239.

Rousseau, Jean-Jacques, Du contrat social ou principes du droit politique (MetaLibri 2008).

Rowe, Peter, Defence: the legal implications: military law and the laws of war (Brassey's Defence Publishers 1987).

Ruddy, F.S., 'International law and the Enlightenment: Vattel and the 18th century', (1968–1969) 3 International Lawyer, 839.

Russell Beattie, Amanda, 'Absolute ends and dynamic rules: being political as human beings', in Anthony F. Lang & Amanda Russell Beattie (eds), War, torture, and terrorism: rethinking the rules of international security (Routledge 2009).

Russell, Bertrand, Common sense and nuclear warfare (Routledge 2001).

Rustow, Dankwart A., 'Political ends and military means in the late Ottoman and post-Ottoman Middle East', in Vernon John Parry & Malcolm E. Yapp (eds), War, technology and society in the Middle East (Oxford University Press 1975).

Rydell, Robert W., 'Science in the service empire: empire in the service of science', in Gregory Blue, Martin Bunton & Ralph Croizier (eds), Colonialism and the modern world: selected studies (Sharpe 2002).

Sachedina, Abdulaziz A., 'The development of jihad in Islamic revelation and history', in James Turner Johnson & John Kelsay (eds), Cross, crescent, and sword: the justification and limitation of war in Western and Islamic tradition (Greenwood Press 1990).

Said, Abdul Aziz, 'Human rights in Islamic perspectives', in Adamantia Pollis & Peter Schwab (eds), Human rights: cultural and ideological perspectives (Praeger 1979).

Said, Edward W., 'Yeats and decolonization', in Terry Eagleton, Fredric Jameson & Edward W. Said (eds), Nationalism, colonialism, and literature (University of Minnesota Press 1990).

Sajoo, Amyn B., Muslim ethics: emerging vistas (I.B. Tauris 2004).

Salacuse, Jeswald W., 'From developing countries to emerging markets: a changing role for law in the Third World', (1999) 33 International Lawyer, 875.

Salem, Isam Kamel, Islam und Völkerrecht: das Völkerrecht in der islamischen Weltanschauung (Express Edition 1984).

Sandoz, Yves, Swinarski, Christophe & Zimmermann, Bruno (eds), Commentary on the Additional Protocols of 8 June 1977 to the Geneva Conventions of 12 August 1949 (International Committee of the Red Cross 1987).

Sardar Ali, Shaheen & Rehman, Javaid, 'The concept of jihad in Islamic international law', (2005) 10 Journal of Conflict and Security Law, 321.

Sardar, Ziauddin & Wyn Davies, Merryl, Distorted imagination: lessons from the Rushdie affair (London 1990).

Sarooshi, Dan, 'Sovereignty, economic autonomy, the United States, and the international trading system: representations of a relationship', (2004) 15 European Journal of International Law, 651.

Sartre, Jean-Paul, Colonialism and neocolonialism (Routledge 2001).

Sarwar, Ghulam, 'State and religion: the Islamic perspective', in Harbans Singh Bhatia (ed), Studies in Islamic law, religion and society (Deep & Deep Publications 1996).

Sassòli, Marco, 'Jus ad bellum and jus in bello: the separation between the legality of the use of force and humanitarian rules to be respected in warfare: crucial or outdated?' in Michael N. Schmitt & Jelena Pejic (eds), International law and armed conflict: exploring the faultlines: essays in honour of Yoram Dinstein (Martinus Nijhoff Publishers 2007).

Sassòli, Marco & Olson, Laura M., 'The relationship between international humanitarian and human rights law where it matters: admissible killing and internment of fighters in non-international armed conflicts', (2008) 90 International Review of the Red Cross, 599.

Scanlon, Thomas M., What we owe to each other (The Belknap Press of Harvard University Press 1999).

Schacht, Joseph, 'Pre-Islamic background and early development of jurisprudence', in Wael B. Hallaq (ed), The formation of Islamic law (Ashgate Variorum 2004).

———, An introduction to Islamic law (Clarendon Press 1965).

Scharf, Michael P., 'Earned sovereignty: juridical underpinnings', (2003) 31 Denver Journal of International Law and Policy, 373.

Scheffler, Thomas, 'West-Eastern cultures of fear: violence and terrorism in Islam', in Kai Hafez & Mary Ann Kenny (eds), The Islamic world and the West: an introduction to political cultures and international relations (Brill 2000).

Schindler, Dietrich, 'International humanitarian law: its remarkable development and its persistent violation', (2003) 5 Journal of the History of International Law, 165.

Schmitt, Michael N., 'The interpretive guidance on the notion of direct participation in hostilities: a critical analysis', (2010) 1 Harvard National Security Journal, 5.

———, 'Military necessity and humanity in international humanitarian law: preserving the delicate balance', (2010) 50 Virginia Journal of International Law, 795.

———, 'Deconstructing direct participation in hostilities: the constitutive elements', (2009–2010) 42 New York University Journal of International Law and Politics, 697.

———, 'The impact of high and low-tech warfare on the principle of distinction', in Roberta Arnold (ed), International humanitarian law and the 21st century's conflicts: changes and challenges (Editions universitaires suisses 2005).

———, 'Human shield in international humanitarian law', (2008–2009) 47 Columbia Journal of Transnational Law 292.

———, 'Precision attack and international humanitarian law', (2005) 87 International Review of the Red Cross, 445.

Schwartz, David Aaron, 'International terrorism and Islamic law', (1991) 29 Columbia Journal of Transnational Law, 629.

Schwarzenberger, Georg, 'The standard of civilisation in international law', (1955) 8 Current Legal Problems, 212.

Schweiker, William, Theological ethics and global dynamics: in the time of many worlds (Blackwell 2004).

Scobbie, Iain, 'Principle or pragmatics? The relationship between human rights law and the law of armed conflict', (2009) 14 Journal of Conflict and Security Law, 449.

Sen, Amartya, Identity and violence: the illusion of destiny (Allen Lane 2006).

Sevea, Terenjit, '"Islamist" intellectual space: "true Islam" and the Ummah in the East', (2007) 35 Asian Journal of Social Science, 575.

Shah, Nasim Hasan, 'Islamic concept of state', in Harbans Singh Bhatia (ed), Studies in Islamic law, religion and society (Deep & Deep Publications 1996).

Shah, Niaz A., Islamic law and the law of armed conflict: the armed conflict in Pakistan (Routledge 2011).

———, Self-defense in Islamic and international law: assessing Al-Qaeda and the invasion in Iraq (Palgrave Macmillan 2008).

———, 'Self-defence in Islamic law', (2005–2006) 12 Yearbook of Islamic and Middle Eastern Law, 181.

Shapiee, Rohimi B., 'Revitalising the siyar (Islamic international law): a challenge for the Muslims', (2008) 4 Journal of Islamic State Practices in International Law, 1.

Shariati, Ali, 'A new approach to understanding of Islam', in Harbans Singh Bhatia (ed), Studies in Islamic law, religion and society (Deep & Deep Publications 1996).

Sharif, Mian Mohammad, A history of Muslim philosophy: with short accounts of other disciplines and the modern renaissance in Muslim lands (Harrassowitz 1963).

Sharma, Shashi S., Caliphs and sultans: religious ideology and political praxis (Rupa 2004).

Shaw, Malcolm N., 'Peoples, territorialism and boundaries', (1997) 8 European Journal of International Law, 478.

Shboul, Ahmad, 'Islam and globalization: Arab world perspectives', in Virginia Matheson Hooker & Amin Saikal (eds), Islamic perspectives on the new millennium (Institute of Southeast Asian Studies 2004).

Siegfried, André, La civilisation occidentale (Clarendon Press 1945).

Simons, Penelope, 'The emergence of the idea of the individualized state in the international legal system', (2003) 5 Journal of the History of International Law, 293.

Simpson, Gerry J., Great powers and outlaw states: unequal sovereigns in the international legal order (Cambridge University Press 2004).

Sitaraman, Ganesh, 'Counterinsurgency, the war on terror, and the laws of war', (2009) 95 Virginia Law Review 1745.

Slim, Hugo, Killing civilians: method, madness and morality in war (Hurst & Company 2007).

Sloane, Robert D., 'The costs of conflation: preserving the dualism of jus ad bellum and jus in bello in the contemporary law of war', (2009) 34 Yale Journal of International Law, 47.

Smith, Rupert, The utility of force: the art of war in the modern world (Allen Lane 2005).

Smyser, William R., The humanitarian conscience: caring for others in the age of terror (Palgrave Macmillan 2003).

Snow, Alpheus Henry, The question of aborigines in the law and practice of nations (G.P. Putnam's Sons: The Knickerbocker Press 1921).

Sonn, Tamara, 'Irregular warfare and terrorism in Islam: asking the right questions', in James Turner Johnson & John Kelsay (eds), Cross, crescent, and sword: the justification and limitation of war in Western and Islamic tradition (Greenwood Press 1990).

Sorokin, Pitirim A., The reconstruction of humanity (The Beacon Press 1949).

Springer, Devin R., Regens, James L. & Edger, David N., Islamic radicalism and global jihad (Georgetown University Press 2009).

Spybey, Tony, Social change, development and dependency: modernity, colonialism and the development of the West (Polity 1992).

Stanley, Brian, 'Christian missions and the Enlightenment: a reevaluation', in Brian Stanley (ed), Christian missions and the Enlightenment (Eerdmans 2001).

———, 'Christianity and civilization in English evangelical mission thought, 1792–1857', in Brian Stanley (ed), Christian missions and the Enlightenment (Eerdmans 2001).

Steele Commager, Henry, The empire of reason: how Europe imagined and America realized the Enlightenment (Anchor Press/Doubleday 1977).

Steiger, Heinhard, 'From the international law of Christianity to the international law of the world citizen: reflections on the formation of the epochs of the history of international law', (2001) 3 Journal of the History of International Law, 180.

Stephens, Dale, 'Blurring the lines: the interpretation, discourse and application of the law of armed conflict', (2009) 12 Yearbook of International Humanitarian Law, 85.

Sterba, James P., Justice for here and now (Cambridge University Press 1998).

Stock, Margaret D., 'Detainees in the hands of America: new rules for a new kind of war', in Michael N. Schmitt & Gian Luca Beruto (eds), Terrorism and international law: challenges and responses (International Institute of Humanitarian Law 2003).

Stoler, Ann Laura, 'Rethinking colonial categories: European communities and the boundaries of rule', in Nicholas B. Dirks (ed), Colonialism and culture (University of Michigan Press 1992).

Strauss, Anselm L., Mirrors and masks: the search for identity (Free Press 1959).

Sultan, Hamed, 'La conception islamique du droit international humanitaire dans les conflits armés', (1978) 34 Revue égyptienne de droit international, 13.

Summers, James J., 'The rhetoric and practice of self-determination: a right of all peoples or political institutions?' (2004) 73 Nordic Journal of International Law, 325.

Tabassum, Sadia, 'Combatants, not bandits: the status of rebels in Islamic law', (2011) 93 International Review of the Red Cross 121.

Tabbarah, Afif Abdulfattah, The spirit of Islam: an interpretive survey of the foundations, graces and teachings of Islam as seen in the light of science and philosophy (Abdel-Hafiz Bsat 1978).

Talbi, Mohammed, 'Les structures et les caractéristiques de l'état islamique traditionnel', in Mohammad Arkoun (ed), L'islam, morale et politique (Desclée de Brouwer 1986).

Tavakkuli Tarqi, Muhammad, Refashioning Iran: orientalism, occidentalism, and historiography (Palgrave 2001).

Thomas, Chantal, 'Causes of inequality in the international economic order: critical race theory and postcolonial development', (1999) 9 Transnational Law and Contemporary Problems, 1.

Thomas, Nicholas, Colonialism's culture: anthropology, travel and government (Polity Press 1994).

Thomson, Ann, Barbary and Enlightenment: European attitudes towards the Maghreb in the 18th century (E.J. Brill 1987).

Tibi, Bassam, 'War and peace in Islam', in Andrew G. Bostom (ed), The legacy of jihad: Islamic holy war and the fate of non-Muslims (Prometheus Books 2005).

———, 'War and peace in Islam', in Sohail H. Hashmi (ed), Islamic political ethics: civil society, pluralism, and conflict (Princeton University Press 2002).

———, The challenge of fundamentalism: political Islam and the new world disorder (University of California Press 1998).

Tillich, Paul, The courage to be (Collins Clear-Type Press 1962).

Tillich, Paul & Thomas, J. Mark, The spiritual situation in our technical society (Mercer University Press 1988).

Tornau, Nikolai Egorovich, Das moslemische Recht: aus den Quellen dargestellt (Rodopi 1970).

Touraine, Alain, Critique de la modernité (Fayard 1992).

Tuck, Richard, The rights of war and peace: political thought and the international order from Grotius to Kant (Oxford University Press 2001).

Umar, Muhammad Sani, Islam and colonialism: intellectual responses of Muslims of Northern Nigeria to British colonial rule (Brill 2006).

Vagts, Detlev F. & Meron, Theodor, 'The Geneva Conventions of 1949 and wars of national liberation', in Detlev F. Vagts, Theodor Meron, Stephen M. Schwebel & Charles Keever (eds), Humanizing the laws of war: selected writings of Richard Baxter (Oxford University Press 2013).

Van Creveld, Martin, The transformation of war: the most radical reinterpretation of armed conflict since Clausewitz (The Free Press 1991).

Van den Berg, Lodewijk William Christiaan, Principes du droit musulman (A. Jourdan 1896).

Vanhullebusch, Matthias, 'The Arab League and military operations: prospects and challenges in Syria', (2015) 22 International Peacekeeping, 151.

———, 'Islamic law and the responsibility to protect', (2010) 4 Human Rights and International Legal Discourse, 191.

Vertigans, Stephen, Militant Islam: a sociology of characteristics, causes and consequences (Routledge 2009).

Veuthey, Michel, Guérilla et droit humanitaire (Institut Henry-Dunant 1983).

Vité, Sylvain, 'Typology of armed conflicts in international humanitarian law: legal concepts and actual situations', (2009) 91 International Review of the Red Cross, 69.

Vogel, Frank E., Islamic law and legal system: studies of Saudi Arabia (Brill 2000).

Voigt, Lydia & Thornton, William E., The limits of justice: a sociological analysis (University Press of America 1984).

von Clausewitz, Carl, On war (Wordsworth Editions Limited 1997).

Wallace, Alfred Russel, 'The origin of human races and the antiquity of man deduced from the theory of "natural selection"', in Michael D. Biddis (ed), Images of race (Leicester University Press 1979).

Walls, Andrew F., 'The eighteenth century protestant missionary awakening in its European context', in Brian Stanley (ed), Christian missions and the Enlightenment (Eerdmans 2001).

Watkin, Kenneth, 'Opportunity lost: organized armed groups and the ICRC "Direct Participation in Hostilities" interpretive guidance', (2009–2010) 42 New York University Journal of International Law and Politics, 641.

———, '21st century conflict and international humanitarian law: status quo or change?' in Michael N. Schmitt & Jelena Pejic (eds), International law and armed conflict: exploring the faultlines: essays in honour of Yoram Dinstein (Martinus Nijhoff Publishers 2007).

———, 'Assessing proportionality: moral complexity and legal rules', (2005) 8 Yearbook of International Humanitarian Law 3.

———, 'Controlling the use of force: a role for human rights norms in contemporary armed conflict', (2004) 98 American Journal of International Law, 1.

Watt, W. Montgomery, Islamic revelation in the modern world (Edinburgh University Press 1969).

———, Islam and the integration of society (Routledge & Kegan Paul 1966).

Waxman, Matthew C., 'The structure of terrorism threats and the laws of war', (2009–2010) 20 Duke Journal of Comparative and International Law 429.

Weeramantry, Christopher Gregory, Islamic jurisprudence: an international perspective (Macmillan 1988).

Weigend, Thomas, 'The universal terrorist', (2006) 4 Journal of International Criminal Justice, 912.

Weiss, Bernard G., 'The madhhab in Islamic legal theory', in Peri J. Bearman, Rudolph Peters & Frank E. Vogel (eds), The Islamic school of law: evolution, devolution, and progress (Harvard University Press 2005).

———, 'Interpretation in Islamic law: the theory of ijtihad', (1977–1978) 26 American Journal of Comparative Law, 199.

Wells, Donald A., War crimes and laws of war (University Press of America 1984).

Westlake, John, Chapters on the principles of international law (Cambridge University Press 1894).

Wheatcroft, Andrew, Infidels: the conflict between Christendom and Islam, 638–2002 (Viking 2003).

Wiktorowicz, Quintan, 'The Salafi movement: violence and the fragmentation of community', in Miriam Cooke & Bruce B. Lawrence (eds), Muslim networks from Hajj to hip hop (University of North Carolina Press 2005).

Wilde, Ralph, International territorial administration: how trusteeship and the civilizing mission never went away (Oxford University Press 2008).

Williams Jr., Robert A., The American Indian in Western legal thought: the discourses of conquest (Oxford University Press 1990).

Wilson, Heather A., International law and the use of force by national liberation movements (Clarendon Press 1988).

Winfield, Richard Dien, Reason and justice (State University of New York Press 1999).

Woodcock, Andrew, 'Jacques Maritain, natural law and the Universal Declaration of Human Rights', (2006) 8 Journal of the History of International Law, 245.

Wouters, Jan & Naert, Frederik, 'Shockwaves through international law after 11 September: finding the right responses to the challenges of international terrorism', in Cyrille Fijnaut, Jan Wouters & Frederik Naert (eds), Legal instruments in the fight against international terrorism: a transatlantic dialogue (Martinus Nijhoff Publishers 2004).

Yamani, Ahmed Zaki, 'Humanitarian international law in Islam: a general outlook', in Hisham M. Ramadan (ed), Understanding Islamic law: from classical to contemporary (Rowman & Littlefield Publishers 2006).

Yilmaz, Ihsan, 'Inter-madhhab surfing, neo-ijtihad, and faith-based movement leader', in Peri J. Bearman, Rudolph Peters & Frank E. Vogel (eds), The Islamic school of law: evolution, devolution, and progress (Harvard University Press 2005).

Zaman, M. Raquibuz, 'Islamic perspectives on territorial boundaries and autonomy', in Sohail H. Hashmi (ed), Islamic political ethics: civil society, pluralism, and conflict (Princeton University Press 2002).

Zaman, Syed Muhammad, 'Place of man in the universe in the world: view of Islam', in Harbans Singh Bhatia (ed), Studies in Islamic law, religion and society (Deep & Deep Publications 1996).

Zawati, Hilmi M., Is jihad a just war? War, peace, and human rights under Islamic and public international law (Edwin Mellen Press 2001).

Zeidan, David, The resurgence of religion: a comparative study of selected themes in Christian and Islamic fundamentalist discourses (Brill 2003).

Zeidy, Mohamed M. El & Murphy, Ray, 'Islamic law on prisoners of war and its relationships with international humanitarian law', (2004) 14 Italian Yearbook of International Law, 53.

Zemmali, Ameur, Combattants et prisonniers de guerre en droit islamique et en droit international humanitaire (E. Pedone 1997).

Zubaida, Sami, 'Islam and secularization', (2005) 33 Asian Journal of Social Science, 438.

———, Law and power in the Islamic world (I.B. Tauris 2003).

Zulaika, Joseba, 'The anthropologist as terrorist', in Nancy Scheper-Hughes & Philippe Bourgois (eds), Violence in war and peace (Blackwell Publishing 2004).

Author Index

Subject Index